The European Parliament

David Judge

and

David Earnshaw

palgrave
macmillan

First published 2003 by
PALGRAVE MACMILLAN
Houndmills, Basingstoke, Hampshire RG21 6XS and
175 Fifth Avenue, New York, N.Y. 10010
Companies and representatives throughout the world

PALGRAVE MACMILLAN is the global academic imprint of the Palgrave Macmillan division of St. Martin's Press, LLC and of Palgrave Macmillan Ltd. Macmillan® is a registered trademark in the United States, United Kingdom and other countries. Palgrave is a registered trademark in the European Union and other countries.

ISBN 0–333–59873–3 hardback
ISBN 0–333–59874–1 paperback

This book is printed on paper suitable for recycling and made from fully managed and sustained forest sources.

A catalogue record for this book is available from the British Library.

Library of Congress Cataloging-in-Publication Data
The European parliament / David Judge and David Earnshaw.
    p. cm. – (The European Union series)
  Includes bibliographical references and index.
  ISBN 0–333–59873–3 (hbk.) – ISBN 0–333–59874–1 (pbk.)
    1. European Parliament. I. Earnshaw, David. II. European Union series
(Palgrave (Firm))
JN36.E947 2003
341.24'24–dc21
                                                      2002193077

THE EUROPEAN UNION SERIES

General Editors: Neill Nugent, William E. Paterson, Vincent Wright

The European Union series is designed to provide an authoritative library on the European Union, ranging from general introductory texts to definitive assessments of key institutions and actors, policies and policy processes, and the role of member states.

Books in the series are written by leading scholars in their fields and reflect the most up-to-date research and debate. Particular attention is paid to accessibility and clear presentation for a wide audience of students, practitioners and interested general readers. The series consists of four major strands:

• General textbooks
• The major institutions and actors
• The main areas of policy
• The member states and the Union

The series editors are **Neill Nugent**, Professor of Politics and Jean Monnet Professor of European Integration, Manchester Metropolitan University; and **William E. Paterson**, Director of the Institute of German Studies, University of Birmingham.

Their co-editor until his death in July 1999, **Vincent Wright**, was a Fellow of Nuffield College, Oxford University. He played an immensely valuable role in the founding and development of *The European Union Series* and is greatly missed.

Feedback on the series and book proposals are always welcome and should be sent to Steven Kennedy, Palgrave Macmillan, Houndmills, Basingstoke, Hampshire RG21 6XS UK or by e-mail to s.kennedy@palgrave.com

General textbooks

Published

Desmond Dinan **Encyclopedia of the European Union**
[Rights: Europe only]

Desmond Dinan **Ever Closer Union: An Introduction to European Integration** (2nd edn)
[Rights: World excluding North and South America, Philippines and Japan]

? **The Political System of the European Union**

J ? McCormick **Understanding the European Union: A Concise Introduction**

Neill Nugent **The Government and Politics of the European Union (5th edn)**
[Rights: World excluding USA and dependencies and Canada]

John Peterson and Elizabeth Bomberg **Decision-making in the European Union**

Ben Rosamond **Theories of European Integration**

Forthcoming

Simon Bulmer and Andrew Scott **European Union: Economics, Policy and Politics**

Neill Nugent (ed.) **European Union Enlargement**

Andrew Scott **The Political Economy of the European Union**

Phillipa Sherrington **Understanding European Union Governance and Policy**

Richard Sinnott **Understanding European Integration**

Also planned

The History of the European Union
The European Union Source Book
The European Union Reader

The major institutions and actors

Published

Renaud Dehousse **The European Court of Justice**

Justin Greenwood **Interest Representation in the European Union**

The major institutions and actors

Fiona Hayes-Renshaw and Helen Wallace
The Council of Ministers

Simon Hix and Christopher Lord **Political Parties in the European Union**

David Judge and David Earnshaw
The European Parliament

Neill Nugent **The European Commission**

Anne Stevens with Handley Stevens **Brussels Bureaucrats? The Administration of the European Union**

Forthcoming

Simon Bulmer and Wolfgang Wessels **The European Council**

The main areas of policy

Published

Michelle Cini and Lee McGowan
Competition Policy in the European Union

Wyn Grant **The Common Agricultural Policy**

Martin Holland **The European Union and the Third World**

Brigid Laffan **The Finances of the European Union**

Malcolm Levitt and Christopher Lord
The Political Economy of Monetary Union

Janne Haaland Matláry
Energy Policy in the European Union

John McCormick **Environmental Policy in the European Union**

John Peterson and Margaret Sharp
Technology Policy in the European Union

Forthcoming

David Allen and Geoffrey Edwards
The External Economic Relations of the European Union

Laura Cram **Social Policy in the European Union**

Sonia Mazey **Women and the European Union**

Steven McGuire and Michael Smith
The USA and the European Union

Anand Menon **Defence Policy and the European Union**

James Mitchell and Paul McAleavey
Regionalism and Regional Policy in the European Union

Jörg Monar **Justice and Home Affairs in the European Union**

Handley Stevens **Transport Policy in the European Union**

Mark Thatcher **The Politics of European High Technology**

John Vogler and Charlotte Bretherton
The External Policies of the European Union

Also planned

Political Union

The member states and the Union

Published

Alain Guyomarch, Howard Machin and Ella Ritchie **France in the European Union**

Forthcoming

Simon Bulmer and William E. Paterson
Germany and the European Union

Carlos Closa and Paul Heywood **Spain and the European Union**

Phil Daniels and Ella Ritchie **Britain and the European Union**

Brigid Laffan **The European Union and its Member States**

Luisa Perrotti **Italy and the European Union**

Also planned

Reshaping the States of the Union

Series Standing Order (*outside North America only*)
ISBN 0–333–71695–7 hardback
ISBN 0–333–69352–3 paperback
Full details from www.palgrave.com

Contents

List of Tables, Figures and Boxes

Tables

Figures

Boxes

List of Abbreviations

ACP	African, Caribbean and Pacific
BSE	Bovine Spengiform Encephalopathy
CAP	Common Agricultural Policy
CFSP	Common Foreign and Security Policy
COREPER	Committee of Permanent Representatives
COSAC	Conference of European Affairs Committees
CRP	Committee on Rules of Procedure
EC	European Community
ECB	European Central Bank
ECSC	European Coal and Steel Community
ECU	European Currency Unit
EDC	European Defence Community
EDD	Europe of Democracies and Diversities
EDF	European Development Fund
EEC	European Economic Community
EFA	Europe Free Alliance
ELDR	European Liberal, Democratic and Reformist Group
EMI	European Monetary Institute
EMU	Economic and Monetary Union
EP	European Parliament
EPC	European Political Community
EPLP	European Parliamentary Labour Party
EPP	European People's Party
EPP–ED	European People's Party and European Democrats
EPU	European Political Union
EU	European Union
EUL	European United Left
IGC	Intergovernmental conference
MEP	Member of the European Parliament
MNP	Member of National Parliament
NGL	Nordic Green Left
NGOs	Non-governmental organizations
ONP	Open network provision
PDS	Partito Democratio della Sinistra
PSE	Party of European Socialists
QMV	Qualified majority voting
SEA	Single European Act
TDI	Technical Group of Independent Members
TEU	Treaty on European Union
UEL	Union of European Left
UEN	Union for Europe of Nations
UKIP	United Kingdom Independence Party

Acknowledgements

It is perhaps appropriate that this book should have been completed almost exactly on the date of the fiftieth anniversary of the establishment of the European Parliament (or more accurately the Common Assembly). In fact, for the authors, the writing of the book seemed to have taken almost as many years! So our first and greatest acknowledgement is to those who have seen the authors age, and aged with them, during the writing process: Lorraine, Ben and Hannah; and Toni and Jo. Our thanks should also be recorded for the patience and forbearance shown by Steven Kennedy at Palgrave and the EU Series editors, especially Neill Nugent, who have waited for so long for this book to arrive.

It is no exaggeration to say that this book would not have been written without Ken Collins. As the chapters demonstrate, his impact upon the development of the Parliament since 1979 has been profound. More importantly, his impact upon the authors has been enormous. He has provided, for over two decades, a practical education in the workings of the Parliament and sustained analysis of its operations, as well as good company. Our thanks also go to others directly associated with the European Parliament and who have provided innumerable answers to our queries and sound advice over the years: Kieran Bradley, Richard Corbett, Francis Jacobs, Niall O'Neill, Mike Shackleton and Martin Westlake.

Fiona Macintyre at Strathclyde demanded, and deserves, a sentence all to herself!

DAVID JUDGE
DAVID EARNSHAW

Introduction

The first, and perhaps most fundamental, question when writing a book is: why bother? This is particularly the case with the European Parliament (EP) when there is already an established text that has been deemed by successive Presidents of the Parliament to be 'the authoritative source' on the EP. This is, of course, the standard reference work written by three parliamentary insiders Richard Corbett, Francis Jacobs and Michael Shackleton. Already in its fourth edition, with a fifth edition in preparation, any other book on the EP has to acknowledge an immense debt to Corbett *et al.*'s *European Parliament* (2000). Equally, recognition of Martin Westlake's work, *A Modern Guide to the European Parliament* (1994), although published nearly a decade ago, will feature at some stage in most writing on the EP. Alongside these standard comprehensive studies now stand a series of books dealing with particular facets of the EP. Recent examples include Blondel, Sinnott and Svenssson, *People and Parliament in the European Union* (1998); Corbett, *The European Parliament's Role in Closer EU Integration* (1998); Katz and Wessels, *The European Parliament, the National Parliaments and European Integration* (1999); and Kreppel, *The European Parliament and Supranational Party System* (2002). In turn, these books reflect merely the English language tip of a multilingual iceberg of texts focused on the European Parliament.

Given these illustrious predecessors, the question 'why bother?' assumes even more importance for the present study. One answer is to be found in the 'Everest syndrome'. And many studies of legislatures throughout the world have sufficed with just such an answer. Thus, just as a standard response of mountaineers to the question of 'why climb Everest?' is 'because it is there', so many academic studies of national legislatures assume that because the institution exists it is intrinsically worthy of study. However, we maintain that academic enquiry should be

1

more adventurous than this and should be driven by intellectual inquisitiveness and analytical curiosity.

One intellectual query driving this book is how appropriate are existing models and categorizations of legislatures and legislative activity for the study of the European Parliament – an institution widely regarded as *sui generis*. Without giving the full answer away at this early stage the short answer is that these models and classifications do, indeed, prove useful in structuring the analysis of the EP. A prime objective of this book, therefore, is to 'locate' the EP within the study of legislatures.

The starting point of our assessment of the EP is thus to decide what are the characteristic features of legislatures and then to discover whether the EP conforms to those characteristics. In identifying three 'universal' functions of legislatures – legitimation, linkage and decision-making – this book assesses the relevance of these functions for the EP and the European Union (EU) across time. In so doing, it becomes apparent that the balance between functions, and the relative emphasis placed upon the performance of these functions by the EP itself, has varied over time.

A further assumption driving this study is that not only does the EP have to be understood as a legislature but it also has to be understood as part of the wider system of EU governance. Where the EP is located conceptually within the EU's institutional structures has a bearing on how well it is perceived to play the roles ascribed to it as a legislature. To understand the EP's linkage functions, or its contribution to the legitimation of EU outputs, or to the EU's legislative process, requires some idea of how the EU as a political system is conceived in the first place.

In locating the EP within wider conceptions of the EU as a system of governance this book acknowledges that the Parliament is part of multiple, complex, interwoven and overlapping institutional networks. In other words, we agree with Peterson and Shackleton (2002:10) that 'the EU's institutions cannot be studied as separate and autonomous entities'. Hence, a basic premise of this book is that the EP, as an institution, can only be understood in terms of its wider interinstitutional interactions. Unfortunately, what complicates this understanding in the case of the EU is that there are no singular institutional structures, only plural institutional forms. Thus, terms that have a certain precision in the context of member states acquire ambiguity in the context of the EU. For example, there is no single executive but rather a 'dual executive' of Commission and Council; nor is there a single legislature but a series of interconnected 'legislative bodies' – in so far as the European Parliament shares legislative functions with the Council and the Commission. From the outset, therefore, we have to recognize that the conceptualization of interinstitutional relations in the EU affects not only the assessment of the past and current performance of the EP but also conditions prognostications about a future 'parliamentarization' of the EU.

Indeed, the implementation of the Amsterdam Treaty in 1999 merely served to heighten beliefs in 'parliamentarization' and the enhancement of 'parliamentary democracy' in the EU. In examining such perceptions the need to recognize the *interconnectedness* of the defining elements of a 'parliamentary model' have to be explicitly acknowledged. As a minimum, criteria by which the process of 'parliamentarization' should be assessed have to be specified.

Our sense of intellectual enquiry leads us to raise some fundamental questions about the location of the EP within the comparative study of legislatures, about its location within notions of EU governance and about the parliamentarization of the EU's system of governance. We claim neither to treat these questions equally nor to answer them in the detail specialists of, for example, integration theories or democratic theories would like. What we do claim, however, is that these are important questions and should at least be raised by students of the European Parliament.

Similarly we raise some important issues surrounding the question of whether or not the EP is a 'proper' Parliament. As the discussion about the location of the EP illustrates, it all depends how a 'parliament' is defined in the first place and what expectations are held of the role and functions of a parliament. In the case of the EP, not only is it relatively new, having been in existence for just over fifty years, but it is also chameleon-like in its capacity to adapt to constant change in the nature of treaty-defined institutional relations, of political constellations (of parties, states, and civil societies), and of informal interinstitutional networks. What becomes evident fairly soon in any analysis of the EP is that global assessments of its powers, legislative influence and linkages with other groups and institutions are extremely easy to assert but difficult to substantiate in the face of such perpetual change.

Indeed, a constant theme of our writing since the early 1990s has been that it is difficult to assess the EP, especially its legislative impact, in aggregate or absolute terms. In practice, assessments of the EP are contingent upon: the chronological period under study; the formal powers and scope of competencies held at that time; treaty-prescribed interinstitutional relations; informal modes of interinstitutional networking; the ideological and national configurations within the EP itself; relations with other EU institutions and member states; and the differentiated nature of EU policy sectors and networks. Thus, in some policy areas the EP is now a true co-legislator with the Council and so is in a radically different relationship to the Council and Commission than it was in the early 1990s, yet in others it remains in essentially an advisory capacity. Similarly, in its linkage and legitimating roles the EP is clearly in a different relationship to both the EU's dual executive and to citizens in member states from that before direct elections in 1979 (and in an altered relationship yet again after the low turnouts at the 1999 election), yet many disconnections remain in terms of public perceptions and knowledge of the EP.

Structure of the book

Locating the European Parliament within wider theories of legislatures and models of the EU's political system is of importance in understanding what role we would expect the EP to perform as a legislature and the broader political context within which it is expected to perform this role. To this end, Chapter 1 examines how the EP can be located within comparative typologies of legislatures, and identifies three universal functions – of legitimation, linkage and decision-making – performed by legislatures. In addition, Chapter 1 also outlines two basic models of governance which provide contextual background for later chapters.

Chapter 2 pursues the analytical prescriptions of Chapter 1 and considers the interinstitutional, contextual and interconnected dimensions of the historical development of the EP. In seeking to 'locate' the EP across time, both as a legislature and within the developing EU integrationist project, a useful historical perspective is provided from which the EP can be viewed in the early twenty-first century.

Chapters 3 and 4 examine the first two of the three 'universal' functions ascribed to legislatures – legitimation and linkage.

Chapter 3 focuses upon the electoral linkage at the core of the process of representation and analyses the concepts of 'demos', legitimacy and democracy within the EU. Chapter 4 then extends the analysis of 'linkage' by looking at how the EP acts as a representative body, and how it links citizens and decision-makers in the periods between elections.

Chapter 5 serves as a pivot in the study. It turns the analysis away from the broader issues of Chapter 4 – of linkage and the representative roles of political parties and the extent of transnational party competition – towards the examination of the role performed by party groups in the internal workings of the European Parliament. Not only do parties link the people to decision-makers but they also link, structure and regularize interactions between decision-makers themselves. Party groups in the EP work within an institutional context that has changed dramatically with successive treaty reforms and enhancements of the legislative role of the EP. Concomitantly, the extension of formal power has increased the importance of exerting institutional controls over the activities of party groups and their members. The identification of a dynamic relationship between the organization of the EP as an institution and the party system and party groups is then used to answer one of the central organizational questions confronting legislatures: how do elected representatives effectively and efficiently organize themselves in order to make collective decisions? In answering this question, Chapter 6 analyses the EP's rules and procedures, its formal institutional leadership positions, and the all-important internal division of labour in the form of its committees.

Chapters 7 and 8 echo the theme of Chapter 1 that any assessment of the EP's formal powers and legislative influence requires recognition of the interconnected, interinstitutional and contextual elements of the exercise of such powers. In this sense, Chapter 7 makes clear that a study of the powers of the EP is intrinsically comparative in nature: in relation to other institutions involved in the EU's legislative process, and in relation to the exercise of these powers across time.

Chapter 8 moves beyond the specification of formal powers to examine the actual influence wielded by the European Parliament in the early twenty-first century. In so doing, the chapter highlights another general theme of the book that the formal dimensions of the EP's influence have to be supplemented by recognition of the informal dimensions of its contribution to the EU's decision-making processes. Indeed, not only is this a historical phenomenon, as revealed in Chapter 2, but it also constitutes a future strategy for the development of the EP.

In 'looking to the future', Chapter 9 concludes with the observation that the first fifty years of the EU have been exercised by the question of 'the future role of the European Parliament', and, undoubtedly, the same question will feature significantly over the next fifty years. The fact that there is neither a simple nor a consensual answer reflects both the contested nature of the EU as a system of governance and the different perceptions of the role of the EP within that system and as a 'legislature'.

In these circumstances, we stand by our initial claim that the EP has to be understood both as a legislature and as part of the wider system of EU governance.

Note on referencing

Given the complexities of the referencing of EU documents we have adopted the following conventions. Wherever possible:

- European Parliament committee reports are noted by PE number. (To ease identification in the references each report is listed numerically by PE number, rather than by PE number by year of publication.)
- Other European Parliament documents (Rules of Procedure, working papers, or information documents) are referenced under 'European Parliament', unless they have a specific author, in which case they are referenced under the author's name.
- European Parliament resolutions are referenced as they appear in the *Official Journal* of the European Communities (OJ) C-series or, if not yet published in the *Official Journal*, the reference and date in Parliament's minutes is provided.
- European Commission documents are referenced by COM number.
- European Council documents are referenced by SN number.

The term European Union (EU) has been used wherever possible, unless its use is historically inaccurate. Similarly, treaty articles are numbered as in the Amsterdam Treaty, except where otherwise indicated.

Chapter 1

Locating the European Parliament

Where is the European Parliament located? The answer seems to be obvious, at least in geographical terms: in Brussels, along with the other major institutions of the European Union – the Council of the European Union and the European Commission. However, as we will discover in the rest of this book, there are no simple answers as far as the EP is concerned. Certainly, there is an impressive parliamentary complex just off the rue Belliard in Brussels, strategically located across from the building which houses the Council of Ministers and close by the Commission buildings. Dominated by the Spaak and Spinelli Buildings the complex contains a futuristic debating chamber (hemicycle) and the offices of the 626 Members of the European Parliament (MEPs) and their staff. It is used for meetings of the Parliament's committees and for plenary part-sessions. However, this impressive complex is matched by another imposing set of buildings in the French city of Strasbourg, some 450 kilometres from Brussels. The Strasbourg complex comprises the Churchill, Weiss and Madariaga Buildings and accommodates MEPs and their staff during twelve weekly plenary sessions each year. So the answer to the original question is: Brussels *and* Strasbourg. Even this is only a partial answer, however, as the full answer is Brussels *and* Strasbourg *and* Luxembourg. Indeed, Luxembourg was the original home of the Parliament before direct elections in 1979, and is still the formal location of the Parliament's General-Secretariat. Thus, even locating the European Parliament geographically is not a simple undertaking.

The European Parliament as a legislature

If there are problems locating the EP geographically it should come as no surprise, therefore, to find that trying to locate the

EP institutionally is an even more daunting prospect. Yet it is a prospect that has to be addressed from the outset, because, very simply, where, how and why the EP is located first within comparative assessments of legislatures and second within the institutional structure of the European Union raises wider issues about democracy, legitimacy, accountability and responsiveness within the EU itself.

What this introductory chapter seeks to do, therefore, is to raise the question of how we would go about trying to 'locate' the EP within the study of legislatures. This perspective – on legislatures – prompts an examination of what the European Parliament 'does', or is expected to do. What needs reiteration here, however, is that the objective of this chapter is to provide 'locational' indicators that can be used to structure the analysis in later chapters. What we seek to do is to examine existing analytical maps in this chapter and then to use these conceptual 'coordinates' to enable the reader in subsequent chapters to locate the EP as a legislature and as part of the EU's political system. Unless we are clear at the outset what the models are, and where the EP is located in each, then we will be unclear what the criteria of assessment are and what expectations we should have of the European Parliament.

The sui generis issue

> The European Parliament is easily misperceived as the Community equivalent of a national legislature. Most members of the European Parliament (MEPs) think that the EP *should* be the Community's legislature, or at least its colegislature alongside the Council of Ministers. (Dinan 1999:267)

Problems will always emerge in the study of the institutions of the European Union, the EP included, precisely because they have no exact counterparts in national political systems. This leads immediately to the *sui generis* issue of whether the European Union is unique in its institutional form and in its trajectory of development. Most concern with the *sui generis* issue, or the '$n = 1$' problem, has been expressed by theorists of regional integration (for an overview see Caporaso *et al.* 1997:1–5). However, the issue is of direct relevance to the EP because of the continuing belief that the European Parliament is 'a unique institution' which happens to 'have an involvement in all the roles associated with parliaments' (Corbett *et al.* 1995:7). But it is worth noting from the outset that this belief is not exclusive to analyses of the EP, for, as Norton (1990:9) notes, 'there is a tendency for scholars to view their particular legislature as *sui generis*'. The starting point of any assessment of the EP, therefore, is to decide what are the characteristic features of legislatures and then to discover whether the EP conforms to those characteristics.

Characteristic features of legislatures

According to Philip Norton (1990:1), what legislatures have in common is that they are 'constitutionally designated institutions for giving assent to binding measures of public policy, that assent being given on behalf of a political community that extends beyond the government elite responsible for formulating those measures'. The value of Norton's definition is that it does not focus exclusively on 'law-making', but instead directs attention to the wider issues surrounding the 'giving of assent' in terms of legitimation, consent and authorization. The definition also recognizes that not all legislatures are directly elected. More particularly, it acts as an analytical pointer towards the multidirectional relationship between a legislature and its broader 'political community' as well as with its involvement with other policy-making institutions.

Implicit within Norton's definition, and in fact explicit in most discussions of what legislatures 'are', is some conception of what legislatures 'do'. In this respect, attention becomes focused on the functions of legislatures, with Robert Packenham (1970:523), for example, proclaiming that 'everyone who has written about legislatures is, explicitly or implicitly, a functionalist'. Packenham, himself, grouped the functions of legislatures into three main categories (based upon his study of the Brazilian legislature) – legitimation; recruitment and socialization of elites; and decisional or influence. Of these functions 'legitimation' was identified as of greatest significance in the political system; while 'decisional' functions – traditionally the primary functions associated with 'legislatures' – were deemed to be of least consequence for the political system as a whole.

Packenham's delineation of functions provided the starting point for many subsequent studies (see, for example, Norton 1990), but its significance for present purposes is that it directs attention away from a preoccupation with 'law-making' and refocuses attention upon the broader roles of legislatures. What becomes clear, rapidly, in Packenham's specification and indeed in any other listing of functions, is that legislatures are not mono-functional bodies concerned exclusively with 'law-making'. In fact, as Packenham emphasizes, 'even if [a legislature] had no decision making power whatsoever, the functions which it performs would be significant' (1970:536).

From the outset, therefore, it needs to be recognized that legislatures are multifunctional institutions. The exact number of functions and their ranking in terms of importance naturally varies from author to author but it is possible to identify three key functions based loosely on the headings provided by Packenham. These are legitimation, linkage and decision-making. This precise listing of universal functions is provided by Copeland and Patterson (1994:154) and will be used throughout the rest of this book (see also Cotta 1974:208–16; Loewenberg and Patterson 1979:43–67). The general significance of this threefold classification of 'key functions' is that

a parliament's very reason for existence is found in them. Failure to fulfil these functions challenges the very basis for the existence of parliaments. A parliament without legitimacy may no longer be considered a parliament; a parliament that lacks any decision-making capacity hardly qualifies for the title; and an entity not formally linked to a broader population is no parliament. (Copeland and Patterson 1994:154)

The threefold classification of functions also points to the fact that parliaments perform their functions in relation to other political institutions and organizations, most particularly political executives in one direction and the electorate and civil society in the other. Thus, at the interstices of government and governance parliaments perform their common functions of legitimation, linkage and decision-making. What we intend to do, therefore, is concentrate upon the three 'universal' functions identified by Copeland and Patterson and assess the relevance of these functions for the EP and the EU across time. In so doing it will be apparent that the balance of importance between functions, and the relative emphasis placed upon the performance of these functions by the EP itself, has varied over time. The best we can do therefore is to follow Copeland and Patterson's (1994:153) advice and 'identify the major functions of parliaments that tend to be universal across both time and space, and [then] identify functions of particular relevance to a polity at a specific juncture in its history'.

'Universal' functions: policy influence, legitimation and linkage

Policy influence

> The simplest and most common comparative statements about legislatures ... usually refer to the importance of the legislature in the policy-making process relative to the importance of non-legislative institutions, commonly those operating through the executive branch of government. (Mezey 1979:23)

Two typologies have dominated the comparative assessment of the policy impact of legislatures and their respective capacities to influence or to 'make' policy. The first was provided by Michael Mezey (1979); and the second was an explicit reworking of Mezey's model by Norton (1990).

Mezey: policy-making strength of legislatures

According to Mezey a legislature can be placed into one of three discrete categories depending on the strength of its policy-making capacities (1979:26). 'Strong' legislatures can modify or reject executive proposals; legislatures with 'modest policy-making power' can modify but cannot reject policy proposals; and those legislatures that can neither modify nor reject policy proposals can be seen to have 'little or no policy-making power'.

In defining the policy-making strength of legislatures, Mezey drew both upon Blondel's (1973) notion of the constraints operating on a legislature, and his earlier concept of 'viscosity' (Blondel 1970:80). For Blondel, 'viscosity' reflected the degree of freedom – or alternatively the compliantness – of a legislature in relation to the executive's processing of legislation. Mezey refined the notion of constraint to mean not simply the 'constraints placed on the legislature that prevent it from influencing the policy-making process, but rather the constraints that the legislature is capable of placing on the policy-related activities of the executive' (Mezey 1979:24–5). In other words, he takes as an indication of the policy role of a legislature the extent to which a legislature restricts the ability of the executive to make policy unilaterally. Ultimately, therefore, Mezey maintains that the 'saliency of the legislature's policy-making role, whether ultimately evaluated as positive or negative, stems at base from its capacity to restrict the process, because that capacity is what compels other institutions to deal with it when they seek to make policy' (Mezey 1979:25).

An equally important part of Mezey's argument, however, is that any evaluation of legislative influence has to deal with 'real rather than paper powers' (Mezey 1979:25). Moreover, any evaluation of the constraints imposed upon executive policy discretion should also include informal mechanisms (for example, private discussions or anticipated opposition) as well as formal procedures for legislative amendment.

Philip Norton: policy-making versus policy-influencing

Philip Norton (1990) refines Mezey's categorization to include the capacity of legislatures to 'formulate' or 'make' policy. This moves beyond Mezey's notion of constraint to take into account the ability of a legislature to substitute its own policy for that of the executive. The essential difference for Norton is between those legislatures that can initiate or formulate legislation and those that cannot. The capacity to 'generate alternative policies' (Norton 1990:179) distinguishes 'policy-making' from 'policy-influencing' legislatures.

In the rest of this book these categorizations will be used to locate the EP diachronically (across time) in Chapter 2, and in comparison with other European parliaments in Chapters 8 and 9. As we will see in later chapters, empirical investigation of the EP's role and functions produces different answers at different times to the question of where is the EP located. What we should be suspicious of from the outset, however, are global

FIGURE 1.1 Policy-making and policy-influencing categorizations

Mezey	Norton
Strong policy-making power A legislature can: • modify or reject executive proposals	**Policy-making** A legislature is able to: • modify and reject measures put forward by government and • formulate and substitute policy for that proposed by government
Modest policy-making power A legislature can: • modify but cannot reject policy proposals	**Policy-influencing** A legislature is able to: • modify and reject measures put forward by government • but cannot substitute a policy of its own
Little or no policy-making power A legislature cannot: • modify or reject policy proposals	**Little or no policy impact** A legislature cannot: • modify or reject measures • generate and substitute policies of its own

Sources: Mezey (1979), Norton (1990).

claims that the EP is not 'a proper parliament'. For the question of what defines a 'proper parliament' is itself a complex issue.

Linkage

If the categorization of legislatures in terms of 'policy-making' or 'policy-influencing' is based upon an assessment of interinstitutional relations (primarily with executives), then, in turn, these relations are influenced by the linkage between a legislature and its wider political and societal environment. The inextricable connections between specific policy role and wider linkage is apparent in Copeland and Patterson's (1994:153) definition of a parliament as 'a group of individuals operating on behalf of others in a binding and legitimate manner and making decisions collectively but with formal equality'. The questions of exactly how, and in what respects, parliamentarians act 'on behalf of others' have been at the heart of representative theories and practice alike (see Judge 1999) and will be at the centre of the discussion in Chapters 3 and 4.

Legitimation

In Mezey's classificatory model a second dimension for distinguishing legislatures was the extent to which 'support' accrued to representative institutions. Support was taken to mean 'a set of attitudes that look to the legislature as a valued and popular political institution' (Mezey 1979:27). Support could be gauged by manifest indicators, such as institutional continuity, elite and public attitudes towards the institution itself, or satisfaction with the policy outputs of a legislature. Equally it could entail 'diffuse support' as part of an abstract 'cultural phenomenon nested within a set of supportive attitudes toward all of the political institutions that make up a political system' (Mezey 1979:31). In this sense the concept of diffuse support is inextricably linked to notions of legitimation. While this is not the place to examine these ideas in detail (see Chapters 3 and 4) the important point is that a parliament's role within a political system (and its location within a comparative categorization of legislatures) is influenced by the 'combination of policy powers and supportive orientations' (Scully 2000a:242). Certainly the role played by the European Parliament in the legitimation of the EU's political system is both important and extremely complex. This complexity is revealed in the discussion of the democratic and legitimacy deficits within the EU (see Chapter 3). For the time being, however, it is sufficient to note Scully's (2000a:244) cautionary statement that: 'A more powerful EP may indeed make the EU more democratic in a technical sense but it has thus far done little to accord the EU as a system of governance the legitimacy which democracy is normally seen to accord'. The location of the EP within the 'EU as a system of governance' will be examined below, but first one further classificatory system based upon 'systems of government' needs some discussion.

'Parliamentary model'

In addition to classification by functions, legislatures can also be differentiated in accordance with the characteristics of the wider political systems in which they perform their functions. One classic point of differentiation has been between 'parliamentary' and 'presidential' systems of government. These two models have been classified in accordance with different institutional configurations between the executive and legislature (Lijphart 1991). Indeed, the significance of this distinction has become more pronounced in analyses of the EU since the implementation of the Amsterdam Treaty in 1999 and a heightened belief in the 'parliamentarization' of the EU and its movement towards a 'parliamentary model' (Dehousse 1998; Muntean 2000; Majone 2002).

One problem common to such analyses, however, is that too often the criteria by which the process of 'parliamentarization' should be assessed are never fully specified. Moreover, there is a tendency to select individual characteristics of the 'parliamentary model' and to proclaim that because the EU displays individual elements of this model it is necessarily evolving towards a 'parliamentary democracy'. What we seek to argue in this book, however, is that a 'parliamentary model' is defined by the very *interconnectedness* of its defining elements. However, before developing this argument, a preliminary specification of what constitutes a 'parliamentary model' is required.

According to Loewenberg and Patterson (1979:56), 'the distinguishing characteristic of legislatures in parliamentary systems of government' is 'the overlap of executive and legislative leaders'. A basic feature of parliamentary systems, therefore, is that political executives are selected by the legislature (Lijphart 1991:3), and, normally, from within the ranks of parliamentary representatives (Lijphart 1984:68, 71). There is thus a fusion of executive and legislative roles. Moreover, 'In a parliamentary system, the chief executive ... and his or her cabinet are responsible to the legislature in the sense that they are dependent on the legislature's confidence and that they can be dismissed from office by a legislative vote of no confidence or censure' (Lijphart 1984:68). The logic of parliamentarism is that the executive should retain the confidence of the legislature because it derives both its legitimacy and its authority from the representative parliament. In this manner there is an intrinsic institutional interconnectedness between the executive and the legislature and the performance of the parliamentary functions of legitimation, linkage and decision-making.

An important corollary of this interconnectedness is the general belief that 'Parliaments are supposed to control the operation of the executive' (Dehousse 1998:598). The exact degree of control is determined, in turn, by the formal and informal constraints that the legislature is able to place upon the executive and vice versa (see Blondel 1973:45–54). These constraints may stem from formal, constitutionally prescribed powers, or from less formal practices, procedures and internal rules of a legislature itself.

In raising the concept of the 'parliamentary model' at this early stage all we seek to do is to reinforce Loewenberg and Patterson's (1979:65) dictum that: 'In conceptualizing the activity of legislatures in functional terms, we are also calling attention to the relationship between what legislatures do and what is done by other structures in the political system'. What we are particularly concerned to emphasize in this book is that the study of the EP, or any other legislature for that matter, has to be: *interinstitutional* – to take account of its relation with other institutions; *contextual* – to take account of the systemic context in which it operates; and *interconnected* – to take account of the multifunctional nature of legislatures.

This is not to claim that all legislatures are unique and cannot be compared, only that there is a danger of extracting isolated variables from different systems and reconstituting or 'stacking them up' in any single legislature to conclude that because some common characteristics can be identified, the aggregate is necessarily a 'parliamentary system'. That the EP performs the defining parliamentary functions of legitimation, linkage and decision-making is not in dispute (though how well it performs these functions is more contentious). What is in dispute, however, is whether the EU's political system *as an entity* conforms to a 'parliamentary model'.

Locating the European Parliament in the European Union's system of governance

Assessments of the role of the EP within the EU are shaped by conceptions of the EU as a system. The schools of thought [on the EU as a system]…orient us toward different approaches to the legitimacy of the EU…They represent useful points of reference for the ongoing debate about the place of the EP within the EU as a whole and its importance for the problem of legitimacy. (Wessels and Diedrichs 1999:135)

Not only does the EP have to be understood as a legislature but it also has to be understood as part of an institutional matrix. In other words, where the EP is located conceptually within the EU's institutional structures has a bearing on how well it is perceived to play the roles ascribed to it as a legislature. It is important, therefore, to keep in mind where the EP is located within broader conceptions of the EU as a political system when trying to assess its location within conceptions of it as a legislature. It makes little sense to make assessments of the EP's linkage functions, or its contribution to the legitimation of EU outputs (Chapters 3, 4 and 5), or to the EU's policy process (Chapters 7 and 8), unless we have a clear idea of what our expectations are of the EP in the first place. Do we expect it to display a direct electoral linkage between the represented and their representatives as in member states? Do we expect representatives at EU level to be authorized and accountable to an EU-wide electorate? Do we expect the existence of a European-wide 'people' or 'demos' in the first instance? Do we conceive of EU institutions in terms that are analogous to existing state-level institutions? Or is the EU's institutional matrix *sui generis* and so requires a new institutional vocabulary and new conceptualizations of legitimacy within the EU? Clearly detailed answers to these questions lie beyond the immediate scope of the present book, but at the very least these questions should be borne in mind when reading the following chapters.

The danger in raising these questions at such an early stage, however, is that the reader may become swamped by the sheer range of models (for example, intergovernmental, federal, cooperative federal, confederal consociationalism, regulatory state, multi-level governance, multi-tiered governance (for overviews see Chryssochoou *et al.* 1999; Rosamond 2000; Hooghe and Marks 2001)). What all of these models share, however, is a recognition that there is dispersion of formal authority among supranational, state and subnational governing institutions and that decision-making is not the sole preserve of elected representative institutions at any single level. In fact, Hooghe and Marks provide a useful organizing frame for our discussion by identifying two main types of governance. 'Type 1 governance' is based upon federal conceptions and is characterized by a limited number of governments operating at a limited number of levels with 'a system of multi-task and mutually exclusive jurisdictions' and with 'a ceiling on the dispersion of authority' (Hooghe and Marks 2001:5). 'Type 2 governance', on the other hand, is based on the proliferation of functionally specific jurisdictions and the organization of governance across a large number of levels. In this model 'formal government has shrunk' (Hooghe and Marks 2001:10) as 'self-rule' on the part of diverse groups and associations has expanded. It is a vision of a decision-making process which is interconnected, non-state-centred, non-majoritarian, and with shared competences among a multiplicity of actors.

In accepting this basic bifurcation of models of governance our intention here is simply to highlight the implications of these models for the conception of the EP. Hence, we do not intend to describe these models in detail, nor do we intend to make judgements upon their respective utility for understanding EU governance. Instead, our intention is far more restricted, and is simply focused upon locating the position of the EP within the institutional matrix identified in each type of governance.

Type 1 governance: the federal analogy

As a 'starting-point for understanding the institutions, politics and policy-making of the EU', William Wallace commends the appropriateness of the 'federal analogy' (1996:445; see also Laffan 1992:8). The use of the word 'analogy' is significant in that the EU should not be conceived of as an unambiguous federal system. Such a system is normally characterized by the existence of a sovereign state, with a constitutional division of powers between different levels of government; and with external sovereignty exercised at the higher level. A bicameral legislature is a common characteristic of such a federal system, with representation in the upper chamber based upon lower levels of government (states). The relationship between the federal level of government and lower levels (states) is regulated through formal mechanisms for constitutional modification, often with a requirement for super-majorities; and through the existence of constitutional courts to adjudicate in disputes over the allocation and exercise of powers between different levels of government (see Elazar 1991:xv; Laffan 1992:7–9). It is not surprising to find therefore that those who actively promote a federalist vision for the EU's future largely subscribe to a model of 'a parliamentary Europe' or aspire to 'full parliamentarization' of the EU (see Abromeit 2002:20).

When analysing the EU's political system, a useful distinction may be drawn between a fully developed federation along the lines of a 'United States model'; a 'confederation' or a 'neo-federal model'; and a 'cooperative federal model'. Taking these models in turn, the United States of Europe variant stipulates a formal–legal division of responsibilities between supra-state/EU-level institutions and state/substate political institutions. An institutional sketch of this model would pencil in a separation of powers at the EU level with the Commission clearly identified as the executive branch, a directly elected EP serving as the first legislative chamber; and with the Council of Ministers acting as a second chamber in areas of concurrent competences between EU and member states (see Wessels 1996b:25–6). The European Court of Justice would serve as a constitutional court with major responsibilities in the adjudication of institutional disputes among the tiers of government and between EU institutions themselves. In this 'United States' model the basic source of legitimation would be a directly elected EP, with the EP serving as the formal linkage between the represented and 'their' government at the EU level. Through elections to a European Parliament the will of the 'European people' would be expressed and their contribution to EU decision-making would be 'unfiltered' (Wessels and Diedrichs 1997:3). There would be no doubt that 'the EP is regarded as the main legitimizing factor of the EU system' (Wessels and Diedrichs 1999:136). The preexisting states and substates, in turn, would have their own designated competences and, through their own democratic processes, would derive legitimation through 'traditional national sources'. They would, however, be 'of secondary importance' (Wessels 1996b:25).

Analysts who acknowledge that the EU has federal characteristics but is not a federal state have turned to concepts of 'confederalism', 'neo-federalism' or 'confederal consociationalism' to understand its institutional configuration. What each of these terms recognizes is a division of decision-making authority among different layers of government. Unlike federalism, where there is a central source of legitimacy grounded in an identifiable demos in a 'union', a confederation is based on the concept of 'dual legitimacy' where the nation states maintain their own democratic legitimacy and continue to claim political sovereignty while allowing a 'pooling of sovereignties' at the EU level. In such a system member states would seek mutual benefits through cooperation over common policies at a supranational level. Such a system would require neither a 'sense of community' among the peoples of the confederation nor the existence of a single demos. Moreover, the 'polycentric and multilogic pattern' of decision-making is associated with a large dose of intergovernmentalism (Chryssochoou 1997:530). In these circumstances, the EP would remain in a secondary relationship to the EU's dual executive institutions (most particularly the Council of Ministers), and national parliaments would share a similar subsidiary relationship to their own national executives. The result would be that 'the main source of democratic legitimacy for EU decisions' rested more 'in the Council of Ministers' representation of national governments – in turn based on their respective national parliamentary structures – than on the powers of the EP as the natural exponent of representative democracy at the regional level' (Chryssochoou 1994:7). However, in the absence of a transnational demos there would be no effective mechanism for the direct democratic control of intergovernmental EU institutions, and in this lacuna are to be found the roots of the EU's 'crisis of legitimacy' and its various 'democratic deficits' (see Chapters 3 and 9).

Type 2 governance: 'multi-level'

According to Peterson and Bomberg (2000:25) multi-level governance has become 'a central point of consensus' among scholars of the EU. The initial premise of this model is that neither the concept of the nation state nor notions of international organizations capture the complexity of decision-making in the EU. The form of governance in the EU is thus both new and unique. What has emerged is a 'new, non-territorial form of governance' (Jachtenfuchs and Kohler-Koch 1997). It is *sui generis* in form, and decision-making is 'through a unique set of multi-level, non-hierarchical and regulatory institutions, and a hybrid mix of state and non-state actors' (Hix 1998a:39). To complicate matters still further the EU is a dynamic system subject to regular constitutional change and institutional innovation. Overall, therefore, 'because the EU as a political system is unique, it is an open process of trial and error to find out what kind of decision-making routines will develop and what will be the relative importance of individual institutions in the game' (Kohler-Koch 1997:3).

The 'multi-level governance' model acknowledges the continuing importance of state-level political systems, and that 'state arenas remain ... the *most* important pieces of the European puzzle' (Marks *et al.* 1996:346, original emphasis), but it also recognizes that the state does not exercise a monopoly of decision-making competences. Instead, these competences are shared by institutions and policy actors at different levels rather than concentrated at the level of individual states. 'That is to say, supranational institutions – above all, the European Commission, the European Court, and the European Parliament – have independent influence in policy making that cannot be derived from their role as agents of state executives' (Marks *et al.* 1996:346). Moreover, an essential part of the 'multi-level governance' model is that states no longer provide the sole interface for national political actors – whether as individuals, groups, private and public organizations or parties – between state and supranational levels.

Another feature of this model is functional differentiation or policy segmentation (see, for example, Peterson 1995:76–80; Kohler-Koch 1997:2–4; Hix 1998a:39–41, Peterson and Bomberg 1999:22–8; Richardson 2001:7–12). Consequently, decision-making in any single policy field is likely to engage the activities of subnational, national and supranational agencies, institutions and non-governmental organizations. Moreover, decision-making comes to be structured around informal contacts, networks and norms, and no longer involves clear hierarchies of power and competences. In this sense, in its very complexity, and in its engagement of a myriad of functional and territorial constituencies at multiple levels, the system has been characterized as a system of 'governance' rather than simply of 'government' (see Jachtenfuchs and Kohler-Koch 1995:5).

Nonetheless, even within this model, formal institutions of politics and government – executive, legislative, judicial institutions and political parties, for example – continue to be of importance, but their significance has now to be understood in terms of their relations with wider forces of governance. When the specific location of the EP is considered in models of multi-level governance two contrasting visions, among many, can be perceived. One is a pessimistic vision of a 'post-parliamentary Europe'; the other is a more optimistic vision of 'a new kind of parliamentary system'.

Post-parliamentary Europe

Judge noted in 1999 that it is commonplace to argue that the position of parliamentary institutions in Western liberal democracies are undergoing systematic erosion in complex systems of governance (see Judge 1999:121–48). In the case of the EU this argument is encapsulated in Andersen and Burns's (1996:234) statement that:

> The EU is, then, a mix between international co-operation with nation state representatives as key actors and particular forms of governance with elaborate, specialised sub-governments, policy networks and lobbying... Parliament is only marginally important even on the formal level.

What is of particular concern for the EP in this model is a 'frustrating and delegitimising gap between representative democracy's responsibility and its lack of structural capability and control' (Andersen and Burns 1996:243). In this gap, alternative forms of legitimacy – of 'output legitimacy' – derived from effective and efficient sectoral policy-making and policy solutions, become of increased importance (see Höreth 1999:259–61; Lord and Beetham 2001:451–2). In one extreme view, 'governance' and 'output legitimacy' crowd out or supercede parliamentary institutions, and representative democracy more generally (Andersen and Burns 1996:242). In this manner, the importance of the EP is seen to be residualized and the EU's political system becomes characterized as 'post-parliamentary'.

The fusion model

An influential strand of multi-level governance analysis is that the institutional structure and the sources of legitimacy within the EU are not directly comparable either to national political systems or to a supranational model of a 'United States of Europe'. Instead, the EU comes to be conceived as a 'multi-level system of governance in which a direct representative element in the shape of the EP is having an important say, as part of a European legitimacy complementary to the national and functional one, but in which the sources and dimensions of legitimacy are progressively getting merged' (Wessels and Diedrichs 1997:9). What is seen to be emerging therefore is a new kind of political system with *sui generis* characteristics (see Wessels 1996a:68; Wessels and Rometsch 1996:364). In essence established perspectives of federalism or intergovernmentalism cannot capture the role of the EP adequately within the EU's novel political system. Instead the EU should be understood as a 'new kind of polity characterized by fusion' (Wessels and Diedrichs 1999:139). The word 'fusion' acknowledges the merging of instruments of governance among national, subnational and supranational actors and institutions. What results is a 'mixed polity' which shares political authority among several levels of governance and 'includes a multitude of different sources of direct and indirect, functional, legal and democratic legitimacy' (Wessels 1996a:59). It is within this context that the role of the EP is identified as departing from established parliamentary models and 'essentially renders the EU a new kind of parliamentary system' (Wessels and Diedrichs 1999:139).

Within this new system there is an assumption of joint decision-making by the European Parliament and the Council. The expectation is that the Commission would increasingly serve as the executive of the EU – with its head elected by both the EP and the European Council, and other Commissioners nominated by the head of the Commission and approved by the EP. Majority voting in all EU institutions would be the norm, with some mechanism to 'unblock' institutional impasses between the legislative institutions of equal status (the Council and the EP). Yet the EP remains 'neither the emergent legislature of a European superstate in the making nor a powerless institution at the center of an intergovernmental system' (Wessels and Diedrichs 1999:143). It occupies an intermediate and somewhat indeterminate institutional position. Indeed, in the multitudinous vertical and horizontal institutional transactions involved in the complex process of 'institutional fusion', the EU's decision-making process is 'hardly understandable' with the concomitant danger that 'its output lacks a deeper-going acceptance' (Wessels and Rometsch 1996:365). There is the danger that 'the ability of the public to identify outcomes with their sponsors and assign responsibility accordingly will diminish' as the 'process of fusion progressively blurs the boundaries between the different actors and makes their roles functionally less distinguishable' (Wessels and Diedrichs 1999:149).

Ultimately, the logic of Wessels and Rometsch's argument leads – in one direction – to a call for the 'extended participation of national institutions – especially of national parliaments' (1996:365). But equally their logic leads, in another direction, to the conclusion that:

> The EP's direct representative capacity will continue to play an important role in this system, potentially bolstering a European legitimacy … The EP will likely never become a central representative institution comparable to national parliaments. Nonetheless, the Parliament's further development will continue to have far reaching implications for EU legitimacy. (Wessels and Diedrichs 1999:149)

In this conception the EU is seen as a complex and highly differentiated institutional system which 'combines several levels of governance and a wide range of actors' and the result of which is a 'mixed polity' and an 'optimal form of government' (Wessels and Diedrichs 1997:8). Unlike the post-parliamentary variant of the new governance thesis, in this 'new kind of polity' the EP is 'an increasingly important component of the EU political system' (Wessels and Diedrichs 1999:148).

Conclusion

Locating the European Parliament within wider theories of legislatures and of the European political system is of importance in understanding what role we would expect the EP to perform as a legislature and the broader political context within which it is expected to perform this role. What is apparent from this preliminary review of theories is that the EP, in conformity with all legislatures, is a multifunctional organization; but unlike other legislatures is a transnational body operating in a system of multilevel governance. This very multiplicity of roles and the multilevel context within which it operates should lead us to view global assessments of the EP and whether it is, or is not, a 'true' or 'proper' parliament (see, for example, Höreth 1999:253) with some caution. As the historical review of the EP's legislative powers in the next chapter reveals, the 'location' of the EP, in terms of policy influence, has changed over time. After the Maastricht, Amsterdam and Nice treaties the EP – with its capacity to 'modify and reject executive proposals' – can now be located in Mezey's category of legislatures with 'strong policy-making power'. But even this new categorization needs to be qualified by recognition that the policy influence of the EP should be disaggregated into its constituent elements. In other words, some acknowledgement has to be made that the EP will be more influential in some policy areas than others, and will be more influential even within the same policy area at some times rather than others (see Judge *et al.* 1994).

If assessments of the policy influence of the EP vary across time and across substantive policy areas, then equally judgements of the efficacy of the EP's legitimating and linkage functions vary in accordance with which model of the EU's political system is utilized. Understanding the location of the EP in the respective models not only helps us to assess the EP's historical contribution, or lack of it, to the legitimation of the EU but also identifies future prognostications as to the development of the EU as a political system and the EP's role in that process. Put very simply, different conceptions of what the EU is now, and what its future development entails, result in different assessments of what role the EP performs in the wider legitimation of the EU and what its future contribution to the 'democratization' of the EU will be. Whether this future is a 'parliamentary' one remains to be seen.

Chapter 2

Historical Evolution: The European Parliament and Ever Closer Union

Chapter 1 introduced a variety of models of legislative functions, and theories about the EU as a political system, with little attempt to locate the EP decisively in any single model or theory. Instead, the categories and variables that might be of use in undertaking such an exercise were simply identified and listed. The purpose of Chapter 1, therefore, was limited to making the analytical prescription that the study of the EP has to be: *interinstitutional* – to take account of its relation with other institutions; *contextual* – to take account of the systemic context in which it operates; and *interconnected* – to take account of the multifunctional nature of legislatures. The purpose of this chapter is to follow this prescription and examine how the location of the EP has varied across time in accordance with changes to its functional roles, its interinstitutional relations with the Commission and Council, and the systemic context in which it operates. It is important to deal with this cross-time analysis at the outset, both to provide a historical perspective on the development of the EP, and to provide a perspective from which the EP can be viewed in the early twenty-first century – without constantly having to refer back to the evolution of the EP in subsequent chapters.

Monnet's ambiguous institutional legacy

The origins of the EU are normally traced back to 1945, though ideas about European integration had persisted throughout the interwar period (see Urwin 1991:4–7; Dinan 1999:12–13). However, the prototype of the institutional structure of the EU is to be found in the European Coal and Steel Community (ECSC) which was established by the Treaty of Paris on 18 April 1951. The ECSC was the result of the initiative taken in May 1950 by

Robert Schuman, the French Foreign Minister, when he proposed the pooling of the coal and steel resources of France and the Federal Republic of Germany specifically, and more generally other West European states which cared to join a new Coal and Steel Community. The details of the genesis of the Schuman Plan need not detain us here other than to note that the diplomatic groundwork and inspiration for this Plan can be located in the French Modernization Plan of 1946, known as the Monnet Plan. Jean Monnet, the French Commissioner General with responsibility for formulating the 1946 Plan, is regarded as the 'architect of the European Community' (see Featherstone 1994:150; Holland 1994:9). Indeed, the enduring achievement of Monnet remains the institutional configuration of EU government.

The hallmark of Monnet's role in the drafting of the Treaty of Paris was the combination of pragmatism and idealism. From the outset Monnet was clear that: 'Europe will not be built all at once, or as a single whole: it will be built by concrete achievements which first create *de facto* solidarity' (Monnet 1978:300). Nothing was more concrete than the establishment of institutions. Indeed, for Monnet, institutions, were the key to successful integration: 'Only institutions grow wiser. They accumulate collective experience' (Monnet 1978:393; see Holland 1994:10; Featherstone 1994:159). If the enduring achievement of Monnet remains the institutional configuration of EU government, there are many who are willing to argue that Monnet's was an ambiguous institutional legacy. On the one side an elitist technocratic model can be discerned, while on the other a federalist democratic vision can be identified.

Elitist/technocratic blueprint

The first institutional blueprint (or map) ascribed to Monnet is essentially an elitist, technocratic model (see Pryce and Wessels 1987:24; Featherstone 1994:150). Monnet's 'method' of institutional building is now commonly associated with 'neofunctionalist' theories of integration (on neo-functionalism see Rosamond 2000:50–73; Cram 2001:55–60). From the outset a distinctive form of interest representation – derived from an expectation of functional consultation, and generating, in turn, an impetus for the creation of new networks focused upon the High Authority – came to be imprinted in the institutional structure of the new European Community. The objective of 'consultation' was to cultivate a 'combination of benevolent technocrats and interest-propelled economic groups to build transnational coalitions in support of European policies and to undermine the scope for national policies' (Wallace 1993:300). The fact that the ECSC existed in a 'political vacuum' with no 'independent legitimacy or direct political authority' (Wallace 1993:300) assisted the growth of these coalitions. Given this technocratic vision, some commentators have been led to argue that there was no provision for a parliamentary assembly in Monnet's original plans (Milward 1984:409). In this view, an Assembly came as a late addition and was proposed shortly after the start of negotiations in order 'to blunt the technocratic edge of the Authority'.

An alternative view maintains that Monnet acknowledged the need for a Common Assembly even before negotiations on the ECSC began (see Hirsch 1987:107, cited in Featherstone 1994:160; Westlake 1994a:71). By this view, while there is no doubt, as Monnet's own *Memoirs* makes clear, that his primary objective was to ensure that the vital first political step was taken by the setting up of the High Authority (Monnet 1978:324), it was also clear that the draft treaty discussed in Paris in June 1950 incorporated 'parliamentary control' in its design (see Oliver Harvey in Bullen and Pelly 1986:216). What is not in doubt, equally, is that the Assembly was designed to operate at the peripheries of the grand European design. While the Common Assembly might have been the first transnational Assembly in Europe, it had no legislative powers and no direct democratic legitimacy derived from direct elections. In terms of Mezey's categorization, noted in Chapter 1, it was easily located at this time in the 'little or no policy-making' group of legislatures, and in Norton's terminology it had 'little or no policy impact'.

Common Assembly: bridge to federal model?

The Assembly's role was prescribed in Articles 20 to 25 of the Treaty of Paris. Articles 20 and 21 stated that the composition of the Assembly 'shall consist of the peoples of the States brought together in the Community ... of delegates who shall be designated by the respective Parliaments'. Article 21(3) recorded that: 'The Assembly shall draw up proposals for elections by direct universal suffrage in accordance with a uniform procedure in all

Member States'. But it was to be the Council which was to 'make appropriate provisions' in accordance with the respective constitutional requirements of member states for the implementation of direct elections. The powers of the Assembly were specified in Article 24 and were essentially deliberative and supervisory.

The powers of the Common Assembly were thus closely circumscribed from the outset. In these circumstances, perhaps it is not surprising to find that the negotiations concerning the Assembly revolved around its composition rather than its powers, given that its powers were only minimally conceived. Equally unsurprising, perhaps, is that national interests predominated in these negotiations. Paramount importance was accorded to the defence of national interests in the treaty negotiations and the sovereignty of national parliaments was underscored throughout.

Locating the Assembly in the ECSC

Before moving on to consider the 1957 Treaty of Rome and later treaty revisions, it is advisable to reiterate the location of the EP in the institutional structure of the ECSC. It was not created to provide democratic legitimation of common policies either in terms of providing the direct consent of the represented, or in terms of authorization of those policies. The Common Assembly was neither directly elected nor directly capable of influencing or authorizing legislation. Instead, it was the Council that was to 'add to and endorse the decisions of the High Authority' (Hayes-Renshaw and Wallace 1997:9). In other words, it was the Council that was designed to play the legislative role normally ascribed to parliaments. Authorization of legislation was to be provided indirectly by ministers of elected national governments meeting in the Council. The outputs of the ECSC decision-making process would thus be legitimated indirectly by national governments, but would also derive their legitimacy in part from technocratic sources. 'Technocratic legitimation' was to derive from the ability of experts, operating in a supranational institution, the High Authority, to reach effective decisions that would promote the economic well-being of member states. In this respect conceptions of 'democratic legitimacy' did not weigh heavily in discussions about the putative institutional structure of the ECSC as it 'was not seen as essential to the task in hand'

(Featherstone 1994:163). Instead, it was believed that 'effective problem solving' would slowly extend the legitimacy of the High Authority. The very name – High Authority – was a significant signal that this supranational agency would gradually extend its authority to undermine the independence (and legitimacy) of member nation states. The expectation was that supranational institutions would be surrounded by a plurality of groups, and that a variety of functional 'stakeholders' would thus emerge in the European policy arena.

Hence, the new Community placed the emphasis firmly upon a 'locking-in' (or *engrenage*) of interested organizations, whether national administrative agencies or functional groups, into the European dual executive structure of the High Authority and the Council, rather than upon securing the direct involvement of national publics through parliamentary representation. It was envisaged that the issue of popular consent and democratic legitimation could be postponed until national publics had experienced the benefits of integration.

Democratic participation through elected representative institutions was thus something for the future. In this context Article 21 of the Treaty of Paris, which provided for the possibility of direct elections, was not mere window dressing. Moreover, Article 25 of the treaty, seemingly innocuous at first sight, conferred upon the Assembly the right to adopt its own rules of procedure. This control over its own procedures was to prove vital to the evolution of the Assembly and later to the European Parliament.

That the EP did evolve into something far more far-reaching in practice was dependent not only upon its membership and its democratic aspirations but also upon the innate rivalry between supranational and intergovernmental organizations which became institutionalized at the heart of the emerging European Community. At this point the interinstitutional dimension of analysis of the EP needs to be remembered and it is to this that we now turn.

Members, integrationist aspirations and interinstitutional relations

The 78 members of the Common Assembly of the European Coal and Steel Community met collectively for the first time in

Strasbourg on 10 September 1952. All members were nominated by their respective national parliaments, and as Wallace and Smith (1995:142) note the membership was partly self-selected as 'the most enthusiastic for European cooperation were happy to volunteer, the most sceptical saw little point in coming forward'. One immediate practical manifestation of this 'euro-enthusiasm' was the decision taken in June 1953 for members of the Assembly to sit according to political affiliation rather than by nationality. Transnational cooperation was reinforced in the decision to provide financial assistance to transnational party groups in the Assembly. From the beginning, therefore, there was an internal dynamic within the Assembly in favour of enhanced supranational cooperation generally, and the maximization of the role ascribed to the Common Assembly under the Treaty of Paris specifically. Moreover the Assembly rapidly established a subcommittee, chaired by Bernard Dehousse, to see how Article 21's provision for direct elections to the Assembly might be implemented (Herman 1980:14).

Given the majority predisposition within the Assembly in favour of the integrationist project, the High Authority rapidly recognized 'how attractive an alliance with the Common Assembly could be, in order to ensure that the two institutions, which were genuinely *communautaire*, were on the same side' (Albert Coppé, Member of High Authority, quoted in Wallace and Smith 1995:142). This attraction was reciprocated with the Assembly constantly urging the High Authority to expand its supranational initiatives (see Urwin 1991:55–6). This mutually enhancing relationship was to remain a characteristic feature of Assembly and High Authority interactions (and later between the Commission and the European Parliament (see Westlake 1994b:225)).

If the predisposition in favour of enhanced integration was evident both internally within the Assembly and externally in its relationship with the High Authority, this predisposition found almost immediate institutionalization. This came about through an invitation from the Council to the Common Assembly to convene a special committee to consider the feasibility of establishing a European Political Community (EPC). The Council's initiative was taken in the context of negotiations over the creation of a European Defence Community (EDC) which was to coexist with the ECSC. While the background to, and details of, the EDC – formalized in the Paris Treaty of 27 May 1952 – are not of concern here, the significant point is that the Common Assembly was asked to draft a blueprint for a future EPC to balance the functional ECSC and the military EDC. Thus, on *only its second day of existence* (11 September 1952) the Assembly created a working party to draft proposals for radical constitutional change. Even if the Council did not expect much to come of these proposals, nonetheless the Assembly's own expectations were raised. From the outset it was given a legitimate role in advancing further political integration.

A draft Treaty Establishing a Political Community was accepted by the Assembly on 10 March 1953 (for details see Urwin 1991:64–5; Nicoll and Salmon 2001:16–17). If the blueprint was more confederal than federal, nonetheless the experience of drafting a new constitutional settlement was 'inculcated in the European Parliament's collective memory' (Westlake 1994a:13). Despite the rejection of the EDC Treaty by the French National Assembly on 30 August 1954, the ECSC survived the wreckage, and, in the process, the Common Assembly had secured, almost by default, the acceptance of the six contracting governments to the principle of direct elections for a European representative institution.

The Treaty of Rome and the establishment of the European Economic Community

In effect the two Treaties of Rome of 1957, along with the Treaty of Paris of 1951, constituted the constitution of the European Communities. The institutional arrangements of the ECSC were consolidated and extended in the 1957 treaties. Reflected in the institutional design of the EEC and Euratom (and ultimately of the Merger Treaty of 1965) was the characteristic mix of the intergovernmental and supranational elements of the ECSC. A supranational body, the Commission, which was the equivalent of the ECSC's High Authority, was given the powers to: formulate recommendations for legislative proposals; 'participate in the shaping of measures taken by the Council'; implement decisions reached by Council; and generally to act as the 'guardian of the treaty' by ensuring 'that the provisions of this Treaty and the measures taken by the institutions pursuant thereto are applied' (Article 155). To counterbalance this supra-national body, a Council, consisting of a representative of each member state at ministerial level, was conferred with the 'power to take decisions' and was charged to ensure the coordination of the general economic policies of the member states (Article 145). The Council of the EEC thus had greater powers bestowed upon it in relation to the Commission than its predecessor in the ECSC. The EEC Treaty also institutionalized the representation of functional interests more explicitly through the creation of an Economic and Social Committee (EcoSoc). This body was to have advisory status and for decades after the Treaty of Rome it insisted upon its co-equal status with the Parliamentary Assembly established for the EEC.

The Assembly's formal powers

The Parliamentary Assembly of the EEC was manifestly the child of the ECSC Assembly. The Articles of the Treaty of Rome pertaining to the Parliamentary Assembly were based on the corresponding Articles of the Treaty of Paris. Article 137 (1957) repeated the wording of Article 20 (1951) that the Assembly 'shall consist of representatives of the peoples of the States brought together in the Community' but added the word 'advisory' to the phrase 'to exercise the advisory and supervisory powers which are conferred upon it by this treaty'. In so doing, the Treaty of Rome acknowledged a marginal enhancement of the new Assembly's powers – an enhancement which was to prove significant in the long term.

The EEC Treaty introduced a formal right of parliamentary involvement in the Communities' legislative process. In 22 articles of the EEC Treaty and in 11 articles of the Euratom Treaty provision was made for the Assembly to be consulted on Commission proposals before adoption by the Council. Unlike the Economic and Social Committee, which also had rights of consultation but which was subject to a deadline imposed by Council for the submission of its opinions, the Assembly was not subject to Council deadlines. This difference was to prove of importance to the later expansion of parliamentary participation in the European policy process.

Once granted a formal role in the legislative process, no matter how limited in practice, parliamentarians sought the incremental expansion of that role through *informal* internal processes and external interinstitutional agreements. Perhaps because the Assembly was granted such a tangential role in the legislative process its very marginality invited its members to seek alternative, informal modes of influence. As we will see below, considerable institutional ingenuity and constitutional dexterity were deployed by members of the Assembly/Parliament in ensuring an incremental accretion of their influence. Such ingenuity and informal modes of influence were to prove a characteristic feature of the development of the European Parliament.

The formal powers of the Assembly over the Communities' budget was enhanced in Article 203 of the EEC Treaty and Article 177 of the Euratom Treaty. Under these provisions the Assembly effectively became a twin arm of the EEC's budgetary authority (Westlake 1994a:15). Article 144 of the EEC Treaty and Article 114 of the Euratom Treaty confirmed the right, granted initially under the ECSC Treaty, of the Assembly to censure and to force the resignation of the Commission as a body. However, the EEC and Euratom treaties extended this right of censure beyond consideration of the Commission's annual report to include, implicitly, all aspects of the Commission's activities. Although frequently dismissed as a 'nuclear weapon' or as a 'sledgehammer' – and, moreover, criticized as a weapon wrongly targeted on the Commission rather than the Council – the linked powers of censure and dismissal were to prove vital to the evolution of the EP (see Chapters 7 and 8). The very fact that the weapon existed was sufficient to ensure that both the Parliament and the Commission had a vested interest in securing interinstitutional cooperation rather than conflict. In this sense, the negative power of censure and dismissal helped to forge a constructive relationship between the Parliament and the Commission. As such it has played a central role in the political and constitutional development of the European Union.

Proposal for direct elections

The EEC Treaty, like the ECSC Treaty before it, provided for the introduction of direct elections. The Assembly itself was to draw up proposals for direct elections which were to be conducted under a 'uniform procedure in all member states'. This right of initiative, in the drafting of a legislative proposal on direct elections, was unique; in all other areas of Community law it was the Commission that enjoyed the formal right of initiative. In conferring this right upon the Assembly the treaties instilled a democratic dynamic in the constitutional arrangements of the Community. As long as there were no direct elections, and as long as there was no uniform electoral procedure throughout member states, then the Community could be deemed somehow to be 'deficient' in participatory terms.

What the commitment to direct elections provided from the outset, however, was an *inherent institutional dynamic* within the Assembly for the practical achievement of direct elections, and a mechanism for a *perpetual normative questioning* of the constitutional construct of the EC/EU itself. Direct elections, following the logic of Monnet, were 'the only way to get the question [of integration] away from officials and into the hands of the people at large, and to make the latter really feel that they were participating in something new' (William Hayter (who was the UK Minister in Paris in 1952) in Bullen and Pelly 1986:889). In the absence of direct elections, or in the absence of popular engagement with the 'European project', the legitimacy of that project and the institutional construct of 'Europe' would remain open to question (see Chapter 3).

In the event it took 22 years before the first direct elections were held in June 1979. The intervening period was characterized by the EP's constant assertion of the principle that a directly elected parliament at the European level would afford democratic legitimacy to the legislative outputs of the Community. Counterposing this view was the belief – most vividly expressed in 1960 by the then French Prime Minister, Michel Debré – that the EC was simply an intergovernmental association of European states. In this vision he did 'not see what direct elections by universal suffrage of a political assembly dealing with technical bodies or with higher civil servants can accomplish' (cited in Westlake 1994a:17). Such resistance took a draft convention (1960), a revised convention (1976), numerous parliamentary resolutions, reports of the EP's Political Affairs Committee (most notably the Pleven and Patjin Reports), threats to take the Council to the Court of Justice (1969) and enlargement of the Community (1973) before it was overcome and European elections were eventually held on 7–10 June 1979. As Nugent observes (1999:220–1): 'That the first direct elections were not held until 1979 is witness to the feeling of some member governments ... that direct elections were rather unwelcome, both because they had supranational overtones, and because they might be followed by pressure for institutional reform in the EP's favour.' As the post-1979 history of the EP reveals, member governments were justified in fearing increased pressure for institutional reform on the part of a directly elected EP. Before examining the period after 1979, however, some of the most important developments in the period 1957–79 need to be noted.

Formal structures and informal changes, 1957–79

The Treaty of Paris and the two Treaties of Rome thus provided the constitutional blueprint for the EEC, EC and EU. For some thirty years after the formation of the EEC the institutional configuration provided by the 1957 treaties was to remain unaltered in essence. Amendments and supplements to the treaties were made and added, but the institutional (im)balance – which pivoted on the initial compromises between intergovernmental and supranational organizations made in the 1950s – was never formally challenged.

If, in this sense, the treaties could be regarded as the 'tablets of stone' for the constitutional development of the EU, they also possessed some of the geological qualities of magmatic rocks – hard on the outside but malleable and fluid on the inside. Whereas formal amendments to the treaties chipped away at the surface of the constitutional stonework, an internal interinstitutional dynamic soon became activated at the heart of the constitutional edifice. For long periods, however, analysts of the EU's development, and particularly of the evolution of the EP, looked only at the formal surface of the treaties and ignored the magmatic interinstitutional changes occurring beneath the surface.

In preface to examining the formal changes that were effected in the 1957–79 period, one informal change, of major symbolic importance, needs to be noted. This was the decision, taken on 30 March 1962, for the Assembly to call itself the European Parliament. However, the formal title 'Assembly' remained unaltered in the treaties until the adoption of the Single European Act in 1986.

Merger Treaty, 1965

In October 1960 the Assembly had adopted a resolution calling for the merger of the three Councils of the different Communities, and the combination of the EEC and Euratom Commissions with the ECSC's High Authority. Westlake (1994a:20) argues that Parliament's reasoning was that 'it, as well as the cause of integration, stood to gain from such a move, since a single Commission, still beholden to Parliament, could only gain in authority'. In 1965 a treaty establishing a single Council and a single Commission of the European Communities was signed and the Treaty came into effect in 1967. The powers exercised by the merged institutions still rested on the founding treaties, though one innovation made in Article 4 was the acknowledgement of a Committee of Permanent Representatives (COREPER) to prepare for Council meetings. With the institutionalization of COREPER the intergovernmental nature of the EEC was reaffirmed.

Budgetary provisions: treaty reforms, 1970 and 1975

Parliament achieved formal recognition as part of the 'budgetary authority' after the Treaty Amending Certain Budgetary Provisions of the Treaties was signed in Luxembourg in April 1970. In adopting a system of 'own resources' financing, the Community required member states to contribute to collective resources while allowing the Council and Parliament jointly to determine the overall limits of expenditure within the revenues made available by member states. The 1970 treaty changes were consolidated by further treaty revision in 1975. The combined effect of these amendments was to secure for the Parliament four major powers. First, the EP acquired, within certain limits, the right to increase or reduce Community expenditure without Council approval; second, it could redistribute spending between budget sectors; third, it was granted the power of rejection of the annual budget or of supplementary budgets; and, fourth, it was given the exclusive right to approve, or not to approve, the way in which the Commission spent the money voted in the budget (for details see Corbett *et al.* 2000:216–17; see also Chapter 7). This exclusive right of discharge was hailed by the EP itself as 'in effect the first full *legislative* power under the EEC Treaty'

(European Parliament 1978:21, emphasis added). Since 1975 the budgetary powers of the Parliament have not been subject to formal treaty revision. However, they have been subject to four interinstitutional agreements (in 1982, 1988, 1993, 1999) which have further enhanced the budgetary and scrutiny capacities of the EP.

Conciliation

In making the EP a joint budgetary authority the treaty amendments of 1970 and 1975 not only gave Parliament the capacity to influence the Council's policy development, but also generated new possibilities for institutional conflict. It was partly to anticipate and avoid budgetary conflicts that a 'conciliation' procedure was introduced by a Joint Declaration of the Council, Commission and Parliament in 1975.

The Council recognized that the new budgetary powers of the EP might be used to prevent the implementation of contested legislation with budgetary consequences. In these circumstances, the Council was willing to negotiate and agree a method of resolving potential conflicts. Under this procedure, if the Council wished to diverge from the opinion of the EP on 'Community acts of general application which have appreciable financial implications', then the issue was to be referred to a Conciliation Committee composed of equal numbers of MEPs and members of the Council. At the conclusion of conciliation negotiations, the Council retained the sole right to adopt the act in question. Ultimately, therefore, Parliament did not have the capacity to force concessions out of the Council, but rather enjoyed the right to ask ministers in the Council to reconsider disputed proposals. Before direct elections in 1979 the conciliation procedure was used on only five occasions, and to little positive effect as far as Parliament was concerned. After direct elections, however, the number of conciliations and their qualitative impact upon Community legislation increased steadily (see below).

Irrespective of its policy impact, which was severely limited in the early years, the conciliation procedure was to prove of importance for four other reasons. First, it acknowledged the need for a linking mechanism between Council and Parliament which would allow the latter to consider financially significant legislative measures before they were formally adopted. In so doing, there was an implicit recognition that 'effective budgetary control calls for some say in legislation giving rise to expenditure' (Committee of Three 1979:76). Second, it provided a direct and unfiltered link between Council members and MEPs. In this sense it implanted Parliament into the direct consciousness of the Council and helped to develop closer working relations with the EP. Third, the Parliament had an incentive to extend the scope of the procedure beyond conciliation on budgetary matters to other important legislative proposals. And MEPs proved adept at extending the reach of the procedure through the creative amendment of its own Rules of Procedure (see European Parliament 1979: Rule 22(a)). Fourth, conciliation provided an institutional dynamic for the EP to press for further interinstitutional agreements in order to extend the procedure. Parliament was assisted in this respect by the Council's willingness to convene 'informal conciliations' and to adopt a flexible interpretation of the phrase 'with appreciable financial implications'. This enabled conciliations to be held on legislation which did not strictly fall within this category.

Again the specific details of the extension of the procedure need not distract us from the general point that the EP, throughout its history, has proved willing to maximize its limited formal powers by seeking creative informal agreements with other institutions and through internal procedural innovations. What the introduction of the conciliation procedure in 1975 vividly illustrates is the use of procedural precedent to lever more far-reaching institutional change at some future date. Without being too overly deterministic it is possible to conclude that the 1975 conciliation procedure 'acted as the precursor of the much more developed system of conciliation that exists under co-decision' (Corbett *et al.* 2000:183).

A directly elected Parliament: small steps and large strides, 1979–87

Immediately before direct elections one authoritative evaluation of the European Parliament concluded that:

The European Parliament is *not* a parliament (or, more accurately *not much* of a parliament) because it fails to meet a series of basic political, constitutional and decision-making requirements concerning the performance of legislative, financial and control powers. (Herman and Lodge 1978:65)

Certainly, at the time of direct elections in 1979 there were many who were either sceptical of the EP's capacity to effect a funda-mental redistribution of power without formal changes in the EP's advisory and supervisory powers, or who believed that increased 'democratization' of the EC's policy-making process was unlikely to result simply from the process of direct elections (see Dinan 1999:84–5; Nicoll and Salmon 2001:31). Both analy-ses were correct in identifying the basic fact that European elec-tions in themselves neither altered treaty-based interinstitutional relations nor enhanced the participation of directly elected rep-resentatives in the EC's legislative process. But both analyses underestimated the dynamic effects of direct elections in stimu-lating MEPs to press for more far-reaching institutional changes.

In practice, direct elections were to have a positive impact at three different levels. The first was at an 'attitudinal' level. MEPs' own expectations were reoriented and the attitudes of the other European institutions to the EP were reappraised. The second was a structural shift in the balance between national parliaments and the EP. The third was an underlining of the tra-ditional strategy pursued by the EP in seeking a dual enhance-ment of its powers: indirectly, through *petits pas* (small steps); and, directly, through promotion of treaty-based fundamental constitutional revision which was to culminate, successively, in the Single European Act (SEA) and the treaties signed in Maastricht, Amsterdam and Nice. However, before examining these treaty revisions, we will examine the incremental advances made by the EP in the period between direct elections in 1979 and the entry into effect of the SEA in 1987.

Attitudinal change

One early, and extremely important, indication of changed atti-tudes on the part of other EC institutions to the directly elected EP came in the Court of Justice's 1980 *Isoglucose* ruling (for details see Kirchner and Williams 1983). The ruling of the Court in Case 138/79 annulled a regulation which had been adopted by the Council before Parliament had formally delivered its opinion. The Court held that the Council had infringed the procedural requirement of the consultation procedure set out in Article 43(2) EEC. The significance of the consultation procedure in the view of the Court was that:

> [It] is the means which allows the Parliament to play an actual part in the legislative process of the Community. Such power represents an essential factor in the institutional balance intended by the Treaty. Although limited, it reflects at Community level the fundamental democratic principle that the peoples should take part in the exercise of power through the intermediary of a representative assembly. (Quoted in Westlake 1994a:24)

In this statement the Court clearly identified Parliament as having its own source of democratic legitimacy. In which case, the Council could no longer disregard Parliament's opinions without being in violation of the treaty. Hence, just one year after the first direct elections, Parliament appeared to have become 'in the eyes of the Court … a vital and major institution within the Community' (Kirchner and Williams 1983:179).

Correspondingly, the attitudinal relationship between the Parliament and the Commission was affected by direct elections. After 1979 the Commission increasingly looked towards the EP for legitimation of its actions and proposals. The result was that 'although the Parliament was still practically dependent on the Commission, the Commission was becoming politically dependent on the Parliament' (Westlake 1994a:25). In the first two years of the new Parliament, MEPs rapidly moved to increase this political dependence through a series of resolutions and through amendments to the EP's Rules of Procedure on 26 March 1981 (see Lodge 1983:30–1; Kirchner and Williams 1983:180–1).

Rule changes and procedural innovation

The 1981 Rules of Procedure doubled the number of rules from 54 to 116. New Rules 35 and 36 were of particular significance in introducing a mechanism of delay into the procedure for producing a parliamentary opinion. In order to maximize the advantage derived from the *Isoglucose* ruling, the new rules allowed for the referral of draft opinions back to the appropriate committee. This provided for the postponement of a vote on a Commission proposal until the Commission had expressed its position on the amendments proposed by Parliament. The threat of delay was particularly potent on those matters requiring an urgent response by Parliament. Thus, in line with Mezey's notion of constraints identified in Chapter 1, the EP, in policy areas covered by consultation, began to edge away from the lowest category of legislative influence, towards the modest influence/power category.

Not only was Parliament provided with a mechanism to lever concessions out of the Commission but also, through pressing for the acceptance of its amendments by the Commission, Parliament sought indirectly to influence the Council's decisions. Council could only change a revised Commission proposal by unanimity. In this manner, not only did the rule changes affect the practice of EP–Commission relations and the perception of each institution held by the other, but they also marked a psychological turning-point in the EP's relations with the Council. If, as Lodge (1983:33) argues, the internal procedural changes rested 'on the premiss that the EP has a moral and political obligation to EC voters to represent their interests by affecting ... the content of EC legislation', then after direct elections this premiss was never explicitly challenged by the Council. Thereafter, the EP gradually became ever more focused in the collective 'mind's eye' of the Council.

Questions

The creative use of parliamentary procedures was also evident in the enhanced inquisitory role the EP accrued to itself over time. Under the EEC Treaty the Commission alone was held responsible for replying 'orally or in writing to questions put to it by the Assembly or by its members' (Article 140). The Council was to 'be heard in the Assembly in accordance with the conditions which the Council shall lay down in its rules of procedure'. Even before direct elections, however, Council accepted (in 1973) that it should answer parliamentary questions and (in 1976) extended this agreement to cover political cooperation meetings of foreign ministers. This acceptance of 'informatory accountability', in the sense of acknowledging the basic right of Parliament to be informed about the actions of Commission and

Council, was further entrenched by the Solemn Declaration on European Union signed in 1983. In accordance with this Declaration Council undertook to answer all parliamentary questions addressed to it. The important point for our discussion is that this symbolic advance was made on the basis of a political convention rather than a treaty obligation.

Legislative initiative

Informal innovations also contributed to the enhancement of the legislative role of the EP (and to the potential relocation of the EP into the modest power category in Mezey's schema and into Norton's 'policy influencing' category) even before formal treaty revisions were effected in the 1980s and 1990s. As noted above, the Commission alone under Article 155 of the Treaty of Rome was empowered to formulate recommendations for legislative action; yet, through astute use of its own rules, the EP created for itself a right of legislative initiative. Parliament adopted procedures – most notably 'own initiative reports' – that enabled it to forward draft proposals for legislation to the Commission (see Judge 1993:190–3; Judge and Earnshaw 1994:264–6). In this manner, the EP was able to insert its ideas at the formulation stage of the legislative process; either to bring a new issue onto the agenda, or to express a view on matters upon which it did not have to be formally consulted. In this sense the EP also began to edge towards Norton's 'policy-making' group of legislatures in its tentative development of a capacity to 'generate alternative policies'. Moreover, as Lodge notes (1989:66) the use of 'own initiative reports' provided a simple device which 'when handled shrewdly by MEPs ... was to prove extremely useful: it was the basis of the draft treaty establishing the European Union in 1984. It was also a useful vehicle for increasing formal EP–Commission contact on a future legislative agenda.'

Interinstitutional agreements

However, before examining the role of the EP in formal treaty revision, one further informal strategy is worthy of examination. As noted above, the Council, Commission and Parliament signed a joint declaration in 1975 to establish a conciliation procedure for legislation with 'appreciable financial implications'. Since direct elections in 1979, Parliament has consistently sought the extension of interinstitutional agreements to regularize its relationship with the Commission and Council. Once having established working conventions and practices with the other institutions, Parliament has been adept at transforming these informal arrangements into something more tangible, particularly during periods of formal treaty revision. A pattern has thus emerged where in the aftermath of treaty amendment, Parliament has been able to secure interinstitutional agreements to ease the implementation of new working patterns and connections between the institutions. In this manner the 1988 agreement on budgetary matters flowed from the implementation of the Single European Act, and negotiations surrounding the introduction of the Maastricht Treaty led in 1993 and 1994 to a series of interinstitutional agreements designed to facilitate the new working relationships among the three institutions. In turn the implementation of the Amsterdam Treaty brought in its wake the 1999 interinstitutional agreement on financial matters and the Framework Agreement on Relations Between the European Parliament and the Commission of July 2000 (see Chapter 7).

Formal treaty reforms

Draft Treaty on European Union

The 'small steps' strategy adopted by the EP after direct elections in 1979 was accompanied by a parallel strategy of promoting a 'qualitative leap' towards further integration. Initially the majority of newly elected MEPs in 1979 were predisposed in favour of taking 'small steps' and of developing the role assigned to them by the existing treaties. Within a very short period, however, the inability of existing European institutions to deal with the problems arising from the 'eurosclerosis' of the 1970s and early 1980s led to demands for comprehensive constitutional reform both from within and outside of the EP (see Capotorti *et al.* 1986:9–10). From outside, a joint initiative of the foreign ministers of West Germany and Italy – Hans-Dietrich Genscher and Emilio Colombo – led to the publication of the Genscher–Colombo Proposals in November 1981. These proposals constituted a draft European Act and sought to identify the principles and institutional reforms which would enhance European integration without a formal revision of the Treaty of Rome. At the heart of these principles was a recognition that the ideal of an EC identity should be promoted, the European Council should act as the source of political guidance within the Communities, there should be greater cooperation on foreign and security matters, and that the position of the EP within the decision-making process should be 'improved' (for details on the proposed improvements see Lodge 1982:279–83). The Genscher–Colombo Proposals made little headway and culminated only in 'a vague, insubstantial assertion of the Community's international identity' in the form of a 'Solemn Declaration on European Union' (Dinan 1999:98). Nonetheless, the Proposals heightened the profile of further political and economic cooperation on the EC's agenda. Moreover, they provided reinforcement of the position of those within the European Parliament who favoured a strategy of far-reaching constitutional reform.

In fact the EP had been kept informed of the Genscher–Colombo deliberations and had offered its strongest support for the ministerial initiative. In parallel, in July 1981, 170 MEPs signed a motion calling for fundamental reform of the EC. This motion was promoted by members of the 'Crocodile Club'. This all-party group of MEPs, which derived its name from the Strasbourg restaurant which had hosted the group's inaugural meeting in 1980, was committed to fundamental reform of the institutional procedures of the EC and a redefinition of the powers of the Community. In addition to the motion calling for Treaty revision, the EP also established in July 1981 a new Committee on Institutional Affairs. The sole task assigned to the new Committee was to draft a new constitutional framework for the EC (Lodge 1984:378).

Altiero Spinelli, one of the founders of the postwar federalist movement, was appointed general rapporteur of the Committee and, along with six co-rapporteurs, produced general guidelines for the reform of the treaties. These guidelines were accepted by Parliament in a resolution of 6 July 1982. At their centre was support for the principle of subsidiarity, and for a new institutional balance which would lead to greater equality between the Council and the EP, and which would further acknowledge the democratic legitimacy of the Parliament. These guidelines were eventually translated into the Draft Treaty on European Union which was adopted by the EP on 14 February 1984 by a vote of 237 to 31.

The first line of the preamble to the Draft Treaty indicated that its purpose was 'continuing and reviving the democratic unification of Europe'. The Draft Treaty aimed to provide a single and comprehensive constitutional text for a new political entity to replace the existing Communities. While keeping the institutional configuration of the EC – Council, Commission, Court of Justice and Parliament (with the European Council elevated to the fifth institution) – the Draft Treaty redressed the EC's intergovernmental imbalance in favour of enhanced democratic participation by a supranational Parliament. This redress was most evident in Article 36 which stated unambiguously that: 'The Parliament and the Council of the Union shall jointly exercise legislative authority with the active participation of the Commission'. Correspondingly, Parliament was to constitute jointly with the Council the budgetary authority of the Union. In both cases, the Council was to lose its capacity to block progress through inaction, as approval had to be given within specified time limits (Articles 38 and 76). Moreover, within the Council, majority voting was expected to become the general rule. The Draft Treaty also specified an enhanced oversight role for Parliament in its relations with the Commission. While the Commission was to retain the right of legislative initiative, it was envisaged that an acceptable legislative programme would have to be submitted to Parliament before the Commission could take office.

Single European Act, 1986

In the event, the institutional blueprint of the Draft Treaty failed to guide the intergovernmental conference convened after the Milan summit of June 1985. What the IGC produced instead was amendment of the EEC Treaty to: incorporate new policy areas (including environment, research and technological development, and regional policy); complete the internal market by 1992; put European foreign policy cooperation on a legal basis; and provide formal recognition of the meetings of Heads of State and Government in the European Council. The discussions in the IGC were pervaded by a general feeling that little policy development, especially in regard to the completion of the single market, could be achieved unless the process of decision-making in the EC was reformed. A synergy was thus engendered – in large part intentionally through the creative perspicacity of Commission President Jacques Delors – between economic reform and institutional reform (see Noël 1989:3–14). The central dynamic of this synergy was a recognition that the project of the 1992 single market could only be effected if the political process of the EC was made more efficient. In turn, it was acknowledged that greater efficiency raised, as its corollary, a need for the further democratization of the decision-making process.

Greater efficiency was to be effected through two linked reforms of the Council. On the one side, unanimity had to be replaced by greater majority decision-making; on the other, the Council had to delegate some of the burden of implementing its own decisions to the Commission. With majority voting, however, came the prospect that ministers from any particular state might be outvoted, thus calling into question the ability of their own national parliaments to control the preferred outcomes of the Council negotiating process (see Westlake 1994a:27). If the lines of accountability between national ministers in the Council and national parliaments became blurred in these circumstances, there was a specific counter logic, therefore, to enhancing the legislative scrutiny and control of the EP. When combined with a more general federalist logic – which was shared by some member states, particularly Germany and Italy, and by the Commission – for an increase in the legislative powers of the European Parliament (see Dinan 1999:118), the case for constitutional reform became overwhelming.

Ultimately, the confluence of these specific and general logics resulted in the introduction of the 'cooperation procedure' in the SEA. This applied to most of the legislation needed to effect the internal market and added, in effect, a second reading to the traditional legislative procedure of consultation (see Chapter 7 for details). The SEA also gave Parliament, through an assent procedure, equal rights with the Council for the ratification of accession treaties and association agreements. However, despite these enhancements of the EP's legislative powers, the incremental procedural changes fell far short of the general powers of codecision envisaged in Parliament's original Draft Treaty.

The response of the EP to this shortfall was predictably critical. Although disappointed with their new powers, MEPs recognized that cooperation was, nonetheless, a *new* power and that, with judicious use, it had the potential for future development. From the outset senior MEPs and officials within Parliament were acutely aware of the strategic political implications of the procedure (as indeed were officials in the Commission, but for different reasons). Both institutions were sensitive to the new interinstitutional dynamic that had been created by the procedure; and both were aware of the changes in institutional priorities and working routines needed to maximize the effect of the SEA.

Interinstitutional dialogue

Whilst seeking to maintain its autonomy and independence, the Commission had a vested interest in ensuring that its own legislative initiatives did not stall because of interinstitutional rigidities or textual ambiguities in the treaty itself. It adopted, therefore, a flexible attitude to Parliament, working out a number of interinstitutional agreements and informal understandings, as well as adopting a more formal 'code of conduct' (at Parliament's urging) in 1990. These changes in attitude and working practices were themselves testimony to the fact that Parliament now had to be taken seriously, not least because of the very practical advantage of securing its support at an early stage of the legislative process. In this context, what happened at the first reading stage of the cooperation procedure, and even before, was the prime concern of the Commission (see below; Earnshaw and Judge 1995a). Equally, Parliament focused its attention upon first reading and changed its rules of procedure in 1986 to ensure that legislation subject to cooperation would 'in theory have absolute priority for consideration in committee' (European Parliament 1987: Rule 47(2)). The rules also acknowledged (in Rule 36(5)) the need to ensure that legislative resolutions focused specifically on procedural points rather than providing a discursive commentary on the text. In addition, provision was made to facilitate the construction of stable political majorities early in the cooperation procedure, which would endure to second reading where absolute majorities were required. Rule 36(3) was changed to allow for the verification of the legal basis of new proposals on a case-by-case basis. Moreover, both institutions, jointly, have been willing to challenge Council when it has overturned their prior agreement on the choice of legal base. What proved to be far more contentious in practice, and indeed to give rise to much tension between the Commission and Parliament, was the issue of 'comitology': that is, the Commission's specification in draft legislation of the type of committee needed to assist it in the performance of executive functions (see Chapter 8).

The new rules adopted by Parliament in 1986 also envisaged a monitoring procedure (Rule 41) whereby the preparation of a common position by Council would be monitored by the rapporteur and chairman of the relevant committee. Some observers hoped, optimistically, that such monitoring would 'serve to check that the Commission is keeping its promises on amendments and effectively upholding amendments it has accepted ... [and serve, indirectly] to prevent the Council from adopting a common position that strays too much from Parliament's position' (Fitzmaurice 1988:395). In practice, however, the reality of EP–Council relations under cooperation diverged significantly from this optimistic prognosis.

Moving beyond the SEA

With hindsight, however, the SEA conformed to the historical pattern of the EP's insatiable quest for 'the democratic unification of Europe' (Draft Treaty preamble). In this quest, dramatic 'qualitative leaps' were aspired to, but 'small steps' were achieved pragmatically and cumulatively to significant effect. Certainly the SEA did not put the EP on a co-equal footing in the legislative process, but what it did do was provide new opportunities for the EP to seek 'further refinements of the cooperation procedure, further amendments to the treaty and the revival of the draft Treaty establishing the European Union' (Lodge 1989:76). With increasing momentum after the elections of 1989, the EP issued a series of reports and resolutions highlighting the constitutional deficiencies of the SEA and calling for further 'democratization' of the EC's institutional structure.

The demands of the EP for a reconsideration of the SEA's institutional legacy were to find increased resonance in certain member states in the context of wider economic and political developments within the Community. The decision to convene an intergovernmental conference on economic and monetary union (EMU) taken by the European Council in 1989, alongside the emerging movement towards German reunification, and the political transitions in East and Central Europe, combined to prompt a general consideration of 'European Political Union' (EPU) within the integrationist debate on 'European Union' (see Wessels 1991:9–11; McAllister 1997:199–228). Predictably, the EP was proactive in seeking to widen the debate to include institutional reform. Particularly influential in this respect were the reports issued by the EP's Institutional Affairs Committee under the names of its rapporteurs David Martin and Emilio Colombo (see Corbett 1993a; Lodge 1994:75; Corbett *et al.* 2000: 299–300).

Rather than propose fully elaborated treaty revisions, Parliament's resolutions adopted on the basis of the Martin reports canvassed pragmatic, but far-reaching, procedural reform and expansion of the EC's competences (OJ C 96, 17 April 1990:114–18; OJ C 231, 17 September 1990:97–105). The key proposals envisaged in the Martin reports included: codecision for the EP with the Council; election of the Commission president by Parliament on a proposal from the European Council; generalized majority voting in the Council; greater cooperation between the EP and national parliaments; a limited right of legislative initiative by the EP; the creation of parliamentary committees of inquiry; reinforcement of Parliament's control over finance; as well as extension of the competences of the EC. The Martin reports ultimately proved crucial in defining the agenda of the IGC convened to consider political union in parallel with the IGC on EMU (Corbett *et al.* 2000:299).

While most member states agreed with the basic objectives of European Political Union – redressing the democratic deficits; expanding Community competences; strengthening subsidiarity; increasing the efficiency of decision-making – significant differences emerged in the IGC on how these were to be implemented (see Pryce 1994:36–52; Nugent 1999:197–202). Although the EP was not a direct participant in the IGCs, it made its views known, nonetheless, through its reports and debates; and pressed, successfully, for the establishment of an interinstitutional committee to serve as a forum for discussions between the three institutions. The EP also pursued a parallel strategy of involving national parliaments in deliberations upon treaty reform. Meetings with the European Affairs committees of national parliaments were convened and, more significantly, a Conference of Parliaments of the Community, or *Assizes* to use a traditional French word, was held in Rome in November 1990 (see Westlake 1995; Judge 1995:89–90). The Assizes proved of some significance in adopting, a month before the IGCs opened, a declaration that endorsed all of the EP's main proposals for treaty revision. At the heart of the Rome Declaration was a call for a Union 'on a federal basis', a Union in which, moreover, the European Parliament would exercise a power of real codecision. In this sense the Assizes 'helped to place firmly on the agenda of the IGC virtually all the issues that had been raised by the EP ... [and] gave ammunition to those governments favourably disposed towards the proposals and helped shape expectations with regard to the IGCs' (Corbett 1992:275).

The Journey from Maastricht to Amsterdam

As the negotiations proceeded and Parliament's exorbitant demands came nowhere near being met, a torrent of speeches and resolutions condemning the IGCs flowed out of Strasbourg ... As expected, the results of the Maastricht summit disappointed Parliament. (Dinan 1999:143)

Manifestly, while the European Parliament did not secure all it wished for, Dinan's dismissive assessment of Parliament's impact needs some qualification on at least two grounds. First, there is little doubt that many of the new treaty provisions, particularly those concerned with the extension of the powers of the EP itself, would not have been included in the Maastricht Treaty had it not been for the unremitting pressure of the EP. Second, Parliament obtained significant changes in the two areas it had identified as in need of specific change: the Community's legislative procedure and its involvement in the appointment of the Commission. Overall, therefore, a more balanced assessment is provided by Corbett (1994:223) in his statement that 'Maastricht constitute[d] an important step forward ... for the European Parliament.' This view was shared by Lodge (1994:80) who concluded that the 'TEU significantly augmented the potential scope of the European Union's popularly elected arm of the legislature'.

In terms of the enhancement of the EP's legislative influence the Treaty on European Union (TEU) was of significance in introducing a new legislative procedure – now almost universally referred to as the 'codecision procedure' – into the European Union's legislative process. Although its scope was more limited and its operation more complex than initially envisaged by Parliament, nonetheless it was greeted by influential commentators as 'a remarkable step forward' (Westlake 1994a:146) and 'of fundamental importance to public perceptions of Parliament's role: it can no longer be accused of lacking teeth' (Corbett 1994:210). For the first time Parliament was now an equal partner in the legislative process, with acts adopted under the procedure jointly signed by the presidents of Council and Parliament, and with an absolute right of veto over significant areas of EU legislation. To echo Mezey's (1979:25) words, a right of veto is 'the most telling constraint that the legislature can place on the policy-making process'. After Maastricht, and under codecision, the EP – with its capacity to 'modify and reject executive proposals' – met Mezey's (1979:26) analytical requirements, noted in Chapter 1, to be located in the category of legislatures with 'strong policy-making power'.

As a consequence, informal interinstitutional linkages expanded in response to codecision. Immediately after the Maastricht Treaty came into effect 'informal conciliations and trialogues – involving the Council presidency, EP committee chairpersons and members of the Commission – emerged as crucial arenas for informal bargaining' (Peterson 1995:86). Informal negotiation also increased 'upstream' – with bargaining occurring earlier in the legislative process. At a broader institutional level, one of the early outcomes of codecision was the conclusion of horizontal agreements between Parliament and Council (and the Commission) on 'comitology' (see Chapter 8) and on 'amounts deemed necessary'. The net result of the dialogue between Parliament and Council was the confirmation of an increasingly bipartite bargaining process and this, in turn, placed the Commission in a considerably more ambiguous, and weaker, position than in the cooperation or consultation procedures. The ultimate logic of the Commission's position was that it needed now to act in a more even-handed manner between Parliament and Council in its search for legislative agreement.

Maastricht also extended and enlarged the assent procedure to new areas and categories where international agreements required Parliament's assent. The powers over the appointment of the Commission were increased (see Corbett 1994:214; Hix and Lord 1996; Hix 1997). The TEU also saw further consolidations of the formal power of the EP in several other ways: first, it conferred a right of legislative initiative upon Parliament in so far as it allowed the EP to request the Commission to bring forward legislative proposals; second, it recognized the petitioning procedures of the EP and empowered Parliament to elect an Ombudsman to deal with matters falling within the competence of the EC; third, it required the President of the Central Bank to provide an annual report to Parliament and gave Parliament the right to be consulted on the appointment of the Bank's President and board members; and, fourth, it enabled Parliament to bring the other institutions before the European Court where its own prerogatives had been infringed.

Alongside these formal enhancements and extensions of its powers Parliament also sought to maximize, through its own internal procedures and through informal pressure, its own contribution to the EU's decision-making process. In conformity with the historical practice of combining 'small steps' with 'qualitative leaps', Parliament continued to work simultaneously for further practical procedural gains and more wide-ranging treaty reforms. In 1993 it negotiated a series of interinstitutional agreements with the Commission and the Council on the EU's finances; 'democracy, transparency and subsidiarity'; implementing the principle of subsidiarity; the proceedings of the conciliation committee; and the Ombudsman (see Corbett 1993b:31–5). A year later it concluded an interinstitutional agreement on committees of inquiry. The year 1994 also saw the adoption of new Rules of Procedure designed to maximize the impact of the formal powers conferred by the TEU. As Judge *et al.* (1994:31) noted at the time, 'internal procedural reform [was] designed to impact more widely on interinstitutional relations'. In this manner, the Commission was prompted to table amendments to its own proposals directly in EP committees, rather than having to wait until after Parliament's formal first reading (European Parliament 1994:Rule 56(3)). Under Rule 32 a two-stage procedure was introduced for the approval of the Commission, which effectively provided for a veto on the Council's choice of

Commission President (see Hix 1997:2). Similarly Rule 33 secured an undertaking from the Commission President that he would present the Commission's programme to the Parliament and that the Council would be invited to attend this presentation. In reviewing the rule changes effected in 1994, Nicoll (1994: 403–10) reached the conclusion that their cumulative effect was to enhance the EP's bargaining position relative to both the Commission and the Council. In particular he noted that 'it was only to be expected that the new rules would give the Council trouble. If they did not, the Parliament would think that it was not doing its job' (Nicoll 1994:409).

The 1996 intergovernmental conference

Similarly, the EP would have considered itself to have been failing in its self-ascribed 'job' had it not continued to press for further treaty reform after Maastricht. In fact, the Maastricht Treaty provided an inbuilt incentive for Parliament – precisely because one of its provisions (Article N) was for the convening of an IGC in 1996 to consider further revision of the treaty. A second incentive came in the simple fact that in the three years since the TEU came into effect 'policy making in the Union ha[d] not settled down into stable and agreed routines' (Laffan 1997:295). A third incentive arose out of a heightened awareness that, without reform, the institutional capacity of the EU could be seriously weakened with the enlargement of the Union to 15 member states in 1995, and potentially 27 within 10 to 15 years (Laursen 1997:61).

The IGC was preceded by the creation of a 'Reflection Group'. Composed of 18 members – one from each member state, one representative from the Commission and two from the EP – the group's main task was to map out the parameters of the debate on the revision of the TEU. The IGC was convened subsequently at the Turin European Council in March 1996. For the first time the EP was accorded a formal role in an IGC. Despite opposition from France and the UK, it was agreed that the Parliament should be given a role similar to that of the Commission. In the event, the President of the Parliament was allowed to address and exchange views with foreign ministers at each of the IGC's monthly meetings, and two representatives from the EP held detailed monthly meetings with ministers' representatives. During the course of the IGC Parliament received copies of all working documents and position papers produced for IGC meetings.

Before the first meeting of the IGC, Parliament and the Commission submitted 'opinions' setting out their respective priorities for the ensuing discussions. The position of the EP was summarized in its resolution of 17 May 1995 on 'The Functioning of the Treaty on European Union with a View to the 1996 Intergovernmental Conference – Implementation and Development of the Union' (OJ C 151, 19 June 1995:56–67). The essence of this position was that Parliament should have equal rights to the Council in all areas of legislative and budgetary competence; have a strengthened role in the fields covered by the first and second pillars (European Communities and Common Foreign and Security Policies) and with regard to EMU; be involved in any decision on its own seat; its assent should be required for members of the various European Courts and the executive committee of the European System of Central Banks; it should have the rights to initiate legal actions and request the opinion of the Court of Justice on the compatibility of international agreements with the treaty; the Commission should be required to respond to Parliament's legislative initiatives; and, finally, that the total membership of the EP should not exceed more than 700.

The Amsterdam Treaty

The result of 15 months of deliberations by the IGC was the Amsterdam Treaty that was agreed by Heads of State and Government on 17 June 1997 and signed later that year on 2 October. The protracted process of revision which culminated in the Amsterdam Treaty is noteworthy in itself. The 1996 IGC marked the third cycle of constitutional revision to be undertaken in just over ten years. Certainly this rolling process of constitutional change throughout this decade facilitated the EP's self-ascribed 'system development' role (see Wessels and Diedrichs 1997:6), if for no other reason than because other EU institutions, and significant member states, were receptive to the *principle* of change, even if they were not necessarily convinced by the specific proposals for reform advocated by the EP. Indeed, a putative institutionalization of the principle of constitutional review and revision within the treaties themselves seems to have emerged in this period. Thus, just as Article N of the TEU made the commitment to hold an IGC on the operation of the treaty in 1996, so, correspondingly, the Amsterdam Treaty (in the Protocol on the Institutions with the Prospect of Enlargement of the European Union, Article 2) called for the convening of an IGC 'to carry out a comprehensive review of the provisions of the Treaty on the composition and functioning of the institutions' at least one year before any future enlargement increases the number of member states to above twenty. In this manner constitutional review, and the opportunity for the EP to champion further change, became embedded in the future (see below).

Provisions relating to the European Parliament

History teaches us that the EP has never been satisfied with the piecemeal enhancements of its powers in successive treaty revisions. The response of the EP to the Treaty of Amsterdam provided no major exception to this general rule. A *Report and Initial Evaluation of the Results* (of the IGC and the New Amsterdam Treaty) (European Parliament 1997a), produced by a working party of the Parliament's General Secretariat, found the outcomes on the EP's powers and position in the legislative process to be less than impressive.

Nonetheless, specific significant advances were secured. Most importantly, the codecision procedure was extended to 23 new cases: eight of these referred to new provisions; the other 15 cases referred to existing treaty provisions to which other procedures had previously applied. After Amsterdam the codecision procedure applied to a total 38 legal bases (with a further extension to two other cases within two years of the treaty coming into force). Codecision was now the general rule where qualified majority voting applied in Council (with the main exception being agricultural policy). At the same time Article 189B (which set out the procedure in the Maastricht Treaty) was amended to streamline the procedure (see Chapter 7). The Amsterdam Treaty virtually eliminated the cooperation procedure (with the exception of EMU matters).

The EP's role in the procedure for appointing members of the Commission was strengthened and its right of approval of the appointment of the President of the Commission was confirmed. Another 'definite success for the EP' (European Parliament 1997b), was the new paragraph 5 of Article 190 which enabled the EP to lay down the regulations and general conditions governing the performance of the duties of its members (albeit 'with the approval of the Council acting unanimously'). The preceding paragraph of Article 190 confirmed the right of the European Parliament to draw up a proposal for elections by direct universal suffrage in accordance with a uniform procedure in all member states. In turn, Article 189 limited the number of MEPs to 700 – the ceiling proposed by the EP.

On the downside, a major regret of the EP, however, was the insertion of the protocol on the location of the seats of the institutions which specified that the European Parliament was to have its seat in Strasbourg, with additional plenary sessions in Brussels. Under this protocol, committees of the European Parliament would continue to meet in Brussels and the General Secretariat of the European Parliament and its departments would remain in Luxembourg. In other words, the EP's demand to decide on its own seat itself was rejected (see Chapter 6). Similarly, nothing came of the idea of increasing the EP's control over 'comitology' (see Chapter 8). Nor was the EP's access to the Court of Justice increased. Moreover, the Amsterdam Treaty did not grant the EP a real right of legislative initiative alongside the Commission, in part because Parliament did not make a direct request to this effect.

Amsterdam: steps towards a parliamentary model?

If the outcomes of Amsterdam are assessed in terms of 'winners' and 'losers' then Elmar Brok MEP, a Parliament representative at the IGC, was in no doubt that 'if there is one winner in the Amsterdam Treaty, then it is the European Parliament' (quoted in Dehousse 1998:603). This view was shared by many beyond the EP itself. Thus, political scientists Moravcsik and Nicolaidis (1998:22) maintained that what was 'particularly striking' about the Amsterdam Treaty 'is the increase in parliamentary power'. Similarly, constitutional lawyer Renaud Dehousse identified the Parliament as 'the institution that has most benefited from the Treaty of Amsterdam' (1998:603). Overall, Nentwich and Falkner (1997:15) concluded that: 'Viewed from some distance, the Amsterdam Treaty brought to an end what the Single European Act began and the Maastricht Treaty continued: making the European Parliament a co-legislator, equally powerful than [sic] the Council ... In both regards, the Amsterdam Treaty marks a seachange.'

Certainly the treaty redressed the procedural imbalance in the codecision procedure between the Council and Parliament by removing the negative veto of the Council inherent in the 'third reading'. 'The elimination of this option underlines that it is only by compromise and agreement with Parliament that Council can adopt legislation' (Corbett 1998:40). But it was still a little premature to see Parliament as an equal 'co-legislator' with the Council when significant policy areas remained beyond the scope of codecision.

A greater interinstitutional redistribution of power was apparent, however, in the relationship between the Commission and Parliament. The extension and simplification of codecision eroded still further the ability of the Commission to control the text of proposals throughout the legislative process (see Nickel 1998; Moravcsik and Nicolaidis 1998:21), and so tipped the legislative balance still further away from the pre-Maastricht Commission–Council dialogue to a post-Amsterdam Parliament–Council dialogue.

In these circumstances, several commentators were willing to argue that Amsterdam marked a further step in the evolution of the EU towards a federal model. Dehousse (1998:624) acknowledged that the EU now had two institutional features – a bicameral legislature and an executive whose appointment and term of office depended on the support of a majority in the lower house – which are 'common to all political systems that seek to combine federalism and a form of parliamentary government'. Similarly, Nentwich and Falkner (1997:4) concluded that the treaty moved the EU a 'little closer to a federal state model with a parliamentary and a state chamber'. But they immediately qualified this statement by arguing that Amsterdam had resulted, so far, in 'a unique type of federal decision-making structure'.

The road from Amsterdam to Nice

IGC 2000: Parliament's aspirations

The signing of the Treaty of Nice on 26 February 2001, following the IGC inaugurated a year earlier in February 2000, constituted the fourth treaty reform within a 13-year period. The imminent enlargement of the EU – to a likely total of 25 member states by 2004 and a further increase to 27 by 2010 – added urgency to the reexamination of the institutional questions left unresolved by the Treaty of Amsterdam (the so-called Amsterdam 'left-overs').

The EP identified two 'interrelated imperatives' for the agenda of the 2000 IGC: first, democratization of the EU's institutions; and, second, improvement in their effectiveness (PE 303.546 2001:17). Underpinning these broad 'imperatives' were three specific institutional questions which had been left unresolved by the Amsterdam Treaty: the scope of unanimous voting in Council under the codecision procedure, the weighting of votes in the Council and the composition of the Commission. The EP outlined its objectives for the IGC in a report by its Constitutional Affairs Committee (rapporteurs Giorgos Dimitrakopoulos and Jo Leinen (PE 231.873 1999)) and in its resolutions adopted on 3 February 2000 (OJ C 309, 27 October 2000:85–6; PE 232.649 2000) and 13 April 2000 (OJ C 40, 7 February 2001:409–19; PE 232.758 2000).

From the outset the EP reaffirmed its belief that:

> the composition, functioning and balance between the institutions of the Union, Parliament, the Council and the Commission, must reflect its dual legitimacy as a union of peoples and a union of States and that an overall balance must be struck between the small and large States and populations; considers therefore that the constitutional principle that the Union of the Peoples is represented by Parliament and the Union of the States is represented by the Council has to be taken account of. (OJ C 40, 7 February 2001:410; PE 232.758 2000)

As the representative institution of the 'Union of the Peoples', the EP drafted a long wish-list of reforms for consideration by the IGC. This list included the incorporation of the Charter of Fundamental Human Rights into the new treaty; the 'constitutionalization' of the existing texts of the treaties by joining them into a single document; consolidation of the EU's international status; and encouragement of closer cooperation when the EU was incapable of collective action.

More specifically, and of more immediate relevance to the concerns of this chapter, Parliament called for the reform of the EU's decision-making processes. The EP's belief in the concept of 'dual legitimacy' and its ultimate objective of bringing the 'rights of the countries making up the Union...into balance with democratic requirements' (PE 303.546 2001:19) found reflection in its calls for the reweighting of votes in the Council along with extended use of the codecision procedure.

The EP's resolution of 13 April proposed that the Commission President should be elected by the EP from among candidates put forward by the Council. The Commission President, in agreement with the member states, would then appoint the other members of the Commission subject to the conditions of the existing investiture procedure. The EP's resolution also called for the Commission President to be able to ask Parliament for a vote of confidence. If a majority of MEPs did not offer their support in such a vote then the Commission should resign. Such enhanced involvement in the appointment and dismissal procedures of the Commission would mark significant steps towards a 'parliamentary model' of governance as outlined in Chapter 1.

In terms of Parliament's own internal organisation, the resolution of 13 April confirmed that the maximum number of MEPs should remain at 700 as agreed at Amsterdam. The EP also declared that the new treaty should 'provide for the possibility' that some MEPs could be elected in a single European-wide constituency, in which case each voter would have two votes – one for a European list and one for a national list of candidates. At least one citizen from each member state should be included on the European list.

The resolution also called for the drafting (within 12 months of the treaty coming into effect) of a statute on political parties which would specify the conditions for the recognition and funding of European political parties. In addition, there was support within the EP for the amendment of Article 289 to allow MEPs to decide by an absolute majority on the location of the EP's seat and all of its meetings.

The EP's views were conveyed at the IGC by Elmar Brok and Dimitris Tsatsos who attended the meetings of the Group of Representatives as observers from the European Parliament. In addition Nicole Fontaine, as President of the European Parliament, participated in an exchange of views before each ministerial session and IGC meetings of Heads of State and Government (see SN 400/00 Presidency Conclusions 2000:1). These arrangements represented an incremental advance in the EP's participation in the 2000 IGC beyond that in the 1996 IGC (see Gray and Stubb 2001:7; Yataganas 2001:248).

The Treaty of Nice

The reaction of the EP to the Treaty of Nice was predictable: the changes were insufficient to meet Parliament's aspirations but at least they were a step in the right direction. Yet, as with Maastricht and Amsterdam, even before the ink was dry on the signatures to the treaty, the EP was looking beyond the new settlement to the 'post-Nice process'. The EP recognized that the 'semi-permanent Treaty revision process' (de Witte 2002) provided it with the opportunity to sustain its traditional integrationist dynamic. MEPs believed that the hesitant steps of Nice could be lengthened and quickened in the 'deeper and wider debate about the future development of the European Union' proposed in the Declaration on the Future of the EU (SN 533/1/00/REV1 2000:Annex IV). In particular, the Declaration recognized 'the need to improve and to monitor the democratic legitimacy and transparency of the Union and its institutions, to bring them closer to the citizens of the Member States'. What was notable was that there was to be wide-ranging debate prior to the next IGC scheduled for 2004 which was to involve the EP alongside the Commission, national parliaments, and 'all interested parties' (such as political, economic and academic groups, and 'representatives of civil society'). These 'post-Nice procedures' were immediately identified as a way of levering further democratic advance for the EP within an enlarging EU (see Corbett 2001; Duff 2001).

Outcomes versus aspirations

Under the revised Article 214 the Commission President was to be nominated by a qualified majority of the Council acting at the level of Heads of State and Government. The nomination was then to be subject to approval by the EP. In essence, the adoption of qualified majority voting (QMV) would prevent a single member state exercising an effective veto over the nomination of the Commission President, as the UK had done with Jean-Luc Dehaene in 1994. Moreover, in accordance with Parliament's stated preferences, the role of the President was to be strengthened. The President was now empowered to decide on the internal organization of the Commission; to change the distribution of portfolios during the term of office; to appoint Vice-Presidents after collective approval by the college; and to enforce, with the support of the college, the resignation of a member of the Commission.

While these reforms were seen by the EP as an enhancement of the 'supranational and independent nature of the Commission' (OJ C 47E, 21 February 2002:110; PE 294.755 2002), and while Parliament's involvement in the appointment procedure was increased marginally, other important proposals – for the parliamentary election of the President and for the Commission to be subject to a vote of confidence – were quickly discarded at the IGC. In this specific regard, the advance towards a more 'parliamentary system' of governance – through effective involvement in the appointment process of the executive – was stalled at Nice.

In terms of the EP's own composition the Treaty of Nice amended Article 189 to revise the total number of MEPs upwards from the ceiling of 700 to 732. The response of the EP itself was unambiguous. The EP berated the absence of any 'demographic logic whatsoever' (PE 294.737 2001:13) to the proposed allocation of seats per member state under the revised Article 190. Moreover, it expressed its concern that there was the possibility that the 732 ceiling 'may be exceeded by a considerable margin' if there were few accessions before 2004 but many between 2004 and 2009 (for details see PE 294.737 2001:11–13). What was clear, however, was that the decisions over the total number of MEPs and the distribution of MEPs per member state remained firmly and exclusively in the hands of the Council. What was also suspected within Parliament was

that the Council had used the composition of the EP to counterbalance the decision reached over the weighting of votes in
the Council (PE 303.546 2001:24). Paradoxically, while this
continued external control over the EP's size and membership,
and its inability to determine its own seat, inhibits the internal
'institutionalization' process, nonetheless Nice did acknowledge
the external significance of the EP in the EU's institutional
matrix (see Yataganas 2001:276).

Indeed, illustrations of the growing significance of the EP
came, first, with the extension of the EP's legal powers to enable
it to challenge acts of other EC institutions before the European
Court of Justice; second, in the incorporation of the legal basis
for a statute (to be adopted under the codecision procedure) for
European political parties and their funding (see Chapter 5);
and, third, with the prospect of the adoption of a statute for
MEPs, the requirement for unanimous decision in Council on
this matter was changed to qualified majority.

However, offsetting these positive outcomes, the EP found
that one of the 'most unsatisfactory aspects' of the IGC was the
failure to accept the principle of linking the codecision procedure to all legislative measures adopted by a qualified majority
in Council (OJ C 47E, 21 February 2002:109; PE 294.755
2001). Parliament's pre-IGC position had maintained that, as
a general rule, there should be qualified majority voting in the
Council, accompanied by codecision with Parliament. This linkage was necessary in Parliament's opinion in order to 'reconcile
efficiency in the decision-making process with the democratic
legitimacy of the procedures' (PE 303.546 2001:27). Yet, the
actual outcome in the Nice Treaty failed to meet the EP's aspirations. Qualified majority voting was to be applied to 35 new
cases (22 immediately upon the entry into force of the treaty and
the others at a later date or after a unanimous decision by the
Council). At no time, however, was the issue of a general linkage between QMV and the codecision procedure involving the
EP considered systematically by member states at the IGC
(PE 294.737 2001:18). In the event, the codecision procedure
was extended only to six areas that had previously required unanimity. Significantly, excluded from codecision were the areas of
financial regulations, internal measures for the implementation
of cooperation agreements, and the Structural Funds and
Cohesion Fund. All of these important policy areas remained

subject to the assent procedure. (The assent procedure was also extended to include Article 7 (TEU) on fundamental rights, and enhanced cooperation under the first pillar.) The exclusion from codecision of the three important areas with major budgetary implications simply perpetuated 'an indefensible mismatch between Parliament's budgetary and legislative powers' in the view of the Constitutional Affairs Committee (PE 303.546 2001:28).

After Nice the EP was formally involved in 66 per cent of all first-pillar matters and 37 per cent of all second- and third-pillar matters (combining all legislative measures subject to the consultation, cooperation, codecision or assent procedures). Moreover, some 25 per cent of the articles of the first pillar were covered by the codecision or assent procedures alone (Wessels 2001:210). In other words, Nice represented a further incremental extension of the scope of the EP acting as a co-equal legislative partner with the Council. While the formal view of Parliament was that this extension was 'manifestly insufficient' (PE 303.546 2001:28), another view was more positive in recognizing that: 'it is only a small extension... but it is an extension, it is better than the status quo and we will come back and fight for more' (Corbett 2001).

Conclusion

The simple point of the historical review in this chapter is that the 'location' of the EP as a 'parliament' has changed over time. Equally, the nature of the integrationist project in Europe, and the EP's location within that project, has also changed over time. 'Seen in historical perspective, the process is impressive in its continuity. In little more than ten years the Parliament has moved from the status of a consultative assembly to that of a fully-fledged legislative body' (Dehousse 1998:605). It has become easier, therefore, to locate the EP in a typology of legislatures as its formal legislative powers have been enhanced through successive treaty amendments. After Maastricht, and certainly after Amsterdam and Nice, the EP – with its capacity to 'modify and reject executive proposals' – can be located in Mezey's category of legislatures with 'strong policy-making power'. Equally, if Norton's criteria of the ability to 'generate alternative policies' is used, after Maastricht, the EP had a formal but restricted right to initiate legislative measures. In this sense it bordered on Norton's category of a 'policy-making' legislature.

What is equally impressive is that the EP has been instrumental in 'relocating' itself within the institutional architecture of the EU. In so doing, it has invoked federal constitutional blueprints and called for 'qualitative leaps' to implement those blueprints. In addition, however, it has also secured incremental, pragmatic and ultimately vital consolidations of its powers through 'small steps' of interinstitutional agreements, informal compromises and the creative use of its own internal procedures. However, while relocating itself in this manner the EP has always been aware that it is not 'part of a finished institutional system, but rather ... part of one requiring evolution or even transformation into something different' (Corbett *et al.* 2000:293). In this sense the evolutionary process is perpetual.

Chapter 3

Linkage, Elections and Legitimacy

> Whatever else legislatures do they connect the people to their government in special ways. (Loewenberg and Patterson 1979:167)

In the context of the EU this general statement, which Loewenberg and Patterson believe is universally applicable to all legislatures, is problematic on at least three counts: first, what constitutes 'the people' of the EU; second, what constitutes the EU's government; and, third, what are the special ways in which this connection takes place. The answer to the third question is provided in fact by Loewenberg and Patterson (1979:166) who maintain that 'the word *representation* describes that relationship'. In this chapter we aim to examine the electoral linkage at the core of the process of representation and in so doing to analyse the concepts of the 'people', European 'demos', legitimacy and democracy. However, as Chapters 1 and 2 made clear, discussion of the EP's role in the representative process of the EU cannot be discussed in isolation from conceptions of its roles as a legislature and of its location within a multi-level system of governance.

This chapter starts by examining some of the normative bases of representative democracy and then proceeds to examine these assumptions in the context of the 1999 elections for the European Parliament. The electoral procedures structuring the 1999 contest, the nature of transnational party competition, the dominance of national political contexts and the concern with low turnout are analysed in preface to a broader-ranging discussion of legitimacy and 'linkage'.

Representative democracy

The starting point of a discussion of representative democracy is 'to clear away the myths of rule by the people' and recognize that democracy is 'a set of political mechanisms' (Hirst 1990:28), or a set of political 'techniques' and 'instruments' whereby popular power is exercised (Sartori 1987:30). Representative democracy in this view is conceived as a *political process*. As a process it is deceptively simple: with 'the people freely choosing representatives, those representatives debating and enacting policy and later standing for reelection, and administrators enforcing that policy' (Murphy 1993:4). In this case, the basic claim to be 'democratic' is dependent upon the process itself.

Those who are willing to call this system 'democracy' do so primarily by stipulating a cluster of institutions and rules which define the relationship between governed and governors in the determination of how representatives are chosen and how popular control is exercised over representatives (see Judge 1999: 9–13). At the centre of this institutional cluster are free competitive elections. Indeed, free competitive elections have been identified as 'the genius of representative democracy' (Kornberg and Clarke 1992:9). If the democratic claims of the system are to be sustained, elections have to be free, with an equal weight assigned to each citizen's vote, and open to all adults who must be able freely to organize, speak and inform themselves of the alternatives. In essence elections decide who will make decisions rather than deciding issues themselves (see Riker 1982:236; Sartori 1989:108).

But elections not only choose representatives but also provide the mechanism for *controlling* them. In this view, elections implant uncertainty in the minds of *representatives*. Representatives are thus aware that they may be only temporary occupants of their positions *unless* they maintain some connection with their voters. Elections become periodic and dramatic demonstrations of the fact that possession of decision-making power by representatives is contingent upon the continuing support of their electorate. The ballot is thus 'the ultimate weapon' (Mayo 1960:78) in enforcing popular control over decision-makers in representative democracy. 'In representative government negation is more powerful than affirmation: the former constrains those in power, while the latter remains an aspiration' (Manin 1997:177).

From this perspective, elections are not primarily 'democratic' as a means of expressing voters' preferences on policy alternatives, but rather as a means of controlling those who effectively choose between policy alternatives. As Beetham (1992:47) points out: 'The fact of the vote casts a long shadow in front of it, as it were. It acts as a continuous discipline on the elected, requiring them to give public account of their actions and to take constant notice of public opinion.' Thus, voting exerts more continuous control than the simple act of casting a vote at first seems to allow. It allows for the peaceful transition of decision-making power and provides the essential mechanism by which that power can be checked.

So far this discussion has been based upon conceptions of representative democracy developed from the historical experience of Western nation states. The fundamental issue is whether such conceptions are appropriate for the study of the European Parliament.

The European Parliament and direct elections

> The obvious starting point is that the European Parliament constitutes the representative–democratic element par excellence in the structure of the Union … the European Parliament is the only body serving the whole Union which is directly elected. (Blondel *et al.* 1998:10)

This might be the obvious starting point but, as we will soon discover, discussion of the EP as a representative–democratic institution brings with it a host of theoretical and practical complications. Before becoming immersed in the complications let us deal first of all with the 'simplicities' of the electoral process itself. For our purposes the most straightforward, if not necessarily the easiest, way to analyse EP elections is to start with the latest election and work backwards, drawing out salient historical and analytical points where appropriate.

1999 elections

Electoral procedures

The 1999 elections were held during 10–13 June 1999 in all 15 member states of the EU. Despite various proposals and draft acts having been adopted on a uniform electoral procedure (see Chapter 2) the 1999 elections were still governed by national legislation. For the first time, however, after the passage of the European Parliamentary Elections Bill 1998 in the UK, all 15 member states used a system of proportional representation. Nine member states used a single national list of candidates (Austria, Denmark, Spain, France, Greece, Luxembourg, the Netherlands, Portugal and Sweden) where the whole country forms a single constituency. The six others (Belgium, Finland, Germany, Ireland, Italy and the United Kingdom) divided their national territory into between four and eleven electoral regions. In Germany parties were allowed to submit either *Land* or federal lists; while in Finland they could submit either a constituency list or a national list.

In terms of voting rights, the 1999 election was the second in which citizens of the EU who resided in a member state of which they were not nationals had the right to vote and to stand as candidates on the same conditions as nationals. In practice this was not the universal right envisaged in Article 8 of the Treaty on European Union, as the concept of residence varies considerably from one member state to another (see European Parliament 1997c). Nonetheless, Article 8 of the TEU is seen by the EP itself to be 'of major significance' as 'the concept of European citizenship has become a practical reality in that the citizens of the Union have acquired a fundamental right, namely the right to vote and to stand as a candidate wherever they reside in the Union' (European Parliament 1997c). Whether this legal right translated into a conception of 'European citizenship' on the part of the voters themselves or whether it is possible to speak of a 'European electorate' will be examined below.

Transnational party groups

While transnational party groups are a powerful force internally within the EP (see Chapter 5), externally, and paradoxically in electioneering terms, they play a subsidiary role to national parties. Thus, as Franklin points out, 'although the European Parliament contains party "groups" that sit together and cooperate in legislative matters, these groups are hardly relevant to the electoral process' (Franklin 2001:203). The selection of party candidates, the electoral campaign and, indeed, electoral success or failure itself, is determined in most member states by the profile of domestic party politics (see Hix and Lord 1997: 85–9).

Where transnational party federations have been active, however, is in producing 'European' manifestos. Typically such manifestos have been 'bland, offering little more than platitudes ... and
[providing] symbolic statements of belief than statements of intent'
(Smith 1999:93). In 1999, for example, the Socialists' (PSE) programme did not 'contain a single concrete promise ... All of the
questions that could raise objections ... [were] either evaded or,
more frequently, treated in extremely vague terms' (Grunberg and
Moschonas 2002:94). In this the PSE was not alone, as all of the
federations were confronted with the difficulties inherent in constructing a common programme on the basis of coalitions of
parties with, often, diverse ideological, language and historical
traditions. Indeed, *European Voice* (17–23 June 1999) noted that
'if voters had got around to reading the manifestos of Europe's
political parties, they would have not found much to inspire
them'. There was little to differentiate the transnational manifestos: all European parties were committed to the euro, to
increased powers in justice and home affairs and to an enhanced
role in foreign and defence policy. While the extent to which
these transnational manifestos are used by national parties varies
among member states, even the most pro-European parties have
been reluctant to use them in their domestic campaigns for the
EP elections.

One paradox of EP elections, therefore, is that voters are
mobilized around national party programmes and affiliations,
yet the successful candidates elected by this process then operate
in the European Parliament in transnational groupings which are
largely unknown to the electorates and in some cases are not
even in existence at the time of the election itself (see Chapter 5).

Second-order elections?

What the experience of the 1999 election, and indeed of all EP
elections since the first direct elections were held in June 1979,
reveals is that transnational and national party systems are
interlinked in complex and ambiguous ways. For those politicians and scholars who believed that direct elections would lead
to the creation of a new European identity on the part of voters,
and hence a novel source of supranational legitimation of the
EU itself, direct elections have proved to be both a practical
disappointment and a conceptual quagmire.

The practical disappointment is that voters have not turned out to vote consistently in high proportions. Those voters who have voted have tended not to vote on EU issues, and transnational parties have not emerged as powerful electoral and mobilizing forces. For many commentators the reason for this is easily identified. EP elections continue to be contested not as 'European elections' but as 'second-order' elections (see Hix 1999:180–4; Smith 1999:21–4).

The perspective of 'second-order national elections' was first used in the analysis of the EP elections by Reif and Schmitt (1980). Their starting premise was that in any state, elections for national representative institutions are normally the most salient for voters and parties alike. In this sense they constitute 'first-order elections'. Other elections, for subnational representative bodies, such as local councils or regional assemblies, are deemed to be less salient for voters and hence can be classified as 'second-order elections'. The major distinction between the two types of election is that 'there is less at stake' in second-order elections than in first-order ones (Reif 1985:8).

Elections to the European Parliament indeed have been characterized as 'second-order' in that national political issues, national parties and the political standing of national governments at the time have dominated the campaigns. What is important to remember is that the second-order model recognizes that the same party system operates in both first- and second-order elections. In other words, the latter cannot be separated from the former in the same political system: 'Concerns which are appropriate to the first-order arena will affect behaviour, even though second-order elections are ostensibly about something quite different' (Marsh 1998:592).

Reif and Schmitt offered three broad characteristics that differentiated aggregate behaviour in European elections from national elections. They believed that in EP elections, turnout would be lower, national government parties would suffer losses, and small parties would do better than in national elections. These descriptive propositions have been tested at both individual and aggregate levels using the experience of various elections since 1979.

Marsh (1998) provides one of the most comprehensive analyses using aggregate data on the 1979 to 1994 elections. He reexamined Reif and Schmitt's propositions about which parties win and lose by examining the performances of governments and of individual parties in EP elections (1998:595). What he found was that 'there are election cycle effects on government support manifested at European Parliament elections' (1998:606). At a general level, EP elections served as pointers to subsequent general elections. At a more specific level, government losses were greatest when EP elections were held at their mid-term and levelled off thereafter. What was particularly striking was that Marsh discovered that these losses increased with each set of EP elections, and that these losses could not be explained in terms of increasing government losses in general elections.

The second proposition that small parties gain at the expense of large parties in European elections also found support in Marsh's analysis. While there was no consistent pattern of increasing support for certain types of small parties at all elections, nonetheless there was sufficient evidence that there had been a shift of votes from bigger to small parties, with very small parties and very large parties being the most obvious 'winners' and 'losers' (1998:606).

While not arguing that the EU is entirely irrelevant for the results of European elections, Marsh was led to conclude that the essential insight of the second-order model was upheld. Models based on second-order propositions did help to explain the performance of parties and governments and thus to confirm that: 'European Parliament elections take place within a wider political context and that their results can be understood in such terms' (1998:606).

Case study: the 1999 EP election in the UK

The June 1999 European election in the UK provides a good illustration of how EP elections have to be understood in terms of their national political context. What it also demonstrates is that the second-order model is not fully specified, with some nuances of national party politics lost in a universal model.

First, the poor performance of the incumbent Labour government seems to support Reif and Schmitt's proposition that EP elections manifest swings against governments. To the extent that governments normally tend to disappoint their supporters, governments would be expected to suffer losses in EP elections.

Certainly the Labour government in the UK suffered significant losses. It was out-polled in a nationwide contest for the first time since 1992. Labour's share of the vote was its lowest for any UK-wide election, and at 28 per cent was lower than its worst ever general election result at the 1983 general election. Yet, this result came at a time when its standing in the opinion polls was still relatively buoyant, and when Labour had managed to out-perform the Conservative Party in local elections held just two months earlier. Moreover, with the exception of the Danish Social Democrats (who tend to lose out routinely to anti-EU parties), Labour's vote fell more dramatically than that of any other major governing party. There was, however, a general negative reaction to all 12 socialist parties in government in the EU in 1999 (see Grunberg and Moschanos 2002:98–100).

What the 1999 result indicates is that Labour had difficulty in securing the support of some of its traditional voters. Labour voters in areas of traditional Labour strength were reluctant to support the party, whereas in seats where Labour had developed its support under the repackaged brand name of 'New Labour' between 1992 and 1997 it had no great difficulty in retaining support. On the basis of these findings Curtice and Steed (2000:246) conclude that Labour's performance is consistent 'with an explanation that argues that the party lost ground because of disillusion amongst some of its traditional supporters with its domestic policy repositioning'.

If this conclusion adds support to the 'second-order' nature of the 1999 election, it is moderated rapidly by Curtice and Steed's finding that the pattern of Conservative performance was not simply dependent upon a knee-jerk anti-government response by voters. Instead, the support for the Conservatives was also conditioned by the party's policy position in relation to the euro. Put at its simplest, the Conservative Party's campaign against the euro attracted voters. In which case, if Labour's traditional supporters were sending a message to their national government, Conservative supporters were sending a different message about Britain's adoption of the euro. The outcome was that 'not only did Britain's two main parties fight very different election campaigns, but they also appear to have secured very different results that had very different underlying messages' (Curtice and Steed 2000:246).

Firmer support for the 'second-order' nature of the 1999 EP election was to be found, however, in the performance of small parties. The Scottish National Party and Plaid Cymru both made substantial gains upon their performance in the previous general election of 1997. But Curtice and Steed found little evidence that the performance of the two nationalist parties had been greatly affected by their stance on the EU. This was not the case, however, for the United Kingdom Independence Party (UKIP) and the Green Party which secured, respectively, 7 per cent and 6.3 per cent of the national poll. Manifestly, in the case of the UKIP, the party secured support on the basis of its anti-European stance. 'There seems every reason to conclude that the UKIP vote was the result of voters casting their ballots on the basis of their views about Europe' (Curtice and Steed 2000:250). The Green Party's success could be accounted for as a second-order willingness on the part of voters to support a small party, especially on the part of those in sympathy with its environmental cause. Yet, as Curtice and Steed note (2000:251), this was not the first time that the Green Party had enhanced its support at EP elections and one explanation 'may be [that] the presence of Greens from other countries in the European parliament gives its European election campaigns a vital credibility it otherwise would have lacked'. Arguably, the Greens also benefit from the strong recognition (as reflected in Eurobarometer surveys) of the transboundary impact of environmental issues and the need for coordinated responses.

In the case of the performance of small parties in the UK in the 1999 European elections there is sufficient evidence to suggest that the second-order model requires some further refinement. Small parties certainly benefited, but this was not simply a matter of size, it was also a matter of policy positions with regard to the EU. But if the EU was of concern to some voters it was so primarily in respect of rewarding or punishing parties according to their defence of national interest in relation to the EU.

Turnout

At 24.1 per cent, the turnout at the 1999 European election was the lowest recorded in any of the five EP elections held in the UK. It also represented the lowest turnout in any EU country (see Table 3.1).

TABLE 3.1   *Voter turnout (%) in EP elections, 1979–99*

	1979	1984	1989	1994	1999
Austria	–	–	–	68[3]	49
Belgium	92	92	91	91	90
Denmark	47	52	46	53	50
Finland	–	–	–	60[3]	30
France	61	57	49	53	47
Germany	66	57	62	60	45
Greece	79[1]	77	80	71	70
Ireland	64	48	68	44	51
Italy	86	84	82	75	71
Luxembourg	89	87	87	89	86
Netherlands	58	51	47	36	30
Portugal	–	72[2]	51	36	40
Spain	–	69[2]	55	59	64
Sweden	–	–	–	42[3]	38
UK	32	33	36	36	24
EU (average)	63	61	59	57	49

[1] Accession elections 1981.
[2] Accession elections 1987.
[3] Accession elections 1996.

The 1999 election seemed to confirm Reif and Schmitt's proposition that turnout would be lower in EP elections than in national elections. In addition, the gap between local and EP turnout was as large as it had ever been. This reflected a historical pattern of lower turnout at European elections than for contemporaneous local elections in the UK.

If the 1999 EP election appeared to be a second-order one in the UK, it does not necessarily mean that this was because of growing voter disinterest in the EU. One suggestion was that electors in some parts of the country were suffering from 'voting fatigue', having been called upon to vote in elections for a parliament in Scotland and an assembly in Wales as well as local elections only a few weeks before the European elections. Low turnout was not, however, exclusively a 'European' phenomenon. A by-election in the Leeds Central constituency which was held on the same day as the European elections, and one which marked the first electoral test of the government in nearly two years, recorded, at 19.5 per cent, the lowest turnout in a Westminster election since the Second World War.

Whatever the specific explanations for the low turnout in the UK, there is a more general concern with the secular downward trend in turnout across the EU over a twenty-year period between 1979 and 1999. Generally, aggregate turnout in 1999 was at an all-time low throughout the 15 member states of the EU, with almost exactly half of voters not casting a vote in the EP elections.

Why the concern with turnout?

> Direct elections ... will give this assembly a new political authority. At the same time it will reinforce the democratic legitimacy of the whole European institutional apparatus. (Tindemans 1976:Section V, A)

This belief that direct elections would necessarily enhance the legitimacy of the entire EU institutional framework has been at the heart of the debate about the democratic deficit in the EU. There was an assumption of an automatic correlation between an increase in democracy (through the act of voting) and an increase in legitimacy (by developing support through the participation of all the electorates of member states). Not surprisingly, given this assumption, there has been an intense concern with the level of turnout throughout the history of direct elections. This was largely because members of supranational institutions (the EP and the Commission) feared that 'a low turnout would undermine the legitimacy of the EP [or] that it might be interpreted as an expression of no confidence in the EC' (Smith 1999:110). Thus the reverse of Tindemans's logic is that if direct elections failed to provide 'a new political authority', then far from reinforcing democratic legitimacy they would simply serve to undermine that legitimacy. Yet, as we will see, the connection between turnout, democracy and legitimacy is neither that simple nor direct.

Explanations of low turnout

As noted above, one explanation is that EP elections are second-order elections. Turnout figures in Table 3.1 are used by some commentators, such as Hix (1998b:35), for example, to argue that the EU is an 'upside-down political system' where the focus of attention is on national politics.

Attitudinal explanations

At an individual level, part of the explanation rests in the attitudes of voters towards the EP and to the EU itself. Blondel *et al.* (1998:238) argue that if voters behaved according to the assumptions of the second-order model then 'participation in European Parliament elections would not add a jot to the legitimacy of the European Union ... more participation would not necessarily indicate a more representative political process at the European level; the effect would depend on the kind of participation involved'. Blondel *et al.*'s survey, based on nearly 13,000 completed questionnaires in nine languages in the wake of the 1994 EP elections, found that the most striking characteristic of voters' general attitudes to the EU was a sense of a lack of involvement rather than opposition. 'Indifference, apathy, and ignorance' characterized attitudes to the EU (Blondel *et al.* 1998:240).

Correspondingly, voters' attitudes to the European Parliament itself were not generally grounded in political knowledge or direct experience of the Parliament. There was a correlation between knowledge of politics and assessments of the EP's power – greater knowledge was associated with higher power ratings of the EP in comparison with national parliaments (1998:241). Moreover, Blondel *et al.* found that the power perceptions attributed to voters in the second-order model are far from being universal (1998:112). Only 28 per cent of their respondents saw the EP as being substantially less powerful than their national parliament, and 20 per cent believed that its future impact would be lower than that of national parliaments. In this respect the majority of respondents did not share the view of the relative powerlessness of the EP which is at the base of the second-order model (1998:112). There were, however, notable differences among member states, with voters in Germany, the Netherlands and Luxembourg rating their own national parliaments as quite powerful and the EP as relatively powerless, while voters in Spain and Ireland rated the EP's power far higher than that of their national parliaments. The basic problem for the EP, however, was that a substantial proportion of its electorate had no image of the Parliament – whether good or bad. In total some 39 per cent of respondents had no affective image of the EP (1998:120).

Blondel *et al.* proceeded to raise the question of how far the probability of voting or non-voting was affected by attitudes to the campaign, the parties and the candidates, as well as more broadly to the EP and the EU. Their answer pointed to two sets of explanations. First, there were circumstantial explanations, with some 40 per cent of respondents citing pressures of time or of work, illness, or absence from home, for example, as reasons for not voting. Second, there were voluntary explanations. Lack of interest was the most common reason in this category, with political distrust, inadequate information and dissatisfaction with the EP electoral system also featuring in the comments of voluntary abstainers (1998:243).

Using a series of bivariate analyses, Blondel *et al.* discovered that variations in turnout were associated with European party and candidate differentials, in other words, attitudes to the EU did make a difference. Thus, in the terminology of the second-order model, turnout did not appear to be determined by whether the voter saw 'less at stake' in European rather than in national elections (1998:244). This finding directly confronts the second-order explanation of low turnout. Moreover, in their multivariate analysis, Blondel *et al.* found that national political attitudes were not the primary influence on turnout and that orientations towards the EU and to the power of the EP played a significant role. Of particular interest was the finding that even those who made adverse assessments of what was at stake in the EU elections or of the power of the EP were not any less likely to vote in European elections. Blondel *et al.*'s research is thus at variance with much of the previous work on the second-order nature of elections.

Institutional explanations

Blondel *et al.* also question some of the orthodoxies surrounding the impact of institutional factors upon turnout. Compulsory voting, the simultaneity of national and European elections, and the nature of the electoral system have all attracted the attention of researchers trying to account for differences in turnout among member states. The starting point of such analyses is to note the differences observable in Table 3.1. Certainly voting is higher in those countries where voting is nominally compulsory – in Greece, Belgium and Luxembourg. And in Italy voting is still defined by the constitution as being a 'civic duty'. The average turnout in these four countries was some 37 per cent higher in 1999 than the average in other member states. But even in these high-turnout countries there was a gap between Belgium and Luxembourg and Italy and Greece. This pattern had been observable in previous elections and underlined the fact that even when voting was nominally prescribed, voters in Italy and Greece chose not to vote in the European elections more than in national elections.

What is also apparent is that in all countries – with the exceptions of Spain, Ireland and Portugal – turnout was lower in 1999 than in 1994. In Ireland a simultaneous referendum, and in Spain the scheduling of a large number of local and regional elections, contributed in part to the increased turnout figures for the EP elections.

While Blondel *et al.* accept that compulsory voting is a major determinant of turnout at European elections (see also Frognier 2002:50), they are more sceptical of claims that proportionality of the electoral system or the timing of national and European elections have much impact. They do acknowledge, however, that concurrent national elections raise turnout at EP elections. This confirms Smith's (1999:120) finding of nearly a 20 per cent increase in participation at European elections when they have coincided with national elections. Similarly, Guyomarch's study of the 1999 EP elections supported this proposition and concluded: 'coincidence with, or proximity to, national elections remain[ed] an important factor in all member states' (Guyomarch 2000:169).

Distance in time between national and European elections has also been identified as a contextual variable influencing turnout. Thus, for example, Franklin (2001:208) maintains that the period of time between national and EP elections is an important variable in explaining the variance in turnout from country to country (see also Franklin *et al.* 1996:317–20). The basic proposition is that voters and parties are less interested in the EP elections if national elections have occurred recently. The longer the gap between national elections, therefore, the greater the potential engagement of voters in the European election. Indeed,

Franklin (2001:209) maintains that the significant decline in turnout in Germany between 1994 and 1999 (60 per cent to 45.2 per cent) can be understood by the close proximity of the preceding national election in 1999. However, Blondel *et al.* question the significance of the 'time elapse' variable in explaining turnout. They maintain that this contextual variable does not appear to have a significant effect on turnout (1998:227). Using both the time elapsed since the last national election and time until the next election Blondel *et al.* found that the timing variable has little impact on turnout. In this regard, their results tend to undermine the second-order view that turnout is related to the electoral cycle in the national political arena (1998:228). Similarly, proportionality of the electoral system is found to have relatively little effect by Blondel *et al.*

Elections, democracy and legitimacy

What is distinctive about legitimation in liberal democratic political systems is that democratic participation is largely conceived in terms of authorization of representatives through the electoral process (see Beetham and Lord 1998:8). In a representative democracy both election (participation) and representation (indirect decision-making) are defining characteristics of the political system. Repeated elections serve as a key incentive in encouraging representatives to take account of the views of the represented.

So far we have consciously referred to 'representative democracy' and the relationship between the people and their representatives, rather than to 'representative government' and the relationship between the people and elected decision-makers in government. This is because, as we will examine below, what constitutes 'the people', and what is meant by 'government' in the EU, is the source of heated contestation. For the moment, however, we will simply focus upon the question of why low turnout and voter participation in EU-wide elections is considered to be a problem of 'legitimacy' within the Union itself.

Even at this starting point the issues of legitimacy and of a 'democratic deficit' in the EU become immediately entangled. Again we will postpone a discussion of both the nature and of the number of 'deficits' until later, concentrating here simply

upon the limited notion that direct elections provide neither sufficient authorization from, nor a clear expression of, 'European'
opinion or public identity to confer legitimacy upon the actions
and outputs of their representatives in the European Parliament.

From the outset direct elections were seen as a means of
enhancing the 'direct legitimacy' of the representatives in the EP.
European elections were identified as the process through which
the actions of MEPs would be authorized and through
which they would be directly accountable to the people who
elected them (see Herman and Lodge 1978:74). What was
particularly important in this argument was the fact that MEPs
alone would be authorized on a 'European' basis, and so be able
to speak on behalf of the 'European electorate'. This was a claim
which neither the Commission nor the Council of Ministers
could substantiate in terms of the bases of their collective tenure
of office. In the words of former President of the Commission
Walter Hallstein (1972:74):

> What is lacking ... is an election campaign about European
> issues. Such a campaign ... would give the candidates who
> emerged victorious ... a truly European mandate from their
> electors; and it would encourage the emergence of truly
> European parties.

Such a rationale for direct elections is based on the claim that
elections would elicit popular support for the process of
European integration. Moreover, as Smith notes (1999:17–18),
'at no time did those who favoured direct elections question that
public support could be rallied or that elections were the way to
rally it'.

Given the subsequent failure of 'truly European parties' to
emerge, for election campaigns to be nationally based rather
than focused on European issues, and the propensity of substantial numbers of voters not to vote, then the counter logic is
that MEPs do not have a convincing 'truly European mandate'.
Indeed, this is the essence of the persistent streak of Euro-
scepticism in most EU member states.

If the consensus before direct elections was that they would
increase the EP's and EC's legitimacy, the actual experience of
European-wide elections has 'lent credence to the view that [they]
might exacerbate rather than mitigate legitimacy problems'

(Lodge 1993:22). This is why turnout and the nature of campaigns become so important. Thus, after the 1999 elections Wilfred Martens, then leader of the European People's Party, recognized that 'in some member states, the legitimacy of the European Parliament has been put into question' (*European Voice* 17–23 June 1999).

Demos or demoi?

The discussion of legitimacy in the EU presupposes a model of representative democracy derived from the practices of modern liberal democratic nation states, where a territorially defined 'people' – commonly identified as a 'national electorate' with some identity rooted in 'nationhood' – elect their representatives in a national assembly or parliament. While a legally prescribed common EU citizenship was introduced under Article 8 of the TEU, there is a notable absence of a shared collective European identity on the part of these legally defined 'citizens'. This lack of a developed sense of European identity and loyalty has been considered 'the most serious of the obstacles to the development of political legitimacy at the European level' (Beetham and Lord 1998:33).

Yet the relationship between identity and the legitimacy of the EU's political system is not unidirectional. An essential element of the case for direct elections was the assumption that a European identity could be *created* through political participation. Similarly, other integrationist projects – through, for example, the development of institutions (European Courts, European Central Bank), symbols (flags, anthems) and substantive policy programmes (student exchanges, regional and social funds) – reflect a logic that political resources can be used to develop a sense of 'Europeanness'. By this logic the fact that European identity is relatively weak and that citizens are basically agnostic on the issue of integration (Blondel *et al.* 1998:64–5; Cautres and Sinnott 2002:11) does not preclude the possibility that the sense of identity can be strengthened and the agnosticism mitigated over time.

At this point in the discussion the work of Joseph Weiler is of relevance. Weiler recognizes that citizenship is as much about social reality and identity of the polity as it is about the politics of public authority (1999:337). For Weiler citizens constitute the *demos* (the people) of a political system:

> *Demos* provides another way of expressing the link between citizenship and democracy. Democracy does not exist in a vacuum. It is premised on the existence of a polity with members – the *demos* – by whom and for whom democratic discourse with many variants takes place ... Simply put, if there is no *demos*, there can be no democracy. (Weiler 1999: 337)

A parliament is a democratic institution in this view because it derives its authority from the *demos* (through the representative process) and hence legitimizes the outputs of that process (Weiler 1997:257). When the EU is examined then it is apparent that there is no nation, no state and hence no *demos*. By the logic of Weiler's statement, without a *demos* there can be no democracy. 'If the EP is not the representative of *a* people, if the territorial boundaries of the EU do not correspond to its political boundaries, then the writ of such a parliament has only slightly more legitimacy than the writ of an emperor' (Weiler 1997:258).

One proposal therefore is to create a *demos*. Thus for example, Lord concludes his book *Democracy in the European Union* with the plea for the development of transnational deliberative politics which could conceivably be built upon the construction of 'a *demos* around shared civic values' (1998:132). The linkage between institutional form and collective identity is apparent in this prescription, but in both theory and practice this is an exceedingly complex linkage to envisage.

Multiple demoi

Rather than conceive of a single *demos*, Weiler suggests that citizens of the EU are best conceived as belonging simultaneously to multiple *demoi*, based upon different subjective identities. One identity is ethno-culturally based and rooted in nationality and the nation state. The other is understood in civic terms and a commitment to shared values which transcend ethno-cultural identification.

There are at least three ways of conceiving multiple *demoi* in the EU. The first is to understand European citizenship in the same way as national citizenship. By this view citizens are located simultaneously in a set of 'concentric circles' of identity, sharing a sense of belonging to, say, Scotland, the UK and Europe, or Catalonia, Spain and Europe. A second conception identifies two *demoi* but this time based upon two different senses of belonging. One is a sense of ethno-cultural identification associated with belonging to a nation, the other is a civic and political understanding. In the case of the EU, the latter sense of belonging would stem from 'European transnational affinities to shared values' (Weiler 1999:344–5). These values would have to have distinctive 'European' dimensions, and Weiler suggests that commitments to human rights and to shared social responsibilities encapsulated in the ethos of the welfare state might serve as the bases of such distinctiveness. Immediately, however, Weiler qualifies this view by stating that these commitments to human rights and to social welfare provision do not really differentiate 'European' values from those of most nation states in the EU. In other words there is little that transcends identity to established nations and states.

A third version of multiple *demoi* is offered by Weiler. Starting from the premises of the second view he argues that it is possible to conceive of a sense of belonging based on different subjective factors of identification. One factor, certainly, would be organic–cultural identification with the nation. The other, as in the second view, would be to shared 'European' values. In the third view, however, the concepts of nationality and state membership are 'totally independent' of European citizenship (Weiler 1999:346). At the heart of this conception of European citizenship is a commitment to supranationalism. What it is based on is 'the discipline of decisional procedures representing a range of interests and sensibilities going beyond the national polity' (Weiler 1999:347).

What this discussion of multiple, variable geometry *demoi* reveals, however, is that the construct of a European *demos* is aspirational. Such a *demos* does not exist. It is at best an 'icon' or 'symbol' to guide the future development of the EU.

Demos, demoi and EU governance

The interlinkage of a European *demos* and the 'discipline of decisional procedures beyond … the national polity' is central to

Weiler's conception of European citizenship. Indeed, this is a circular relationship: a *demos* is the democratic foundation for representation and the legitimation of the political system of the EU and its policy outputs; yet that *demos* can only be developed out of recognition of the legitimacy of the EU's 'decisional procedures' themselves. If this is a circular relationship it also appears to confront the EU with a catch-22 predicament in trying to enhance its institutional legitimacy.

In assessing the legitimacy of the EU's 'decisional procedures', both citizens and academic commentators alike often draw directly upon existing liberal democratic, state-based notions of what such procedures entail (see Hix 1999:166–8). Notably for our discussion, parliaments are central to these notions of legitimacy. Dehousse (1998:609) makes this point in his statement: 'as parliaments are regarded as the main providers of legitimacy, executive authority must derive from, and be responsible to the legislature'. Correspondingly, one persistent strand of argument in the enhancement of the EU's legitimacy has revolved around increasing the European Parliament's contribution to democratic authorization, accountability and representation (Lord 1998:15; Beetham and Lord 1998:6–9).

Proposals for the democratization of the EU have been many and varied. Almost all of them, however, are concerned with the enhancement of representative *government* rather than with representative democracy as such. Attention thus becomes focused upon the capacity of elected representatives to authorize and hold decision-makers to account, as well as to influence decisions and public policies made by 'government'. This concern is reflected in Weiler's belief that 'the basic condition of representative democracy is, indeed, that at election time the citizens "can throw the scoundrels out", that is replace the government' (1999:350). A prior condition, many would argue, is that parliaments should authorize government in the first place. On either count – whether authorization or holding government to account – the fundamental problem is that there is no 'government' to authorize or to throw out.

The EU has a dual executive in which the Council and Commission share, asymmetrically, executive responsibilities for the formulation, initiation and oversight of the implementation of policies. Traditionally the democratic authorization of the Council–Commission executive was located in the indirect legitimation afforded collectively to the Council through the process of individual national elections of its members. The EU's dual executive was thus authorized indirectly by the electorates of each member state voting in national elections. If this claim to democratic authorization was tenuous for the Council it was even more so for the Commission. The President of the Commission is nominated by the 'common accord' of the member states' governments, and each Commissioner is chosen individually by national governments. While the consultative and confirmation rights of the EP have been enhanced since Maastricht and Amsterdam (see Chapters 2 and 8), electorates in the member states still have no direct say in the selection of Commission members as they neither vote for individual Commissioners nor directly affect the choice of Commission President.

A key element of the 'democratic deficit' identified at the heart of the EC in the 1990s was 'the weaknesses and deficiencies in inter-institutional relations and specifically to the idea of inadequate parliamentary influence over the Commission and Council ... [in particular] the impact of Euro-elections on the composition of decision-making institutions [was] seen to be flawed' (Lodge 1993:22). The connection between authorization of an executive and the relevance of parliamentary elections was explicit in most proposals to address the 'deficit'. In his pamphlet on *European Union and the Democratic Deficit* (1990:26), David Martin MEP recognized that: 'At present, European elections are genuinely about electing a Parliament, but the affect of casting one's vote is less immediately perceptible to the voter. To allow the Parliament to elect the President of the Commission would go some way to rectifying that situation.'

This connection was still being made in early 1999 by Julie Smith, who argued that the changes in the appointment procedure incorporated in the Maastricht and Amsterdam treaties marked 'a considerable advance towards an elective [authorization] function and one which could be expressed to the voters in relatively simple terms, potentially giving them a greater interest in EP elections' (1999:68). But, as the June 1999 election demonstrated, that potential remained unfulfilled. In part this is because of the self-reinforcing logic of second-order elections; for, as long as national parties contest European elections primarily on domestic issues, there is no real incentive to emphasize the authorization capacity of a supranational institution.

Another basic characteristic of representative government is the ability of elected representatives to influence the policy choices of executives in accordance with the wishes expressed by voters through competitive elections. In practice in most liberal democracies this distils into a process of competitive party government. At best the EU is an embryonic system of party government (see Hix 1999:186). At worst, some argue that such a system is neither possible nor necessary in the political culture of the EU (see Blondel *et al.* 1998:253).

Without entering into the details of the debate about the development of competitive party government, at this stage at least (see Chapter 5), the relevant part of this debate for present purposes is its emphasis upon giving the EP greater powers in the EU's legislative process (Hix 1999:167). In practice, paradoxically, the EP does play a more influential policy role than many of its national counterparts (see Earnshaw and Judge 1996:101–2). The potential to exploit this at election time is mitigated, however, by voter ignorance and the inability of transnational parties to claim credit for what are essentially interinstitutional, intergovernmental policy outputs rather than clearly identifiable outputs of party government as such. As noted earlier in this chapter, there appears to be only a tenuous connection between perceptions of the power of the EP and electoral turnout. Despite the EP's enhanced powers, and despite recognition of this fact by knowledgeable voters, most voters still have little knowledge of the role or impact of the EP. The fact that the EP is not dismissed as a 'write-off in itself or relative to national parliaments' does not automatically lead to the stimulation of involvement or participation in European elections (Blondel *et al.* 1998:241).

Dual legitimation, dual deficit: the European Parliament and national parliaments

> [T]he European Union is based on a system of dual legitimacy: the first legitimacy is based on the democratic institutions of member states ... Gradually a second source of legitimacy has been building up, mainly based on the direct elections to the European Parliament. (Neunreither 1994:312)

So far we have focused almost exclusively in this discussion of elections and legitimacy upon the 'European level' and the role of the European Parliament. However, throughout, the connections between the processes of representation at a national level and at a supranational level have intruded either implicitly or explicitly into the discussion. Moreover, conceptions of what sort of political system the EU is – whether 'type 1 governance' or 'type 2 multi-level governance' (see Chapter 2) – have provided a sub-conscious structuring of the debate. Thus, for example, analysis of a 'European people/demos' and 'European legitimacy' res-onates with federalist notions of EU-wide democratic representa-tion and legitimation derived from the EP (see Chapter 1). Correspondingly, an intergovernmental perspective threads through the analysis of 'second-order elections' and the assump-tion of limited legitimation derived from the EP. What matters are national electoral contests and national policy outputs.

The idea of a dual legitimacy, noted above by Neunreither, is intuitively attractive but upon further consideration generates a series of paradoxes and conceptual tensions. These complications are outlined at length by Beetham and Lord (1998:84–93), but the essence of their analysis is that the EU has 'created mutually com-plicating relationships between democratic legitimation at the national and European levels' (1998:84). Attempts to link the two levels of legitimation is not a simple problem of aggregation – of adding EU representative democracy on to existing national processes of representation. In the first instance, there are 15 national political systems displaying different characteristics (for example, majoritarian versus consensus decision rules; struc-tures of legislative–executive relations; experiences and phasing of democratization; and the weighting of territorial and functional representation). In the second instance, the development of European representative processes, without an underpinning elite or public commitment to EU-wide electoral competition, may question the legitimacy of outputs of that process despite their actual responsiveness to public needs. Despite these difficulties the EU has consciously sought to develop dual legitimation in prac-tice; not least through an increasing recognition that both national parliaments and the European Parliament have roles to play in providing authorization, representation and accountabil-ity in the Union (see Chapter 9).

Multiple legitimation

Wessels and Diedrichs believe that the notion of 'dual legiti-macy' does not go far enough (1997:8). They claim instead that the EP is but one element of 'multiple legitimation' within the EU, it is simply 'only one of several loci of legitimacy in the fused polity' (1999:148). The 'fused polity' is one in which it is difficult to trace accountabilities and where responsibility for any specific policy is diffuse (Wessels 1997:274). The fusion thesis assumes that national, subnational and supranational actors interact at several levels of governance in a complex and highly differentiated political system (see Chapter 1). Not surprisingly, given the emphasis upon multi-level complexity, Wessels and Diedrichs find that the orthodoxies of federalist (supranational) and realist (intergovernmental) perspectives provide inadequate conceptualizations of legitimacy in the EU. Instead, as noted in Chapter 1, they argue that the EU is becoming a new kind of parliamentary system (1999:139). In this new system 'national and subnational institutions keep their legitimacy while at the same time the EP might acquire a share of basic acceptance and identification by the citizens. Complementary and mutually reinforcing processes of legitimacy-building are possible' (1999:148). In this 'new polity' legitimacy derives from a 'pluralistic citizenship' (Wessels and Diedrichs 1999:148). A merging of different sources of legitimacy is claimed to be apparent with the EP making an important contribution as 'a direct representative element ... as part of a European legitimacy complementary to the national and functional one' (Wessels and Diedrichs 1997:9). Ultimately, however, it is predicted that, while the EP is unlikely to become a central representative institution comparable to national parliaments, its direct representative capacity will play an important role in bolstering 'a European legitimacy'. The important point is that the model underlines the institutional complexity and multi-level nature of the EU and highlights the elemental point that legitimacy is not a zero-sum construct where either national parliaments or the EP are the single source of 'European legitimacy'. There are other foci of legitimation and other forms of representation.

Conclusion

The simple formulation of Loewenberg and Patterson noted at the start of this chapter, about the linkage role of legislatures, only captures part of the complex linkages between 'the people' and government in the EU. Equally, a simple linear model of parliamentary legitimation proves inappropriate in the EU. Empirically, the sources of legitimation within the EU are multi-level and, some would claim, are as much concerned with 'output legitimacy' – in terms of technocratic and efficient decision-making – as with 'input' notions of legitimacy derived from the processes of electoral linkage. Normatively, however, the EP 'seems to be predestined to be the main bearer of legitimacy in the Union' (Höreth 1999:250). In part, this is because of the sheer normative strength of existing conceptions of legitimation derived from established representative democratic praxis in member states and the subsequent transposition of these ideas to the EU level. The simple fact remains that most of the political debate (in contrast to the academic debate) 'about the legitimate political order in Europe remains primarily focused on the European Parliament' (Höreth 1999:250). This is hardly surprising given that: 'quasi-statehood and representative democracy are the two signposts that orient the debate' (Kohler-Koch 2000:528). These indicators reflect the common experiences of member states and provide institutional frames for future development. These are frames, moreover, which do not rely upon the normative aspirations surrounding notions of 'pluralistic citizenship' or 'associational democracy', and which do not entail a radical rethinking and reshaping of forms of governance.

Thus, while much academic attention has been focused upon the prescription of a future European polity which will be different and new, and which draws upon multiple (and often conflicting) sources of legitimacy (see Héritier 1999:280; Höreth 1999:264–5), politicians have preferred to follow a simpler logic. In this logic, in Beate Kohler-Koch's (2000:521) words, the question of EU development 'is reduced to looking for a frame to match surface indicators: representation is linked to parliament, political control to increasing parliamentary powers, and political efficiency to increasing governmental control'. In other words, politicians prefer constitutional choices rooted in their existing experiences. Not surprisingly, the best solution to problems of legitimacy in the EU, identified by many parliamentarians at least, is for further parliamentarization of the EU's political process. Exactly what further parliamentarization involves, and what impact it will have upon legitimation within the EU, will be examined in later chapters. More immediately, however, Chapter 4 examines the practice of representation and 'what' MEPs represent when they act on behalf of their electorates.

Chapter 4

Linkage, Representation and MEPs

Chapter 3 examined the linkage provided by direct elections between Members of the European Parliament and citizens of the European Union. In this chapter we develop the analysis of linkage by looking at how the EP acts as a representative body, and how it links citizens and decision-makers in the periods between elections. However, this immediately raises the question of what is 'representation'? It also immediately leads us to sidestep a detailed discussion of the various meanings of representation (see Pitkin 1967; Judge 1999) in favour of addressing the specific ways in which citizens are *re*-presented in the European Parliament by their elected members. In particular, we will concentrate upon the *foci* of representation – upon 'what' is to be represented when elected politicians act for the represented.

Four main foci are usually identified in the literature on representation. These are political parties, functional groups, territorial constituencies and broader social groupings (see Wahlke *et al.* 1962; Loewenberg and Patterson 1979:170–8; Judge 1999). The focus of representation identified by any particular legislator is not, however, simply a matter of individual choice; it is also, as Loewenberg and Patterson (1979:192) observe, 'determined for them by the electoral system through which they are chosen and by the political culture of the nation in which they live'. On both counts – given the nature of European elections and the difficulties of conceiving of a European nation or *demos* as discussed in Chapter 3 – the identification of foci of representation may prove to be more problematic for MEPs than for members of national parliaments (MNPs). We will return to this issue later in the chapter, but for now we need to examine the extent to which MEPs do in fact identify and act on behalf of each of the four main foci noted above. Taking these in reverse order we will look in turn at: microcosmic, constituency, functional and party notions of representation.

Microcosmic representation

As we noted in Chapter 3 the concept of representation is inextricably linked with the concepts of legitimacy and legitimation. In that chapter it was argued that direct elections are an integral part of the legitimation process and provide, simultaneously, the representatives themselves; authorization for the actions of representatives; and, in mediated form, information upon popular preferences. In addition, the periodic nature of elections also provides incentives for representatives to remain informed about popular preferences in between times.

If we assume that representation is essentially about political action – about how and why representatives can act for others, and so 'make present' those who are not actually present at the point of decision – then we have to start by considering 'how' the people are made present in the first instance. One answer, at the institutional level of the representative assembly, is that the composition of the institution itself 'reflects' the composition of the wider electorate – in so far as there is some correspondence between the social characteristics of the population at large and the membership of the legislature. Representation, in this sense, is initially concerned less about what the legislature does than about how it is composed. Ultimately, however, composition is deemed of importance precisely because it affects the outputs of representative institutions. Thus, as Pitkin (1967:63) recognizes, 'proportionalists...are interested in what the legislature does; they care about its composition precisely because they expect the composition to determine the activities'.

The linkage between the 'composition' and 'action' of representative assemblies, between inputs in terms of representativeness and outputs in terms of legislation and policies, is most apparent in microcosmic notions of representation (see Judge 1999:20–46). Exactly just such a linkage is explicit in Pippa Norris's research into the backgrounds of candidates at European elections when she notes that 'Theories suggest that the process of recruitment, determining who becomes an MEP, is likely to shape the decision-making and legitimation functions of the European Parliament' (1999:88). Norris proceeds to note that the extent to which the composition of the legislature reflects that of the electorate from which it is drawn is of importance for at least two reasons. First, 'legislative bodies which fail to reflect society may be perceived as symbolically less legitimate'. Second, 'the social background of members has the power to influence the policy priorities, role perceptions and attitudes of legislators' (Norris and Franklin 1997:185–6). Ultimately Norris concludes that:

> [A] central function of parliament is to act as a linkage mechanism, connecting citizens and the state, and legitimating decisions made by governments. In this regard social representation may be critical. How far does the European Parliament look like a microcosm of European Society? (Norris 1999:96)

A microcosm of European society?

A stereotypical representative in any European national parliament is now predominantly middle-aged, male, and a 'professional politician with a middle class background, medium to high levels of education, significant political experience, and the likelihood of extended parliamentary service' (Cotta and Best 2000:505). Not surprisingly, therefore, research on the socioeconomic background of MEPs shows that they too are predominantly middle-aged, with those aged between 40 and 59 constituting, respectively, 70 per cent and 72 per cent of MEPs in 1994 and 1999 (Mather 2001:189). Correspondingly, the 1994 and 1999 cohorts of MEPs were predominantly drawn from professional occupations (57 per cent and 64 per cent respectively), with public sector employees, especially teachers and university lecturers, being proportionately overrepresented in both 1994 and 1999 (see Norris 1999:93–4; Mather 2001:188). In contrast, manual workers accounted for only 6 per cent of 1994 MEPs and 4 per cent of 1999 MEPs, and those from agricultural backgrounds constituted just 2 per cent and 3 per cent of MEPs in 1994 and 1999 respectively.

Some 18 per cent of MEPs in 1994 and 19 per cent in 1999 came from professional 'political' careers – having served in some official legislative, party or government capacity (Mather 2001:188). Moreover, a further 28 per cent of MEPs in 1999 had also served as elected representatives to their own national parliaments at some stage in their political career. In fact, in five national delegations – Luxembourg, Portugal, Sweden, Finland and Ireland – former or current national parliamentarians were in the majority. However, only 40 elected MEPs in 1999 were simultaneously members of their own national parliaments, and, of these, seven came from the UK (two from Northern Ireland and five from the House of Lords), and a further 22 came from Italy. Indeed, one-quarter of Italian MEPs continued to hold dual mandates. The 1999 Italian delegation also had the distinction of including two former prime ministers, Ciriaco de Mita and Silvio Berlusconi. (In fact, after the Italian election of May 2001, Berlusconi returned once more to national politics as prime minister.) Likewise, the French, Portuguese and German delegations included the former prime ministers Michel Rocard, Mario Soares and Hans Modrow (former East Germany). Indeed, some 10 per cent ($n = 64$) of 1999 MEPs had held national ministerial office before entering the EP (Corbett *et al.* 2000:51).

An interesting aside at this point is that not only does the EP's membership contain a number of leading ex-national politicians, but, given experience to date, there is the distinct possibility that a number of *future* leading national politicians are also included in its membership. In recent years many national governments have included at least one ex-MEP. In 2002, for example, ex-MEPs were included *inter alia* in the Dutch, French, German, British, Greek and Spanish governments: Laurens Jan Brinkhorst and Gijs de Vries (Dutch agriculture and junior foreign minister, respectively), Jean Pierre Raffarin and Nicole Fontaine (French prime minister after the May 2002 presidential election, and French industry minister after the June 2002 parliamentary election, respectively), Heidi Wieczorek-Zeul (German development minister), Geoff Hoon (British defence minister), Christos Papoutsis (Greek minister of maritime transport), and Ana Palacio (Spanish foreign minister). Moreover, the 1999–2004 Commission also included three former MEPs (Busquin, Reding and Vitorino).

In addition, the 1999–2004 Parliament included over 50 regional office-holders and regional presidents. The Italian delegation alone included two serving mayors and several former mayors. More generally, many MEPs had been elected at some stage in their career to serve as local councillors (with 35 per cent of MEPs in 1999 having been elected to local or regional government (Mather 2001:191)).

While prior national political experience is thus a notable, but minority, feature of the career trajectories of MEPs, so too is prior membership of the EP itself. Thus in 1999 only 286 of the 626 MEPs (45.7 per cent) had served previously as MEPs, and only 14 had served continuously since 1979. Within these overall totals, however, there were significant variations among the national delegations. At one extreme, 70 per cent of German MEPs were incumbents, while, at the other, only 24 per cent of Italian MEPs had served in the EP before 1999.

Representation of women

If MEPs are as unrepresentative as national MPs in socioeconomic terms they are also disproportionately male – again in parallel with the gender profiles of all 15 national parliaments. At the 1999 EP election 194 women (31 per cent) were returned as MEPs. However, as Table 4.1 reveals, there is substantial variation of female representation from one member state to another, with Sweden, Finland, France and Germany having more than twice the proportion of female MEPs as returned from Italy, Portugal and Greece. While there is a strong correlation between the proportions of female MEPs and female members of respective national parliaments (Norris 1999:99), in 14 member states the proportion of women representatives returned at the 1999 EP elections was greater than that in the closest national elections (in Denmark the respective percentages were almost identical at 37.5 and 37.4 per cent).

While the proportion of female MEPs increased from 27 per cent in 1994, it has been estimated that it will be 2044 before women obtain 50 per cent representation in the EP (calculated on the rate of increase since the first direct elections (Norris 1999:98)). In the meantime, two simple questions remain to be answered: first, why so few women in the European Parliament; and, second, does it matter?

The first question can be answered in terms of the standard variables accounting for the underrepresentation of women in any Western legislature: opportunity structures of the wider

TABLE 4.1 Female representatives: European Parliament and national parliaments

Country	European Parliament				National parliaments			
	Date of election	Seats	Women	% women	Date of election	Seats	Women	% women
Sweden	June 1999	22	10	45.5	Sep. 1998	349	149	42.7
Finland	June 1999	16	7	43.8	March 1999	200	73	36.5
France	June 1999	87	37	42.5	May 1997	577	63	10.9
Germany	June 1999	99	38	38.4	Sep. 1998	669	207	30.9
Austria	June 1999	21	8	38.1	Oct. 1999	183	49	26.8
Denmark	June 1999	16	6	37.5	March 1998	179	67	37.4
Netherlands	June 1999	31	11	35.5	May 1998	150	54	36.0
Ireland	June 1999	15	5	33.3	June 1997	166	20	12.0
Luxembourg	June 1999	6	2	33.3	June 1999	60	10	16.7
Spain	June 1999	64	21	32.8	March 2000	350	99	28.3
Belgium	June 1999	25	8	32.0	June 1999	150	35	23.3
UK	June 1999	87	21	24.1	June 2001	659	118	17.9
Greece	June 1999	25	5	20.0	April 2000	300	26	8.7
Portugal	June 1999	25	5	20.0	Oct. 1999	230	40	17.4
Italy	June 1999	87	10	11.5	May 2001	630	62	9.8
Total		626	194	31.0				

Source: http://www.ipu.org/wmn-e/classif.htm.

political and party systems; discriminatory tendencies in the 'supply and demand' of candidacies; gender stereotyping; access to resources and support networks; political motivation; and institutional receptiveness (in terms of facilities and working conditions within legislatures) (see Norris and Lovenduski 1995; Norris and Franklin 1997). But equally, the question can be inverted to ask why there is a better representation of women in the EP than in most national parliaments.

One traditional answer has been that males have been reluctant to pursue a political career in the EP given the continuing perception of its relative weakness in comparison to national parliaments. Freedman (2002:179) summarizes this argument thus: 'where there is power there are no women; and where there is no power there are women'. Her survey of women MEPs in the 1999–2004 Parliament appeared to confirm that national parties were 'more willing to make an effort to present women candidates for European rather than for national elections, largely because of a continuing belief by many national politicians that the European institution is not a site of effective power, so that there is less competition for places' (Freedman 2002:181). Another important factor, however, is the genuine commitment to the policy objective of closer European integration shared by many women MEPs. In this sense they perceived membership of the EP less as a 'career' than as a means to 'contribute actively to the construction of the European Union' (Evelyn Gebhart, PSE, Germany, quoted in Freedman 2002:185).

For those who answer the second question, 'does it matter?', in the affirmative the fundamental question is one of democracy itself: how can 'the people' be adequately reflected if one half of them are effectively excluded from formal positions of decision-making? The response is normally a rhetorical assertion that it is only 'fair', it is only 'right', that women should be represented more proportionately. This response is couched in terms of 'democratic justice' (Norderval 1985:84), or of 'symbolic equity' (Norris and Lovenduski 1989:107). Increased female representation is conceived as an end in itself, and the 'problem' is self-evident: for it is 'patently and grotesquely unfair for men to monopolise representation' (Phillips 1995:63).

A second response focuses upon the effects of female under-representation upon the legitimacy of the wider political system as a whole. The claim is made that if representation is designed to secure legitimation for political regimes then 'political decisions made by all-male or predominantly male governmental processes can no longer serve this legitimizing function' (Darcy *et al.* 1994:18). In which case the exclusion of women may undermine 'the democratic legitimacy and public confidence in institutions' (Norris 1996:89; Norris and Lovenduski 1995:209).

But claims for more proportionate representation based upon 'fairness' logically stand independently of the actual impact of increased female representation upon policy outputs. Rarely, however, is the case for 'symbolic equity' pressed by itself and without reference to claims for the substantive impact of increased female representation upon policy outputs. The underpinning assumption is that female underrepresentation 'means that women's interests are poorly represented' (Norderval 1985:84). In other words, it is driven by a belief that more women decision-makers and representatives would have an impact upon the substance of public policy. The belief is that women have identifiable interests as women. The 'bottom line' argument is that gender parity matters if the inclusion of women leads to a change in what representatives do.

Women MEPs in the 1999 Parliament certainly believed that they constituted a 'critical mass' which could affect both the functioning of Parliament and its policy agenda. Freedman's sample of women MEPs identified the constant search for consensus within the EP's committees and political groups, and the non-adversarial style of deliberation in plenary, as both a reflection of, and conducive to, a distinctive style of female representation (2002:184–5). Equally women MEPs held the 'definite opinion' that they were capable of placing women's issues on the EU's agenda.

These ideas find direct reflection in the work of the EP's own Committee on Women's Rights and Equal Opportunities. Freedman (2002:187) maintains that the continued existence of the committee 'is evidence of the way in which women MEPs have contributed to agenda setting'. It produced, for example, no less than eight own-initiative reports (see Chapter 7) and eight reports on Commission Green Papers and strategy documents between 1999 and 2002. However, many MEPs, including younger female MEPs, discount the policy impact of the Women's Rights Committee. This belief is reinforced by the infrequent drafting of legislative reports by the committee. Indeed, in the first half of the 1999–2004 Parliament, the committee was responsible for just three reports on proposed legislation (two by codecision, one by consultation).

Despite these reservations the mere existence of a committee serves as a powerful symbol for at least one MEP (Glenys Kinnock PSE, UK) who noted that: 'women's issues are not peripheral but actually central to the work we do here' (quoted in Freedman 2002:188). Certainly, the Women's Rights Committee maintains an active propagandist role on the issue of increased women's representation.

Territorial constituency

In the study of legislatures there is common agreement that 'parliamentary representation involves a territory' (Hibbing and Patterson 1986:992), or that, as Loewenberg and Patterson (1979:170) maintain, the representation of geographic areas has been 'the primary focus of representation for legislators in many countries'.

One immediate problem confronting any analysis of territorial representation in the EU is, of course, the problem of defining a 'constituency'. Eleven member states use single national constituencies for EP elections, four others use regional constituencies, and Germany, while using a single electoral constituency, lists its successful MEPs by party group by *Länder*. As Table 4.2 reveals, on average, each MEP represents some 550,551 people, with significant variations around this figure – most notably in Germany (with 828,667) and Luxembourg (with 71,500). When compared to national parliaments the ratio of representative to population in the EP is significantly higher. In the UK, each Westminster MP represents on average 92,718 people, while their UK counterparts in the EP represent an average of 681,000 constituents. In Germany the respective ratios are 1 : 123,180 and 1 : 828,667, in France 1 : 102,194 and 1 : 677,770, and in Luxembourg 1 : 7,150 and 1 : 71,500. The simple fact, therefore, is that MEPs on average have to 'represent' far more individual constituents than do national politicians. However, the problem confronting MEPs is that not only do they have to represent more people, they tend to be less

TABLE 4.2   *Ratio of MEPs to population (1999 election)*

Country	Number of MEPs	Population per MEP
Germany	99	828,667
UK	87	681,000
France	87	677,770
Italy	87	662,207
Spain	64	615,531
Netherlands	31	508,387
Greece	25	421,320
Belgium	25	408,520
Portugal	25	399,200
Sweden	22	402,455
Austria	21	384,857
Denmark	16	332,063
Finland	16	322,500
Ireland	15	249,600
Luxembourg	6	71,500
Total EU	626	550,551

Source: PE 294.737 2001.

informed about the preferences of their electors and vice versa are less 'visible' to the people they represent than their counterparts in national parliaments (see Blondel *et al.* 1998:93; Raunio 1999:190; Mather 2001:191–2).

Trying to establish exactly how representatives 'act on behalf' of their electors in territorial constituencies has been a preoccupation of legislative scholars for decades (see Judge 1999:149–57). In essence, however, two main concerns have dominated the literature: one is with 'policy responsiveness' or 'policy advocacy' (see Jewell 1983:320; Norton and Wood 1993:25–8); and the other is with 'service responsiveness'.

On the one hand, a concern with 'policy responsiveness' focuses academic attention upon the congruence between the opinions of constituents and the views and voting behaviour of their representatives in parliament. As the main focus of the EP is, by definition, 'European policy' – that is, policy instruments to deal with European-wide problems (Marsh and Wessels 1997:229) – then one reasonable measure of establishing the congruence of opinions between MEPs and their electorates is to examine attitudes on major European-wide issues such as unification, the single currency and border controls. Indeed, in evaluating the extent of difference between the attitudes of MEPs and their electorates, Marsh and Wessels (1997:231) conclude that: 'MEPs as a whole are more favourable to unification, more supportive of a European Currency, and more inclined to weaken border controls than are voters'. In this respect there is limited policy congruence between the opinions of the represented and their representatives in so far as 'MEPs are unlike publics in their views on European integration' (Marsh and Wessels 1997:239). This leads Marsh and Wessels (1997:231) to conclude that in comparison to national parliaments 'congruence is considerably lower at the European level' and that 'distortions in representation result in elites who are unduly favourable to European integration'.

On the other hand, a concern with 'service responsiveness' draws attention to what is commonly referred to as the 'welfare officer role', with representatives carrying out 'casework' on behalf of aggrieved constituents. As Norton and Wood (1993:29) observe in the context of the UK: 'carrying out constituents' wishes will more often mean raising a matter of personal concern to a constituent or group – particularly at the level of detail, amenable to administrative redress – than expressing views on grand issues of national [or in the case of the EP supranational] policy'. A further dimension of 'constituency service' is the 'promotion' of collective constituency projects, such as local industrial and economic development, environmental improvement or some other social project. Included within this conception of 'service' is what Eulau and Karps (1977:242) term 'allocation responsiveness' whereby representatives seek 'legislative allocations of public projects that involve advantages and benefits ... accruing to a representative's district as a whole'.

The first vital link in the chain of service responsiveness is the simple ability of constituents to contact their representative in order to articulate their concerns and grievances. Research by Mark Shephard and Roger Scully (2002) reveals that, while information is readily available via the EP website about how to contact MEPs in Brussels or Strasbourg, specific constituency contact information is less readily available and varies among national delegations. Their analysis of the web pages of national

EP Information Offices, and of the EP itself, found that while 90 per cent of MEPs provide a postal address in their own countries, only 59 per cent provide a national phone number, 55 per cent a national fax number, and only 36 per cent a national email address (Shephard and Scully 2002:161).

In the event, actual requests by electors for information from, or action by, MEPs appears to be remarkably limited. Most respondents (53 per cent) to a survey of MEPs in 2000 (for details see Scully and Farrell 2001) reported that they received no more than ten such requests per week. Only in Ireland (50 per cent) and the UK (36 per cent) were 50 or more requests received per week (Shephard and Scully 2002:163). These findings confirm earlier survey results which revealed that contacts between MEPs and electors were 'extremely low' (Bowler and Farrell 1993:55).

In view of these figures, perhaps not surprisingly, the majority of MEPs in the 2000 survey did not rank the representation of the individual interests of individual constituents highly among their representative roles. Only in Ireland, the UK and Germany did a majority of MEPs emphasize the importance of such individual constituency representation. Nonetheless, the vast majority of respondents, 90 per cent, maintained a 'constituency office' (Scully and Farrell 2001:Table 4) and placed great importance on 'representing all of the people in their constituency'.

The effects of constituency size are apparent in so far as MEPs from 'countries with either regional constituencies or regional listings attract more citizen contact than those from countries with national constituencies and national listings' (Shephard and Scully 2002:171; for similar findings pre-1999 see Bowler and Farrell 1993). Similarly, regionally elected MEPs were found to assign greater importance to the representation of the interests of individual constituents than were MEPs elected from national lists. Moreover, given the fact that single national constituencies predominate, the majority of MEPs in the survey appeared to treat representation of 'all of the people in a constituency' and representation of the 'national interest' as largely synonymous. Thus, a very close correspondence was apparent in the rankings assigned to the importance of both collective constituency representation and representation of the national interest (see Shephard and Scully 2002:166–8).

However, the linkage between constituency size and conception of representative role is not necessarily as direct as suggested by these findings, as a 'cultural' variable may also be discerned. Thus, for example, UK MEPs, although elected on a closed regional list system in 1999, consistently scored higher than other MEPs in their weekly involvement in constituency work, maintenance of a constituency office, and overall levels of contact with citizens (Scully and Farrell 2001:Table 4). Indeed, Scully and Farrell (2001) note that British MEPs as a group constitute a 'distinct outlier' from most other national groups in the EP, and that this 'may be suggestive of a "cultural" difference in modes of representation'. This cultural effect was also noted by Katz (1997:218) who found that respondents from Britain and Ireland placed greater emphasis upon the role of the MEP as constituency representative than did respondents from other member states. This was explicable, in part, by the importance of constituency service in the role conceptions of representatives in both countries (see Wood and Young 1997).

Functional/interest representation

The third 'focus' of representation – the representation of interests – has become of increasing concern for legislatures in an age of mass democracies. Historically, most Western parliaments were able to accommodate the representation of 'functional' or 'sectional' interests pragmatically alongside territorial, individualistic or party notions of representation. Yet, the tensions between the promotion of sectional interests and the defence of wider 'general' or 'public' interests by elected representatives continued to dog both the theory and the practice of representation in most liberal democracies (see Judge 1999:97–120). Equally the challenges posed by group representation to established conceptions of parliamentary representation – most notably in the formulation of 'post-parliamentary governance' – have raised fundamental normative questions about the impact of policy networks upon established liberal democratic decision-making processes in the EU and its member states. These broader issues are raised elsewhere in this book, but in this chapter we are concerned more specifically with the role of the EP and its representatives in linking organized interests and 'decision-makers' in the EU. This concern leads to an examination of the micro-dimensions of interest representation focused upon individual MEPs and their linkages with outside interests, and the macro-dimensions of interest representation at an institutional level.

Lobbying the EP

Exactly what constitutes 'interest representation' is the cause of heated academic debate but need not detain us here. All that needs to be noted is that the range of interests represented in Brussels is vast. It has been estimated that there are some 10,000 lobbyists in Brussels (*European Voice* 17–23 February 2000:8). In terms of the number of active groups and organized interests, Simon Hix (1999:192) calculated that in the mid-1990s there were in excess of 1,600, with three main types: 561 individual companies with their own public affairs units, 314 'Euro groups', and 302 public affairs consultancies and law firms. By 1998, however, Greenwood (1998:587) identified 700 'Euro groups', 200 firms with their own public affairs units, and 25 public affairs consultancies operating in the Belgian capital. In addition, there were some 135 territorial authorities active in Brussels (Greenwood 1997:9). Both estimates are exclusively 'Brussels-focused' and do not take into account the wide range of national groups throughout the EU which also seek to influence EU policies from afar. The most effective collectively organized interests and lobbyists know that 'Brussels is very much an insider's town' (Greenwood 1997:5). They are aware that knowing who to speak to, and when, are vital resources in the informal interpersonal and interinstitutional networks operating in the Belgian capital.

Certainly there are frequent interactions between MEPs and organized interests. Indeed, the indispensability of interest representation is pointed out by Kohler-Koch who notes that because of MEPs' information deficiencies and time constraints 'they have to be open to lobbying' (1997:6). The sheer scale of interaction was revealed in one survey of MEPs in 1996 which discovered that some 67,000 contacts occurred between MEPs and interest groups each year (Wessels 1999:109). A more recent survey of MEPs, in 2000, recorded that over half of MEPs had weekly contact with interest groups; and around a third had weekly interactions with lobbyists (Scully and Farrell 2001: Table 4).

The three Ts: transmission, translation and timing

'Interest representation' and 'lobbying' in parliaments are normally justified in terms of information transmission, translation and timing. The transmission of information from interest organizations to MEPs is deemed essential as it provides predigested information for elected representatives who are often non-experts in the particular policy area under consideration. This 'briefing' function also allows specific groups and organizations to translate often complex and technical information into accessible data for busy elected representatives. Indeed, as one Italian MEP noted, successful lobbyists supply 'information in ... a clear fashion so that the [MEP] doesn't have to be an expert in the field' (quoted in Burson-Marsteller 2001:19).

As important as transmission and translation of information, however, is the timing of its dissemination. The timing of the provision of information at the appropriate point in the EU's legislative cycle is a key resource of groups and lobbyists. Kohler-Koch (1997:9) is in no doubts that 'Timing is considered to be most essential for successful performance' and that in turn the 'timing of interest representation is dominated by the procedural rules of EU decision making'. Certainly, with the extension of the codecision procedure (see Chapters 2, 7 and 8) lobbyists have become increasingly aware of the need to 'act more quickly to get their views across to MEPs'. As Elaine Cruickshanks, Chief Executive Officer of the consultancy Hill and Knowlton International, notes, 'players from the Council of Ministers and the Parliament are brokering deals much earlier under the codecision procedure' (quoted in *European Voice* 17–23 February 2000:8).

In the case of the EP, timing is particularly acute when amendments to Commission proposals are tabled in committee (see Chapter 8). Committees that have heavy legislative loads are especially colonized by representatives of organized groups and consultants. The sessions of the EP's Environment or Industry committees, for example, regularly attract several hundred interest representatives. But the provision of information is not simply 'supply-led' but is also 'demand-led'. Committee rapporteurs, committee chairmen, vice-chairmen and shadow rapporteurs are particularly prominent 'targets' for the supply of information and, in reverse, are significant 'consumers' of information from outside organizations. Rapporteurs in drafting their reports routinely seek information not only from other EU institutions but also from interest associations and lobbyists (see Chapter 8). In addition, committee members often request draft amendments from interested organizations when the groups concerned have not already suggested their own favoured amendments. As a consequence, the process of amendment in committee is often characterized by intensive negotiation, dialogue and compromise not only among committee members but, crucially, between MEPs and affected interests across Europe.

In these interchanges the preferences of MEPs and lobbyists alike are for issue-specific briefings and the provision of detailed amendments at appropriate times. Of most use for both sides in the MEP–interest relationship is contact on 'issues of particular interest' and 'propositions for amendments to the directives under discussion' (Kohler-Koch 1997:Figure 5). The clear preference in the EP is for direct, personal, well-timed and pertinent contact, with lobbyists providing targeted information on specific legislative amendments. This contrasts markedly with the lobbying styles focused on the Commission – where continuous, long-standing and permanent relationships based around technical content are most valued by lobbyists and Commission officials (see Mazey and Richardson 2001:220).

MEPs and interest representatives trade not only substantive information on policies but also exchange 'interinstitutional' information. The reciprocal trading of information on the thinking and scheduling of legislation within the Commission or Council is a vital commodity in the MEP–lobbyist relationship. Of particular currency in this exchange is information on the work patterns of, and rate of legislative progress in, the various committees engaged in processing specific directives. Representatives of interest associations and lobbyists often provide informal monitoring for MEPs of the asymmetries of committee activity on a particular directive. They track the different deadlines imposed by the various committees for the tabling of amendments; variations in the speed of processing proposals across committees; and possible divergences of policy emphases in the different committees dealing with the same issue. In this way, interest groups with a mastery of the EP's procedural complexities and a developed surveillance capacity provide not only substantive policy briefing but also inter- and intra-institutional intelligence for MEPs.

Lobbying: 'problem' and regulation

The reciprocal transmission of information from organized interests to MEPs, and the subsequent enhancement of the informational resources within the EP, has many benefits. Nonetheless, there remains a deep-seated concern that 'reconciling the demands of self-interested private interests with the wider interests of civil society [is] a central problem of democratic life' (Greenwood and Thomas 1998:487). Historically, interest representation has been regarded as a particular 'problem' for parliaments. Elected assemblies have institutionalized the norms of the equal status and voting weight of individual representatives, and the transparency of deliberation. In practice, however, the interactions between organized interests and elected representatives often reflect inequalities of access to, and provision of, information, and translucent rather than transparent bargaining. In these circumstances fears about the representation of 'sinister interests', to use John Stuart Mill's phrase ([1861] 1910:254), are articulated and demands for regulation emerge.

Exactly such fears and demands emerged after direct elections and have increased with each successive increment in the EP's legislative powers. In an environment in which MEPs 'retain close links with particular sectors or interest groups which will help to condition their choice of priorities' (Corbett *et al.* 2000:58), what concerns MEPs and outsiders alike is just how close these links are, and what kind of resources and incentives are used to 'condition the choice of priorities'. These concerns over the unregulated activities of lobbyists intensified in the 1980s as reports of lobbyists having almost unrestricted and privileged access to EP buildings, their occupants, parliamentary proceedings and many of their facilities led MEPs to consider restricting and regulating the activities of representatives of organized interests. Accusations that the voting independence of a small number of MEPs had been impaired by their pecuniary involvement with outside interests simply fuelled these concerns (see Greenwood 1997:81; Shephard 1999:156).

The institutional response of the EP to such accusations was to instruct its Committee on Rules of Procedure and the Verification of Credentials and Immunities (CRP) to 'submit proposals with a view to drawing up a code of conduct and a public register of lobbyists accredited by Parliament' (PE 200.405

1992:1). The CRP's rapporteur, Marc Galle, produced a report which recommended that there should be: an annual register of lobbyists; a code of conduct; the exclusion of lobbyists from certain areas of the EP's buildings (most notably MEPs' offices and library facilities); an examination of the role of intergroups; and the introduction of an annual register of the financial interests of MEPs and their staff (PE 200.405 1992). However, these recommendations failed to reach the full EP plenary – falling over the extreme difficulty in providing a precise definition of lobbying. The attempt to provide a restricted definition of 'lobbyist' (PE 200.405 1992:4) simply 'led the discussion down a blind alley and ... prevent[ed] the adoption of concrete measures' (Gil-Robles, Draftsman of the Opinion of the Committee on Social Affairs and Employment, PE 216.869 1996).

Despite the failure of the Galle recommendations to reach the EP plenary in the 1989–94 Parliament, the CRP requested authorization to return to the issue of lobbying almost immediately after the 1994 election. In November of that year Glyn Ford was appointed rapporteur. After protracted deliberations the EP amended its rules in 1996 (and inserted a new annex in 1997 (Annex IX)) on lobbying in Parliament (Rule 9) (for details see Greenwood 1997:90–100; Shephard 1999:162–4).

The main purpose of the 1996 rule changes was to make the activities of interest representatives more transparent by establishing a public register of lobbyists. Henceforth, lobbyists were effectively defined as individuals who sought an annual access pass to the EP's buildings. Instead of providing a detailed definition of 'lobbyist', this approach invoked a self-selecting, and pragmatic, logic. This logic found reflection in new Rule 9(2) which provided for the issuing of distinctive photo-ID passes to 'persons who wish to enter Parliament's premises frequently with a view to supplying information to Members within the framework of their parliamentary mandate in their own interests or those of third parties' (PE 216.869 1996). Holders of such passes were entitled only to attend public meetings of the EP and had no special access other than that 'applicable to all other Union citizens' (PE 216.869 1996; European Parliament 2002:Rule 9). In return lobbyists were required to respect a code of conduct and sign a register which was to be made available to the public on request.

While the Ford report and the subsequent code of conduct for lobbyists focused upon the 'external' dimension of the linkage between outside interests and MEPs, a parallel inquiry was conducted into the 'internal' dimension of the 'interests' of MEPs themselves. In August 1994, at the same time as the CRP requested authorization to produce a report on lobbying, it had also requested to report on the declaration of financial interests by MEPs. Eventually, Jean-Thomas Nordmann was appointed rapporteur. Indeed, by 1996 these internal and external dimensions had coalesced to such an extent that they were regarded as a 'coherent package' in the CRP and in deliberation in plenary (Greenwood 1997:95).

Under Rule 9(1) each MEP was expected to make a detailed personal declaration of professional activities and any other remunerated functions or activities, and of 'any support, whether financial or in terms of staff or material, additional to that provided by Parliament and granted to the Member in connection with his political activities by third parties, whose identity shall be disclosed' (European Parliament 2002:Rule 9). In addition, when speaking in the EP, an MEP with a direct financial interest in the subject under debate was required to disclose that interest to the meeting orally. MEPs were also required to have completed the annual financial declaration of interests before they accepted nomination as an office-holder of Parliament or one of its bodies, or participated in an official delegation.

From the outset the Register of Financial Interests was open for inspection, but it could only be accessed in Luxembourg, and Strasbourg and Brussels when Parliament was meeting there. However, many MEPs, most notably Glyn Ford, campaigned forcefully to have the document made publicly available. A decision to this effect was taken in principle in late 1999, followed by a formal announcement in February 2000 when David Martin, Vice-President of the EP, acknowledged that the public should have 'easy access' to the Register (*European Voice* 24 February–1 March 2000:2).

At the time it was noted that the 'change would not happen overnight' (*European Voice* 24 February–1 March 2000:2); but it took a further year of sustained campaigning, both inside and outside of the EP, before details from the Register were finally published on the official parliamentary website in July 2001. Even then, individual permission from each MEP had to be sought before their financial declarations were published on the web. And initially some 39 MEPs did not append a declaration of financial interests to their individual web pages. At the other extreme some MEPs, like Gary Titley (Labour MEP for the North West Region of England), noted assiduously their each and every sponsored attendance at sporting and social occasions.

The 'institutional lobbyists'

In addition to 'mainstream' lobbying by interest representatives, the 1990s also witnessed a dramatic increase in the lobbying of the EP by the Commission and national governments. In recognition of the EP's enhanced legislative capabilities in that decade the Commission and national governments acknowledged the necessity of maintaining a dialogue with appropriate MEPs.

The characterization of national and Commission officials as 'lobbyists' in the context of EU decision-making is certainly not new. In 1993 David Spence, for example, identified the national official as 'clearly a lobbyist of European institutions and other Member States' officials' (1993:47). Within the EP Ken Collins, then Chair of the Environment Committee, in his address to the hearing organized by the Rules Committee into lobbying in 1992, noted the difficulties in defining lobbyists. He argued that, as far as the EP was concerned, a definition should include not only 'delegations of the Council' but also 'Commission officials defending their proposals vis-à-vis Members and parliamentary committees ... representatives of local and regional authorities [and] representatives of third countries' (PE 155.236 1992:Annex, i). Thus, while the depiction of national officials as lobbyists is not new, the greater attention paid by them to the EP is relatively new. Whereas over a decade ago Spence devoted just one short paragraph to the role of the UK permanent representation in Brussels in following EP affairs, such a cursory treatment would be unlikely in the 2000s.

EU governments willingly provide policy briefings to their own national delegations in the EP. One EP committee chairman, in an interview in the 1994–99 Parliament, observed that: 'My permanent representation – the Dutch – is giving us a lot of good briefing, written briefings, so I have good information about what's on the agenda; about what is the opinion of my own country' (quoted in Earnshaw and Judge 1997:555).

Traditionally, and as confirmed by this MEP, much national briefing was essentially formal, taking the form of written memoranda outlining the view of national administrations on Commission proposals, or on parliamentary reports once tabled for the EP's plenary (see also Humphreys 1997). What has changed since then, however, is that national officials and politicians have started to seek to influence EP proceedings more intensively, at an earlier stage, and in tandem with their evolving position in the Council of Ministers. There is also a recognition that national governments should provide tailored briefings for committee rapporteurs, other key committee actors, constituency MEPs, committee members and, ultimately, all MEPs in the run-up to plenary, together even with a voting list 'so that those who agree with your position overall know how to vote for it in detail' (Humphreys 1997:200).

Moreover, it is not unusual for individual permanent representation officials to suggest legislative amendments to their respective national MEPs in committee. Invariably these amendments parallel current national negotiating positions in the relevant working group of the Council. In this sense, national officials have started to intertwine themselves firmly into the pattern of interest representation within the EP. In addition, officials of the permanent representations sometimes also operate *collectively* in seeking to influence the EP. To this end, permanent representation attachés, who are responsible for relations with the EP, meet before each plenary session to coordinate their positions and identify targets for direct lobbying. Obviously, at this stage, national officials will reflect primarily the position arrived at in Council. Such lobbying may be intensive. In the run-up to the EP's vote on the Members' Statute in May 1999 (a vote which ultimately went against the view of Council), one of the permanent representation parliamentary attachés commented to one of the authors that he had 'done nothing for a month but lobby the Parliament on the members' statute'.

Party representation

> According to modern – or, if one prefers, elitist – democratic theory, representative democracy without political parties is close to impossible. (Thomassen and Schmitt 1999:130)

In most parliamentary systems political parties form the primary mechanism of linkage between the electors and their 'government', and so conjoin the two distinct concepts of 'party' and 'government' into the notion of *party government.*

'Party government' offers, in effect, an idealized view of responsible government: one where the actions of parliamentary elites are legitimized by the electoral choice of voters mediated through the programmes of parties. The idea of 'party government', or more accurately 'competitive party government' (Schumpeter [1943] 1976), is deceptively simple and follows a logical sequence: first, each party presents to the electorate a policy programme in the form of a manifesto; second, voters make an informed choice between the competing parties on the basis of this programme; third, the successful party (or coalition) seeks to translate this programme into practice once in government; and, fourth, the governing party (or coalition) is then judged by the electorate on its success in implementing its promises at the next election.

The implications of this model for individual representatives is that they will contest elections on the basis of an agreed aggregate policy programme, and once elected will support policies in conformity with that programme and the party leadership charged with implementing that programme. The internal cohesiveness of parties within the representative parliament is thus a crucial condition of party government. What underpins the notion of party representation is a defence of party discipline and cohesive behaviour of party representatives in parliament (see Judge 1999:70–1).

When the model is applied to the EU, however, there are manifest divergences between the model and the political reality of the EU. There is no competitive party system at the European level which is analogous to competition in national state elections and which forms the basis for the selection of a government (see Chapter 3). Nor is there an EU government as such. Nor do parliamentary parties operate in a simple, bifurcated context where decisions are based on either support for, or opposition to, the policy programme of the majority party (or parties) in the EP.

That being said, however, there are elements of the model which illuminate the present workings of the EU as well as pointing to the potential development of the party system at the

EU level. To identify these convergences it is necessary to examine the two different party organizational structures at this level. The first are the transnational party federations. The second, and of more direct relevance to the present discussion, are the party groups within the EP.

In a formal sense a European party system exists with 'party families' of socialists, Christian democrats, liberals, regionalists and green parties organized into transnational party federations. In a practical sense the importance of these transnational federations in delimiting representative roles for their members is remarkably limited. As noted in Chapter 3, although the transnational federations coordinate EU-wide manifestos, these bland statements hold little resonance for most voters. If the notion of 'party representation' is based upon political parties supplying different policy platforms for voters to choose from, then, in Thomassen and Schmitt's (1999:133) opinion, 'at the European level this does not happen' (see also Franklin 2001:202–4). Similarly, the transnational federations do not form the basis of electors' choices.

The paradox of the party system in the EU is that while European party federations outside the EP are of restricted significance, the party groups within the EP are of vital importance to the daily operations of the Parliament. Party groups determine the composition of leadership positions within the Parliament, such as the President and Vice-President, and committee chairs. They also determine the agenda of the EP, the allocation of speaking time in debates, and the appointment of committee rapporteurs in the processing of legislation (Ladrech 1996:292; Hix 1999:176; Corbett *et al.* 2000:59). In this sense, internally within the EP, a 'truly European party system clearly exists' (Thomassen and Schmitt 1999:134).

While the internal organization of party groups and their wider structural implications for the EP itself will be considered in Chapter 5, the primary concern here is with how and why MEPs act as party representatives within the EP. Recent research by Katz (1999) into the role orientations of MEPs found that they were more likely to give priority in decision-making in the EP to their party than to voters. Admittedly, party influence was ranked well below the use of 'own judgement' by MEPs (Katz 1999:64), but, nonetheless, the influence of party voters was greater than among respondents from national MPs in Katz's sample. Moreover, MEPs placed greater emphasis upon the influence of their party as an *organization* than upon the views of party voters. In part, this reflects the difficulties encountered by MEPs in discerning voter preferences on EU policies from the outcomes of essentially 'second-order' elections (see Chapter 3). In part also, it reflects the ambiguities of party representation in the EP – whether party is conceived in terms of national party delegations, or of EU-wide party groups in the EP. This confusion is perpetuated in Katz's own survey as he combines answers of MEPs to two different partisan organizational foci – 'the view of your national party' and the 'view of your EP group' (Katz 1999:63). So while there is a significant 'partisan' dimension in the role orientations of MEPs it remains unclear how far these orientations point towards the development of a bifurcation of roles in the EP commonly associated with 'party government' (see Chapter 5).

The 'how' of representation: representative style

Thus far we have examined the main foci of representation – of 'what' is represented, whether social groups, territorial constituencies, functional interests or political parties. But the other dimension of representation – the 'style' of representation – of 'how' representatives act on behalf of the represented also needs some consideration. Typically the actions of representatives have been located on a continuum from the position of 'independent trustee' through 'politico' to 'mandated delegate' (Wahlke *et al.* 1962). At the respective ends of this continuum the representative is held either to act independently of voters' opinions or interests; or, alternatively, to take instructions from his or her electors (see Judge 1981, 1999). In between, a representative may act as a 'politico' and adopt either a trustee or a delegate style at different times on different policy issues.

When MEPs were asked to rank the factors most likely to influence their decisions – own judgement, the views of own party voters, or the view of national party or EP group – some 74.7 per cent ranked their own judgement in first place (Katz 1999:64). One initial plausible explanation of the pronounced preference for 'trustee' role orientations in the EP might very well be the absence of 'party government' and the corresponding absence of notions of party representation. One difficulty with this explanation, however, as noted above, is that (if trustee orientations are ignored) then party is clearly identified by MEPs as of importance for the performance of their representational roles. Another difficulty is the simple fact that MPs in national parliaments, with systems of party government, also rank highly a trustee orientation (71.8 per cent). This leads Katz to conclude that representatives might simply identify a socially approved answer, or, more persuasively, that they are able to accommodate notions of independence within a broader frame of 'party representation' (1999:64). In other words, the practice of representation is not unidimensional and representatives may draw upon a range of ideas about representation and adopt a series of orientations (see Judge 1999:58–60). In this regard MEPs are certainly not unique.

Conclusion

One objective of this book is to assess the extent to which the EP can be located within the academic analysis of legislatures. Certainly, the EP provides the only direct linkage between EU decision-makers and the 15 electorates of the EU. In this sense, as the only directly elected supranational representative institution in the EU, it is unique. Despite this unique position it displays, nonetheless, characteristics of representation commonly associated with national parliaments in Western liberal democracies. Whether this is a 'good thing' is open to question. For example, those 'proportionalists' who believe that the EP should be a microcosm of European society are disappointed to discover that MEPs are, in aggregate, just as middle-aged, middle-class and Caucasian as their counterparts in national parliaments. Equally, those concerned with the potential of 'interest representation' to subvert the 'democratic' wishes of the electorate are just as wary as their national counterparts of the representation of 'sinister interests' and the need to regulate the relationships between representatives and the lobbyists, the political consultants, and the public affairs executives who inhabit the corridors of the EP. If anything, the enhanced legislative impact of the EP in the past decade has simply intensified these concerns in Brussels and Strasbourg.

Even the belief that the EP at least was distinguishable from national parliaments in the weakness of notions of 'party representation' and the underdevelopment of a parliamentary party system has been undermined in the light of recent research. Thus, as Katz discovered, MEPs were more likely than national MPs to afford priority to their party than to voters in reaching legislative decisions. Not least because 'for MEPs ... party becomes more important in articulating and interpreting the interests of citizens' given the voters' limited information about the EU and the low levels of participation at EU elections (Katz 1999:65).

If the role orientations of MEPs display marked characteristics of 'party representation' then so too are their daily activities in the EP structured by their party group affiliation. Given the influence of party groups in structuring the conceptions of roles and the actual voting behaviour of MEPs, then one analyst at least believes that 'the post-1999 EP operates very much like any domestic parliament in Europe' (Hix 2001b:685). While this is an overstatement, as there remain marked differences between the EP's party system and national parliamentary systems based upon party *government* (see Marsh and Norris 1997:154–6), nonetheless it highlights the importance of party in the representative process of the EP. And it is to one particular aspect of party representation – party groups – that we now turn in Chapter 5.

Chapter 5

Party Groups in
the European Parliament

Chapter 4 raised some of the issues surrounding the representa-
tive/linkage role of political parties and the extent to which
notions of transnational party competition are appropriate for
the study of the EU. In this chapter we examine the role played
by party groups in the internal workings of the EP. Not only do
parties link the people to decision-makers but they also link,
structure and regularize interactions between decision-makers
themselves. In this respect the EP is no different from most other
parliaments and legislatures in that parties provide the organizational lubricant for the smooth operation of the institution.
A clear link can be discerned between the effective organization
of the EP and the structure of party groups within that institution.
Indeed, the best way to analyse party groups, for our purposes
at least, is as aggregations of individual representatives as an institutional response to the complexities of decision-making in an
environment characterized by information overload, linguistic
proliferation, territorial diversity, ideological heterogeneity and
technological complexity.

The very structure of decision-making itself in the EU – both
in the nature of its legislative procedures and in its multi-level
dimensionality – affects the organizational imperatives of party
groups within the EP. The nature of the EU legislative process is
such that it requires fluid parliamentary majorities across policy
areas and across legislative procedures. This is in contrast to the
fixed and consistent majorities required in many national parliaments in support of, or opposition to, a party government.
Moreover, the nature of interinstitutional bargaining in the EU is
such that the EP has to engage simultaneously with intergovernmental and supranational (and sometimes national) institutions
and so has to be able to accommodate and articulate national
and transnational demands in tandem. Hence, party groups

within the EP cannot be understood in isolation from the institutional context in which they have developed and within which they function.

Development of transnational party groups

Transnational party groups have been such a long-standing feature within the EP that it is worthwhile remembering that there were alternative organizational forms that could have been adopted. One possibility was, of course, for MEPs to organize as national blocs (Henig and Pinder 1969:476–7). Another was simply for representatives to sit as individuals – as independent trustees. Indeed, the original 78 nominees to the ECSC Common Assembly sat in alphabetical order and carried symbols of neither national nor party allegiance. But neither organizational precept – individualism or nationality – offered an effective solution to the institutional requirements of a body charged with the monitoring and supervision of a supranational executive. From the outset, therefore, there was an institutional predisposition in favour of transnational cooperation within the Assembly. Indeed, as noted in Chapter 2, within the first six months of the Common Assembly's creation, party groups had formed, and by June 1953 they had been officially recognized in the Assembly's standing orders. Even before the official formation of groups there had been agreement amongst delegates that the committees of the Assembly should 'reflect political tendencies as well as the balance between nationalities' (Raunio 1996a:65).

The three major West European, postwar party constellations of Christian Democrats, Socialists and Liberals provided the initial groupings in the Assembly. These three groups have been in continuous existence ever since, and have remained the largest groups in the EP. Moreover, the absence of other groups in the formative years of the Assembly from 1953 to 1965 helped to inculcate 'a tradition of political group oligopoly' (Westlake 1994a:185). Since then, a number of other groups have emerged and maintained a continuous existence across several parliaments (Union of European Left (UEL) and Greens), and a number of others have come and gone (for details see Corbett *et al.* 2000:59–70; Hix and Lord 1997:77–9). Still others emerged in the 1999–2004 Parliament (see below). Nonetheless, throughout, the oligopoly of the major groups has remained largely intact.

Certainly, the limited number of party groups has provided organizational benefits in the form of the routinization of working practices and has brought 'stability, consistency, and functional efficiency to the Parliament' (Raunio 1996a:67). In return, the party groups have been conferred with specific institutional rights and privileges in terms of financial assistance, staffing and accommodation (see below). In this manner, there have been incentives for Parliament as an institution, for party groups and for members themselves to consolidate transnational cooperation internally within the groups.

Over time the exact number of transnational groups in the EP and their longevity and composition have been influenced by several key variables. First, group formation was influenced by successive enlargements in 1973, 1981, 1986 and 1995, which brought more MEPs, more parties and more ideological diversity into the EP. Second, the changed political priorities in member states – with advances of parties of the centre right in the 1980s and of the social democratic left in the late 1990s, and with the development of environmental, nationalist and regionalist parties – also impacted on the group profile within the EP. Third, the end of the Cold War affected not only the structures of national party systems but also 'led to a reconfiguration of forces and relationships within the EP' (Ladrech 1996:301). This new freedom, for example, brought the Italian PDS into the Socialist Group in October 1992, after leaving the group it had dominated, the United European Left.

Rules on size and formation

In response to the changing constellation of parties finding representation in the EP there has been a succession of rule changes to regulate the size and formation of groups. Before 1999, a group could be established exclusively from MEPs drawn from a single member state. In the major overhaul of the Rules of Procedure in 1999 the minimum number of MEPs required to form a group was linked for the first time to a distribution of group members across more than one member state (Rule 29(2)). In 1994 the then ruling party in Italy, Forza Italia, had formed from its own representatives the EP group Forza Europa. At that time the minimum threshold for group formation was 26 members from one member state. After enlargement in 1995 the minimum threshold was increased to 29 where MEPs came from a single member state. In 1999 the minimum threshold was reduced to 23 with MEPs drawn from at least two member states. The threshold was reduced still further to 18 if members came from three member states, and to 14 if drawn from four or more member states.

With the next enlargement of the EU the distinction between groups with members from two, three or even four member states would 'no longer [be] meaningful' (PE 304.283 2001:7). In which case, the Constitutional Affairs Committee, at the end of 2001, proposed an amendment to the EP's rules that would require a political group to be comprised of members elected in at least a fifth of the member states and with a minimum size of 16 members (5 per cent of membership). This rule change was designed to 'guarantee the transnational nature of Groups' (PE 304.283 2002:8), and was agreed by the EP in June 2002 (to enter into force on 1 July 2004).

Under Rule 29, the basic requirement governing the composition of groups is that their members share broad 'political affinities'. This requirement has existed in the rules since the earliest days of the Common Assembly, and its significance is that it prevents heterogeneous collections of MEPs nominally joining together to accrue the organizational and financial benefits of group membership. This point was illustrated in July 1999 when five MEPs from the French Front National along with seven Radicals from Italy (Lista Emma Bonino) and other unattached representatives tried to establish a Technical Group of Independent Members (TDI) during the EP's constituent session. The TDI Group was rejected in the plenary session on 14 September 1999 on the grounds that its membership did not display the necessary requirements of 'political affinity'. However, not only was the group ideologically diverse but its members also proclaimed openly that they did not share 'political affinities'. In fact the Court of Justice subsequently noted that the TDI had 'totally ruled out working in the legislature towards the expression of common political intentions, ideas or objectives, however minimal' (Judgment of the Court of First Instance, Joined Cases T-222/99, T-327/99 and T-329/99, 2 October 2001:para. 110).

Also, in September 1999, in contrast to the 'technical' groups of earlier parliaments (see Corbett *et al.* 2000:60–3), it was proposed that the parties of the right and far right join with the Italian Radicals of the Lista Emma Bonino. A further attempt by Italian non-attached members to allow for the formation of a 'Mixed Group' – to allow the 26 non-attached MEPs from nine parties in six member states to benefit from the procedural and financial advantages of a political group – also failed to secure the necessary parliamentary support.

However, Jean-Claude Martinez and Charles de Gaulle of the Technical Group challenged Parliament's rejection in the Court of First Instance. On 25 November 1999 the President of the Court ruled that the Technical Group could remain in existence until the Court's judgment was delivered (Case T-222/99). The Technical Group was formally terminated in October 2001 after the Court rejected the appeals of Martinez and de Gaulle against the EP's decision not to recognize the existence of the TDI Group (Joined Cases T-222/99, T-327/99 and T-329/99). EP President Nicole Fontaine announced, on 3 October 2001, that the EP's decision of 14 September 1999 was 'once again fully effective' (EP Debates 3 October 2001) and by the end of the week the TDI had been removed from the EP's listing of political groups.

In the intervening period between September 1999 and October 2001, Parliament's Committee on Constitutional Affairs examined the whole issue of technical and mixed groups and adopted a report in June 2000 which was subsequently modified in September of that year (PE 232.762 2000). The report proposed amendments to the Rules of Procedure in an attempt to clarify the position of non-affiliated parties and individual MEPs in relation to parliamentary organs and procedures and to address anomalies where these existed. The starting premiss of the Committee was that 'the system of political groups must not create unfairness or discrimination *vis-à-vis* those Members who do not form part of a group' (PE 232.762 2000:8). This principle was later upheld by the Court of First Instance (Joined Cases T-222/99, T-327/99 and T-329/99, 2 October 2001:paras 59 and 202).

However, the Committee reiterated its support for the principle that members of political groups should share some political affinity and that mixed and technical groups infringed this principle. In the Committee's opinion, the way to reconcile the

organization of MEPs from disparate ideological backgrounds
into political groups in accordance with the 'political affinities'
principle rested in the proposition that:

> the requirement that groups are set on the basis of political
> affinity does not mean that Parliament must judge whether
> the members of a group have such affinity; the very fact of
> creating a group together pursuant to Rule 29 means that the
> Members concerned accept that they have political affinity;
> Parliament's non-recognition of a group consequently only
> concerned a case where a particular group explicitly denied
> any political affinity. (PE 232.762 2000:11)

On this basis, the Constitutional Affairs Committee proposed
that an interpretation be added to Rule 29(1) to recognize that
it was up to MEPs, when forming a group, to 'accept by definition that they have political affinity'. Only in those instances
where group members denied 'political affinity' would it be necessary for the EP to make a decision on conformity. The committee's report and the amendment of Parliament's rules was
eventually adopted in plenary in June 2002. Also amended, to
remove the most apparent areas of discrimination, were the
rules that related to the rights of independent members (notably
those relating to the threshold for tabling resolutions to wind up
debate and representation on conciliation delegations).

Parliamentary-specific activities

Party groups within the EP are best regarded as 'parliamentary
specific' (Ladrech 1996:294) in that their intra-parliamentary
activities are largely divorced from the standard campaigning
and electioneering functions associated with political parties in
nation states. As we saw in Chapter 3, EU elections are still basically contested on national political terrains with national political parties jealously guarding the right to select candidates for
the EP and to structure subsequent campaigns. Where transnational party federations have been active is in the formulation of
transnational manifestos and, to a limited extent, in the coordination of campaigns. Nonetheless, the actual detailed organization and running of the campaigns in each member state has

been left to national parties. A division of labour has thus emerged between national parties, transnational party federations and political groups in the EP. A Court of Justice ruling in 1986 – that EP groups could not use funds derived from the EP budget (under item 3708) to fund election campaigns – simply reinforced this division of labour. The Court ruled that it was *ultra vires* for Parliament, via its political groups, to support any kind of election campaign in the absence of a uniform electoral system (see Case 294/83, the *Green Group* v. *European Parliament*, judgment of 23 April 1986). Since that ruling EP funds have been used in principle only for the dissemination of group information and have been suspended even for such activity 30 days before a European election.

One of the consequences of this division of labour has been a fracturing of the normal liberal democratic linkage between the activity of representatives in Parliament and their electoral accountability. In the EU, what MEPs do, or what their party groups do in the EP, is not the primary determinant of reelection (Hix and Lord 1997:89), or, for MEPs, of reselection. Yet, paradoxically, party groups are the primary organizational determinant of what happens in the EP. Precisely because political groups are the backbone of the EP's internal organization significant rights and financial resources have been conferred on them by the institution itself. Thus, in addition to the funds previously provided under budget item 3708 for informational purposes, the groups also received financial assistance under item 3707 for administrative and secretariat support. In 2001 all funding for the political groups was placed on a single budget line, item 3701. This was a result of criticisms made by the Court of Auditors about the legality and regularity of transactions made by the political groups. The Court proposed, in its Special Report (13/2000), that all appropriations for the groups be placed under a single budget heading 'to end the highly theoretical distinction between political and information activities' (Court of Auditors 2000:11 in OJ C 181, 28 June 2000). In 2002, nearly €35 million were provided under this budget line (OJ L 29, 31 January 2002:241); and when expenditure on technical facilities, office accommodation, meeting rooms and other organizational support is added the total support for political groups amounts to approximately 13 per cent of the EP's €1.03 billion budget.

Towards a European party statute

The problems discovered by the Court of Auditors in respect of the legality and regularity of the financial transactions of political parties, and the recommendation that 'consideration should be given to drawing up transparent rules to be applied to the financing of these parties' (OJ C 181, 28 June 2000:para. 64), served to highlight the need for a regulation on the statute and financing of European political parties. However, identification of the need for such a legal statute dated back to at least December 1996 and the adoption of a resolution on the constitutional status of European political parties (OJ C 20, 20 January 1997:29).

Article 191 of the Maastricht Treaty had acknowledged that: 'Political parties at European level are important as a factor for integration within the Union. They contribute to forming a European awareness and to expressing the political will of the citizens of the Union.' But there was no accompanying operational clause that would allow for the implementation of this article. Hence, the Commission proposed, during the 2000 IGC, that Article 191 be amplified further, and transformed into a legal base suitable for the adoption of a statute relating to the formation and funding of European political parties. This mirrored the proposal made by Parliament in its November 1999 resolution on the IGC (OJ C 189, 7 July 2000:224). As a result, the Nice Treaty negotiators added a second paragraph to Article 191, providing for a statute for European parties to be adopted, via codecision:

> The Council, acting in accordance with the procedure referred to in Article 251, shall lay down the regulations governing political parties at European level and in particular the rules regarding their financing.

The IGC also agreed a declaration which sought to guard against the EU acquiring competency in party funding rules nationally, and which reiterated that EU finances 'may not be used to fund, either directly or indirectly, political parties at national level'.

However, pending the ratification of the Nice Treaty, and in anticipation of the entry into force of the new second paragraph of Article 191, the Commission submitted a proposal at the beginning of 2001 (COM[2000]898). The proposal was based on Article 308 of the Amsterdam Treaty, and envisaged the creation of interim rules for a statute and for the financing for European political parties. But other pressures served to prompt the Commission into action. First, in February 2000 the Presidents of the European People's Party and European Democrats (EPP–ED), European Socialists (PSE), the European Liberal, Democratic and Reformist Group (ELDR), and the Greens/European Free Alliance (Greens/EFA) had jointly proposed to the President of the Commission that such a regulation should be proposed forthwith by the Commission. Second, the Court of Auditors' report had considered subsidies from the EP budget to the extra-parliamentary parties to be illegal (see above). In reaching this verdict, the Court had effectively closed off subsidies from the party groups to their extra-parliamentary organizations. Third, 'the cost of promoting democracy in the countries applying for accession' (COM[2000]898 2001: recital 3), and the role that European parties were expected to play in the run-up to the first European elections in the new member states, was a compelling reason for regularizing EU funding of European transnational party organizations. Fourth, Parliament, during the 2001 budget procedure, had already created a new budget line (B3-500) with a token entry for the financing of European political parties. In adopting this budget line Parliament noted that 'the Commission is requested to submit as soon as possible a proposal with a statute for European political parties, in order to implement the Treaty' (OJ L 56, 26 February 2001:874).

The Commission's proposal provided for any European political party or 'union of such parties' to register its statute so long as it is established in the EU; has established, or intends to create or participate in, an EP political group; and its programme and activities respect the principles of democracy, fundamental rights and the rule of law (COM[2000]898 final:Article 1). To receive financing from the EU budget, a European party 'or its national components' must be represented in the EP, or national or regional parliaments in at least five member states, and receive at least 5 per cent of the votes cast at the most recent European elections in at least five member states. At least 25 per cent of the party's budget would be required to come from sources other than the EU budget. The Commission suggested that initial funding would be in the order of €7 million per annum, on the basis of five existing European parties. Parliament, in its subsequent vote on the Commission's proposal, tightened up some of its provisions. Notably, the EP inserted the requirement that any donations and other contributions to European parties be transparent – so effectively outlawing anonymous donations. Moreover, it insisted that only European parties or 'long-term European' unions of parties would be eligible for registration and thereby funding, on the grounds that alliances between parties solely to attract EU funds should be prevented (EP texts adopted 17 May 2001).

During the second half of 2001 the Belgian presidency of the EU prioritized the Commission's proposal. The impending discussion of the proposal by the 29 October 2001 General Affairs Council generated further joint correspondence by the leaders of the European parties (Cassola for the Greens, Cook for the PSE, Hoyer for the ELDR, Maes for the Democratic Party of the Peoples of Europe–European Free Alliance, and Martens for the EPP) to the Belgian Council Presidency and Commission President Prodi. In their correspondence the party leaders suggested that an annual EU budget allocation of €15 million would be more realistic, and indicated that an additional funding allocation for 'start-up costs' might be necessary. They also declared their support for 'the objective of giving European political parties an autonomous organisational and financial basis' and indicated their determination 'to further develop parties at EU level as complementary elements of EU democratic life' (Council of Ministers, Copy of Letter, 12738/01, 26 October 2001).

Structures and staffing

The structure and staffing of each party group is linked, obviously, to its size. Generally, the larger groups tend to have larger bureaux (executive committees) and more staff. The structure of group bureaux is not specified in the EP's rules, and each group's organization is different. In general, the bureau in each group is composed of a chair, president or leader (and in the case of the Greens in the 1999–2004 Parliament, co-chairs), vice-chairs and treasurer along with other members. Procedures for selecting and/or electing group bureaux differ across the groups but in all cases the basic principle is one of reconciling intra-group national and political interests. In the larger groups the position of group leader is agreed in negotiations held by national party leaders shortly after European elections. These agreements are normally part of a larger package which includes the group's candidate for EP President, the parliamentary group's leader, the group's treasurer, group secretary-general, and the leader of the extra-parliamentary party confederation. Thus, in 1999, EU socialist party leaders decided upon octogenarian former PM Mario Soares (Portugal) as Socialist candidate for the EP presidency, Enrique Barón Crespo (Spain) as group leader, Torbun Lund (Denmark) for treasurer, Christine Verger (who had previously worked in the *cabinet* of Commission President Delors) as secretary-general of the group, and Rudolf Scharping to be followed by Robin Cook (each for two and a half years) as leader of the Party of European Socialists (previously Confederation).

Group bureaux also frequently include parliamentary officers such as EP Vice-Presidents, quaestors or committee chairs. Leaders of national delegations within groups are also frequently members of their group bureau. Over the years the role of national delegation leaders within EP party groups has increased. On some occasions, on the most politically sensitive issues, intra-group decision-making is conducted initially among leaders of national delegations (manifestly at the expense of formal group procedures).

In the larger groups there is also a mechanism for ensuring a prorata reflection of the size of each national delegation in the number of members in the bureau. For example, in the EPP–ED there is one coopted bureau member for every ten members per national delegation; and in the PSE ordinary members, formally at least, are elected on a proportional basis according to their party representation in the group. The PSE also has a rule that the number of women on the bureau has to be at least proportional to the number of women in the group as a whole. In 2000, women occupied 39 per cent of PSE bureau positions.

Group chairs are normally elected from the larger national delegations. After the 1999 election each group, with the exception of the Liberals, elected new EP leaders. The respective chairs in 2002 were: for the EPP–ED, Hans Gert Poettering, a German CDU member; for the PSE, Enrique Barón Crespo, a Spanish

PSOE member; for the Liberals (ELDR), Graham Watson, a UK
Liberal Democrat (who replaced Pat Cox, an Irish Independent,
after his election to the EP's Presidency); for the Confederal
Group of the European Left/Nordic Green Left (EUL/NGL)
Francis Wurtz, a French Communist; and for the Group of
Europe of Nations, Charles Pasqua from the French RPFIE.
The Greens/European Free Alliance had two chairs – Monica
Frassoni of the Belgian Ecolo, and Daniel Cohn-Bendit of Les
Verts. In turn, the Europe of Democracies and Diversities had
three co-chairs (reflecting its status as little more than a marriage
of convenience among diverse partners): Jens-Peter Bonde
(JuniBevaegelsen) from Denmark; Jean Saint-Josse (Chasse,
Pêche, Nature, Traditions) from France, and Hans Blokland
(GPV) from the Netherlands.

The position of group chair is of considerable importance
within the EP. In addition to providing internal political leadership, chairs also represent the group in its external dealings with
other groups, most notably in the EP's Conference of Presidents.
Many necessary deals are struck, and alliances forged, in informal
meetings of group chairs. Nonetheless, the scope for independent
action by group chairs is limited in practice by the need to maintain consensual and collective decision-making within the group.

Group meetings

The important role of group chairs and of the bureaux in securing intra-group agreement on policy and institutional decisions is
evident in 'group weeks'. These are scheduled into the EP's annual
cycle and are held in Brussels in the week before plenary sessions
in Strasbourg. In addition, each group meets on several occasions,
normally four, throughout the Strasbourg plenary week and prior
to plenary sessions in Brussels. Elaborate arrangements are in
place within each group to allow time to formulate and articulate
common perspectives on the issues before Parliament and to
mobilize support. In this process the group chair, bureau members
and, especially, national delegation leaders play a key role in
aligning the policy preferences of national delegations and of the
transnational group itself. Indeed, the traditional working pattern, within the EPP–ED and PSE at least, is for group chairs to
structure group debates on important issues around statements
from leaders or spokespersons of national delegations.

Group meetings also allow for the coordination of EP committee decisions with group positions. Hence, 'group weeks' also include collective meetings of the committee coordinators for each group (effectively the group 'spokespeople' on each of the EP's committees), with committee chairs from the group usually in attendance. The committee coordinators' meeting is normally scheduled early in a 'group week', and the outcomes of these deliberations guide subsequent discussion in the group as a whole. In this manner, party group preferences (which reflect broader party and national stances) are reconciled, or at least accommodated, with EP committee positions. In the course of intra-party deliberations committee coordinators and committee chairs serve to attune their respective group positions to the policy preferences formulated within their committees.

The regularity of group meetings, their format and the attempt therein to reconcile various political preferences – party, nationality, committee – provide vivid evidence of the necessity of ensuring a style of 'qualified supranationalism' and collective internal decision-making (see Hix and Lord 1997:128). This style seeks to maximize transnational agreement while allowing for reasoned national and other political divergences from the group position when necessary. Continual consultation within the bureaux and within the wider group is thus a defining feature of group leadership in the EP.

The need for protracted consultation and the frequency of group meetings serve in turn to restrict independent action by group leaders. What is apparent also is that on those occasions when the processes of consultation and collective deliberation unravel, the position of the group leader becomes precarious. This was well illustrated by Pauline Green's fate as Leader of the PSE after the 1999 Commission crisis and the European elections of that year. Her interventions in the Commission crisis and her apparent responsiveness at that time to instructions from her national party leadership in London led to open criticism of her leadership. More particularly, after the significant reduction in the numbers of UK Socialist MEPs after the 1999 election Pauline Green was forced to stand down as leader of the Socialist Group (see *European Voice* 17–23 June 1999).

Each group is entitled to a number of administrative and support staff. The precise number varies in accordance with the size of the group, as well as with the number of working languages used by each group (see Corbett *et al.* 2000:82). In 2002 a total of 553 party group posts were budgeted for. The largest group, the EPP–ED, employed over 150 officials, while the smallest, the Group for a Europe of Democracies and Diversities (EDD), had only 16. Naturally, political affiliation and nationality are important criteria in securing a post in a group, but objective selection criteria of written and oral tests and language tests are now the norm in the larger groups. Most group officials are employed on temporary contracts but enjoy some *de facto* job security. (However, the entire staff of the European Democratic Alliance group was made redundant in 1999 when its largest contingent of French Gaullist MEPs transferred en masse to the EPP group.) Notably, several group officials have used their group position to launch their own careers as MEPs. Some examples from MEPs in the 1999–2004 Parliament include Richard Corbett of the PSE, Caroline Jackson of the EPP–ED, and Monica Frassoni of the Greens.

Composition of groups

Figure 5.1 shows the location of the seven political groups in the EP in September 2002. Table 5.1 indicates the number of MEPs from each member state in each political group.

European People's Party and European Democrats (EPP–ED)

In 1999 the EPP–ED, with 233 MEPs, overtook the PSE to become the largest group for the first time since the introduction of direct elections. This newly found preeminence was to have significant repercussions for the legislative orientation and the working patterns of the EP. Equally, this growth in size had its own internal repercussions for the EPP–ED in that its ideological coherence became more dissipated.

At its inception the EPP was a fairly cohesive grouping of Christian Democratic parties from the six founding member states (for details see Fitzmaurice 1975:69–85; Pridham and Pridham 1981). Uniformly, the national Christian Democratic parties were predominantly centre-right and pro-federalist in

FIGURE 5.1 Location of political groups

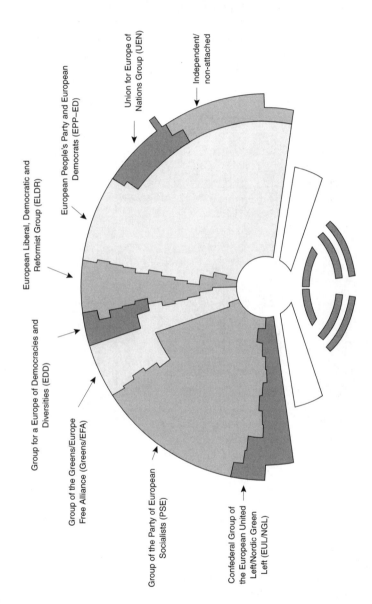

European Liberal, Democratic and
Reformist Group (ELDR)

European People's Party and European
Democrats (EPP–ED)

Union for Europe of
Nations Group (UEN)

Independent/
non-attached

Group for a Europe of Democracies and
Diversities (EDD)

Group of the Greens/Europe
Free Alliance (Greens/EFA)

Group of the Party of European
Socialists (PSE)

Confederal Group of
the European United
Left/Nordic Green
Left (EUL/NGL)

TABLE 5.1 *Political groups by member state (at 16 September 2002)*

	Austria	Belgium	Denmark	Finland	France	Germany	Greece	Ireland	Italy	Luxembourg	Netherlands	Portugal	Spain	Sweden	United Kingdom	Total
EPP-ED	7	6	1	5	21	53	9	5	35	2	9	9	28	7	37	234
PSE	7	5	2	3	18	35	9	1	16	2	6	12	24	6	29	175
ELDR		5	6	5				1	8	1	8		3	4	11	52
GREENS/EFA	2	7		2	9	4		2	2	1	4		4	2	6	45
GUE/NGL			4	1	15	7	7		6		1	2	4	3		50
UEN			1		3			6	10			2				22
EDD			2		9						3				2	16
IND	5	2			12				10				1		2	32
Total	21	25	16	16	87	99	25	15	87	6	31	25	64	22	87	626

Source: www.wdb.europal.eu.int/ep5/owa/p_meps2.repartition?ilg=EN&iorig=home.

orientation. Successive enlargements, however, incorporated within the EPP a number of other centre-right parties which neither subscribed to Christian Democratic values nor shared a federalist vision for Europe. The extent of ideological diversity of the group found reflection in its change of name after the 1999 election to the Group of the European People's Party and European Democrats. The name change was prompted in large part by UK Conservative MEPs who were keen to signal the changed ideological balance inside the group.

The extent to which the balance tipped in favour of rightist parties in the EPP–ED in 1999 can be seen in Table 5.2. While the largest contingent in the EPP remained the traditional backbone of the German CDU with 43 members, the second largest national party delegation after 1999 was the UK Conservatives with 36 MEPs. This was a UK delegation characterized by internal divisions over European integration and which contained an increased number of overtly Eurosceptic members. The third largest national party delegation was the Italian Forza Italia with 22 members (23 by 2002), a populist rightist party with several of its MEPs openly 'Gaullist' in defence of national sovereignty. Indeed, seven other Italian right-wing parties found representation in the EPP–ED. The rightward drift was starkly revealed with the decision of the Austrian ÖVP to join in a domestic governing alliance with the far-right Freedom Party (with the ÖVP's 7 MEPs still retaining membership of EPP–ED). The group leader, Hans Gert Poettering, openly acknowledged the 'great variety within the group' (cited in GPC 2000:18) but did not see such diversity to be a significant problem. However, some traditional Christian Democrats within the group were less sanguine about the diffusion of the original principles of the EPP and established shortly after the election a loose grouping, the Schuman Group, to combat the rightward drift and 'to regroup those who strongly believe in European integration and centre politics' (Gil-Robles, cited in GPC 2000:17).

Group of the Party of European Socialists (PSE)

Until 1999 the PSE had been the largest group in the EP since the first direct elections in 1979. However, with only 180 MEPs returned in June 1999, some 53 fewer members than the EPP–ED, it was forced to relinquish its pole position. Most of the

TABLE 5.2   *European People's Party and European Democrats (EPP–ED) at 16 September 2002 (n = 234)*

	Number of members		National parties
Austria	7	7	ÖVP (Österreichische Volkspartei)
Belgium	6	3	CVP (Christelijke Volkspartij)
		1	PSC (Parti Social Chrétien)
		1	CSP–EVP (Christliche Soziale Partei–Europäische Volkspartei)
		1	MCC (Mouvement des Citoyens pour le Changement)
Denmark	1	1	(Det Konservative Folkeparti)
Finland	5	4	KOK (Kansallinen Kokoomus)
		1	SKL (Suomen Kristillinen Liitto)
France	21	9	UDF (Union pour la Démocratie Française)
		5	RPR (Rassemblement pour la République)
		6	DL (Démocratie Libérale)
		1	Independent
Germany	53	43	CDU (Christlich Demokratische Union)
		10	CSU (Christlich-Soziale Union in Bayerne.V)
Greece	9	9	ND (Nea Dimokratia)
Ireland	5	4	FG (Fine Gael)
		1	Independent Rosemary (Dana) Scallon (Connacht-Ulster)
Italy	35	23	Forza Italia
		4	PPI (Partito Popolare Italiano)
		2	CCD (Centro Cristiano Democratico)
		2	CDU (Cristiani Democratici Unito)
		1	UDEUR (Unione Democratici Europei)
		1	RI–DINI (Rinnovamento Italiano/Dini)
		1	SVP (Partito Popolare Sudtirolese)
		1	Partito Pensionista
Luxembourg	2	2	CSV (Chrischtlech Sozial Vollekspartei)

TABLE 5.2 *Continued*

	Number of members		National parties
Netherlands	9	9	CDA (Christen Demokratisch Appel)
Portugal	9	9	PPD/PSD (Partido Social Demócrata)
Spain	28	27	PP (Partido Popular)
		1	CIU/UDC (Convergencia i Unió/Unió – Democrática de Catalunya)
Sweden	7	5	M (Moderata samlingspartiet)
		2	KD (Kristdemokraterna)
United Kingdom	37	36	Conservative Party
		1	UUP (Ulster Unionist Party)

decline in PSE numbers from 221 immediately before the 1999 elections was accounted for by the loss of 33 UK Labour Party MEPs (see Butler and Westlake 2000). Immediately after the 1999 election the largest national delegation was the German SPD with 33 MEPs. By 2002 and with the inclusion of two former Green MEPs (Ozan Ceyhun and Wolgang Kreissl-Dörfler) the SPD group numbered 35. The UK Labour Party with 29 was the second largest delegation in 1999, followed by the Spanish PSOE with 22 MEPs, and then the French Parti Socialiste with 18 members. By September 2002 the defection of Richard Balfe from the UK Labour delegation to the EPP–ED (via independent status; see below), and the movement of four French MEPs to the EUL/NGL further reduced PSE representation to 175.

As with the EPP–ED, the PSE draws its members from all 15 member states. Nonetheless, the PSE remains far more ideologically coherent than the post-1999 EPP–ED – despite a marked ideological difference between the traditional socialism of the French PS and the 'modernizers' in the UK Labour group. In addition, the PSE's parliamentary strength was reinforced by the fact that, in 2000, socialist governments dominated in the Council of Ministers. Eleven of the 15 member states had socialist parties in government and a total of nine socialist prime ministers.

TABLE 5.3 *Group of the Party of European Socialists (PSE) at 16 September 2002 (n = 175)*

	Number of members		National parties
Austria	7	7	SPÖ (Sozialdemokratische Partei Österreichs)
Belgium	5	3	PS (Parti Socialiste)
		2	SP (Socialistische Partij)
Denmark	3	3	SOC (Socialdemokratiet)
Finland	3	3	SDP (Suomen Sosialidemokraattinen Puolue)
France	18	16	PS (Parti Socialiste)
		1	PRG (Parti Radical de Gauche)
		1	MDC (Mouvement des Citoyens)
Germany	35	35	SPD (Sozialdemokratische Partei Deutschlands)
Greece	9	9	PASOK (Panellinio Socialistiko Kinima)
Ireland	1	1	Labour Party
Italy	16	1	SDI (Socilialisti Democratico Italiani)
		15	DS (Democratici di Sinistra)
Luxembourg	2	2	LSAP (Lëtzeburger Sozialistesch Aarbechterpartei)
Netherlands	6	6	PvdA (Partij van de Arbeid)
Portugal	12	12	PS (Partido Socialista)
Spain	24	22	PSOE (Partido Socialista Obrero Español)/Progresistas
		2	PDNI (Partido de la Nueva Izquierda)
Sweden	6	6	S (Socialdemokratiska arbetarepartiet)
United Kingdom	29	28	Labour Party
		1	SDLP (Social Democratic and Labour Party)

European Liberal, Democratic and Reformist Group (ELDR)

With 51 MEPs from ten countries the ELDR was the third largest group in the post-1999 Parliament. Its membership was geographically concentrated with some 80 per cent representing northern countries and with only 11 of its MEPs coming from the two southern countries of Italy and Spain. With the exception of the Italian I Democratici (and two independent MEPs), all national party delegations were members of the transnational federation of the Liberal, Democratic and Reformist parties of the European Community. In being reelected as ELDR Group leader in 1999, Pat Cox, an independent member from Ireland, continued in his unique position as the only leader of a political group not to be a member of a national political party. More importantly for our purposes however, the ELDR under Cox's leadership entered a coalition with the EPP–ED immediately after the 1999 election and effectively became 'kingmaker in a hung parliament' (GPC 2000:20; see below).

Confederal Group of the European Left/Nordic Green Left (EUL/NGL)

With 41 members EUL/NGL was the fifth largest parliamentary group after the 1999 election. However, by 2002, its membership had increased to 50 as a result of defections from other groups (see above), so making it the fourth largest group in the EP. Its members represented communist, former communist or left-socialist parties in ten member states. The extension of the group's title to include 'Nordic Green Left' was the result of the admission of Swedish and Finnish members after enlargement in 1995. The group's territorial scope was widened further in 1999 with the election of six MEPs of the PDS, the former East German Communist party, and one member of the Dutch Socialistische Partij. EUL/NGL's varied membership, combined with intra-group ideological rifts and differing perspectives on EU integration, tended to undermine its concerted action in the 1994–99 Parliament. This trend continued in the early period of the 1999–2004 Parliament, with even lower levels of EUL/NGL voting cohesion (see below). In part this was because the

TABLE 5.4 *European Liberal, Democratic and Reformist Group (ELDR) at 16 September 2002 (n = 52)*

	Number of members		National parties
Belgium	5	3	VLD (Vlaamse Liberalen en Demokraten)
		2	PRL–FDF (Parti Réformateur Libéral–Front Démocratique des Francophones)
Denmark	6	1	RV (Det Radikale Venstre)
		5	V (Venstre)
Finland	5	4	KESK (Suomen Keskusta)
		1	SFP (Svenska Folkspartiet)
Ireland	1		Independent Pat Cox (Munster)
Italy	8	4	I DEMO (Democratici)
		1	IdV (Italia dei Valori)
		1	NPS (Nuvo Partito Socialista)
		1	PRI.LIB (Partito Repubblicono Italiano)
		1	UV (Union Valdôtaine)
Luxembourg	1	1	DP (Demokratesch Partei)
Netherlands	8	6	VVD (Volkspartij voor Vrijheid en Democratie)
		2	D66 (Democraten 66)
Spain	3	2	CIU:CDC (Convergencia Democrática de Catalunya)
		1	CE (Coalición Europea): CC (Coalición Canaria)
Sweden	4	1	C (Centerpartiet)
		3	FP (Folkpartiet Liberalerna)
United Kingdom	11	11	Liberal Democrats

EUL/NGL's group procedures are rudimentary in comparison with those of the larger groups. The tendency is for its component parts to act independently, even individually. As the word 'confederal' in the group's title suggests, while the EUL/NGL's members undoubtedly share a political affinity, individual priorities and concerns tend to outweigh the pressure for group cohesion (see Lazar 2002:91–2).

TABLE 5.5 *Confederal Group of the European United Left/Nordic Green Left (EUL/NGL) at 16 September 2002 (n = 50)*

	Number of members		National parties
Denmark	4	1	SF (Socialistisk Folkeparti)
		1	Independent
		1	Juni.B (JuniBevaegelsen)
		1	Folk.B (FolkeBevaegelsen Mod EU)
Finland	1	1	VAS (Vasemmistolitto)
France	15	3	PCF (Parti Commmuniste Français)
		3	Independents (elected on Bouge l'Europe List)
		5	LO/LCR (Lutte Ouvrire/Ligue Communiste Révolutionaire)
		1	Mouvement des Citoyens
		2	Parti Radical de Gauche
		1	Socialiste Independent
Germany	7	6	PDS (Partei des Demokratischen Sozialismus)
		1	Independent
Greece	7	2	SYN (Synaspismos tis aristeras kai tis proodou)
		3	KKE (Kommounistiko Komma Elladas)
		2	DIKKI (Dimokratiko Kinoniko Kinima)
Italy	6	4	RC (Rifondazione Comunista)
		2	CI (Comunisti Italiani)
Netherlands	1	1	SP (Socialistiese Partij)
Portugal	2	2	PCP (Partido Communista Portugues)
Spain	4	4	IU (Izquierda Unida)
Sweden	3	3	V (Vänsterpartiet)

Group of the Greens/European Free Alliance (Greens/EFA)

Before the 1999 election the Greens had 27 representatives in the EP. After the election they had 38 MEPs. For the first time the

TABLE 5.6   *Group of the Greens/Europe Free Alliance (Greens/EFA)
at 16 September 2002 (n = 45)*

	Number of members		National parties
Austria	2	2	Grüne (Die Grünen – Die grüne Alternative)
Belgium	7	2	Agalev
		3	Ecolo
		2	VU (Volksunie–ID 21)
Finland	2	1	VIHR (Vihreät)
		1	Independent
France	9	9	V (Les Verts)
Germany	4	4	Grüne (Bündis 90/Die Grünen)
Ireland	2	2	GP (Green Party)
Italy	2	2	Federazione dei Verdi
Luxembourg	1	1	Dei Greng
Netherlands	4	4	Groen links
Spain	4	1	CE:PA (Coalición Europea: Partido Andalucista)
		1	CNEP/PNV (Coalitión Nacionalista Europa de los Pueblos–Partido Nacionalista Vaso)
		1	CNEP/EA (Coalitión Nacionalista Europa de los Pueblos–Eusko Alkartasuna)
		1	BNG (Bloque Nacionalista Gallego)
Sweden	2	2	MP (Miljöpartiet)
United Kingdom	6	2	Green Party
		2	Scottish National Party
		2	Plaid Cymru

British Greens gained seats (two MEPs). Other successes
included the election of nine French Greens, the return of two
Irish Greens and increased representation for the Austrian and
Finnish parties. On the other hand, the German and Swedish
Greens lost seats (five and two respectively). By September 2002
the German Greens had lost three more members, two to the

PSE and one to the EUL group. When combined with the region-alist parties in the European Free Alliance the group had a total membership in 2002 of 45 MEPs from 13 countries, making it the fifth largest group in the EP.

The European Free Alliance, since 1981, had provided an overarching frame for parties seeking greater regional autonomy or independence. Before joining with the Greens in 1999 it had been a member of successive Rainbow Groups, and latterly in the 1994–99 Parliament of the European Radical Alliance. A total of five regionalist parties joined the Greens/EFA Group, and, for the first time, included representatives from the major nationalist parties in the UK – the SNP and Plaid Cymru.

Union for Europe of Nations (UEN)

In 1999, 90 per cent of the 30 members of the UEN came from just three countries: France, Italy and Ireland. In contrast, Portugal and Denmark provided just three members between them. By 2002 the UEN's membership was substantially reduced after the departure of members of the French RPFIE to join the non-attached members. The total number of RPFIE MEPs was thus reduced from 12 immediately after the 1999 election to three in 2002.

As Fieschi (2000:524) notes: 'The Europe of Nations group is a motley gathering.' It includes dissident French Gaullists, Italian nationalists with fascist roots, and Irish Fianna Fáil MEPs. The group claims to be 'united by the values of respect for the individual which form the basis of European civilization' and is convinced that the EU 'can only be built and prosper if sovereignty and national democracy are respected' (www.europarl.eu.int/uen/en/stru). However, as many clues to the group's 'political affinities' are to be found in UEN statements about what it does not favour, as much as in an examination of what it does favour. Most particularly it does not favour 'a Federal Europe which would subject sovereign nations and take away the identity of European Peoples'. In this respect the Eurosceptical stance of some members of the UEN is not too distant from the smaller Group for a Europe of Democracies and Diversities (see below).

TABLE 5.7   *Union for Europe of Nations Group (UEN) at 16 September 2002 (n = 22)*

	Number of members		National parties
Denmark	1	1	DF (Dansk Folkeparti)
France	3	3	RPFIE (Rassemblement pour la France et l'Indépendence de l'Europe)
Ireland	6	6	FF (Fianna Fáil)
Italy	10	9	AN/Segni (Alleanza Nazionale/Patto Segni)
		1	MSI (Movimento Socilae Italiano)
Portugal	2	2	CDS–PP (Centro Democratico Social–Partido Popular)

Group for a Europe of Democracies and Diversities (EDD)

The EDD was a new group formed after the 1999 election and was 'open to members who were critical of further European integration and centralization' (www.europarl.eu.int/edd). The EDD's 16 MEPs represented five parties from four member states. The largest contingent of six representatives was from the French list Chasse, Pêche, Nature, Traditions. Representing hunters, fishermen and rural voters, this list was specifically opposed to EU legislation infringing the privileges of blood sportsmen. These French rural Eurosceptics were joined by three Eurosceptic Danish members from the former Europe of Nations Group (one of whom subsequently left the group), and by two of the three UK Independence Party MEPs elected in 1999 who favour UK withdrawal from the EU. In addition, the EDD also included MEPs from three separate fundamentalist Calvanist parties. Ultimately, the group's claim to 'political affinity' stemmed from a nebulous belief 'in a stable and democratic Europe of nation states built on the diversity and cultures of its peoples' (www.europarl.eu.int/edd). Not surprisingly, perhaps, the EDD had greatest difficulty in articulating and supporting a cohesive programme of action in the EP (see below).

TABLE 5.8 *Group for a Europe of Democracies and Diversities (EDD) at 16 September (n = 16)*

	Number of members		National parties
Denmark	2	2	Juni.B (JuniBevaegelsen)
France	9	6	CPNT (Chasse, Pêche, Nature, Traditions)
		3	RPF (Rassemblement pour la France)
Netherlands	3	3	RPF/SGP/GVP (Reformatorische Politieke Federatie/Staatkundig Gereformeerde Partij/ Gereformeerde Politiek Verbond)
United Kingdom	2	2	UK Ind (UK Independence Party)

TABLE 5.9 *Independent/non-attached members at 16 September 2002 (n = 32)*

	Number of members		National parties
Austria	5	5	FPO (Freiheitliche Partei Österreichs)
Belgium	2	2	Vl. Blok (Vlaams Blok)
France	12	5	FN (Front National)
		6	RPFIE (Rassemblement pour la France et l'Indépendance de l'Europe)
		1	Independent (elected on RPFIE list)
Italy	10	7	Lista Bonino
		3	LN (Lega Nord)
Spain	1	1	EH (Euskal Herritarrok)
United Kingdom	3	1	DUP (Democratic Unionist Party)
		1	UKIP

Non-attached members

As noted above, the Technical Group of Independent Members was formed on 19 July 1999 with the expressed intention of enabling its members to access resources available to party groups to assist them in the performance of their parliamentary duties. After the disbanding of the Technical Group in October 2001 (see above), all but two of its members reverted to non-attached status. Richard Balfe, a defector from the British Labour Party, stood as an independent candidate for the post of Quaestor in January 2002 (see Chapter 6). Balfe later joined the EPP–ED upon joining the UK Conservative Party in March 2002. The bulk of the remaining non-attached members in 2002 comprised seven Italian Radicals and five members of Jean-Marie Le Pen's Front National. A third member elected on the UKIP list (Michael Holmes) joined the non-attached members after his resignation from the party in March 2000.

National party delegations

As noted above, the transnational party group system within the EP has been underpinned by institutional incentives: both direct material incentives of financial and administrative assistance and the benefits derived from the maximization of institutional power and associated policy influence. Nonetheless, the fundamental bedrock of the party group system in the EP has remained individual national parties.

'Size matters' in the EP party groups. The larger national delegations are in a very strong bargaining position within the groups (see Raunio 1996a:72). Leadership positions (for the EP's bureaux and for nominations to parliamentary posts) are normally distributed in accordance with broad principles of proportionality within groups among national delegations (using the d'Hondt method). In turn, leaders of national delegations are elected by their respective national party colleagues and represent their parties in intra-group negotiations and often take decisions on their behalf in the bureaux. Elaborate mechanisms are in place to tie national delegations into party group agreements. Indeed, decisions at group level are routinely preceded by discussions within national party delegations. As noted above, meetings of national delegations are consistently held in 'group weeks' and during plenaries, with preliminary negotiations among national delegations normally taking place before important group decisions are taken.

Correspondingly, parallel meetings and contacts between leaders of national delegations and their own domestic parties are an essential part of the decision-making process within party groups. Indeed, as the EP's legislative role expanded and became more institutionalized in the 1990s, contacts between MEPs and their national parties increased and became more routinized (Raunio 2000:220–1). Another stimulus came with the upheavals in national politics associated with the ratification process of the Maastricht Treaty. Given the unpreparedness of national parties and the 'intellectual vacuum' surrounding the debate about EU integration at the time, party groups were presented with the opportunity to assert their status in relation to their national counterparts (Ladrech 1996:299). As the issue of integration came to prominence in domestic politics, so EP party groups found their policy positions to be both more pertinent to national deliberations and also the subject of increased attention by national party officers.

In the larger delegations contacts with national parties are formalized through EP leaders serving on the executive bodies of the national parties (Raunio 2000:213). Thus, for example, the Leader of the UK's European Parliamentary Labour Party (EPLP) sits on the party's National Executive. However, informal modes of communication are equally important, with national party leaders and their officers maintaining regular phone contact with their counterparts in the EP's larger delegations. Government parties are especially sensitive to maintaining regular contacts with their respective EP party leaderships. In the UK, for example, the Labour government in 1997 initiated a system of European Parliamentary Private Secretaries through whom ministers receive regular updates on developments within the EPLP and in the EP more generally (Scully 2000b). In turn, this evolved into a system of 'link' persons whereby a Labour MEP from each of Parliament's committees is formally identified as responsible for liaising with the corresponding national government department in London. In addition, the UK Labour Party's General Secretary and other party officers regularly visit Brussels and Strasbourg to evaluate emerging opinion in the EPLP (Hix and Lord 1997:127). Not only do national delegations feed national party perspectives into transnational group deliberations; they also serve as informational conduits in the reverse direction – between the EP and domestic political parties. In fact, as Scully (2000b) points out, 'One of the major contributions that MEPs make is to help their national parties and governments *understand* the issues operating at the European level.'

Ultimately, however, national affiliation and national party perspectives have less of an impact on voting behaviour in the EP than party group affiliation. Of course there are exceptions to this general rule, but their very infrequency simply serves to illuminate the 'normal rule' of intra-group accommodation and the search for inclusive decisions. A good example of the disruption to normal group activities came in July 2001 with the EP's rejection, after conciliation, of the directive on company law concerning takeover bids (OJ C 65, 14 March 2002:57; see Chapter 8). By the time of the final plenary vote on the directive, the largest national delegations, and for that matter most of the smaller ones, articulated and defended a national position. Certainly, German MEPs displayed national solidarity after extensive lobbying by the German government (and the personal involvement of Chancellor Schröder). As a result only one German MEP (Christophe Konrad, EPP–ED) voted in favour of the directive. British MEPs were equally united, but this time in support of the takeover directive. Certainly, those British MEPs who were absent from the vote, given the tied outcome at 273–273 with 22 abstentions, were subject to significant British media attention (see, for example, *Financial Times* 6 July 2001).

Issue voting and intra-group cohesion

If 'Departures from party loyalty are observable in all legislative parties in democratic countries' (Loewenberg and Patterson 1979:229), then one expectation would be that such 'departures' would be greater in transnational parties than national ones (see Attina 1990:576–8; Hix 2001a:57–8). One specific set of problems undermining cohesion in transnational party groups in the EP is that 'their subcomponents are not merely factions or tendencies, but fully formed political parties in their own right, with proud histories as self-governing organisations in the national arena' (Hix and Lord 1997:141). Moreover, the incentives for national parties to exert influence over their MEPs' voting decisions have increased in parallel with the enhancement of the legislative powers of the EP. In these circumstances a secular trend towards increased intervention by national parties to control the activities of their European representatives might well be anticipated.

Offsetting such a trend, however, is the reality that the very protractedness of intra-group bargaining in the EP enhances the independence of national party delegations from direction by their party leaderships 'back home'. The constant process of negotiation and deliberation between national delegations normally results in compromises most group members are willing to support and if necessary vote for in plenary. This is why so much time is devoted in the larger groups to building consensus by incorporating and reconciling the views of national delegations to agreed group positions. Scully (2000b) illustrates, for example, how the very complexity of the EP's political environment – with over 120 parties from 15 member states operating in seven transnational political groups – makes it usually both extremely difficult and organizationally inefficient for national parties to bind their MEPs to strictly defined and predetermined policy preferences. Only where issues are closely delimited, clearly defined and with limited possible outcomes are national party mandates likely to produce anticipated results. One such recurring issue has been the choice of the Commission President. Empirical analysis of the EP's vote on the confirmation of Jacques Santer as Commission President in 1994 and of Romano Prodi in 1999 found that although there was a clear ideological divide on this issue, MEPs were strongly influenced by the preferences of their national parties (Hix and Lord 1996; Gabel and Hix 2002).

Yet, in the early years of the 1999–2004 Parliament such issues were few and far between. While national influence increased, its effectiveness tended to be limited by the inherent and enduring features of EP decision-making. In the context of bargaining within the EP – where the possible outcomes are infinite and as (in rational choice terminology) the dimensionality and the number of actors increase – it is more problematic and less efficient for national delegations to be tied to predetermined national bargaining positions. In these circumstances domestic parties generally have little to gain from mandating their representatives in the EP. To do so would 'simply condemn them to being outvoted, and [to deny] them the flexibility to negotiate their way into winning coalitions' (Hix and Lord 1997:129). In which case, as Scully argues, a lack of bargaining flexibility in such multi-actor, multi-dimensional bargaining can be harmful (Scully 2000b:18). A plausible option for most parties is thus 'to see their MEPs enjoying a limited, or conditional independence' (Scully 2000b:19). Exactly how far the limits of this 'conditionality' extend has yet to be mapped empirically, but what is clear, nonetheless, is that the relationship between national parties and transnational groups is one that is complex, often contradictory, evolving, and certainly untidy.

Coalition formation and party competition

More detailed empirical analysis has been conducted on the variables influencing partisan cohesion and coalition formation. In the most detailed study to date of party cohesion in the post-1999 EP Hix (2000a, 2001a,b) tests four different hypotheses. The first concerns the incentives party group leaders can offer group members to support the group line. These incentives primarily revolve around control of the policy agenda and the allocation of leadership positions, such as committee chairs and rapporteurships. Given that the larger groups have greater influence over both the EP's agenda and the allocation of official positions, one hypothesis is that the voting behaviour of individual MEPs would be structured according to party group alignment and that this would be particularly the case in the larger groups.

A second, and counterposed, proposition is that while party group leaders may exercise internal control in the EP, national party elites also exert powerful external control through candidate selection and wider party patronage. In fact, given the relative weakness of internal 'whipping' systems in the EP, there are few sanctions available to party group leaders to curb dissent by national delegations on policy issues with a high salience in domestic party arenas. Existing studies of pre-1999 parliaments bear testimony to the fact that, where there were conflicts between party group and national party preferences, MEPs were more likely to vote in accordance with the latter rather than the former (Brzinski *et al.* 1998).

The third hypothesis derives from a standard assumption that the voting rules in the EP enhance both intra-group cohesion and intergroup cooperation (see below). The formal requirements of the cooperation and codecision legislative procedures – for absolute majorities at their later stages – leads to a recognition by MEPs that the EP can positively influence EU legislative outputs only with internal group unity and the creation of cross-group minimum-winning-coalitions. In other words, only a 'grand coalition' between the two major party groups, EPP–ED and PSE, is certain to guarantee the outcome favoured by the EP where an absolute majority of MEPs (314 of 626) is required. The procedural rules would thus appear to prompt voting cohesion within and between groups, and, as Raunio (1996a:149) concludes therefore, the institutional rules of the EP '[put] pressure on the political groups to achieve high levels of cohesion when votes are taken'.

The final hypothesis examined by Hix is that the nature of the policy issue may itself affect group cohesion and coalition formation. The expectation is that different coalitions will be found in different policy domains – such as EU integration and EU institutional issues, socio-economic issues and socio-political matters (Hix 2001a:8).

Cohesion in the 1999 Parliament

Writing before the 1999 election Hix noted that 'party groups have become increasingly cohesive despite the fact that the number of national delegations has increased' (Hix 1999:176). Hix's assessment was based on 'index of agreement' data, where a score of 100 means that all members of a group voted the same way and a score of 0 indicates that the group vote was split equally. However, one methodological issue needs to be noted before considering voting behaviour in the EP, and this is that the data used in such studies is drawn from roll call votes.

In practice, there are two major limitations in using roll call votes. One is, as Hix himself concedes, that 'roll call votes do not tell the complete story of voting behaviour in the EP' (Hix 2001b:667–8). Decisions in committees and many votes in plenary are conducted by a show of hands, or through electronic voting which records aggregate voting behaviour. Estimates vary as to the actual extent of roll call voting. In the 1994–99 Parliament Kreppel and Tsebelis (1999:941) estimated that only 15 per cent of votes involved a roll call, while Hix (2001b:667; 2002:6) places the proportion of roll calls at one-third of all votes. The second limitation on the use of roll call votes is that they tend to be called by party groups (although 32 individual MEPs may call a vote) and the results are biased in favour of the groups calling the vote (Carrubba and Gabel 1999). Groups are prone to call a roll call vote to record their partisan position on a specific issue, or to draw attention to the policy position of another group, or as a measure of intra-group cohesion and policy unity (see Corbett *et al.* 2000:149; Kreppel and Tsebelis 1999:941–2). These limitations need to be borne in mind when analysing the empirical studies of voting behaviour. Nonetheless, roll call votes allow for some inferences to be made about voting cohesion in the EP.

Not withstanding these methodological limitations, analyses of roll call votes reveal that, historically, there has been a high degree of party cohesion among the party groups in the EP and that there has been an increase in cohesion as the legislative powers of the EP increased after the Maastricht and Amsterdam treaties. One compelling reason for the high levels of cohesion across the EP is the absence of party government and its attendant bifurcated voting patterns either in favour of or in opposition to the government. In the absence of an executive presence in the legislature, the votes of MEPs represent their collective opinions upon Commission proposals or Council decisions. In this context high majority voting (with average majority size between 60 to 70 per cent) – which is unusual in most national parliaments – is unexceptional in the EP.

In the first six months of the 1999–2004 Parliament, however, there was a marked decline in party group cohesion, with the average, non-weighted, 'agreement' score falling to 70, the lowest recorded since 1984 (Hix 2000a). Perhaps not surprisingly, given the ideological diversity of the UEN and the EDD noted above, these two groups recorded the lowest scores with 58 and 41 respectively. Both major party groups saw a fall in cohesion with the PSE and the EPP–ED scoring respectively 85 and 81 in this period, though over the longer period between June 1999 and December 2001 cohesion levels in both parties recovered from the initial dip (see Hix *et al.* 2002). Certainly in absolute terms the EPP–ED remained less cohesive after 1999 and in part this can be explained by the fact that UK Conservatives voted against the group position in nearly one-third of roll call votes in the early part of the parliament. This led some within the EP to argue initially that 'the institution is now dominated by a group which lacks many of the characteristics of even the loosest group' (Ludlow, in GPC 2000:17). This was, however, an overstatement as even after 1999 the EPP in relative terms (controlling for the overall level of cohesion in the EP as a whole) was more cohesive than in any other parliament since 1984 (Hix *et al.* 2002:13).

Intergroup coalitions

In the absence of a simple split between government and opposition parties in the EP, variable legislative coalitions have formed around specific policy positions. This does not mean necessarily, however, that voting patterns are unpredictable. In fact, the reverse is the case. Traditionally, there has been an underlying consistency and predictability to voting in the EP. A system of 'political group oligopoly' has operated where the PSE and Christian Democrats have constituted a winning coalition to meet the requirements, both political and procedural, for the exercise of legislative influence.

Kreppel (2000a:344–5) finds substantiation of this 'tradition of oligopoly', or more accurately perhaps of 'duopoly', in her findings that the PSE and EPP joined together on 60 to 70 per cent of votes, depending on the type of procedure, in the period 1987–96. Further confirmation of this 'duopoly' was provided by Hix and Lord (1997:139) in their study of a sample of 59 plenary votes in 1994–95. In this period they found that a majority of PSE and EPP MEPs voted together on 75 per cent of occasions. Plus, more often than not, PSE and EPP MEPs were joined by a majority of ELDR group members (PSE–ELDR 81 per cent; EPP–ELDR 75 per cent).

What needs to be explained therefore is both why the PSE–EPP duopoly emerged with such regularity, but equally why, on something like one-third of votes, no agreement was reached between the major party groups? One common explanation of the formation of the PSE–EPP duopoly and 'grand coalitions' is as a response to the absolute majority requirements of certain legislative and budgetary procedures. As Corbett *et al.* (2000:91) point out, 'Usually, the Socialists and EPP must negotiate compromises if Parliament is to have an impact'. In practice, therefore, there is a reinforcing dynamic between procedural rules and the political configuration of the PSE–EPP coalition which is 'centripetal and stabilising' (Hix and Lord 1997:162).

Not only are political bargains and compromises essential to exert legislative influence but the parameters of this consensus do not extend far beyond the centre of partisan policy preferences within the EU. Admittedly there are ideological divisions and a left–right divide is apparent on approximately one-third of votes (a divide which was even more pronounced after 1999 (see below)), but, overwhelmingly, centrist consensual policy positions have tended to prevail in the EP.

The potential of the absolute voting requirement 'to force political moderation' in the EP has recently been noted in the empirical analyses of Kreppel and Tsebelis (1999:958). They particularly found this to be the case with legislative amendments when the largest political group has to realign its original preferences to a position nearer the centre to attract support from the second largest group. In this specific sense, voting rules clearly have some impact – but are not the exclusive or the primary explanation of coalition formation. Kreppel (2000a:346; original emphasis), for example, argues that 'it is the *institutional system* of checks and balances which require ideological moderation for effective legislative influence'. Her contention is that the level of cooperation between the major party groups of the PSE and EPP is best explained by the simple fact that the EP has to work with the Commission and Council to process legislative outputs. Both of these other bodies institutionalize consensual and non-confrontational decision-making processes, and within this wider institutional context it is rational for groups within the EP to conform to a non-adversarial style of decision-making. Thus, in 'a political system where numerous, ideologically diverse actors have "veto power" ... over the legislative process we should expect gradual and moderate change to be the norm' (Kreppel 2000a:346). In other words, the process of interinstitutional bargaining impacts upon the internal bargaining between party groups in the EP (see also Hix and Lord 1997:148).

But the impact of voting procedures and interinstitutional context is neither uniform nor unidirectional. Manifestly the PSE and EPP traditionally have been unable to agree on approximately one-third of votes. The circumstances under which a duopoly or 'grand coalition' failed to emerge differs according to both stage of voting and policy area. As a general proposition, groups are more likely to work together on final proposals and resolutions than on individual legislative amendments (Kreppel 1999:19). As the real power of the EP rests in its capacity to amend legislation, it is hardly surprising that votes on amendments are more often contentious and more politically charged. Indeed, it is frequently the case in both committee and plenary that, while amendments tabled may be hotly contested in separate votes by the EPP and the PSE (and other groups), when it comes to the vote on the final resolution, consensus prevails, with the EPP and PSE (and others) voting in favour.

Moreover, the substantive area of legislation may affect the type of coalition formed. Kreppel and Tsebelis (1999:959–60) found, for example, that a PSE–EPP coalition formed more frequently when dealing with legal and environmental matters than with social and energy issues, and almost disappeared on economic issues. In fact, a clear left–right ideological divide emerged between the PSE and EPP on economic policies.

If the dominant voting pattern in the 1994–99 EP was a coalition centred around the PSE, EPP and ELDR then the next most frequent pattern was one of left–right bipolarization (Hix and Lord 1997:13). An analysis of the earlier 1989–94 Parliament also concluded that the 'major division in the EP is Left–Right' (Kreppel and Tsebelis 1999:961). Thus, despite a 'tradition of oligopoly' there are some issues (accounting consistently for more than 30 per cent of votes) upon which the two largest party groups have been unable to reach agreement. As we will see in Chapter 8 these instances of polarized voting have attendant political and legislative costs.

Coalitions in the 1999–2004 Parliament

Some of these costs became more apparent in the 1999–2004 Parliament with one assessment of the first year of the new

Parliament concluding that:

> The victory of the centre-right in [the 1999] European elections profoundly changed the political make-up of the new Parliament. The established 'grand coalition' between Socialists and Christian Democrats has died a sudden death and as a result the institution is now more divided between left and right than at any time in its history. (GPC 2000:2)

To paraphrase Oscar Wilde, however, the demise of the EPP–PSE duopoly was 'much exaggerated'. The EPP–PSE coalition was still observable in 69 per cent of votes between June 1999 and December 2001, and was thus at roughly the same level as in the 1994–99 EP (Hix *et al.* 2002:36).

While the PSE and EPP–ED are clearly differentiated on the left–right dimension there still remains a fluidity and contingency to this divide. In practice the complex pattern of coalition formation across issues identified by Kreppel and Tsebelis (1999:959–60) continued into the post-1999 EP with Hix (2001a:27–8) finding that grand coalitions were more likely to predominate on issues relating to integration and external relations, but less evident on socio-economic and socio-political questions. In other words, different coalitions form on different policy issues (Hix 2001b:684). When coalition formation under different voting rules is examined, Hix's data reveal that there was, on average, a clear left–right division regardless of voting rules in the first 12 months of the 1999–2004 Parliament. Within this overall picture, however, there is a high variation around the left–right split (Hix 2001a:25).

The position of the ELDR on this left–right continuum is pivotal. In the first six months of the 1999–2004 EP the ELDR chose the EPP–ED as its voting partner in 70 per cent of votes and the PSE in 62 per cent of votes (Hix 2000a:3). This initially tipped the ideological balance in favour of the centre right, with the ELDR pragmatically voting for the largest party group in anticipation of policy concessions. However, over the longer period of June 1999 to December 2001 the pattern of coalition formation resembled very closely that of the preceding Parliament with the ELDR aligning with the PSE on 73.9 per cent of votes (73.8 in 1994–99) and with the EPP–ED on 71.3 per cent votes (72.0 per cent in 1994–99) (Hix *et al.* 2002:36).

Conclusion

One obvious conclusion of this chapter is that politics in the EP is dominated by party groups. Moreover, these pan-European groups remain overwhelmingly cohesive in their voting behaviour despite their internal heterogeneity. As noted earlier, there are no fewer than 129 national parties represented in the EP, with the largest group, the EPP–ED, having 35 national party delegations. Added to this heterogeneity, the fact that national parties still control nomination procedures for EP candidacies removes a traditional incentive for greater party cohesion which is available to most party leaders within national legislatures (see Bowler *et al.* 1999:8). On top of these disincentives, the absence of party government in the EU also is a force moderating political group cohesion in the EP.

For these reasons EP groups remain less cohesive than party groups in member states' legislatures (see Raunio 2002:265). Nonetheless, empirical evidence reveals that MEPs vote predominantly along partisan rather than national lines. In so doing, MEPs frequently structure their voting behaviour along a policy dimension which corresponds to a traditional 'left–right' ideological conflict in most national party systems. In aggregate, while different party coalitions form on different policy issues, and while the left–right ideological split has been more pronounced in the 1999–2004 Parliament, a willingness to seek consensus between the two largest groups is still the dominant feature of voting behaviour in the EP. The willingness of the major party groups to cooperate with each other is, in part, a reflection of the realities of interinstitutional bargaining in the EU policy process. Simply stated, an ideologically polarized EP would be unable to generate the necessary majorities at the later stages of the legislative process to impact upon EU policies. In these circumstances 'the party groups are forced to produce moderate proposals if they are to have any influence at all' (Kreppel 2002:216).

Party groups work within an institutional context that has changed dramatically with successive treaty reforms and enhancements of the legislative role of the EP. In part, the securing of formal legislative power has underpinned the informal commitment of party groups to seek consensus in order to maximize the policy impact of the EP. In part also, the extension

of formal power has increased the importance of exerting institutional controls over the activities of party groups and their
members. In this sense, as Kreppel postulates, there is a dynamic
relationship between the organization of the EP as an institution, the party system and the party groups:

> exogenous increases in the legislative authority of a parlia-
> ment directly affect the development of the internal organi-
> zational structures, the party system (coalitions + number of
> parties) and the internal development of the parties them-
> selves (albeit weakly). Each of these in turn then indirectly
> affects the evolution of the others. (Kreppel 2002:218–19)

It is to the internal organizational structures that we now turn
in Chapter 6. Before doing so, it is worth committing to memory (for Chapter 9) the conclusion that, in party terms, 'The
post-1999 EP operates very much like any domestic parliament
in Europe ... The EP *is* what most voters would consider a real
"parliament" ' (Hix 2001b:685; original emphasis).

Chapter 6

Internal Organization

How legislators choose to organize themselves is one of the most fundamental issues confronting parliamentarians and students of legislatures alike. Different forms of legislative organization impact differently upon the internal relations between individual representatives, and upon the external relations of parliaments with other political institutions within the wider political system. Moreover, the choice of rules and procedures affects both the process of legislative decision-making and the nature of legislative outputs themselves. Not surprisingly, therefore, long before 'new institutionalism' (and its rediscovery of the importance of political institutions) became fashionable in academic circles, questions of legislative organization and institutional design had been of historic concern to parliamentarians and legislative scholars alike.

The central organizational question confronting legislatures is: how do elected representatives effectively and efficiently organize themselves in order to make collective decisions on the multiplicity of complex issues demanding their attention? In other words, what are the strategies available to legislators to cope with informational overload and environmental uncertainties? As already seen in Chapter 5, one powerful institutional device for dealing with the problems of collective decision-making has been the organization of political parties. In this chapter, however, attention will be focused upon the organizational form of Parliament itself: upon its rules and procedures, upon formal institutional leadership positions, and upon the all-important internal division of labour in the form of its committees. The importance of legislative organization should not be underestimated, for not only have issues of institutional design and organization remained a preoccupation of historic parliaments and new assemblies alike but, as Krehbiel (1991:2) points out, they have continued to shape:

> the collective expression of policy objectives, the level of
> expertise that is embodied in legislation that seeks to meet
> legislative objectives, the effectiveness with which legislation
> is implemented, and, ultimately, the importance of the legis-
> lature in the governmental process.

Legislative organization seeks to manage complexity. Most
legislatures start, at least, from a fairly simple institutional configuration: whether bicameral or unicameral. A 'legislature'
remains, nonetheless, a singular institution; most parliaments
take for granted their location in a single city, and, in most
national assemblies, representatives communicate with each
other in a single language, or a highly restricted range of official
languages. In the case of the European Parliament, however,
none of these assumptions hold. It is a co-legislator in partnership with an external intergovernmental institution – the
Council – which in turn, arguably, is part also of a dual executive. It has three geographical locations. It is unique in being the
only transnational directly elected representative institution in
the world. It is one of the largest elected chambers in the world.
And it has eleven official working languages which produce
110 possible language combinations for representatives to communicate effectively with each other. Hence, even before confronting the standard interinstitutional and policy complexities
facing all legislatures, the EP has to deal with its own specific
organizational complexities arising from a peripatetic existence
and a multilingual and multinational composition.

Seat

It has long been lamented by MEPs themselves that they have
no direct control over where the Parliament sits. The right to
determine where the European Parliament meets is conferred by
the treaties upon national governments (Article 289 (ex 216)).
The Amsterdam Treaty reaffirmed and detailed this right:

> The European Parliament shall have its seat in Strasbourg
> where the 12 periods of monthly plenary sessions, including

the budget session, shall be held. The periods of additional plenary sessions shall be held in Brussels. The committees of the European Parliament shall meet in Brussels. The General Secretariat of the European Parliament and its departments shall remain in Luxembourg. (Protocol on the location of the seats of the institutions, Amsterdam Treaty)

Yet, most MEPs, if given the choice, would prefer a single seat for the European Parliament, and many would prefer Brussels to Strasbourg. If this is the case then why do MEPs still lead a peripatetic existence and why has a 'single seat' still not been agreed?

The simple answer, long acknowledged by the Council itself, is that 'the decision on a seat is essentially of a political nature' (Council letter, 20 December 1974, quoted in Earnshaw 1985:79). If the question of a single seat for Parliament remains unresolved, at least the issues have been clarified and the number of options have been reduced over the years. One option, that was effectively removed as early as 1981, was a triangular rotation of meetings between Strasbourg, Brussels and Luxembourg. Since that date Parliament has refused to schedule its plenary sessions in Luxembourg (with few exceptions, the last being in 1986 when the Strasbourg chamber was being enlarged).

The original triple location emerged at the inception of the ECSC when the dual executive of the Council and the High Authority was located in Luxembourg. It made some sense, therefore, to locate the secretariat of the Common Assembly in close proximity to the staff of the Council and the High Authority. Yet, representatives to the Common Assembly convened initially in the only fully-equipped multilingual parliamentary building available at the time – the Parliamentary Assembly of the Council of Europe in Strasbourg. As most members of the Common Assembly also sat in the Council of Europe's Assembly there was a reinforcing pragmatic reason for meeting in Strasbourg. Plus, Strasbourg had a historic claim to host representatives of supranational European institutions as it was imbued with 'the spirit and memory of Europe' (President of the EP, EP Debates 15 December 1999) – which continues to be evoked today – and served as a powerful spatial symbol of Franco-German postwar reconciliation. Moreover, as long as the Assembly was seen primarily as a deliberative body, there was no immediate necessity for its members to interact directly with, or be physically located close to, the executive institutions and the bureaucracies of the EC. Significantly, however, when Assembly members performed their consultative functions in the legislative process – with the emphasis upon scrutiny of executive actions through the committee system – they preferred to work close to where the executive action was. And, after the Treaty of Rome in 1957, the centre of the EC's legislative 'action' increasingly became Brussels.

The routine of holding committee meetings in Brussels, and of scheduling plenary sessions in Strasbourg, with occasional plenaries in Luxembourg, became the established working pattern in the decade after the Treaty of Rome. However, in the subsequent decade – from 1968 up until direct elections in 1979 – Parliament began to hold more plenary sessions in Luxembourg, not least because of the convenience of holding its meetings where its secretariat was based (Corbett *et al.* 2000:28).

Gradually, however, after the first direct elections in 1979, Luxembourg lost out to Strasbourg despite considerable investment in a new parliamentary building (hemicycle) to accommodate the enlarged parliament on the Plateau du Kirchberg. In fact, within six months of the formation of the new directly elected EP, its members questioned the intergovernmentalist restrictions placed upon Parliament's location. MEPs asked the Political Affairs Committee and its rapporteur, Mario Zagari, to examine this issue. Eventually, in July 1981, on the basis of Zagari's report, MEPs adopted a resolution in favour of a single seat. As an interim measure, they agreed to restrict plenary sessions to Strasbourg and committee meetings primarily to Brussels.

Not surprisingly, the Luxembourg government, given its substantial financial investment in a new hemicycle, contested Parliament's decision in the Court of Justice. In February 1983 (Case C-230/81) the Court ruled that the EP had no obligation under the status quo to meet in Luxembourg, and in the same month the EP voted to convene an additional part-session in Brussels rather than in Luxembourg. A subsequent attempt by Parliament, in July 1983, to move its secretariat away from Luxembourg foundered, however, on a successful challenge made by the Luxembourg government in the Court of Justice (Case C-108/83).

Thereafter, various attempts to further rationalize the location of the EP, through parliamentary resolutions in October 1985 and January 1989, resulted in further court cases initiated by the Strasbourg and Luxembourg authorities. Both feared that Parliament's support of building projects in Brussels, and the increased scheduling of sittings in the Belgian capital, would residualize the EP's presence in their respective cities (C-258/85 and joined cases C-213/88 and C-39/89).

These fears were only heightened when, in January 1992, the EP's President signed the lease for a new parliament building in Brussels. (Later, in 1996, the President of the EP made an agreement with the Luxembourg prime minister which guaranteed that the number of EP staff based in the Duchy would not fall below 2,000. This commitment secured around half of the EP's Secretariat in Luxembourg until the end of 2004.) The ultimate intention of Parliament was to reduce the number of meetings in Strasbourg and schedule additional meetings in Brussels. The response of the French government was swift and decisive. At the Council summit in Edinburgh in December 1992 the French government secured an agreement that Strasbourg should be considered the normal venue for the EP's monthly part-sessions. What was unusual about the Edinburgh declaration was the exact specification of the number of meetings to be held in Strasbourg. The Parliament immediately questioned the legality of the European Council's decision (in its resolution of 16 December 1992 OJ C 21 1993:107) and demonstrated its opposition to any detailed intervention in the scheduling of its internal affairs by ignoring the decision and scheduling only eleven and ten sessions in Strasbourg in 1993 and 1994. When the EP scheduled only eleven Strasbourg sessions in 1996 the French government sought the overturn of this decision in the Court of Justice. In October 1997 the Court ruled that only after twelve sessions (or eleven sessions in election years) had been scheduled in Strasbourg could additional sessions then be held in Brussels (C-345/95).

This minimum number of Strasbourg meetings was incorporated in the protocol of the Amsterdam Treaty noted above, but controversies still continued to erupt over the number of days required to constitute a plenary session, and the possible compression of two plenaries into a single week. Indeed, on 14 June 2000 MEPs voted by 277 to 232 with 28 abstentions to discontinue Friday sittings of the Strasbourg plenary. Amendments that went even further, and proposed the reduction of Strasbourg sessions to two days and the extension of Brussels plenaries to five, were ruled inadmissible on the grounds that votes relating to the calendar of sessions must respect the treaties. Nevertheless, the intent was clear. One Luxembourg Socialist MEP, Jacques Poos, identified the ultimate aim of many MEPs who voted in favour of this motion to be 'an end to Strasbourg's tenure as the seat of the European Parliament' (EP Debates, Vote, 14 June 2000). Similarly, Luxembourg Liberal Colette Flesch denounced the 'nibbling aimed at circumventing the treaties' (quoted in *Agence Europe*, 14 June 2000). Earlier, at the official opening of the new Louise Weiss building in Strasbourg in December 1999, an open letter signed by more than 200 MEPs had requested that the 2000 IGC confer upon Parliament the right to decide its own location (*European Voice*, 13–19 April 2000:7). In March 2000 Parliament's Committee on Constitutional Affairs proposed that Article 289 of the EC Treaty should be amended to allow the EP to decide 'by an absolute majority of its members, on the location of its seat and all its meetings' (PE 232.758 2000:6). The Committee's proposal was incorporated into the EP's resolution of 13 April 2000 on proposals for the IGC and supported in plenary by 401 in favour, 77 against and nine abstentions. However, it was not accepted by member states (see Chapter 2).

Costs of multiple seat

The costs of maintaining a triple seat are substantial. The construction costs of the new building opened in Strasbourg in 1999 were over €435 m; and it costs Parliament annually over €22 m to lease the building for just 60 days of sittings per year. In turn, Parliament's new buildings in Brussels cost over €1 billion to construct. The recurrent costs are also substantial, with the 2002 Budget providing for €154.8 m for building rental and associated costs (such as insurance, cleaning and maintenance and security). A further €104.6 m were set aside for accelerated repayment of existing buildings (PE 300.037 2001: chapter 20).

The cost of transporting members, staff and documentation between the two sites has been estimated at €145 m per year, while the variable costs of an ordinary five-day session in Strasbourg are about 33 per cent higher than in Brussels, in addition to the other, much higher, costs due to buildings and hotel expenses (PE 305.659 2002:11). Not surprisingly, many MEPs fear that 'Strasbourg projects a deeply negative message that the Parliament is prepared to waste time and money... There is simply no justification for European taxpayers to pay for a needless travelling circus' (Roy Perry MEP (EPP–ED, UK), quoted in *Agence Europe* 14 April 2000). In addition to the financial costs of investment in, and maintenance of, two hemi-cycles, associated office accommodation, leisure and recreational facilities, and logistical expenses, there are also the time-costs attendant upon communicating and commuting between split sites. Again, it is not uncommon to hear MEPs complain of having to 'pack our bags every three weeks in this ridiculous way' (Andrew Duff, MEP (ELDR, UK), quoted in *Agence Europe*, 14 April 2000).

Speaking in tongues

Representatives in the European Parliament communicate with each other in eleven working languages. This results in 110 possible language combinations. Not surprisingly there is a separate Directorate-General for translation and interpretation services within the EP's Secretariat which in 2002 employed some 584 permanent translators and some 258 permanent interpreters (with over 1,000 auxiliary interpreters). In 1999 it was estimated that the EP required some 50,000 interpreter days to conduct its business (www.europarl.eu.int/interp/public/interep_en. htm). Overall, up to one-third of all parliamentary staff are employed to provide linguistic services.

In a continent where language has played such an historic role in helping to define and bolster conceptions of nationhood, it is hardly surprising to find the vigorous maintenance of linguistic identities in an institution constituted of representatives from the many diverse and disparate cultural and linguistic traditions of Europe. Equally unsurprising is the defence of linguistic equality in the EP's rules of procedure and various resolutions adopted by Parliament.

The principles of linguistic sovereignty have held particular resonance in the EP at times of enlargement. In May 1994, for instance, in the face of new elections and the 1995 enlargement, a resolution was adopted which upheld the 'right to use one's own language' in the EP (Resolution 6 May 1994 OJ C 205 1994:529). At the same time the 'strict equality' in the use of all the EU's official languages was reaffirmed; as was the undesirability of implementing language restrictions in an 'institution composed of elected representatives'. The issue of the number of official languages resurfaced later in two reports for Parliament's Bureau. The first was on multilingualism in the EP, and was drafted by Jean-Pierre Cot in 1999. The second, on preparing the EP for enlargement, was submitted to the Bureau in early 2001 by EP Vice-President Guido Podesta. While the Cot report countenanced radical change and the limiting of interpretation into only a single or restricted range of languages (see Corbett *et al.* 2000:37), the Podesta report reaffirmed 'multilinguacy, and especially the principal of equality between languages' in the EP. Podesta's report added that, with enlargement, it would be necessary 'to continue to guarantee that MEPs may speak and hear their own language in all the meetings and that all the documents are translated into these official languages' (quoted in *Agence Europe* 25 January 2001).

Enlargement eastwards certainly brings new linguistic challenges. Most obviously, the number of languages increases, potentially to 22 with a possible 462 language combinations. The requirement for flexibility in these circumstances is acknowledged within the EP, but flexibility does not go so far as to 'remove the right of every member to speak his or her own language' (PE 304.283 2002:amendment 62, justification). However, the latest enlargement will result in the representation in Parliament of small numbers of MEPs with their own language – for example six Estonian, seven Slovenian, and eight Latvian members. Before enlargement eastwards the Danish and Finnish MEPs constituted the smallest linguistic communities.

Thus, with the prospect of some of the new languages being used by very small numbers of MEPs, Parliament's review of its rules, following Nice and preceding enlargement, envisaged interpretation in committee only from and into languages actually 'used and requested' by members (PE 304.283 2002:amendment 62, Rule 117(3). Such a pragmatic approach formalized the existing practice whereby interpreters often refrained from interpretation into languages if no appropriate member is listening.

The importance of linguistic equality is institutionalized in the EP's Rules of Procedure. Rule 117(1) holds that 'all documents of the Parliament shall be drawn-up in the official languages'. Rule 139(6) makes it clear that untranslated amendments will not be put to a vote if 12 or more MEPs object, and Rule 74(1) records that the receipt of a Council or Commission position under the cooperation and codecision procedures will only be announced when all necessary documents have been 'duly translated into the official languages'. The need for precision in understanding detailed, technical and complex legislative documents is one powerful reason for maintaining linguistic equality. In the case of legislation processed under the codecision procedure, for example, a small group of parliamentary lawyer linguists liaise with their counterparts in the Council to ensure equivalence in the various language versions of legislative texts.

More generally, a text has to be available for translation ten days in advance of any formal parliamentary meeting in which it is to be considered in all languages. Nevertheless, there are frequent complaints from MEPs of documents only being available in the more widely used languages, or only being available at the very last minute. It is not uncommon for debate in committee to be postponed because one or more language version of committee papers is not available. In addition to the problem of time lag, concern has also been voiced that 'the quality of the translations produced by Parliament's translation service in various policy areas betrays a lack of specialisation'. In making this criticism the EP's Committee on Budgets asked Parliament's Bureau, in March 2000, to ensure that 'translation standards keep pace with the increasingly specialised work carried out by the institution' (PE 232.976 2000:13–14).

Interpretation has traditionally been conducted under a matrix system whereby each language is interpreted into every other language. As a matter of principle many MEPs identify simultaneous translation into their mother tongue as a legitimate defence of their national and linguistic identity. Even when fluent in another language (most commonly French or English) MEPs from smaller member states, such as Denmark or Finland, have insisted on direct interpretation, and translation of documents, into their own language at formal parliamentary meetings.

Away from the formal proceedings in the chamber and committee rooms the translation and interpretation conventions within political groups are less rigid. Even those groups with members from all 15 EU states (the PSE and EPP–ED) use only four languages (English, French, German and Spanish), and the ELDR, with representatives from ten countries, uses just French and English. Similarly, within the EP's own secretariat, there is a convention of using just French and English. And there is a growing tendency for original texts sent to the Parliament's translation services to be produced in either of these two languages. In fact, French and English now account for two-thirds of original texts sent for translation. In contrast, the Greek, Portuguese, Swedish, Finnish and Danish languages account for less than 2 per cent of all translated texts.

Costs

The 2002 budget provided an appropriation of €22.4 m for interpreters and conference technicians. The actual costs in 2001 had been €24.95 m (PE 300.037 2001:Item 1870) with a further €10.62 m set aside for external translation (and associated technical work, typing and printing costs (PE 300.037 2001:Item 1872)).

In addition to the financial costs there are also efficiency costs associated with working in so many different languages. As noted above, concern has been expressed about the quality of translation of technical and specialist texts. Misunderstandings between members and the tabling of unnecessary amendments are two common results of imprecise translations (see Corbett *et al.* 2000:35). There is an additional problem of translators trying to identify the precise linguistic meaning of often technical amendments across the full range of the EU's legislative competences. Incomprehension and a lack of spontaneity can sometimes be observed in debates in plenary and committees as a consequence of cultural nuances and inflexions being lost in the literal interpretation of words. The cut and thrust of deliberation, and the value of rhetoric, is certainly lost in simultaneous interpretation of multilingual debate. Moreover, the whole process of decision-making is affected by the time constraints imposed by the working hours of interpreters. Fixed working hours for plenary and for committees are agreed between interpreters and Parliament.

Any extension of these hours has to be authorized in advance, and only occurs in exceptional circumstances.

Obviously, the associated costs of translation and interpretation would be increased with the enlargement of the EU to 25 member states by 2004. Ten new states would bring ten additional languages and increase the possible language combinations to 420. The prospect of finding qualified linguists capable of translating, for example, Hungarian into Danish caused some concern for MEPs (see PE 289.524 2000:11).

Formal parliamentary leadership

> The organization of legislatures is very different from the organization of bureaucracies. Legislatures organize themselves, they are not organized by outside authorities. Legislatures are organizations of members who are nominally equal to each other, who do not, therefore, stand in the relationship of authority and subordination to each other as do members of hierarchical organizations. (Loewenberg and Patterson 1979:164)

Nevertheless, universally, legislatures have designated leadership roles and, hence, hierarchical organizational structures. What distinguishes legislatures from many other organizations, however, is the fact that elected representatives select their own leaders. The EP is no exception to this general rule. Similarly, the EP is no exception to the rule that parties and parliamentary committees provide the main, invariably parallel, and sometimes competing, foundations of legislative leadership structures. The concentration of power in the reinforcing structures of party groups and of formal committees correspondingly finds reflection in the official leadership positions in the EP.

These positions have at their pinnacle the individual office of President and the collective offices of the 14 Vice-Presidents. Operating in tandem with the Presidency are the collective bodies of the Conference of Presidents, the Bureau, the College of Quaestors, the Conference of Committee Chairmen, and the Conference of Delegation Chairmen. The Conference of Presidents and the Bureau provide direction and supervision of the broad managerial, administrative and financial dimensions of the EP's operations. The Conference of Chairmen and the Conference of Delegation Chairmen have more specific concerns with the organizational dimensions of the EP relating to the processing of substantive legislative and policy outputs.

The Presidency

In a comparative study of presiding officers in democratic assemblies Stanley Bach (1999:210–13) identified five activities in which all such officers are expected to engage. First, there was the ultimate responsibility for the management of the assembly; second, responsibility for the allocation of the assembly's resources among members and party groups; third, organizing the agenda and working schedule; fourth, chairing plenary sessions and interpreting Rules of Procedure; and fifth, controlling debates. Bach also identified a sixth role exercised by many presiding officers and that was to act in a partisan capacity. (It should be noted, however, that in many legislatures the presiding officer is expected to detach himself or herself from overt party activity.) However, in legislatures where the partisan character of the position of presiding officer is openly recognized, then it 'is deemed both natural and proper for the majority party to choose its leader (or one of its leading members) to occupy the primary position of authority in the body it controls' (Bach 1999:212–13).

Choice of President

In the case of the EP, the choice of the President is clearly influenced by party political considerations. The President in the first half of the 1999–2004 Parliament was Nicole Fontaine, a member of the largest political group, the EPP–ED. Since direct elections in 1979, a convention has emerged whereby the President, along with other parliamentary officers, is chosen every two and half years. Elections for these posts are held in the month after the June EU ballot, and then in the January session two and a half years later. Moreover, since 1989 there had been a tacit agreement between the two largest groups, the PSE and EPP, to alternate the two presidential terms, with the largest group holding the office in the first term and the smaller group holding it in the second. Thus, in 1989, the EPP supported the socialist Enrique Barón Crespo and in return the PSE did not contest the 1992 mid-term election against the EPP's candidate Egon Klepsch. In the 1994–99 Parliament the split presidency continued with Klaus Hänsch of the PSE serving in the first half and José Maria Gil-Robles serving in the second half of the term.

The agreement between the two largest political groups foundered, however, in the wake of the 1999 EP election. The PSE decided to contest the elections for the first time in a decade on the stated grounds that the EPP's rightward ideological trajectory and its internal instability had undermined the tacit understanding between the two groups (*European Voice* 15–21 July 1999:3). The age of the Socialist candidate, Mário Soares, who would have been 77 in 2002, was also a factor in prompting the contest in 1999. In the event, the EPP–ED worked out a 'constitutive agreement' with the ELDR (see Chapter 5), part of which was a deal to divide the presidency – with Nicole Fontaine of the EPP occupying the post for the first half of the term and the ELDR leader Pat Cox serving as President in the second half. In the event, Cox was challenged by four other candidates in January 2002, eventually beating the PSE contender David Martin by 298 votes to 237.

During her period in office, Nicole Fontaine continued the tradition of EP Presidents actively sustaining a partisan political persona, and she also willingly defended French national interests. For example, in June 2000, after MEPs voted to abandon Friday sittings at Strasbourg in the following session, Mrs Fontaine issued a press statement regretting the decision (www.europarl.eu.int/president/press/en/cp0086.htm). Her response to criticisms, that it was unseemly for the President of Parliament to openly question a decision reached by a majority of MEPs, was simple and nationalist. In her words, it was 'the least a French president of the assembly could do' (quoted in *European Voice* 20–26 July 2000:14). Earlier Mrs Fontaine had adopted an overtly political stance (but in this instance not a partisan position as her opinion diverged from that of the majority of the EPP group) in support of EU sanctions against the Austrian Conservative government. In doing so she asserted the 'right of the Parliament president to voice his or her political convictions' (*European Voice* 20–26 July 2000:14).

Functions of the EP President

Box 6.1 provides the functions performed by the EP's President. Most of the five activities identified by Bach are evident in this list: management of the assembly; allocation of its resources; organization of the agenda and working schedule; chairing plenary sessions and interpretation of the Rules of Procedure; and control of debates. Similarly Bach's expectations that presiding officers generally represent the assembly in its formal relations with other government institutions and external bodies finds confirmation in Box 6.1. A cursory glance at the President's list of engagements in any one month would reveal a punishing schedule of symbolic and ceremonial meetings with heads of state and visiting dignitaries; meetings with heads of government and ministers of member states; publicity and promotional opportunities; visits to states both within and beyond the borders of the EU; and the performance of internal parliamentary managerial functions.

BOX 6.1   Functions of the President of the EP

- Responsible for the application of the Rules of Procedure of Parliament, and, to this end, plays a steering role in all the activities of Parliament and its bodies.
- Signs the EU budget into being following Parliament's vote on it at second reading. During the procedure, the President chairs the EP/Council conciliation delegations.
- May, under the EP/Council codecision procedure, chair the EP/Council conciliation committee. Jointly with the President-in-Office of the Council, the President signs all legislative acts adopted by codecision.
- Addresses the European Council prior to each of its meetings, stating Parliament's viewpoint on the subjects on the agenda in the framework of a debate with the heads of state and government.
- When an intergovernmental conference is held for the reform of the treaties, the President takes part in the meetings of the government representatives where these are organized at ministerial level.
- Represents Parliament in its international relations, and, in this connection, undertakes official visits within and outside the EU.

Source: www.europarl.eu.int/president/function/en/default.htm.

In addition, the EP President plays a significant role in representing the EP in its interinstitutional relations with the Council and Commission as well as in its wider interactions with international agencies and institutions. A fair degree of discretion is often afforded to the President in performing this interinstitutional role. Thus, for example, in February 2002, newly elected President Pat Cox decided not to follow the recommendation of the Parliament's Legal Affairs Committee to ask the European Court of Justice to review the legal base of the European Company Statute. Cox explained that his decision was an expression of 'political faith' in the Council. Indeed, not to have taken this decision would have delayed still further a measure which had been before the Council for over 30 years (see *Agence Europe* 1 February 2002). Moreover, he noted that: 'We talked a great deal in the course of the weeks before we elected a president about making our House more political. I hope that this act of political faith will say that we bring primacy of politics to what we do for the next stretch' (EP Debates, 4 February 2002).

The Vice-Presidents

The President is assisted by 14 Vice-Presidents who act formally as substitutes for the President in his or her absence. In this capacity they chair plenary sessions, and act as surrogate representatives for the President in the conduct of the EP's external relations. They also participate in the work of the Bureau in their own right (see below). To stand any chance of election, nominees for Vice-President invariably have to have the official backing of the political groups. The rank ordering of the allocation of responsibilities among the Vice-Presidents and groups is also primarily determined by the political groups. Thus, in the 1999–2002 period, Socialist group members held the three highest ranked portfolios (David Martin (UK), Renzo Imbeni (Italy) and Gerhard Schmidt (Germany)). Thereafter, the next eight posts were shared between PSE and EPP members, with the three lowest preference posts occupied by members of smaller groups (Jan Wienbenga (ELDR), Alonso Puerta (EUL-NGL) and Gérard Onesta (Greens/EFA)). In January 2002, following the election of Pat Cox as President, the portfolios of the

Vice-Presidents were reorganized and Giorgos Dimitrakopoulos (EPP, Greece) and Charlotte Cederschiöld (EPP, Sweden) joined David Martin at the head of the rankings.

Each Vice-President concentrates upon specific duties. In addition, three Vice-Presidents are appointed to serve as permanent members of the Conciliation Committee with the Council (see below), and two serve as leaders of the EP's representatives on the Conference of European Affairs Committees (COSAC) (see Chapter 9).

Quaestors

After the election of the Vice-Presidents, MEPs are balloted upon the election of five 'Quaestors'. As Westlake (1994a:195) describes the position: 'The continental tradition of quaestor, alien to Westminster, is intended to safeguard backbenchers' rights, and the five quaestors in the European Parliament act very much in this tradition'. The Quaestors are responsible for administrative and financial matters of direct concern to the performance of the role of the individual MEP and act in accordance with guidelines laid down by the Bureau (European Parliament 2002:Rule 25). Like the Vice-Presidents, nomination for election as Quaestor is usually made by the political groups. One recent exception came, however, in 1999 when a British Labour MEP, Richard Balfe, failed to secure the PSE's support of his candidature. Balfe subsequently stood independently of PSE support and was elected. Though a member of the PSE – and a Quaestor – he did not, accordingly, sit in the bureaux of the PSE. In January 2002 Balfe was reelected as a Quaestor, on this occasion standing as an Independent candidate. The other Quaestors in 1999–2002 were Mary Banotti (EPP), Godelieve Quisthoudt-Rowohl (EPP), Daniel Ducarme (ELDR) and Jacques Poos (PSE). In January 2002 Ducarme was replaced by Miet Smet (EPP).

The responsibilities of Quaestors cover the allocation of offices, provision of equipment, employment conditions of MEPs' assistants, security arrangements, official cars and financial questions on expenses and fees. Such matters often excite strong passions among MEPs, and, as a consequence, meetings of the Quaestors 'are particularly robust affairs' (Corbett *et al.*

2000:103). In addition, Quaestors serve in a consultative capacity in the Parliament's Bureau.

The Bureau

The Bureau is the regulatory body that is responsible for Parliament's budget and for administrative, organizational and staff matters. Its membership consists of the President and Vice-Presidents along with the Quaestors (who sit in on its meetings in a non-voting capacity). Members are elected for a term of two and a half years. The main duties of the Bureau are listed in Box 6.2 but, in practice, the Bureau operates in the 'political shadow' of the Conference of Presidents (Westlake 1994a:195).

BOX 6.2 Main duties of the Bureau (Rule 22)

- Take financial, organizational and administrative decisions on matters concerning members and the internal organization of Parliament, its Secretariat and its bodies.
- Take decisions on matters relating to the conduct of sittings.
- Decide the establishment plan of the Secretariat and lay down regulations relating to the administrative and financial situation of officials and other servants.
- Draw up Parliament's preliminary draft estimates.
- Adopt the guidelines for the Quaestors.
- Be the authority responsible for authorizing meetings of committees away from the usual places of work, hearings and study and fact-finding journeys by rapporteurs.
- Appoint the Secretary-General.

Source: European Parliament (2002).

Conference of Presidents

The Conference of Presidents is one of the organizational power-houses in the EP with responsibility for the broad political direction of Parliament (see Box 6.3). It meets regularly, approximately twice a month, and consists of the President of Parliament and the chairs of the political groups (including a delegate from the non-attached Members). Traditionally non-attached Members did not

---

BOX 6.3   Main duties of the Conference of Presidents (Rule 24)

- Take decisions on the organization of Parliament's work and matters relating to legislative planning.
- Responsible for matters relating to relations with the other institutions and bodies of the European Union and with the national parliaments of member states.
- Responsible for matters relating to relations with non-member countries and with non-Union institutions and organizations.
- Draw up the draft agenda of Parliament's part-sessions.
- Responsible for the composition and competence of committees and temporary committees of inquiry and of joint parliamentary committees, standing delegations and ad hoc delegations.
- Decide how seats in the Chamber are to be allocated.
- Responsible for authorizing the drawing up of own-initiative reports.
- Submit proposals to the Bureau concerning administrative and budgetary matters relating to the political groups.

Source: European Parliament (2002).

have the right to vote. However, following the dispute over the creation of the TDI Group (see Chapter 5) the Constitutional Affairs Committee proposed in 2001 that Rule 23(3) should be amended to allow the non-attached Members of the Conference to vote in accordance with the specific mandate of other non-attached Members (PE 232.762 2001:9). Parliament subsequently rejected this proposal.

The Chair of the Conference of Committee Chairs also attends on a non-voting basis (see below). Conference meetings are held behind closed doors in order to facilitate consensual agreements (Rule 23(3)). When a consensus cannot be reached, however, votes are taken and weighted in accordance with the number of members in each political group.

The prime purpose of the Conference is to 'cut deals between the Groups regarding Parliament's business' (Corbett *et al.* 2000:103). Given the preeminence of the EPP–ED and the PSE, the duopoly of power noted in Chapter 5 finds institutional expression in the meetings of the Conference of Presidents. Smaller groups can easily be outvoted and so have an incentive to find consensual outcomes. The political and partisan sensitivity of agreements worked out in conference is reflected in the fact that minutes of its meetings are carefully checked and approved by its members before dissemination to all MEPs. This both reinforces the perception of consensual outcomes and also minimizes the political fall-out likely to result from divergent interpretations of conference deliberations.

Conference of Committee Chairs and Conference of Delegation Chairs

A monthly meeting brings the chairs of parliamentary committees together to discuss organizational matters common to all committees and to help formulate draft plenary agendas (Rule 26). Because the committee chairs are significant politicians in their own right, drawing their authority from their formal parliamentary status but also buttressed by their position within a political group, they are a powerful force within the EP. With 'their collective finger on the Parliament's legislative pulse' (Westlake 1994a:194) the chairs play a considerable role in ensuring the stability of the EP's legislative biorhythms by settling demarcation disputes between committees, resolving common difficulties and monitoring progress of legislation through the committee cycle. The Conference elects its own chair, who, in turn, attends the Conference of Committee Presidents as the committee chairs' representative.

The EP has an extensive system of delegations which link Parliament with other parliamentary institutions and countries outside the EU. At the start of the 1999–2004 Parliament there were 34 delegations. These were grouped into 20 interparliamentary delegations and 14 delegations to joint parliamentary committees, which in turn were subdivided into two categories – Europe and Non-Europe. The former are delegations with countries that have applied to join the EU and have signed 'Europe' agreements. The latter include Parliamentary Cooperation Delegations with Kazakhstan, Kyrgyzstan, Uzbekistan, Tajikistan, Turkmenistan and Mongolia, and interparliamentary delegations with countries in the Americas, Asia–Pacific and the Middle East. In addition the EP is represented in the Joint Assembly of the African, Caribbean and Pacific regions and the EU (ACP–EU) which brings together 71 African, Caribbean and Pacific countries and the EU.

Each delegation has its own chair and two vice-chairs who are elected by the plenary along with committee chairs (see below) on the basis of nominations made by the political groups to the Conference of Presidents. Delegation chairs meet once a month in the Conference of Delegation Chairs to discuss common organizational and scheduling issues.

Secretariat

Parliament's work is organized by a Secretariat, headed by a Secretary-General, with a permanent staff of over 4,210 in 2002 (PE 300.037 2001:13) grouped in eight Directorates-General. Of these officials, as noted above, up to one-third are employed in the linguistic services. A further 530 or so are staff employed, and recruited directly, by the political groups (see Chapter 5). The permanent officials of the EP are thus relatively few in number and are recruited directly by external open competitions. Upon appointment they become European civil servants who are subject to the Official Code of Conduct and a vital part of their employment conditions is their independence (http://www.europarl. eu.int/codex/default_en.htm).

While the EP's Staff Regulations do not allow for posts to be reserved for nationals of any specific member state, there is an attempt, especially at the highest grades, to ensure some approximate proportionality among nationalities. Thus, of the eight heads of the Directorates-General, six represented different nationalities. In 2002, a British national, Julian Priestley, headed the Secretariat as Secretary-General. Priestley was appointed to this post in 1997 and, indeed, was only the fifth incumbent since 1958. Party affiliation, however, is not precluded and leading officials may have clear party pedigrees. Indeed, Priestley had stood as a Labour Party candidate in the Plymouth Devonport constituency in the 1983 UK general election.

Despite 'carrying out their duties in a politically neutral way' (Corbett *et al.* 2000:172), the highest officials within the Secretariat have acquired a reputation as 'convinced and mainly devout supranationalists' who act as 'an institutional memory (particularly important in a Parliament with high levels of membership turnover) and the administrative and legal champions of their institution' (Westlake 1994b:173). Throughout the history of the EP its permanent officials have been proactive in the creative exploitation of Parliament's formal powers and informal procedures. In particular, 'activist' officials have sought appointments in the legal service and to the secretariats of the most prestigious and influential parliamentary committees (see below).

Formal organization: committees

Analysing committees

Longley and Davidson (1998:2), in their review of developments in parliamentary organization, identify committees as the major loci of innovation in the processes and structures of representative assemblies. They note that: 'Parliamentary committees figure significantly on all continents and in most countries of the world, increasingly serving as the main organising centre of both legislation and parliamentary oversight' (Longley and Davidson 1998:2). This observation simply confirms the truism noted by Mattson and Strøm (1996:303) that: 'By broad consensus, committees are considered one of the most significant organizational features of modern parliaments.'

Explanations of exactly why committees are such ubiquitous features of modern parliamentary organization vary significantly. Recent analyses, grounded in 'new institutional' perspectives, recognize that committees provide 'economies of operation' (Mattson and Strøm 1996:251; Strøm 1998:24). As formal mechanisms for instituting a division of labour among representatives (of nominally equal status), committees facilitate decision-making in legislatures. This leads to 'efficiency gains' whereby legislation is processed and oversight is effected more expeditiously than if the plenary as a whole had collectively involved itself in deliberation and scrutiny. Moreover, it also enhances the prospects of legislative effectiveness through the encouragement of specialization and expertise and, hence, the maximization of institutional capacity to deal with the problems of complexity, technicality and information overload.

If, however, there is basic agreement about the benefits to be derived from 'economies of operation', there is disagreement about the precipitants of specialization through a committee-based division of labour. Over the 1990s three major analytical perspectives emerged to explain this institutional form: the 'distributive', the 'informational' and the 'organizational'. The distributive perspective, derived primarily from studies of the US Congress, conceives of a legislature as 'a collective choice body whose principal task is to allocate policy benefits' (Krehbiel 1991:3). The emphasis in the distributive perspective is on how legislators secure favourable distributions (in terms of policy outcomes) through exchange and concerted action. Legislators seek to control those institutional forms and parliamentary procedures which allow direct benefits to accrue to their constituents. The logic behind this perspective is that legislative organization revolves around committees because this institutional form helps to fulfil individual legislators' distributive goals. The dominant concern is with who receives benefits from legislative policy choices and at whose expense. The question asked about legislative institutions is subsequently: how can institutional design assist legislators to capture gains from trade? The answer, in short, is that a committee system is the institutional solution for securing the necessary exchanges and bargains.

The second, 'informational', perspective, however, conceives of committees as more than distributional devices based on a division of labour. They are also 'specialization-of-labour devices' (Krehbiel 1991:80). Hence, a key difference from a distributional perspective is that 'committee types, rules, and resources arise from within informational models because of the constitutional provision that the legislature determines the rules of its proceedings' (Krehbiel 1991:80). In this view, institutional arrangements reflect a need to acquire and disseminate information – with committees providing the necessary incentives for legislators to specialize in order to achieve their political and personal goals. In other words the development of policy expertise on the part of individual legislators can be conceived as a potential collective good (Krehbiel 1991:5). The ultimate challenge of legislative institutions, therefore, is to secure gains from specialization while minimizing the degree to which enacted policies deviate from majority-preferred outcomes. In short, Krehbiel's argument is that uncertainty of policy outcomes engenders institutional arrangements that reward expertise and specialization.

While the 'informational' model developed by Krehbiel emphasized the organizational logic behind the creation and maintenance of a strong committee system, it did so without direct reference to parties. This omission was addressed subsequently by

Cox and McCubbins (1993) in their reevaluation of the role of committees in a partisan context. They maintained that committees are the extensions of party control within the legislature. McCubbins also proceeded – with Kiewiet (Kiewiet and McCubbins 1991), and Lupia (Lupia and McCubbins 1994, 1998) – to develop an 'organizational' approach to legislative committees by utilizing principal–agent theory. The question to be answered this time was: how can legislators realize the potential benefits of delegation without abdicating their control over policy? (Lupia and McCubbins 1994:368). An essential ingredient of their explanation was that 'Legislative rules, procedures, and practices, though created for other purposes, often establish the conditions for learning' (1994:369). In which case, institutional design becomes the key to the existence of competition between information providers (1994:363).

What is important in McCubbins's work, both with Kiewiet and with Lupia, on agency and delegation is that it is explicitly comparative – prompting analysis of legislatures in relation to other institutions of governance and in relation to other legislatures in other political systems. In fact, an earlier comparative analysis, if less sophisticated than that of the American 'new institutionalists', had been made a decade earlier. In 1981 Judge sketched an 'elementary model' of legislative specialization which identified three macro-variables and a number of micro-variables which might affect the development of committee systems in different legislatures. The macro-variables were: first, the nature of authority hierarchies within a legislature; second, the nature of ideological or partisan competition; and, third, the compatibility of representative theories and practices with a formal division of labour (Judge 1981:46–8). It was hypothesized that where a decentralized, horizontal pattern of authority existed within a legislature – where leadership was segmented into different and competing hierarchies, among party, political executive and intra-parliamentary structures – then the conditions for an extensive division of labour would be more favourable than where centralized, vertical and hierarchical patterns of leadership prevailed. Second, it was stipulated that where partisan competition was essentially a zero-sum game, where all major issues were reducible to a choice between two mutually exclusive alternatives, as in an adversarial 'Westminster' party system, then legislative decision-making was simplified, and the necessity for developing specialized knowledge as a criterion of choice could be deemphasised. At the other extreme, where structured ideological or partisan factors played little or no consistent part in the determination of choice, then decision-making would be more dependent upon the possession of expertise and so enhance the perceived need for specialization.

Judge also recognized that macro-variables had to be supplemented with a consideration of the motivations and goals of individual representatives. Thus, for example, it was acknowledged that macro-organizational structure impacts on micro-orientations and the attainment of individual objectives – to the extent that different authority structures and normative systems in different legislatures help to explain different patterns of specialization (see Judge 1981:60–2). This assumption, that a specialization strategy may facilitate the fulfilment of personal goals, later found reflection in the work of a new generation of EP legislative scholars (see Hix *et al.* 1999:2). In attempting to hypothesize why MEPs seek to join particular committees they surmised that the behaviour of representatives could be influenced by three different sets of career goals: reelection, policy impact and office-seeking (1999:12). From these standard assumptions they suggested that reelection-seeking MEPs would value membership of committees which 'deal with domestically salient matters'; policy-seeking MEPs would wish to serve on committees that 'are relevant to individual policy concerns'; while office-seeking members would 'prioritise the most prestigious committees' (1999:24). The expectation of Hix *et al.* was that 'policy-seeking MEPs, and office-seeking members to a somewhat lesser extent [would] seek and gain rapporteurships in order to influence the EP's positions and to gain intra-committee prestige'.

What the above discussion highlights is the simple fact that the development of the EP's committee system would be expected to reflect a balance of exogenous and endogenous variables. What the following discussion focuses upon is the formal structure of the EP's committees and the working routines and styles that have developed within the different committees.

Committee structure

From the outset the EP operated primarily through a committee system. Despite its advisory remit and its remarkably limited legislative functions, nonetheless the Common Assembly of the ECSC established seven standing committees in its first year of existence. The number of parliamentary committees increased to 13 after the establishment of the EEC and Euratom in 1958, and increased again to 16 after direct elections in 1979. Thereafter, the number increased gradually to 20 before a review of the committee structure in 1999 reduced the number to 17.

What merits our attention, however, is not the number of committees, but rather their longevity and their institutionalization at the centre of the EP's decision-making processes. Simply stated, in accordance with the discussion of the academic analyses of committee formation above, the absence of authoritative executive leadership in the EP (given that there was no 'government' to support or oppose), and the absence of unambiguous party direction (given the competing and occasionally conflicting voting cues of national and transnational party groups), required representatives in the EP, from the very beginning, to establish alternative institutional devices through which to reach rational decisions.

At the start of the twenty-first century, the EP's specialized committees are at the heart of its legislative, and non-legislative, work. Chapters 7 and 8 examine in detail both how the committees operate and their contribution to the decision-making processes; here, however, we will concentrate upon the organization of the committees themselves.

1999 review of committees

Immediately before the June 1999 election the committee structure of the EP was systematically reviewed for the first time since direct elections in 1979. (An earlier, far less systematic and unsuccessful attempt to rationalize the committee structure had been proposed in the 1989–94 Parliament by the then PSE Group leader Jean Pierre Cot.) The 1999 review was prompted, in part, by the incremental increase in the numbers of committees over the years (from 16 in 1979 to 20 in 1999); in part also by the changed legislative priorities of the EP resulting from the Amsterdam Treaty; and, in part too, to redress some of the imbalances in workload that had arisen from the initial functional allocation of committee responsibilities. The Amsterdam Treaty meant, for example, that the legislative responsibilities and hence workload of some committees – such as the Regional Policy, Transport and Tourism Committee – would be enhanced. Having learnt from the experiences of the Environment, Public Health and Consumer Protection Committee and the Legal Affairs Committee immediately after the Maastricht Treaty, whose workloads had increased dramatically upon the introduction of the codecision procedure, an attempt was made in 1999 to lessen the disparities of overall workloads among committees.

In the event this rationalization of the committee structure was only partially fulfilled. Proposals were considered which would have reduced the number of committees to between 12 and 14, yet in the event 17 remained (European Parliament 1998; see Table 6.1). Ultimately, any attempt to rationalize the committee structure needed to find a careful balance between the desire of MEPs to inflate the number of committees and positions available (especially but not exclusively through special pleading for their special interests), and the practical limitations imposed by the limited number of interpreters, and the availability of meeting rooms and of parliamentary time. Tension was also apparent not only about the existence of certain committees but also over the respective remits of each committee. Thus, for example, one of the most controversial aspects of the 1999 review was the transfer of responsibility for the legal protection of consumers to the Legal Affairs Committee from the Environment Committee (though the latter retained responsibility for the broader aspects of consumer policy). The strength of feeling over this issue was reflected in the comments of long-standing Environment Committee member, Françoise Grossetête (EPP–ED, France): '[allocating the legal protection of consumers to the Legal Affairs Committee] shows ignorance of the reality of the policy being pursued in favour of consumers ... all consumer policy should be assigned to the Committee on Environment and Public Health' (quoted in *Agence Europe* 22 April 1999).

The extent of variation in committee workload can be seen in Table 6.2. Despite the 1999 reorganization there remains a marked imbalance in the workloads of the various commitees with five of the 17 accounting for half of all adopted reports. Table 6.2 lists the number of reports produced by each committee between July 1999 and July 2002. There are two main broad categories of reports: legislative and non-legislative.

TABLE 6.1 *Parliamentary committees and chairs, 2002*

Parliamentary committees and chairs, 2002	Full members
Foreign Affairs, Human Rights, Common Security and Defence Policy	69
Elmar Brok (EPP–ED)	
Budgets	40
Terence Wynn (PSE)	
Budgetary Control	21
Diemur Theato (EPP–ED)	
Citizens' Freedoms and Rights, Justice and Home Affairs	49
Jorge Salvador Hernández Mollar (EPP–ED)	
Economic and Monetary Affairs	42
Christa Randzio-Plath (PSE)	
Legal Affairs and the Internal Market	34
Giuseppe Gargani (EPP–ED)	
Industry, External Trade, Research and Energy	56
Carlos Westendorp y Cabeza (PSE)	
Employment and Social Affairs	51
Theodorus Bouwman (Verts/ALE)	
Environment, Public Health and Consumer Policy	60
Caroline Jackson (EPP–ED)	
Agriculture and Rural Development	39
Joseph Daul (EPP–ED)	
Fisheries	23
Struan Stevenson (EPP–ED)	
Regional Policy, Transport and Tourism	58
Luciano Caveri (ELDR)	
Culture, Youth, Education, the Media and Sport	37
Michel Rocard (PSE)	
Development and Cooperation	33
Joaquim Miranda (GUE/NGL)	
Constitutional Affairs	35
Giorgo Napolitano (PSE)	
Women's Rights and Equal Opportunities	39
Anna Karamanou (PSE)	
Petitions	28
Vitaliano Gemelli (EPP–ED)	

TABLE 6.2 *European Parliament committee reports, July 1999 to July 2002*

	Consultation	Codecision (reports in 1st reading)	Codecision (recommendations in 2nd or 3rd reading)	Assent	Green papers, strategy documents, Commission reports, etc.	Budgetary procedure	Discharge procedure	Own-initiative	Rules of Procedure	Verification of Credentials	Immunity	Appointment procedure	Interinstitutional agreement	TOTAL
Foreign Affairs	11	2	1	3	56			14						87
Budgets	20	2	1		3	43		2					5	76
Bugetary Control	9	2			13		25	3					1	52
Citizens'	78	5	3		18			4						109
Economic	19	20	8		40			13				1		101
Legal Affairs	15	11	22	2	12			4	1	1	10		1	79
Industry	36	20	14	12	25			4						111
Employment	5	9	17		29			6						66
Environment	14	66	75		19			9						183
Agriculture	41	6	2		6			5						60
Fisheries	45				14			4						63
Regional Policy	3	38	27	4	29			3						104
Culture	4	5	8	19				9						45
Development	4	4	6	2	12			7						35
Constitutional	3			2	4			9	10				3	31
Women's	1	1	3		8			11						24
TOTAL	308	191	187	44	288	43	25	107	11	1	10	1	10	1226

Source: Calculated from http://www.europarl.eu.int/committees/home_en.htm.

The legislative category can be broken down further in accordance with the legislative procedure in operation – consultation, cooperation, codecision or assent (see Chapter 7 for details). Within these legislative categories the number of codecision reports was heavily skewed towards six committees, with the Environment, Regional Policy, Legal Affairs, Economic, Industry and Employment committees accounting for around 87 per cent of all codecision reports. Indeed, in the first half of the 1999–2004 Parliament the Environment and Regional Policy committees between them accounted for over half of all codecision reports. The second 'non-legislative' category includes 'own-initiative' reports, reports examining consultation papers and strategy documents produced by the Commission, as well as those relating to budgetary procedures and interinstitutional agreements.

Membership

The 1999 review of the committee structure was implemented in the July session of the new Parliament. This conformed to established practice where the number of committees, the size of their memberships and the allocation of responsibilities is decided at the first July session of a newly elected parliament. Individual committee assignments are then allocated in accordance with Rule 152:

> Members of committees and temporary committees of inquiry shall be elected after nominations have been submitted by the political groups and the Non-attached Members. The Conference of Presidents shall submit proposals to Parliament. The composition of the committees shall, as far as possible, reflect the composition of Parliament.

As is the case in other legislatures, there is intense competition to serve on some committees and less competition to serve on others (see Neuhold 2001:4, McElroy 2002:10). In the first three parliaments, the Foreign Affairs Committee (despite limited formal powers) and the Budgets Committee (with more extensive formal powers) were particularly regarded as high-status committees, and competition for seats on these committees was intense. More recently membership of the most proactive legislative committees, such as Environment and Economic and Monetary Affairs (EMAC), has been heavily contested.

Most MEPs serve as a full member of one committee and as a substitute on another. Substitute members normally have full speaking and voting rights (if acting as a replacement for an absent full member). They may also serve as rapporteurs and draftsmen (especially if they have acknowledged expertise in the policy area under consideration). Some committees are deemed to be 'neutralized committees' which, because of their technical focus (for example, Rules (before the 1999 review) and Petitions) or specialist concern (for example, Budgetary Control), would be unlikely to attract sufficient members to serve on them if MEPs were limited to full service on only one committee. The pay-off for membership of a 'neutralized committee' is that it does not prejudice an MEP's chances of becoming a full member of another committee.

Ultimately, as with most other legislatures, the choice of committee is not an unrestricted preference of the individual representative. Instead, committee assignments are determined by political groups in rough proportion to their respective numerical strengths in plenary. Groups also endeavour to maintain a proportionate national balance within their representation on committees. As a result, 'the composition of committees generally reflects the national and ideological composition of the chamber' (Bowler and Farrell 1995:227). In addition, an informal, if weak, seniority principle operates in the larger groups where longer-serving MEPs may press prior claims over newly elected MEPs to appointment on the most prestigious and oversubscribed committees.

Within the broad parameters set by party groups, individual representatives seek appointment to specific committees. The mix of individual career preferences and personal goals plays a decisive part in the choice of committee assignments (Corbett *et al.* 2000:107). The most powerful incentives prompting service on particular committees have been found to derive from personal interest in a policy area and/or prior occupational experience. As Bowler and Farrell (1995:231–4) found from their investigation of committee assignments in the 1989–94 Parliament, and as Mamadouh and Raunio (2000:8) confirmed for the 1994–99 Parliament, occupational and interest-group attachments were 'the only consistently significant determinants driving committee membership'. In combination the criteria deployed by party groups and individual group members in the allocation of committee assignments allows for the development of 'a process of coordinated – even controlled – specialization' (Bowler and Farrell 1995:241). This echoes the earlier contention of Judge (1981:38–40, 46–8) that the practices of 'party representation' and shared party values may facilitate a division of labour among members of the same party group in a legislature.

Committee bureau

Once committee members have been selected, each committee then elects its own bureau (of chair and three vice-chairs). The bureau, especially the chair, plays a powerful role both internally within the committee, and in the committee's external relations in the EP itself and in its dealings with other EU institutions and national governments and interests beyond the EP. As is the case with other formal office-holders in the EP, committee chairs hold office for half-parliamentary terms and are thus subject to reelection midway through a parliament. In practice, this has resulted in a considerable turnover of committee chairs for most committees. During the lifetime of the 1994–99 Parliament, for example, 16 of the 20 committees changed their chair.

Although formally 'elected', in practice, committee chairs and vice-chairs are chosen on the basis of negotiation amongst political groups. Groups choose which committees to chair in accordance with the proportional d'Hondt system – whereby the order of allocation is determined by alternation between the political groups according to size. Thus, after the 1999 election, the EPP–ED, as the largest group, could claim the first, third, fifth, seventh, tenth, thirteenth, fifteenth and seventeenth choice of committee chair. The PSE, as the second largest group, gained the second, fourth, sixth, eleventh, fourteenth and sixteenth choices. The ELDR had the eighth choice, the Greens had the ninth, and the EUL/NGL had the twelfth choice.

In making its choices the EPP–ED ranked the Environment, Public Health and Consumer Policy Committee as its first choice, with Caroline Jackson (EPP–ED, UK) subsequently becoming chair. Undoubtedly, this was a reflection of the prestige and legislative importance built up by the committee over the years. Mrs Jackson as an active and long-standing member of the Environment Committee, with significant knowledge of the substantive issues and modes of working of the committee, was an obvious contender for the chair of the committee. As the second largest national contingent in the EPP–ED the British Conservatives had a claim to one of the group's key chairs; and, undoubtedly, support for Mrs Jackson's nomination within the EPP–ED was aided by the fact that, unlike many of her British Conservative colleagues, she was not a Eurosceptic.

Offsetting its first choice – of a prime legislative committee – the EPP–ED selected the Committee on Foreign Affairs, Human Rights and Defence as its second choice. Although having no legislative powers, this committee was guaranteed to have a high political profile in the post-Amsterdam EU. Moreover, it was also seen as an 'ideal consolation prize for German Christian Democrat MEP Elmar Brok, who failed in his bid to become the leader of the Christian Democrats' (*European Voice*, 22–28 July 1999).

The PSE, in making its four main choices in 1999, opted for a rank-order of Economic and Monetary Affairs (chaired by Christa Randzio-Plath, PSE, Germany), Budgets (Terry Wynn, PSE, UK) Trade and Industry (Carlos Wetensdorp y Cabeza, PSE, Spain) and Employment and Social Affairs (Michel Rocard, PSE, France). The ELDR chose to chair the Citizens' Freedoms and Rights, Justice and Home Affairs Committee, the Greens opted for Agriculture, and the EUL/NGL chose the Development and Cooperation Committee.

At mid-term, in January 2002, six committees elected new chairs. Jackson, Brok, Randzio-Plath and Wynn retained their positions at the head of the leading committees, but Rocard was replaced by Theo Bouwman (Greens, Netherlands) as chair of the Employment Committee. Rocard became chair of the Culture Committee in a move that was seen 'as something of a failure for the Socialist Group' (*European Voice* 24 January 2002). In turn, Joseph Daul (EPP–ED, France) became chair of the Agriculture Committee and Giuseppe Gargani (EPP–ED, Italy) became chair of the Legal Affairs Committee. Luciano Caveri (ELDR, Italy) took over as chair of the Regional Policy Committee. Ana Palacio Vallelersundi (EPP–ED, Spain) was elected to chair the Committee on Citizens' Freedoms and Rights, Justice and Home Affairs, though in July 2002 she became the Spanish foreign minister, and was replaced by Jorge Salvador Hernández Mollar (EPP–DE, Spain).

Once the chairs have been selected a similar process of proportionate inter-party distribution of vice-chairs then takes place. In the case of the EPP's first-choice committee in 1999, Environment, Carlos Lage of the PSE gained the first vice-chair, Alexander de Roo of the Greens/EFA was appointed second vice-chair, and Ria Oomen-Ruijten of the EPP–ED picked up the third vice-chair. At mid-term in 2002 de Roo remainded as a vice-chair on the Environment Committee but Lage and Oomen-Ruijten were replaced by Anneli Hulthén (PSE, Sweden) and Mauro Nobilia (UEN, Italy). In the case of EMAC, the PSE's first choice in 1999, the vice-chairs were William M. Abitbol (EDD, France), José Manuel García-Margallo y Marfil (EPP–ED, Spain) and Philippe Herzog (EUL/NGL, France). In 2002, John Purvis (EPP–ED, UK) replaced William Abitbol.

Final decisions on committee office-holders are taken at the first plenary session following the European election and any revisions, contingent upon the wider choice of presidency and bureau, are made by the political groups at that time. The grip of political group control is just as apparent at the mid-term review of committee leadership positions. Political groups have been prone to reallocate committee bureau positions at mid-term to reflect the internal political balance among their own members. One consequence of this propensity of political groups to rotate committee leadership positions is the undermining of specialization, reputation for expertise and a 'collective memory' of procedural and institutional affairs at the top of the committee structure. The one clear exception remains Ken Collins (PSE, UK) who served as chair of the Environment Committee for 15 out of the 20 years he served as an MEP. Only Willy de Clerq as the chair of the External Economic Relations Committee from 1989 to 1997 came anywhere close to Collins for accumulated service as chair of a single committee. In contrast, other important committees have changed their committee chairs with remarkable regularity. The Legal Affairs Committee had 12 chairs in the period 1979–2002, while the Employment (Social Affairs) Committee had 11 and Foreign Affairs had 10 chairs in the same period.

Group coordinators

Political group coordinators play an important role in coordinating the activities of group MEPs in and across committees. Together with the committee's bureau, group coordinators arrange a committee's agenda, and facilitate the working of the committee by discussing forthcoming votes, the tabling of amendments and broader political problems before they surface in the full meeting of the committee. In particular, coordinators negotiate the distribution of rapporteurships among the groups represented on the committee. In turn, it is then the responsibility of the group coordinator to allocate a specific report within his or her own group. The group coordinator also decides which substitute member may vote in the absence of a full committee member from the group. Generally the coordinator is responsible for orchestrating the activities of group members on a committee and for performing many of the functions associated with 'party whips' in other legislatures: convening pre-meetings to formulate the group's position on forthcoming votes in the full committee, working out a schedule of speakers, ensuring attendance at key votes, and communicating information on the progress and outcomes of committee deliberations to the wider group. The performance of all of these tasks, however, is complicated by the internal segmentation of groups along national as well as ideological lines.

Allocations of rapporteurships are based loosely on the principle of proportionality. Within each committee the allocation between groups is based usually on an informal 'points' system. Each group receives a quota of points in proportion to its numerical strength in the committee. (In the Budgets Committee, however, the points quota is determined in accordance with the number of group MEPs in Parliament as a whole.) Corbett *et al.* (2000:117) provide a concise summary of the normal procedure:

> Reports and opinions to be distributed are ... discussed by the committee coordinators who decide the number of points each subject is worth, and then make bids on behalf of the Group, the strength of their claim being based in theory (but not always in practice) on the relationship between the number of points already used by the Group and their original

quota. A controversial issue may be the subject of competing bids.

But the precise bidding system varies among committees, not least because the process is entirely informal. In the Environment Committee, for example, the point value of a report depends on the number of groups willing to bid. If four groups express an interest then the point value is four, and if two groups make a bid the value is two points. Less contentious reports normally have a value of two or three points, with opinions having a value of one point. The 'neutralized committees' mentioned above rarely use a points system, while others, such as the Research, Technological Development and Energy Committee in the 1994–99 Parliament, operated a strict hierarchical points system for different types of report, with the committee secretariat deciding the value (for details see Mamadouh and Raunio 2000:14–15). Some reports, which no group particularly wants, may have a zero points value. Yet another model is provided by the Legal Affairs Committee, where codecision proposals 'cost' two points, consultations and reports on Commission Green and White Papers one point, and opinions for other committees half a point. The Legal Affairs Committee has also adapted the system further, and at second reading a group 'pays again' to retain the report. In theory, therefore, the rapporteurship could thus change between readings. Normally, however, rapporteurships remain with the same group (if not necessarily with the same person) at second reading.

Overall, the allocation system works effectively with very few formal votes taken in committees to decide rapporteurships. As Ken Collins, former chairman of the Environment Committee, noted in interview, the selection of rapporteurs is 'a combination of a kind of auction and a kind of elaborate game of poker' (Wurzel 1999:12). In this game coordinators play side-games whereby a particular political group's bid for a particular report may secure support (or acquiescence) from other coordinators because of their implicit approval of the bidding group's potential nominee as rapporteur. Equally, there is the counter proposition, that a coordinator may allow a particular report (sought by a less able member of the same group) to be allocated to another group to ensure that the committee ultimately receives a well-drafted report. When the chips are down in this game of poker, however, the biggest groups hold the biggest stakes and operate an effective duopoly in the allocation of the most politically controversial and prestigious reports.

Once a group secures a particular report it is then allocated to a specific member of the group. At this point considerations of nationality and expertise, sometimes as conflicting principles, come into play. A detailed study of the distribution of reports and rapporteurships in committees found that, on the one side, 'the size of national delegation predicts rather well its share of reports' (Mamadouh and Raunio 2000:25). Equally, on the other side, it was also confirmed that 'within committees certain MEPs are recognised as experts on specific issues, and that these representatives are assigned as rapporteurs on these topics' (Mamadouh and Raunio 2000:30). Particularly among group coordinators and members who have served on the same committee for many years, nationality is often discounted and is ranked well below other selection factors such as specialization within the committee, negotiation skills, and respect among other political groups. Obviously, overall, some balance will be maintained among group members of different nationalities – but this is seldom explicit. Similarly, where a particular issue has a specific national dimension it can work against – as well as in favour of – members of that nationality becoming rapporteur. Exactly how reports are dealt with, and how rapporteurs fulfil their roles, will be examined in detail in Chapter 8.

Temporary committees/Committees of Inquiry

Under Rule 150, 'Parliament may at any time set up temporary committees, whose powers, composition and term of office shall be defined at the same time as the decision to set them up is taken; their term of office may not exceed twelve months, except where Parliament extends that term on its expiry' (European Parliament 2002). There are two basic types of temporary committee. First, there are committees formed in accordance with Rule 150 and whose powers and mode of operation are determined exclusively by Parliament. Between 1979 and 1999 seven such committees were established. These dealt with such matters as European economic recovery (1983), budgetary resources (1984), 'making a success of the Single Act' (1987),

Community legislation necessary to permit German unification (1990), the 'Delors II' package (1992), employment (1994/5), and the monitoring of action taken subsequent to the report of the BSE Committee of Inquiry (1997). After the 1999 election a temporary committee was created in July 2000 to assess the implications of a communications interception system known as ECHELON. In January 2001, another committee was established to examine developments in the field of human genetics and other new medicine technologies. A further temporary committee was established in March 2002 to analyse the management of, and the impact of, the foot and mouth crisis.

The second type of temporary committee is the Committee of Inquiry. Soon after direct elections in 1979 the EP started to use such committees to draw attention to specific policy issues and to assert its rights of scrutiny over the actions of other Community institutions. Nine Committees of Inquiry were established between 1979 and the adoption of the Maastricht Treaty. These ranged from the handling of nuclear materials, through transfrontier crimes linked to drug trafficking, and the use of hormones in meat, to racism and fascism. However, these investigatory committees had no formal standing or legal recourse beyond the EP itself. In other words, the committees were dependent upon the voluntary cooperation of other EU institutions and national authorities in the pursuit of their inquiries.

This changed with the addition of a new article to the EC Treaty at Maastricht which provided a legal base for the EP's Committees of Inquiry and specified that provisions relating to the right of inquiry should be worked out by common accord by the Council, Commission and Parliament (see Shackleton 1998:116–17). Eventually, after detailed negotiations extending over 15 months, an interinstitutional agreement was reached between the three institutions and, shortly thereafter, Parliament revised its internal rules to accommodate the new provisions. At the beginning of 1996 the first Committee of Inquiry – into the Community's transit regime – was established under the chairmanship of John Tomlinson (PSE, UK). The committee had 17 full members and 17 substitutes, and met 37 times over a period of 13 months. While the transit committee was conducting its extensive inquiry, a second Committee of Inquiry into the BSE crisis was established in July 1996. The BSE committee was chaired by German Christian Democrat Reimer Böge. It held 31 meetings and produced its report (in February 1997 with Manuel Medina Ortega as rapporteur) within six months of its inception.

In his detailed assessment of the impact of the transit and BSE committees Shackleton (1998:123–7) draws a contrast between their limited formal powers and their impact on both public and policy debates as well as upon actual policy outcomes. In comparison to Committees of Inquiry in most member states' parliaments, the EP's committees' powers to call witnesses, enforce their attendance and elicit evidence were severely circumscribed. Nevertheless, both committees secured significant press and media coverage and made an impact upon specific policy programmes and upon the EU's policy process itself (for details see Shackleton 1998:125–7).

Conciliation Committee

As will be seen in Chapter 7, codecision is the most significant legislative procedure in the EU (and the details of this procedure will be examined in the next chapter). At this point in the discussion of the internal organization of the EP, however, it is advisable to examine the structure and workings of the Conciliation Committee. This committee effectively constitutes the final stage of the codecision procedure itself (for full details see European Parliament 2001a).

The Conciliation Committee is an interinstitutional body and, unlike the other committees considered in this chapter, is not, therefore, an exclusive parliamentary organization. Representatives of both the EP and Council meet in the Conciliation Committee with the express purpose of reaching agreement on a joint text on the legislative proposal under consideration (see Chapter 7). Representatives of the Commission are also present at the meetings of the committee, which are mostly held in Brussels.

The Conciliation Committee has a total membership of 30, with 15 members of the Council or their representatives and an equal number of MEPs. Parliament's Conference of Presidents determines the political composition of the EP's delegation at the beginning of each legislature, but not the precise membership (which varies with each committee). In the 1999–2001 period there were six EPP–ED representatives, five from the PSE, one ELDR, one Greens/EFA, one EUL/NGL and one rotating representative from the UEN, EDD and TDI groups (until the TDI was disbanded in October 2001). Although nominally having a membership of only 15 members, by the time political advisers, technical experts, legal experts and other support staff are represented some 70 to 80 people may actually be in attendance at the Conciliation Committee (Garman and Hilditch 1998:280).

The membership of the EP's delegation is appointed for each separate conciliation, with the exception of the three Vice-Presidents of the Parliament who serve as permanent members of the Conciliation Committee. (The permanent members constitute part of the quota of the respective political groups.) In the first half of the 1999–2004 Parliament the three Vice-Presidents who served on the Conciliation Committee were Renzo Imbeni, James Provan and Ingo Friedrich; in the second half Provan and Friedrich were replaced by Giorgos Dimitrakopoulos (EPP–ED, Greece) and Charlotte Cederschiöld (EPP–ED, Sweden). The rapporteur and the chair of the committee responsible are members, and most other members are selected by the party groups from the committee responsible or from committees that have provided an opinion on the directive under consideration (under Rule 82). Moreover, the delegation normally includes the group spokespersons on a specific proposal, and party group coordinators in the main committee responsible are often appointed. Representatives from the Commission also are normally invited to the meetings of the EP delegation (and of the Council delegation).

On average, up to five meetings of the EP's delegation may be necessary prior to formal Conciliation Committee meetings. These 'prior meetings' provide opportunities to discuss future strategy or the outcomes of negotiations (in trialogue or other informal meetings: see Chapter 8). These delegation meetings are usually held in Strasbourg.

The delegations are supported by a Conciliations Secretariat. The main tasks of the Secretariat are to prepare and organize the meetings of the delegations, prepare background notes for delegation members, assist in the running of the conciliation procedure, draft compromise texts, and prepare reports for plenary on the outcomes of Conciliation. Perhaps more importantly, the Secretariat maintains and develops contacts with all of the leading participants in the conciliation process – especially with relevant officials in the Council and Commission, and with the secretariats of relevant EP committees, with Parliament's legal service, and with the Jurist Linguist Unit to ensure the legal verification of the texts throughout the codecision process. The Conciliations Secretariat also plays an important role in informing MEPs and interested publics of the process of conciliation itself and of the progression and processing of legislation under the codecision procedure. The importance of Parliament's conciliation unit in oiling the wheels of the conciliation process is noted by Garman and Hilditch (1998:280–1) who highlight the significance of the exploratory meetings convened between the conciliation units of Parliament and the Council which ultimately facilitate compromises in the Conciliation Committee itself.

As for the full Conciliation Committee, any number of meetings may be convened within the six- or eight-week deadline stipulated in the codecision procedure. The maximum number to date has been four meetings – on the Fifth Research Framework Programme in 1998.

Rules of Procedure

> Parliaments ... are divided internally into various subgroups, such as chambers, parties, and leadership bodies. Legislative output depends on the powers vested in these subunits of parliamentarians. Legislative organisation is not simply a matter of what substructures exist: what ultimately matters are the rights or authorities given to these units. Moreover, the rights are tied up with sometimes arcane and complex rules by which the legislature does its work. (Strøm 1995:69)

As Chapter 2 revealed, Article 25 of the ECSC Treaty conferred upon the Common Assembly the right to adopt its own rules of procedure. That right was to prove vital to the evolution of the Assembly and, later, to the European Parliament. Indeed, throughout the history of the Parliament MEPs have proved adept at extending the reach of their powers and influence through the creative amendment of the EP's own Rules of Procedure. Moreover, Chapter 2 also underscored the point made by Evans (1999:632) that 'Seemingly minor decisions about rules made early in a legislature's existence…can have profound consequences for institutional development'.

Indeed, a 'philosophy' has been discerned behind the rules which has sought the strengthening of the EP's position in the legislative process 'from the beginning to the final decision' (Romer 1993:2–3), as well as making its internal organization more efficient and, more widely, maximizing its interinstitutional impact (see Judge *et al.* 1994:31). This 'philosophy' was clearly expressed by Richard Corbett, in his report as rapporteur on the rule changes to be effected upon the introduction of the Amsterdam Treaty:

> Parliament has traditionally taken the Treaties and tried to stretch them like a piece of elastic, in order to enhance the efficiency and democratic accountability of the Union. Of course Parliament cannot contravene the Treaties in its Rules of procedure but the Treaties inevitably leave scope for interpretation and room for imagination. (PE 229.204 1999:87)

Between 1979 and 2002, well over 1,000 rule changes were proposed by the Rules/Constitutional Affairs Committee (Kreppel 2002:107–20, PE 229.204 1999; PE 304.283 2001). Admittedly, some two-thirds of these amendments were minor, technical or clarificatory, and a substantial proportion were never adopted. Many more were inspired by significant treaty revisions – the SEA, Maastricht, Amsterdam and, eventually, Nice. Nonetheless, in quantitative terms alone they reflect the internal dynamism of the institution and the perpetual quest for the enhancement of the EP's standing within the EU's interinstitutional structures. Moreover, in qualitative terms, the incessant rule changes have reflected at least four major organizational requirements of the EP, which have varied over time and in their relative emphasis (see Kreppel 2002:104–5): first, to increase the efficiency of its internal organization (in terms of leadership structures, committee division of labour and so on); second, to regulate and institutionalize party group activities (in terms of the prerogatives of large groups, protection of the rights of small groups and the organizational requirements of technical groups and non-affiliated members); third, to address increments in the EP's powers and competencies arising from treaty revisions; and, fourth, to sustain an integrationist dynamic (in terms of setting the agenda of future interinstitutional relations by innovative procedural changes as illustrated, for example, by the development of the nomination process of the Commission).

Intergroups

'Intergroups' are unofficial groupings of MEPs who share a common interest in a particular cause or interest. With the exception of the intergroup of Elected Local and Regional Representatives no other intergroup has formal status within the EP. Despite the 'unofficial' nature of these groups, some 100 were in existence in 2000 (*European Voice* 6–12 April 2000:24; for an indicative list see Corbett *et al.* 2000:165). There is such diversity amongst intergroups in terms of size, membership, frequency of meetings, links with political groups and outside interests that it is difficult to make generalized statements about their activities.

Nonetheless, Corbett *et al.* (2000:158) list the benefits of intergroups for the EP as enabling MEPs to focus on a 'particular set of issues of specific national, constituency or personal concern', to specialize, to make contacts with outside interest groups on an informal basis, and to facilitate political contacts outside their own political groups. There are, however, also certain disbenefits associated with intergroup activity. Indeed, concern with the operations of a few intergroups and their close connections with outside lobbies led the Conference of Presidents in 1995 to ratify an agreement to reaffirm and underline the unofficial status of such groups. Intergroups were expected to make clear that they were not organs of the EP, they did not speak on behalf of Parliament, they could not use the EP's logo or its official title in any communications or printed materials. Specific rules were also drafted in the same year to bring intergroups into line with the rules concerning lobbyists and the declaration of financial interest of MEPs and their assistants (see Chapter 3). In 1999 further restrictions were placed on the creation of intergroups when they were required to have the support of party group leaders before they could be constituted.

In addition to the concerns that some groups merely served as a 'front' for certain organized interests, there was also concern that the sheer scale and activism of intergroup networks constituted 'a rival centre of attention to official parliamentary activities, and in certain circumstances may undercut the latter' (Corbett *et al.* 2000:158). Thus, on occasion, the clash of timing of intergroup meetings with official parliamentary committee meetings and plenary debates has adversely affected attendance at the latter. Similarly, outside speakers occasionally quibble at attending committee meetings after appearing at intergroup sessions.

Plenary

As noted earlier, the EP is required by the protocol to the Amsterdam Treaty to schedule 12 plenary sessions a year (formally titled 'part-sessions') in Strasbourg, with additional plenary sessions held in Brussels. Effectively, with the ending of Friday sittings in 2000, each Strasbourg plenary part-session lasts just three and a half days. Not surprisingly, this episodic and curtailed working schedule heightens the premium placed upon formalism in the EP's plenaries.

Moreover, in formal terms, the treaties only recognize Parliament as a collectivity in plenary under its President. Thus, although the working methods and organization of the EP revolve around the committees and political groups, only decisions reached in plenary have the imprimatur of Parliament. In other words, while committees are indisputably the practical locus of decision-making, the outcomes of their deliberations still have to receive the formal approval of the EP as a whole. Final votes on legislative proposals can only take place in plenary.

The formal preeminence of plenary is reflected in the fact that the proceedings on the floor of the chamber are published verbatim in the *Official Journal*. In contrast, as Westlake notes (1994a:201), debates within committee are simply minuted and distributed only within the committee itself. (However, one of the innovations in Parliament's rule changes in June 2002 was to ensure, exceptionally, the production of a verbatim report of the presentations of the President of the European Central Bank made to Parliament's Economic and Monetary Affairs Committee.) The formal recording of plenary proceedings also partly explains the often stunted and formalistic contributions to debate – as speakers are strictly apportioned across political groups, time limits are rigidly enforced, and, correspondingly, individual speeches tend to be regimented and frequently scripted (see Chapter 7). Moreover, given the time constraints and the need to record accurate decisions, voting is usually separated from debate, confined to specific voting times, and ordered in accordance with standard procedures for the taking of votes (see Corbett *et al.* 2000:148–51).

Conclusion

This chapter has examined how the EP has responded to the complexities of making collective decisions in a peculiarly heterogeneous environment. The EP's peripatetic existence and its use of eleven working languages has only served to exacerbate the generic problems encountered by all elected representative bodies in processing highly complex and often technical issues in an informed manner.

The absence of a 'government' removes one authority hierarchy from within the EP, which in most other Western parliaments provides an identifiable decision-making cue for individual members – simply whether to support or oppose the position adopted by the 'government'. Other hierarchies of party and parliamentary leadership roles have thus developed, and conjoined, to mitigate the centrifugal organizational forces at work in the EP. Most importantly of all an internal division of labour, structured around committees, has developed to offset these forces. The committees provide the main institutional mechanism for the processing of legislative proposals. Notably, they enjoy considerable autonomy under the rules of the EP, and as nodal points of influence they have organizational consequences for party groups. So much so, that party groups seek both to control the memberships of the committees and to coordinate their own internal activities around the work of committees.

One of the themes of this chapter, and more generally of the book, has been that institutional design and organizational adaptation has been a persistent feature of the EP. At a formal level, the specification of decision-making procedures in the treaties has had internal organizational ramifications, and successive treaty reforms have stimulated attendant organizational changes within the EP. Equally, however, at a more informal level, the creative amendment of the EP's own Rules of Procedure has mirrored an institutional dynamism and an almost perpetual quest for the enhancement of the EP's standing within the EU's interinstitutional structures.

Chapter 7

Formal Powers

> Although we must expect the real influence of legislators will be at variance with their constitutional powers, we nevertheless need to know what scope constitutions give to legislatures before we can consider some of the more complex problems of legislative influence. (Blondel 1970:30)

Heeding Blondel's words this chapter examines the formal powers conferred upon the EP before the complexities of legislative influence are analysed in Chapter 8. Almost by definition, such an examination is comparative in nature as it requires an assessment of the powers of the EP in relation to other institutions involved in the EU's legislative process, and also invites some assessment of the powers of the EP in comparison to those of national parliaments. In particular, in line with Mezey's ideas outlined in Chapter 1, this chapter will examine the capacity of the EP to constrain the legislative activities of the 'dual executive' of the Commission and Council. However, this does not mean that constraints are to be analysed solely in negative terms – of preventing action – but should also be seen as positive incentives to promote cooperative interinstitutional collaboration. Moreover, as Chapter 2 revealed, the formal powers of the European Parliament have to be viewed in tandem with informal modes of influence. How these formal and informal dimensions interact will be examined in Chapter 8; in the meantime the powers of the EP will be outlined in relation to the processing of legislation, budgetary control, appointment and dismissal of EU institutions, and scrutiny and control of EU institutions.

Legislative powers

Starting in the twenty-first century: codecision

Codecision2

Most studies of the legislative role of the EP start with a historical review of the incremental advances made since the inception of the EC. Equally most studies note the limited formal legislative powers of the EP before the SEA, Maastricht and Amsterdam Treaties. In fact, some studies still seek to argue that, even after Amsterdam, 'The EP suffers from its hapless image as a powerless, money-wasting "talking shop"' (Peterson and Bomberg 1999:43). But what this chapter argues is that an analysis of the EP in the early twenty-first century should start with the formal powers currently possessed by the EP, and a recognition that the EP is presently and undisputedly a co-legislator in important policy areas with the Council of Ministers. The 'hapless image' is no longer linked to legislative reality. The present reality is that the EP is a major player in the legislative process. For this reason we start the examination of formal legislative powers with the codecision procedure.

Since the Amsterdam Treaty came into effect on 1 May 1999, codecision has become what the EP itself describes as the 'normal legislative procedure' or 'the standard procedure' (http://www.europarl.eu.int/presentation/en/powers.htm). The post-Amsterdam procedure is the second version of codecision, the first being introduced after the Maastricht Treaty, and hence is often referred to as 'codecision2'. Despite the fact that the second version is widely regarded as remaining a highly complex procedure (see Figure 7.1), it represents a considerable simplification of the initial codecision procedure.

Some 38 areas of Community action, extending over 31 treaty articles, are covered by the procedure. In 2001 this meant that over 50 per cent of Commission proposals tabled under the first pillar were processed under codecision (http://www.europa.eu.int/abc/doc/off/rg/en/2001/pt0031.htm #anch0019) with this proportion set to rise further once the Nice Treaty was ratified and implemented.

The Nice Treaty extends codecision to a further seven policy areas where qualified majority voting in Council has been

204

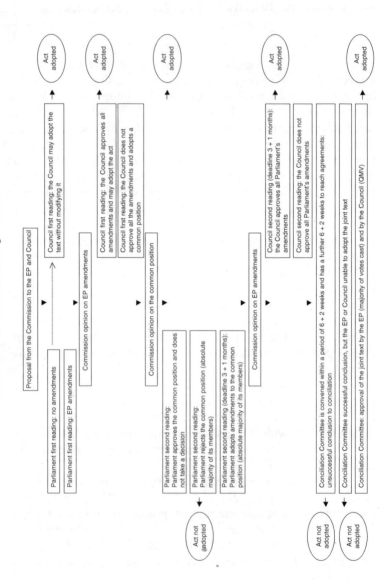

FIGURE 7.1 Codecision2 procedure

introduced. These include incentives to combat discrimination (Article 13), judicial cooperation in civil matters (Article 65), specific industrial support measures (Article 157), economic and social cohesion actions outside the Structural Funds (Article 159), and the statute for European political parties (Article 191). In the case of visas, asylum and immigration policy (Articles 62 and 63) the move to QMV and to codecision is only partial and scheduled to occur at a later date.

Significantly, however, codecision does not apply in all areas where the Council acts by qualified majority. Agriculture and trade policy are the two most glaring exceptions. Indeed, in the case of trade policy the EP has no formal involvement other than, post-Amsterdam, it is to be consulted on extending the provisions of Article 133 to services and intellectual property. Nevertheless, gradually, through the 1990s and into the twenty-first century, the consensus has grown within and beyond Parliament that not only should codecision become the 'normal' procedure but also that it should eventually apply in all cases where Council acts by qualified majority.

The simplest way of conceiving of the procedure is in terms of three stages, or readings, with eight termination or 'exit' points for legislative outcomes.

Under Article 251 the whole process starts with the Commission proposing legislation to the European Parliament and the Council. The Commission retains the sole right of legislative initiative in the case of most treaty articles under the first pillar. The draft regulation, directive or decision is then examined in Parliament, primarily by the relevant parliamentary committee (see Chapters 6 and 8), and, where appropriate, amendments to the Commission's text are tabled before the plenary adopts an 'opinion'. Council simultaneously considers the Commission's proposal and subsequently decides whether to accept or reject the EP's amendments. If no amendments are proposed or, alternatively, if all the amendments contained in the European Parliament's opinion are acceptable to Council, then Council may, by qualified majority, adopt an act at this early stage. These represent the first and second, successful, exit points.

If, however, Council seeks to amend the Commission's proposal and selectively adopt some EP amendments, or not, then its decision is communicated to the EP in the form of a 'common position'. Article 251 requires that the EP should be fully informed of the reasons which led Council to adopt its common position. In turn, the Commission informs Parliament of its response to the Council's amendments.

Once the common position is forwarded to Parliament, a three-month time limit is activated, within which Parliament can, variously: unconditionally approve it or fail to take a decision; reject it by an absolute majority of its members; or amend the common position again by an absolute majority of its members. At this second reading stage, if the EP approves the common position, or alternatively does not take a decision, then an act is adopted in accordance with the common position. This is the third, successful, exit point. If the common position is rejected the legislation falls. This is the fourth exit point, and the first at which there is an unsuccessful legislative outcome. Where amendments are proposed, the amended text is returned to the Council and to the Commission. The Commission has to decide whether to accept or reject Parliament's amendments.

If the Commission favours the amendments, and if Council decides to accept all of Parliament's amendments, a qualified majority in Council will secure the adoption of the text. Alternatively, unanimity is required in Council to adopt the EP's amendments for which the Commission does not offer its support. In either case, this is the fifth exit point. Where the Council rejects one or more of the EP's amendments the proposal is automatically referred to the Conciliation Committee. Negotiations on a compromise text have to be conducted within a period of six weeks. The role and composition of the Committee is set out in Article 251:

> The Conciliation Committee, which shall be composed of the members of the Council or their representatives and an equal number of representatives of the European Parliament, shall have the task of reaching agreement on a joint text, by a qualified majority of the members of the Council or their representatives and by a majority of the representatives of the European Parliament. The Commission shall take part in the Conciliation Committee's proceedings and shall take all the necessary initiatives with a view to reconciling the positions of the European Parliament and the Council. In fulfilling this task, the Conciliation Committee shall address the

common position on the basis of the amendments proposed by the European Parliament.

If conciliation fails to produce an agreed joint text the sixth exit point is reached and the act falls. Otherwise bargaining between Council and Parliament produces a joint text which incorporates agreement on individual EP amendments. This text is agreed independently of the opinion of the Commission, though it may 'take all the necessary initiatives with a view to reconciling the positions of the European Parliament and the Council' (Article 251). At this point, the European Parliament, acting by an absolute majority of the votes cast, and Council, acting by a qualified majority, each have a period of six weeks in which to adopt the joint text. This constitutes the seventh and final positive exit point. An eighth and negative termination point is reached where one of the co-legislative institutions votes against the joint text and the act fails.

The importance of codecision2 is that it provides the EP with a veto which it lacked under preceding legislative procedures. Failure to reach agreement between Council and the EP now effectively results in the failure of legislative proposals. The prospect of producing a negative outcome serves to focus the collective minds of Council and Parliament to reach positive compromises. As Corbett *et al.* (2000:189) note: 'This right to say "no", whether at second reading or during conciliation, gives Parliament a bargaining position which it hitherto lacked regarding Community legislation.' Previously, under codecision1, the legislative power differential had operated in Council's favour.

Codecision1 and cooperation

At this point it is worth noting the main difference between the two versions of the codecision procedure. Codecision1 itself had been 'one of the most significant constitutional changes contained in the Treaty of Maastricht' (Corbett *et al.* 2000:188) and was a development from, and an extension of, the cooperation procedure introduced by the Single European Act. (The general use of codecision2 has largely supplanted the cooperation procedure which, after Nice, now only applies to four EMU provisions: Articles 99(5), 102(2), 103(2) and 106(2)). Despite its shortcomings, the codecision1 procedure enabled the EP, for the first time, to prevent the adoption of EU legislation, even when Council unanimously supported it.

The first stage of codecision1 paralleled the preexisting cooperation procedure, with the EP producing an opinion on the Commission's proposal before Council adopted its common position. However, codecision1 introduced the 'legal innovation' whereby the Commission formally sent its proposal directly to Parliament at the same time as it sent it to the Council (see Chapter 2). Before Maastricht, the Commission had sent its proposal to Council – which subsequently consulted Parliament. Unlike codecision2, however, there was no provision for an agreement to be reached at first reading without Council adopting a common position.

At second reading, under cooperation, a unanimous Council could, with the agreement of the Commission, overrule Parliament's rejection of a common position. If Parliament's amendments were supported by the Commission and incorporated into a revised proposal, then Council could either adopt the revisions by qualified majority, or, alternatively, modify the agreed proposal by unanimity. Any amendments not supported by the Commission also required unanimity to be adopted by the Council. In either case, the Council had the last word on Parliament's amendments.

Codecision1 introduced the convening of a Conciliation Committee if Council did not approve all of Parliament's amendments. A Conciliation Committee could also be convened where the EP declared its 'intention to reject' Council's common position, but the Amsterdam Treaty deleted this complex provision. (In fact, this provision had rarely been applied in practice.)

Where a joint text was agreed in conciliation both Council (by qualified majority) and Parliament (by simple majority) were required to adopt the measure in accordance with the joint text. Failure to approve the text in this way resulted in the proposed act being 'deemed not to have been adopted' (Article 189b(5), now Article 251b(5)) as happened on the biotechnology patenting directive in 1995 (see Chapter 8). This was perceived to be a problem at the time by the French President in Office of the Council, Alain Lamassoure, who regretted 'the European Parliament's rejection of the compromise ... due to an internal problem within that institution. This vote reveals a problem of method in the codecision procedure' (quoted in *Agence Europe* 3 March 1995). But this 'problem' remained inherent within the codecision procedure as Parliament in plenary, rather than its representatives in the Conciliation Committee, had the final say on the legislative measure.

If conciliation did not result in agreement, and Council reconfirmed its common position unchanged, Parliament had either to accept Council's text, or to reject it by an absolute majority. In theory, Council could adopt the text unilaterally in such circumstances. On the only occasion it chose to do so, on voice telephony, the EP managed to construct an absolute majority and confirm rejection (see Chapter 8).

Consultation

As noted in Chapter 2, the consultation procedure was the initial legislative procedure from which the cooperation and codecision procedures ultimately derived. What Chapter 2 also revealed was that the capacity of the EP to affect legislation under this procedure was entirely conditional upon both the Commission and the Council incorporating parliamentary amendments into a proposal. Even after Amsterdam, the consultation procedure featured in no less than 66 treaty provisions (Maurer 1999a:9) and continued to be applied to significant areas of EU policy such as: agriculture, the harmonization of indirect taxation, private sector competition, the harmonization of national provisions affecting the internal market and specific measures relating to industrial policy, nuclear energy and radiation, as well as to fiscal aspects of environmental policy. Asylum and immigration issues were also subject to consultation (for a full list see Corbett *et al.* 2000:184). The Amsterdam Treaty also introduced a new form of consultation under the third pillar (Article 34(2)(b,c,d) (ex Article K.6 TEU)) for the purpose of approximation of laws and regulations relating to police and judicial cooperation. Under the new procedure Council can set a deadline of not less than three months within which Parliament has to submit its opinion. If an opinion is not provided within the deadline then Council can proceed to adopt the measure unilaterally.

Assent procedure

The assent procedure was introduced by Articles 8 and 9 of the Single European Act and subsequently extended in both the Treaties of Maastricht and Amsterdam. Assent is simply 'an "authorisation" without which a legislative act cannot be definitely adopted by the Council' (Maurer 1999b:46). In the first instance, under the SEA, Parliament's assent was required before Council could enact association agreements with third countries and the accession of new member states. Maastricht and Amsterdam added further areas to the scope of the assent procedure: sanctions for the breach of fundamental human rights; special tasks entrusted to the European Central Bank; amendments to the protocol of European System of Central Banks; specific aspects of the organization of the Structural Funds and the creation of the Cohesion Fund; uniform procedures for European elections; and international agreements under Article 300(3) covering specific institutional frameworks, budgetary implications, or entailing amendment of legislation adopted under codecision. In turn, the Nice Treaty required the assent of the EP under Article 7 (TEU) before the Council could decide that there was a clear risk of a serious breach of fundamental rights. Assent was also extended to enhanced cooperation under the first pillar. The assent procedure now covers aspects of both external relations and internal EU legislative competences. In total, the assent procedure is present in 13 treaty provisions (see Maurer 1999a:9). In two cases, relating to the duties of the Ombudsman and the general conditions governing the duties of MEPs, the assent of the Council is required for Parliament to act. In these specific cases, the assent procedure is reversed.

Corbett *et al.* (2000:204) describe the assent procedure as 'a cruder form of codecision in that there is no scope for Parliament to put forward amendments to the measure in question'. Indeed, one weakness of the assent procedure is that it does not provide a mechanism whereby the EP and the Council can settle their differences. In fact, some commentators argue that the power is a 'nuclear' one and hence MEPs are reluctant to use it (Smith 1999:76). Nonetheless, it is a significant power and comparable with the ratification procedures possessed by most national parliaments in relation to international agreements. Moreover, it is not simply negative. As Dietmar Nickel (1999:5) argues:

> we are confronted with a misunderstanding ... power is often construed as being the negative use, a decision not to do something. This is just wrong. You use your assent power for instance for an enlargement as much when you vote in favour as when you say no.

Ultimately the most pressing constraint upon the EP's negative use of the assent procedure is simply that in most instances withholding assent is a blunt weapon if Parliament is anxious to see association agreements, enlargement or other favoured internal legislation come into effect.

Initiation of legislation

The EP has, through 'own-initiative reports' under Rule 163 and members' 'motions for resolution' tabled under Rule 48, been able to participate indirectly in the initiation of legislation (see Chapter 2; Judge 1993:191–3; Judge and Earnshaw 1994:263–6). Own-initiative reports are drafted by the responsible committee and adopted by a majority of MEPs present at plenary as with other reports and resolutions. Since 1982 the Commission has agreed in principle to pursue any parliamentary initiative to which it did not have major objections. On the occasions when it has objected the Commission has explained its position to Parliament. More generally it has also reported regularly to the relevant committee on progress made on parliamentary initiatives. The classic example of the EP's legislative initiative remains the ban on the import of baby seal skins (as early as 1982), though more recent examples include the 1998 proposal to ban tobacco advertising which had its origins in a parliamentary initiative in 1990.

The Maastricht Treaty granted the EP a comparable right to that of the Council to initiate legislative proposals. Under Article 192 the EP, acting by an absolute majority of its members, is empowered to request the Commission 'to submit any appropriate proposal on matters on which it considers that a Community act is required for the purpose of implementing this Treaty'. Parliament's experience with the procedure has been mixed. One of the earliest examples of the use of the provision was Parliament's request in May 1994 that a liability regime for environmental damage should be established in EU law. Parliament's proposal followed an earlier Commission proposal on civil liability for damage caused by waste, which had sat before Council for some years before eventually being withdrawn, and a Commission Green Paper on environmental liability published in 1993. Parliament also held a joint hearing with the Commission on environmental liability during the same year. However, only in January 2002 – nearly eight years after the original parliamentary initiative – did the Commission submit a legislative proposal providing for environmental liability. Even then, the Commission was only prompted into action by Parliament's threat to derail another of the Commission's proposals – on the deliberate release of genetically modified organisms – if the proposal on liability was not submitted.

A somewhat more expeditious application of Article 192 (then 138b) occurred with legislation on the settlement of claims arising from traffic accidents outside the claimant's country of origin. Adopted in October 1995, Parliament's resolution under Article 138b sought a Commission proposal to harmonize national provisions relating to liability in car insurance, and thereby to protect consumers and the victims of traffic accidents. Some half a million tourists are involved in accidents in a member state other than their own each year, and an obvious legal vacuum existed in EU law in settling accident claims. In October 1997 the Commission brought forward a proposal (COM[97]510 final), in line with Parliament's request, and this was approved in Parliament's first reading in July 1998. In December of that year Council reached a political agreement on the proposal, and reached a formal common position in May 1999. Parliament's second reading took place in December 1999, and the measure was agreed in conciliation in March 2000, with formal adoption in May 2000.

In early 2000 the boundaries of Article 192 were pushed still further. On this occasion, the European Ombudsman (see below) creatively proposed, in a special report submitted to the EP President, that Parliament should use the procedure to request the Commission to submit a proposal for a regulation on a code of good administrative conduct in the EU institutions (*Agence Europe* 20 April 2000).

Budgetary powers

Chapter 2 chronicled the acquisition of significant budgetary powers by Parliament after the creation of the EC's 'own resources' in 1970 and further treaty revision in 1975. While the formal powers have remained little altered in over thirty years, Parliament's influence upon the EU's finances has extended with the signing of successive interinstitutional agreements. The first was signed in 1988 and by 1999 four had been signed in total (see Chapter 2).

Julie Smith (1999:74) notes that 'The EP's role in budgetary affairs is highly significant, since it has a much larger say than most national parliaments.' If anything, however, the EP's budgetary powers are the reverse of those traditionally exercised by parliaments. Whereas national parliaments have historically focused upon exercising control over the raising of revenues – under the rallying cry of 'no taxation without representation' – and thereby subsequently and indirectly influencing expenditure decisions, the EP has exercised control over expenditure but has had little say over the raising of revenue. This 'peculiarity' in the exercise of the EP's budgetary powers is a reflection of the EU's own unique financial arrangements. The EU has four revenue sources aggregated in its 'own resources': customs tariffs and other duties collected in trade with non-member states (15 per cent of revenue); agricultural levies, premiums and other duties collected within the framework of the Common Agricultural Policy (CAP) (2 per cent); currently up to 1 per cent of the VAT base in member states (38 per cent); and a contribution from member states, calculated from a base rate of their respective gross national products, and reflecting their ability to pay (43 per cent). The remaining 2 per cent consists of miscellaneous revenue and surpluses from the previous year (for details see Laffan and Shackleton 1996:94; Nugent 1999:393–4).

Whereas Parliament has had no power to vary revenues, since the treaty revision of 1975 it has accumulated significant powers over expenditure. Even so, Parliament's control over expenditure has been limited by the technical, and largely artificial, distinction made in the EU between 'compulsory' and 'non-compulsory' expenditure. Expenditure which results directly from the application of treaty obligations is deemed 'compulsory'. In contrast, 'non-compulsory' spending has been defined as 'avoidable expenditure where the Union enjoys broad discretion as to the level of expenditure that it incurs' (Corbett *et al.* 2000:225). Exactly what this distinction meant in practice was the cause of a 25-year battle between the EP and Council. Throughout that period Parliament consistently challenged the distinction made between the two types of expenditure. It had a vested interest in doing so, as MEPs had only limited scope to influence non-compulsory expenditure. Effectively this meant that some 80 per cent of the EU's spending, most notably the Common Agriculture Policy, was largely shrouded from EP scrutiny and control. In fact, the annual budgetary cycle was characterized by differences over the classification of expenditure as the EP sought to expand the areas over which it had influence. Correspondingly, it also sought to increase expenditure in those areas in which it could make the final allocation (regional policy, education, transport, social policy). On both counts the EP had some considerable success. By 1999 55 per cent of EU expenditure was classified as non-compulsory with the Structural Funds accounting for 35 per cent of the total EU budget.

The issue of the classification of expenditure came to a head in 1995, when the Council sought to annul the budget adopted by the EP in the Court of Justice (Case C-41/95). Both the Council and the Commission maintained that Parliament had adopted 131 amendments on compulsory expenditure – which it had no right to amend. Given the disagreement between the two arms of the budgetary authority, the Court ruled in December 1995 that the budget process was incomplete. The reasoning was that as agreement had not been reached the act was illegal and hence the budget was invalid. The Court did not make a judgment upon the respective classifications of compulsory or non-compulsory expenditure but referred the matter of definition back to the two institutions comprising the budgetary authority. Following this judgment, protracted negotiations between the Council and Parliament resulted in Annex IV of the 1999 Interinstitutional Agreement which clarified the classification of expenditure. Moreover, the 1999 Agreement specified that the preliminary draft budget should contain a proposal for the classification of each new budget item and each item with an amended legal base. If there was disagreement over the proposed classification then the two institutions agreed to 'examine classification of the budget item concerned on the basis of Annex IV' (OJ C 172, 18 June 1999:point 31).

At the same time as MEPs campaigned to increase the proportion of non-compulsory expenditure they simultaneously sought to increase the maximum level of expenditure permissible under the treaties. According to Article 272 Parliament, with the agreement of the Council, can propose an increase in the annual maximum rate of increase in non-compulsory expenditure calculated by the Commission prior to the submission of its preliminary draft budget for the following year. In making its calculation the Commission is required to take into account macro-economic indicators in member states such as levels of economic growth, government spending and the rates of inflation. In 2000 and 2001 the maximum rate of increase was calculated at 3 and 3.3 per cent respectively.

Given the relatively low voting hurdles that had to be jumped (at least in comparison to increasing own resources) there were few disincentives for MEPs not to seek to increase the maximum rate of increase. 'The result was that the Parliament spent much of the 1980s up to 1988 trying to convince the Council to agree to an increase in the maximum rate' (Westlake 1994a:125). In reverse, the Council spent much of the 1980s trying to curb spiralling EU expenditure, largely fuelled by agricultural transfers, in the face of severe macro-economic problems in member states. In 1985 the differences between the Council and Parliament reached a climax when the EP's President signed a budget for 1986 which exceeded the calculated maximum rate by more than 600 million ECUs. Council challenged the EP's unilateral action in the Court of Justice (Case C-34/86) and received confirmation in the Court's ruling that any new maximum rate had to have the explicit agreement of both arms of the budgetary authority. When, in 1986, Parliament again amended non-compulsory expenditure above the maximum rate, the EP's President did not sign the budget this time in acknowledgement that the increase had not been agreed with the Council. Within a few months an agreement was eventually reached which increased the maximum rate of increase from 8.1 per cent to 8.149 per cent, and which allowed both institutions to claim some sort of credit (for details see Corbett *et al.* 2000:227).

In view of the persistent annual disputes over the maximum rate of increase, as well as those over the classification of expenditure, it was generally acknowledged that some reform was required of the budget process. Reform eventually came in the context of the reexamination of the EU finances in the 'Delors-1 Package' (see Laffan and Shackleton 2000:219–21) when an Interinstitutional Agreement on 'budgetary discipline and the improvement of the budgetary procedure' was signed between the Council, the Commission and the EP. This Agreement entered into force in July 1988 and largely resolved two of the main points of friction between the institutions. First, it adopted a five-year financial perspective in which it was agreed to respect the expenditure levels proposed in six categories of expenditure. Within this five-year horizon a detailed financial framework for each year could then be agreed. Importantly, this arrangement severed the linkage between increases in compulsory expenditure and reductions in the amounts available for non-compulsory expenditure. Effectively the Council conceded a substantial increase in non-compulsory expenditure, with a specific commitment to the doubling of expenditure on the Structural Funds, by the end of the first five-year period. Such a commitment could only be fulfilled, however, if the normal calculation of the maximum rate of increase was exceeded. Moreover, the Interinstitutional Agreement included the provision that the institutions could agree to exceed the permissible maximum rate in advance of any specific annual agreement. In so doing, the 1988 Agreement 'transformed the argument about the maximum rate of increase' (Corbett *et al.* 2000:228). In the event, however, it did not remove all disputation from the budget process.

In particular, Parliament's attempts to maximize the rate of increase continued to meet with opposition from the Council. Ever willing to advance a creative interpretation of procedures, the EP argued that it could increase spending to the maximum permitted level in each category and then assume that the overall total was acceptable to the Council. Council on the other hand proved unwilling to accept this assumption and threatened to challenge it in the Court of Justice in 1992. This threat was dropped when the matter was resolved after the 1992 Edinburgh European Council.

As part of a wide-ranging package on the financing of the EU up to 1999, the Edinburgh Council determined specific annual financial allocations for each of six expenditure categories, and established new revenue ceilings to allow for an overall increase of 1.27 per cent of GNP by 1999. A further part of the package was Council's concession that it would accept in advance, within the overall ceiling, the maximum rates of increase for non-compulsory spending voted by Parliament. In return, Parliament conceded the principle that maximum rates of increase would be set below the absolute ceilings in each category to accommodate any necessary additional expenditure in any one year (OJ C 172, 18 June 1999).

Certainly the 1999 Interinstitutional Agreement marked a transformation in the budgetary process. As Corbett *et al.* (2000:218) note:

> The two institutions increasingly seek mutually acceptable outcomes based on a shared perception of each other's role, rather than Parliament attempting to use the Treaty articles to impose its will on the Council. The combined effect of the financial perspective and the new rules and procedures has been to reinforce substantially the smooth running and predictability of the budgetary procedure.

The 1999 Agreement marked not only the resolution of the differences over technicalities – of classification of expenditure and maximum rate of increase – but also confirmed the changed priorities of the EP in the use of its budgetary powers. In turn these changed priorities reflected wider changes in the interinstitutional relationship between Council and Parliament. The EP's initial strategy of maximizing its policy influence through the budgetary process (at a time of limited legislative powers), and the ensuing endemic competition with the Council, gave way to cooperation with the Council on management issues (Laffan and Shackleton 1996:95). The initial focus on the authorization of expenditure has given way to greater concern with monitoring how it is spent and in curbing fraud and financial mismanagement (see below).

Treaty-prescribed powers

As noted above, under Article 272 the EP is a twin arm, alongside the Council, of the 'budgetary authority'. What this means in practice is that Parliament is able to propose modification to compulsory expenditure, within defined limits, but is dependent upon Council's acceptance of its proposals. In other words, the final say on such expenditure rests with the Council. On 'non-compulsory expenditure', however, the EP has the last word.

The procedures through which these powers are effected allow the EP to propose amendments when debating Council's draft budget at first reading. The Council has 15 days in which to respond. Where the Council informs Parliament that it accepts these amendments without modification the EP's President is empowered to declare that the budget has been finally adopted (European Parliament 1999:Annex 4, Article 4). Council may, by qualified majority, modify and refer back to Parliament its amendments on non-compulsory expenditure. When the draft budget returns to the EP after the Council's second reading, Parliament can no longer modify compulsory expenditure but it can, by three-fifths of votes cast, amend Council's modifications to non-compulsory expenditure. When this process has been completed and Council has acknowledged that the outcome is in conformity with the financial provisions of the treaties, it is the responsibility of the President of the Parliament to sign the budget into law.

Where agreement cannot be reached between the two arms of the budgetary authority on amendments to the draft budget, Article 272 ultimately empowers the EP to reject the draft budget as a whole. On three occasions, in December 1979, 1982 and 1984, Parliament expressed its dissatisfaction with the draft budget by finding the necessary two-thirds majority for rejection and so requiring Council to submit a new draft. On these occasions a complex procedure was activated which allowed the Commission to continue spending on the basis of 'provisional twelfths'. This provision allows the Commission to spend each month the equivalent of one month's expenditure as in the preceding year's budget or as projected in the draft budget before it was rejected. In effect this allows the Union to continue functioning but does not allow for increased expenditure or new projects to be undertaken. Given Parliament's general predisposition in favour of both increased spending and new financial commitments there is a disincentive for MEPs to use the procedure, a disincentive which has increased with the signing of each successive interinstitutional agreement.

Discharge

As noted above, Parliament has increasingly become concerned to ensure sound financial management in the implementation of the EU's budget. In this task the EP is assisted by the Court of Auditors which conducts detailed audits of the accounts of all EU bodies. The Court of Auditors examines the accounts of all revenue and expenditure and verifies their 'legality, regularity ... and examines whether financial management has been sound' (PE 167.189 1997:2). The Court then produces an annual report which includes separate sections detailing the activities of each of the institutions in that financial year. In addition, since the Maastricht Treaty, the Court of Auditors has been required to issue a 'statement of assurance on the reliability of the accounts and the legality and regularity of the underlying transactions for each financial year' (Court of Auditors http://www.eca.eu.int/EN/coa3.htm). The annual report and the statement of assurance are subsequently forwarded to the EP, which, since 1975, has had the exclusive right to approve (grant a discharge) or disapprove (not grant a discharge) the Commission's implementation of the budget. The actual processing and assessment of the Auditors' reports is entrusted to the EP's Committee on Budgetary Control, which recommends whether or not Parliament should discharge the Commission's handling of the budget.

'The power to grant or not to grant discharge therefore represents the strongest expression of Parliament's political control over the Commission as regards its responsibility in implementing the budget' (PE 229.285 1998:5). In fact, so great was the negative power implicit in a refusal to grant discharge that neither the Treaties nor the Communities' Financial Regulation formally contemplated the consequences of such a refusal (Corbett *et al.* 2000:254). On the only occasion before 1999 that Parliament refused to grant discharge, in November 1984, the Commission was within weeks of its planned termination of office and hence the procedural logic – that a motion of censure or the Commission's resignation would follow – was not fulfilled.

The connection between failure to grant discharge and the resignation of the Commission will be examined in Chapter 8. Here, however, it is the 'positive' dimension – the power to grant discharge – which needs some further examination. Corbett *et al.* (2000:253) make clear that discharge 'is much more than an annual ritual: it is as much a *power* as a procedure'. It is a formal statement that the EP accepts the manner in which the Commission has implemented the budget. In making its judgment Parliament has asserted its right to require the Commission to provide all necessary information (given treaty status in Article 206(2)) and to ensure that the 'Commission should take all appropriate steps to act on observations by the European Parliament relating to the execution of expenditure' (Article 206(3)). In recent years the EP, acting through its Committee on Budgetary Control, has used the process of discharge to investigate allegations of financial mismanagement, fraud and irregularities. In so doing, it has encountered problems in eliciting information from the Commission and in securing an adequate response to its observations and recommendations (see PE 226.077 1998). In these circumstances the EP devised a strategy of postponing a decision on discharge, and thereby giving notice to the Commission that it expected missing information to be provided or remedial action to be taken, or both, by a given deadline. Implicit in the postponement of discharge was a threat. This threat was made explicit in the Budgetary Control Committee's report on the postponement of discharge for the 1996 financial year (PE 226.077 1998:20):

> in proposing that the discharge be postponed, it is by no means your rapporteur's intention to start a witch hunt against the Commission leading eventually to its inevitable resignation. On the contrary, this is constructive criticism, and your rapporteur ... just wants to set the ball rolling. The Commission must be aware, however, that if it fails to heed the barking of the watchdogs, no-one will protect it from the bloodhounds.

This warning proved to be prophetic in view of the ensuing events over the discharge of the 1996 budget and the subsequent resignation of the Santer Commission in 1999 (see Chapter 8).

Appointment and dismissal

The Commission

It was noted in Chapter 1 that a basic feature of parliamentary systems is that political executives are selected by the legislature. In this sense there is a fusion of executive and legislative roles. Moreover, 'In a parliamentary system, the chief executive ... and his or her cabinet are responsible to the legislature in the sense that they are dependent on the legislature's confidence and that they can be dismissed from office by a legislative vote of no confidence or censure' (Lijphart 1984:68). The logic of this system, therefore, is that the executive should retain the confidence of the legislature because it derives both its legitimacy and its authority from the representative parliament. An important corollary of this logic is the general belief that 'Parliaments are supposed to control the operation of the executive' (Dehousse 1998:598). The exact degree of control is determined, in turn, by the formal and informal constraints that the legislature is able to place upon the executive and vice versa (see Blondel 1973:45–54). This returns us to Mezey's (1979:25) notion of constraint identified at the beginning of this chapter and in Chapter 1. The constraints of concern here are those that the EP can exercise over the formation and dismissal of the Commission. There are both negative and positive dimensions to these powers, and variations in the degree of constraint attendant upon the exercise of these powers.

Appointment of the Commission

Historically the EU's process for the appointment of the Commission was intergovernmental, consensual and driven by domestic political considerations (Jacobs 1999:3). Initially the EP had no say in the appointment process, but then through gradual increments attained the dual right to be consulted upon the choice of the Commission President, and also to assent to the choice of the College of Commissioners as a whole.

Article 214(2) of the Amsterdam Treaty went further:

> The governments of the Member States shall nominate by common accord the person they intend to appoint as President of the Commission; the nomination shall be approved by the European Parliament.
>
> The governments of the Member States shall, by common accord with the nominee for President, nominate the other persons whom they intend to appoint as Members of the Commission.
>
> The President and the other Members of the Commission thus nominated shall be subject as a body to a vote of approval by the European Parliament. After approval by the European Parliament, the President and the other Members of the Commission shall be appointed by common accord of the governments of the Member States.

The main change effected in the Amsterdam Treaty was that the appointment of the President of the Commission was no longer simply contingent upon consultation with Parliament but was now dependent upon the formal approval of the EP. In turn the influence of the President over the choice of the College of Commissioners was enhanced. This was taken a step further in the Nice Treaty. Under the provisions of Nice the President is to be nominated by the European Council acting by qualified majority. The appointed President and Council (again acting by qualified majority) then adopt the list of proposed Commissioners. After approval of the body of Commissioners by the EP, Council ultimately appoints the Commission, again by qualified majority.

In practice, however, these changes marked an incremental advance on already existing procedures adopted by the EP after the Maastricht Treaty. After Maastricht the EP as a whole, rather than just its enlarged Bureau, was involved in the consultation process in the choice of Commission President. Moreover there was a formal vote to record Parliament's verdict. In drafting its new rules to take account of the Maastricht changes the EP decided that it would 'elect or reject the Commission by a majority of the votes cast' (Rule 33). Implicitly the EP maintained that if a negative vote was recorded then the nominee would be withdrawn (Hix 2000b:98). This interpretation found confirmation in 1994 when Jacques Santer, at the time that his nomination for Commission President was initially canvassed, made it clear that he would withdraw if Parliament voted against him. Further confirmation came from the then Council Presidency (Germany) that a new candidate would have to be found in the event of a negative vote by the EP (Hix 2000b:98).

In addition, the Maastricht Treaty synchronized the Commission's term of office with that of Parliament. The appointment of the President, and of the Commission as a whole, was now designed to coincide with that of a new parliament. The intention was that the coterminous mandates of the EP and the Commission would facilitate 'parliamentary scrutiny and control as well as the feeling of Commissioners that they were accountable to Parliament' (Corbett *et al.* 2000:235–6). To maximize parliamentary control the EP sought to establish the principle of 'prior authorization' whereby individual Commissioners-designate would appear before its committees to identify the Commission's policy priorities. In amending its Rules of Procedure, new Rule 33 requested 'nominees proposed for the various posts of Commissioners to appear before the appropriate committees according to their prospective fields of responsibility'. These hearings were to be held in public, and, significantly, were scheduled before the confirmation vote was to be taken. Each Commissioner-designate was requested to make a statement to the relevant committee and answer questions. The main objectives of the hearings, as described by the EP itself, were:

> to prepare the way for the final EP vote on the Commission as a whole by providing insights into the personalities and views of the various nominees. The hearings process also helps to strengthen the democratic accountability and legitimacy of the Commission and, in case of approval of the Commission, to establish a working relationship between Parliament's Committees and the relevant Commissioner at the earliest possible moment. Finally they also serve as an initial benchmark for examining the subsequent performance of the Commissioner concerned. (see http://www.europarl. eu.int/dg3/com/en/default.htm)

January 1995 saw the first use of 'confirmation hearings' for Commissioners, when the newly enlarged Parliament scrutinized nominees for the Santer Commission. No formal votes were held at the end of each committee hearing, simply because the EP had no power to reject individual nominees. Instead, each committee chair wrote to the President of the Parliament expressing the committee's evaluation of each Commissioner-designate. In turn, the President of the Parliament convened a press conference to discuss the published conclusions of the committees. Although negative comments on individual Commissioners were voiced (particularly on Bjerregaard and Flynn), they had little tangible effect on the outcome of the vote on the Commission as a whole, other than the reallocation of one aspect of Commissioner Flynn's portfolio (see Corbett 1995:40–1). Nonetheless, at the time, Fitzmaurice (1994:183) identified the new Maastricht confirmation provisions as possibly 'one of the most significant of the institutional reforms' in that they 'could imply a more parliamentary Commission in the long term'.

The second confirmation hearings were held in September 1999 when the new Parliament considered nominees for Romano Prodi's Commission. The basic format of the 1995 hearings was retained. All hearings were held in public with nominated Commissioners making brief ten-minute oral statements followed by question-and-answer sessions in the respective committees lasting up to three hours. Live transmission of proceedings were relayed to overflow rooms, and full verbatim transcripts, translated into all official languages, were placed on the Internet site of the Parliament. Each committee then made its assessment in a closed session at the end of the hearing with the committee chair forwarding the results in writing to the President of Parliament.

One significant innovation in the 1999 hearings was a common written questionnaire which all nominees were required to return two weeks in advance of the scheduled committee meetings which began on 30 August. Each questionnaire was divided into approximately five sections: personal and professional experience relevant to the prospective role as Commissioner; independence in terms of any restraining personal and national commitments; views on the future development of the European Union; conceptions of the Commission's democratic accountability to the European Parliament; and specific questions on policy portfolio(s) to be held by the individual Commissioner. The replies varied in length from 16 pages (Pedro Solbes Mira, Commissioner-designate for Economic and Monetary Union) to 103 pages (Franz Fischler, Commissioner-designate for Agriculture). In the middle range, at 51 pages, was the written response of Loyola de Palacio, the Commissioner- and Vice-President-designate for Transport, Energy and relations with the European Parliament. Mrs de Palacio had to answer specific questions not only from the Committee on Regional Policy, Transport and Tourism but also from the Committees on Constitutional Affairs, on Industry, External Trade, Research and Energy and on Petitions, as well as additional questions tabled by political groups.

In general, the responses were cautious, with a common line clearly visible on the questions relating to the individual responsibilities of Commissioners and their accountability to the EP. All nominees stated that they would resign if the Commission President called upon them to do so (see below), and all offered a variation upon Mrs de Palacio's answer to the question: How do you envisage the nature of your responsibility to the European Parliament?

> Under the Treaty, the Commission is, collectively, politically accountable to the European Parliament. On the other hand, all members of the Commission must account to Parliament for their actions and submit to its political control; for this purpose they remain at the full disposal of Parliament and appear before parliamentary committees as often as necessary, supplying all the information which Parliament requires in order to exercise control: in other words, they are democratically answerable to Parliament. (http://www.europarl. eu.int/ hearings/pdf/com/answer/depalaci/default_en.pdf)

Ultimately, however, as Gareth Harding observed in *European Voice* (9–15 September 1999): 'As with all job interviews, the problem is that candidates will say almost anything to get the post. Promises to provide MEPs with all documents and appear before parliamentary committees at every available opportunity therefore have to be taken with a pinch of salt.'

What also characterized the interview process were the increased levels of preparation on both sides from those apparent in 1995. A further characteristic was the increased partisanship of proceedings, with EPP MEPs openly critical of the overall left-of-centre bias of the incoming Commission and of specific Socialist Commissioner-designates. In particular, Phillipe Busquin, former Walloon Socialist leader, encountered sustained hostile questioning from EPP members of the Industry Committee on his alleged proximity to a number of domestic political scandals. In return, Socialist MEPs responded in kind with fierce criticisms of Spanish Christian Democrat Loyola de Palacio, and succeeded in delaying for a short period the decision on her nomination.

Certainly, the hearings provided insights into the 'personalities, views and experience of the nominees', as well as opportunities for partisan point scoring, but they were also designed to review the proposed structure of the Commission as a whole and whether the portfolios were the most appropriate ones. More particularly, the hearings were supposed to provide an opportunity for the EP to assess the Commission's proposed overall policy programme and its policy priorities (http://www.europarl.eu.int/dg3/com/en/default.htm). In effect, this was to allow for benchmarks to be identified by which the subsequent performance of the Commission could then be assessed.

Clearly, the logic of 'control through selection' shines through the EP's stated purpose of its confirmation hearings. The reasoning is simple in that it is believed that the post-Amsterdam appointment process would increase not only the EP's influence over who is appointed as President (and subsequently as Commissioners and to which specific portfolios) but also that it would enhance Parliament's impact on the Commission's policy agenda by securing the prior 'authorization' of the executive's programme. While such 'conditionality' is simple to conceive of in theory, in practice, as the experience of the 1999 Parliament illustrates, it rapidly becomes enmeshed in the complexities of 'party politics' (see Chapter 8 and below).

Nonetheless, even if the positive dimension of 'prior authorization' has yet to be fully explored, the implicit negative sanction of the hearings remains. Very simply, nominees for the Commission would be hard pushed to resist their rejection as a result of the hearings. As one of the Commission nominees involved in 1999 hearings noted: 'Mais on imagine mal qu'un [ou une] commissaire pressenti[e] ait pu se maintenir si la commission parliamentaire qui l'avait auditionné[e] avait émis un avis formellement négatif' ('But one cannot imagine that a nominated Commissioner could be able to remain if the parliamentary committee which had heard him or her had formally adopted a negative opinion') (Lamy 2002:40).

Censure and dismissal of the Commission

Under Article 201 the EP has the capacity to force the Commission to resign as a body if a motion of censure is carried by a two-thirds majority of the votes cast, representing a majority of the members of the European Parliament. Yet the EP has never actually used this formal power, 1999 notwithstanding. In part, this is because of the procedural inhibitions on the exercise of this power, whereby a double majority is required in Parliament to secure the collective dismissal of the Commission. In larger part, however, the failure to adopt a motion of censure is because the power of dismissal is a 'nuclear weapon' in Parliament's procedural armoury. As noted repeatedly throughout this book Parliament and Commission historically have shared a common institutional perspective which has been reinforced by close working arrangements and interinstitutional agreements between the two institutions. In Hix's words (1999:47), 'the EP is aware that the Commission, as a fellow supra-national institution, is more often an ally against the Council than an enemy'. As a result, Parliament has proved reluctant to deploy the negative weapon of censure. Moreover, the fact that the weapon is targeted at the Commission collectively, and aimed at the College of Commissioners as a whole, means that it is an indiscriminate weapon.

The dismissal of individual Commissioners is not countenanced in the censure procedure. Indeed, this is the obverse of the appointments procedure, for just as the EP consents to the formation of the College of Commissioners as a collectivity, and not to the appointment of individual Commissioners, so MEPs censure the Commission as a whole and not as individual Commissioners. Despite several attempts before 1999 to extend the right of dismissal to individual Commissioners, successive IGCs and treaty revisions failed to incorporate such a provision (see Corbett 1998:324; Spence 2000:9–10). One reason was the reticence of national governments to see any parliamentary encroachment upon their capacity to nominate Commissioners and to press for specific portfolios. Another reason was the continuing commitment within the Commission to Monnet's original principle that collegiality enabled the Commission to stand collectively against pressures from national governments (Spence 2000:10). If collegiality was designed initially as a protective shield – to ensure a realm of policy independence for individual Commissioners when confronted by contrasting policy preferences by national governments – it also served simultaneously to shelter Commissioners from accountability to Parliament. Nonetheless, Parliament itself has also continued to subscribe to the initial Monnet view 'that it is essential to ensure the complete independence of the Commission, its role as guardian of the treaties and its collective responsibility' (PE 232.758 2000).

The fact that a censure motion has not been successful has not prevented the EP from tabling such motions. Nine motions had been tabled before the censure vote in January 1999 – five since direct elections. All failed to come close to meeting the double majority requirement of the procedure. The closest censure vote before the 'Commission crisis' was on the handling of the 'BSE crisis' in 1997 when 73 per cent of MEPs voted but only one-quarter (118) of those who voted supported the motion (see Lord 1998:89; Maurer 1999a:54–5).

These earlier votes appeared to confirm Westlake's assessment that such motions were used as 'proof that the [nuclear] weapon exists rather than of any serious intention to use it' (1994a:115). The key to understanding the censure 'weapon', therefore, was 'the ever-present threat of potential sanction' (Westlake 1994a:115). It ensured that both the Parliament and Commission had a vested interest in securing interinstitutional cooperation rather than conflict (see Judge and Earnshaw 1999:7). Indeed, the Commission from the outset was extremely sensitive to any suggestion that the power might be used. In this sense, the negative power of censure and dismissal helped to forge a positive and constructive relationship between Parliament and the Commission. As such it has played a central role in the political and constitutional development of the European Union.

Perhaps, not surprisingly given the events surrounding the resignation of the Santer Commission, the negative dimension of individual resignations and the individual responsibility of Commissioners preoccupied the incoming Commission President in 1999. Prodi anticipated that Parliament 'might in future require guarantees from individual Commissioners that they would resign if an individual motion of censure by the Parliament required it' (Spence 2000:10). The occasion for such guarantees to be requested would be during Parliament's confirmation hearings. As the report of the 'Three Wise Men' made clear (in its examination of the 'institutional problems which needed to be tackled' before enlargement):

> Recent events have raised the question of the individual responsibility of Commissioners and of reconciling it with the collective responsibility of the Commission. President Prodi is dealing with this in an informal manner by requesting in advance the agreement of Commissioners to resign if he so requires. The group believes that this informal arrangement should be formalised in the treaty, so as to confirm the authority of the President, with due respect for the collegial character of the Commission. This would also clarify the respective powers of Parliament and President regarding the performance and tenure of Commissioners. (von Weizsäcker, Dehaene and Simon 1999:8)

Ultimately, however, the informal arrangement instigated by Prodi left the fate of individual Commissioners in the hands of the President rather than in those of the EP. It was this arrangement that was tested during the course of the confirmation hearings in September 1999, with each Commissioner-designate being asked if they would be willing to resign at the request of the President. Nonetheless, it needs to be remembered that Parliament itself still did not possess the formal power to censure, dismiss or initiate a vote of confidence in individual Commissioners. Indeed, as noted above, it remains committed to the notion of the collective responsibility of the Commission. But to many, both within and outside of the EP, 'after the [1999] resignation it became clear that censorship of individuals was essential' (Spence 2000:10).

As noted in Chapter 2, the Treaty of Nice strengthened the role of the President, but Parliament's involvement in the appointment procedure was increased only marginally. Its most radical demands – for the parliamentary election of the President by the EP and for the Commission to be subject to a vote of confidence – received only scant attention at the 2000 IGC. In this specific regard, the advance towards a more 'parliamentary system' of governance was stalled at Nice.

Appointments to other EU bodies

In addition to its formal powers over the appointment of the Commission the EP is also involved in the nomination processes for the Court of Auditors, the European Ombudsman, the European Monetary Institute, the European Central Bank, and the executive boards of some EU agencies (such as the European Medicines Agency and the European Environment Agency). As Westlake (1998:432) notes 'all [of these powers] are interrelated and, in procedural terms have borrowed from each other'. But Westlake's assessment needs to be qualified in two ways. First, a distinction needs to be made between, on the one hand, appointments to quasi-parliamentary institutions such as the Court of Auditors, the European Ombudsman and, on the other, to quasi-executive bodies such as the European Monetary Institute and the European Central Bank. Second, there was little procedural borrowing in the appointment procedure of the European Ombudsman.

The European Ombudsman

The post of European Ombudsman was introduced by the Maastricht Treaty. The Ombudsman is empowered to investigate complaints of maladministration by Community institutions or (non-judicial) bodies. Any EU citizen or 'any natural or legal person' residing in a member state may contact the Ombudsman directly or alternatively route their complaint through an MEP. The duties of the Ombudsman are regulated by Parliament and are annexed to the EP's Rules of Procedure. (The Commission expressed its opinion on the rules governing the performance of these duties and they were also approved by the Council.) The Ombudsman is 'parliamentary' in the literal sense of being appointed by Parliament. Indeed, Westlake (1998:437) refers to the office as the 'parliamentary ombudsman'. The EP exercises exclusive control of the nomination process, with member governments, unusually in EU appointments, having no input. Moreover, the Ombudsman's term of office is coterminous with that of the EP itself and nominations are made by MEPs immediately after each parliamentary election. In making its decision on the appointment of the Ombudsman public hearings are held in the Petitions Committee, which take the form of interviews with all of the nominated candidates. A list of interviewed candidates is then presented, in alphabetical order, for decision by the full Parliament. In this regard the parliamentary appointment process of the Ombudsman is distinctly different to the EP's other appointment procedures. The vote is decided by simple majority, though at least half of all MEPs have to be present. In the event of a tie the rules provide for the eldest candidate to be appointed.

Jacob Söderman was elected as the first Ombudsman and he was reelected, narrowly, for a second term in October 1999. The Ombudsman's office is located in the EP buildings in Strasbourg. Söderman works closely with the Petitions Committee to which he presents an annual report as well as reporting to plenary. His budget is annexed to the EP's budget.

In the event of the Ombudsman no longer fulfilling 'the conditions required for the performance of his duties or is guilty of serious misconduct' then, at the request of the European Parliament, he may be dismissed by the Court of Justice (http://www.euro-ombudsman.eu.int/home/en/default.htm).

Court of Auditors

The Court of Auditors was established in 1975 with the merger of the two separate audit bodies of the EEC and Euratom and the ECSC. Under the treaty (Article 248(4)) the Court of Auditors exists to help the twin budgetary authorities (Parliament and Council) 'in exercising their powers of control over the implementation of the budget'. The EP had pressed hard for the creation of a single audit body and as a result 'has always had a proprietorial, and almost paternal, attitude towards the Court' (Westlake 1994a:47). From the outset, the EP was given the right to be consulted in the appointment of its members (Article 247). This was the first time that the Parliament had been involved in the EU's appointment process, and, in line with its wider expansionist procedural creativity (see Chapter 2), sought to maximize its influence beyond the formal power of consultation. This it did by establishing the practice after direct elections of using its Budgetary Control Committee to hold hearings, loosely based on the American tradition, in which nominees were questioned on their experience and views. Recommendations were then made by the committee to the EP as a whole for its decision on whether or not to approve the nominees.

What should be remembered at this point is that there was no treaty provision for such hearings, and there is no formal obligation upon nominees to appear before the committee. What the EP was able to count on, however, was the political calculation that any candidate who refused to attend a hearing would be highly unlikely to receive positive parliamentary support. More of a gamble was what would happen if Parliament expressed a negative opinion upon a nominee. This occurred for the first time in 1989 when the nominees of the French and Greek governments failed to receive a favourable opinion. The outcome was inconclusive as the French replaced their initial candidate while the Greek government ignored Parliament's opinion. Some within the EP identified the French response as setting an 'important precedent' (Westlake 1998:433) and as a reinforcement of Parliament's position (Jacobs 1999:5), but such assessments were strongly qualified by events in 1993. On this second occasion, the EP's opposition to a nominee from Portugal and to the reappointment of the Italian government's nominee was completely ignored by the Council, thus revealing 'the inherent weakness of the European Parliament's position' (Corbett 1999:5) when its informal procedures collided with formal treaty prescriptions.

European Monetary Institute and the Central Bank

With the implementation of the Maastricht Treaty in 1993 the formal consultation of the EP was extended to include the nomination of the President of the European Monetary Institute (Article 117) and nominees for President, Vice-President and members of the executive board of the European Central Bank (Article 112). Formally the EP had equal consultative rights with the Council in assessing the merits of the nominee for the

President of the European Monetary Institute. In practice, however, the European Council acted on the basis of a proposal from the ECOFIN Council (Westlake 1998:433). Despite his appointment being a foregone conclusion, the nominee, Baron Alexandre Lamfalussy, was asked to respond to a written questionnaire and was subjected to three hours of questioning in the Committee on Economic and Monetary Affairs. Similarly, Lamfalussy's successor, Wim Duisenberg, was subjected to the same rigorous process of scrutiny in 1997. Again what is of significance is that both candidates were under no formal obligation to appear at the parliamentary hearings, but both responded quickly and positively to the invitation to do so. Certainly, in the case of Lamfalussy's appearance before the Economic and Monetary Affairs Committee a key precedent had been established.

The precedent set by hearings held for the President of the European Monetary Institute proved to be of direct relevance to the appointment process of the European Central Bank (ECB). In adopting the process of 'confirmation hearings' the EP sent the message to Council that it would seek to maximize its powers beyond the mere consultation afforded to it under the treaty. In particular, given Parliament's dissatisfaction with the limited political control of the ECB conferred in the Maastricht Treaty, it was predictable that the EP would seek to define the terms of any future dialogue with members of the ECB – and to do so through the medium of the confirmation hearings. In this respect the written questionnaire sent to all nominees (1998 was the only occasion when all candidates were appointed at the same time) was of vital importance. The questionnaire covered the topics of the personal and professional background of the candidates, issues of monetary and economic policy, decision-making processes of the ECB, and, more pointedly, the issue of the democratic accountability of the ECB. Indeed, one of the positive results of the process was the commitment of the President-designate Wim Duisenberg to maintain a regular dialogue with the EP and to appear before its Economic and Monetary Affairs Committee on at least a quarterly basis. Moreoever, Duisenberg announced that he would withdraw his candidature if the EP failed to approve his nomination. These concessions have rightly been seen as strategic advances in securing enhanced accountability of non-elected EU bodies to

the EU's only directly elected institution (see Corbett 1999:12).
Westlake (1998:437) was even more up-beat in his assessment
of how these advances were secured: 'Once again, Parliament
brilliantly exploited the potential of its own internal rule-
making autonomy in order to create effective [confirmation]
procedures.' Certainly, in the absence of any legal requirement
for the ECB to report to (other than for the President of the ECB
to provide an annual report to Parliament) or to explain its
policy actions to Parliament, nonetheless it has been able to
secure – through the confirmation process – informal practical
undertakings to this effect (see de Haan and Eijffinger 2000:402).

Power of scrutiny

> In the legislatures of the contemporary world ... some methods
> of exerting pressure are relatively 'vague' and address
> themselves to a problem, normally without specifically
> suggesting a solution. (Blondel 1973:110)

Two of the most common methods in this regard are debates
and questions. Undisputedly, the EP has sought to develop the
classic parliamentary power to force the executive to be
available to the Parliament and to compel its 'responsiveness to
parliamentary questions, its participation in debate and its public defense of its position' (Mezey 1979:110–11). As with all
other legislatures the EP has developed procedures to
obtain information from the executive (Loewenberg and
Patterson 1979:148–9). Yet the EP faces the peculiar difficulty
of confronting a 'dual executive' – of Commission and Council,
only half of which has any direct treaty-prescribed responsibilities to Parliament – and a series of other executive agencies and
bodies (most significantly the European Central Bank) which
have limited formal requirements to account to the EP. The
growth of executive powers has only compounded the EP's difficulties; yet it has also simultaneously strengthened its resolve
to extend the general parliamentary powers of oversight.
Over time, therefore, the EP has developed a 'small arsenal of
traditional parliamentary powers for scrutinising the activities
of, and holding to account ... Community institutions'
(Westlake 1994a:174).

Questions

The right of Parliament to question the Commission was incorporated in the Treaty of Rome (Article 23). The Treaty provided for written and oral questions to the Commission. However, there was no provision for questions to the Council, though a convention developed after 1973 whereby Council agreed to answer MEPs' questions. This undertaking to answer all parliamentary questions was confirmed by the Council in the 1983 Solemn Declaration (see Chapter 2).

Questions addressed to the Commission tend to elicit fuller and less circumspect replies than those put to the Council. In part, this is because of the difficulties encountered by the Council's Secretariat in drafting – and COREPER in agreeing – an agreed response on behalf of all representatives on the Council (as well as encompassing the views of the Commission). To accommodate the amount of consultation required among Permanent Representatives, MEPs are required to give the Council at least three weeks' advance notice of a question for an oral answer with debate. The Commission on the other hand is expected to provide oral answers with only one week's notice. Replies from the Commission and Council to oral questions are followed by a debate and may prompt the adoption of a resolution. Given the limited time available at plenary sessions, considerable limitations have been placed upon the tabling of oral questions. Under Rule 42 they may be tabled only by a committee, a political group, or at least 32 MEPs. The Conference of Presidents then decides whether the tabled questions should be placed on the agenda and in what order. Given these restrictions relatively few oral questions with debate reach the agenda each year (see Table 7.1).

Questions for oral response may also be asked during a 60- to 90-minute period set aside respectively for the Commission and Council at designated times during plenary sessions. These sessions have become known as 'question time' after the procedure in the UK's House of Commons – from where the idea was borrowed after the first contingent of UK MEPs arrived in 1973. Since that date question time has become a permanent feature of plenary sessions. Even so it remains 'a much-maligned and much misunderstood procedure' (Westlake 1994a:176). In all but isolated instances the EP's question time lacks the excitement and

TABLE 7.1   Type of question by year

Type of question	1999			2000			2001		
	Comm.	Council	Total	Comm.	Council	Total	Comm.	Council	Total
Oral with debate	58	17	75	89	56	145	77	45	122
Oral question time	523	308	831	650	354	1,004	596	376	972
Written	2,606	263	2,869	3,678	485	4,163	3,302	413	3,715

Source: Commission General Reports 1999, 2000, 2001.

political drama of some of the heated adversarial exchanges in the UK's House of Commons. Nonetheless, insiders are unwilling to dismiss the procedure out of hand, claiming instead that it remains 'a useful vehicle' (Corbett *et al.* 2000:249) primarily because it is 'one of the very few areas of Parliament's activities where the backbencher may enjoy direct, formal interaction and debate with a commissioner or minister' (Westlake 1994a:177). A total of 831 questions were answered at question time in 1999, 1,004 in 2000 and 972 in 2001 (see Table 7.1). In practice, however, such interaction is often stunted and perfunctory (see Raunio 1996b:359) despite repeated attempts at enlivening question time. Other, more productive, 'mini' question times are now a common feature of several committees where Commissioners and their officials respond orally to questions from committee members.

Oral questions are far less numerous, however, than written questions. In 1999, 2000 and 2001 respectively 2,869, 4,163 and 3,715 written questions were tabled (see Table 7.1). Rule 44 states that questions for written answer may be tabled by any Member and are forwarded to the institution concerned via the EP's President. Questions which do not require detailed research are expected to be answered within three weeks (and are deemed to be 'priority questions'). Each MEP may table one priority question each month. 'Non-priority questions' are to be answered within six weeks. All written questions and answers are published in the *Official Journal of the European Communities*. Unanswered questions are also listed in the *Official Journal*. Often the Commission views the deadlines imposed by Parliament to be unrealistic, and leaves written questions unanswered beyond the deadlines stipulated by the

EP. (Nevertheless, the drafting of answers to written questions is a high priority of the Commission services.) If the time limit is infringed the MEP tabling the question has the option of requesting that the issue be placed on the agenda of the appropriate committee at its next meeting.

The real value of written questions, as Raunio (1996b:362–3) points out, is that 'it forces the Commission to produce a reply, and members thereby receive an official statement from the Commission which they can afterwards use for their own purposes'. They also provide a means whereby MEPs can inform the Commission, and Council, of concerns and grievances experienced by their electorates or issues which they feel should receive greater attention by the EU's executive. In this way written questions serve the same purpose as other forms of questions and act as a two-way channel of communication between elected representatives and the EU's dual executive. That questions are of significance in symbolizing the responsibility of the Commission and Council to answer to Parliament is not in doubt. What is less certain, however, is how effective this channel is in practice. Empirical evidence from the early 1990s recorded that some members believed that the Commission put little effort into replying to MEPs' questions and that often 'vague and imprecise answers' were produced (Raunio 1997:142). Other MEPs were willing to concede that the 'Commission's record in answering the questions ha[d] improved over the years' (Raunio 1997:142). Perhaps as important as the quality of replies, however, is the sheer ability of individual MEPs to ask written questions on a matter of their choosing, largely unfettered by political group or other collective institutional constraint. In this sense, questions 'represent one of the last rights of the backbencher and one of the last means available to the MEP to have her or his case represented in public' (Raunio 1997:143). Equally, however, it should be noted that relatively few written questions originate directly and unambiguously from individual MEPs. Organized interests, corporate interests, lobbyists, citizens and national officials (and even Commission officials) have all been known to suggest the tabling of written questions by MEPs for the Commission and Council to answer. Yet this is also often a two-way process with MEPs who are sympathetic to or interested in a particular case frequently asking those who are lobbying them to draft a written question. This can be to underscore parliamentary support and interest in an issue, or simply to extract information from the Commission or Council that might otherwise remain outside of the public domain.

Debates

Debate has been a classic function of legislatures through the ages. The term 'parliament' derives from the French verb 'parler' meaning to speak. There is a strong tradition of legislative analysis which holds that, regardless of their legislative powers, parliaments are above all deliberative bodies. They act as forums within which executive policies and political issues can be discussed and assessed by elected representatives (see Judge 1999:29–30). In this manner, debate as a procedure is part of the 'vague' means of exerting influence identified by Blondel (see above). It is a very general part of the functions, identified in Chapter 1, of 'control' and 'administrative oversight' exercised by parliaments (see Packenham 1970:534; Mezey 1979:76–7). Indeed, for most commentators deliberation is not simply a 'function' of legislatures but is also conceived as a 'power' (see Westlake 1994a:181). In the case of the EP this power is enhanced by the fact that it controls its own agenda – unlike many national parliaments. This enables debates to be conducted on subjects of Parliament's own choosing and to a schedule of its own timing.

The EP has developed the procedure of debate, largely through informal and creative interpretation of its formal powers, to oblige the EU's dual executive to debate specific policies and wider matters of concern to representatives. Up until July 2002 Rule 50 allowed for a political group or at least 32 members to ask the President in writing for a debate to be held on a topical and urgent subject of major importance. Such debates became a part of the cathartic function of the EP – and served as a means of 'letting off steam on pressing matters' (Westlake 1994a:181). Despite the Commission and Council being actively involved in these debates, and frequently being pressed for action in resolutions adopted at the close of the debates, the practical impact of debate was extremely limited. Genuinely important topical and urgent questions have tended increasingly to be dealt with under Commission or Council statements (see below).

From July 2002 topical debates have been more closely focused on 'breaches of human rights, democracy and the rule of law' (European Parliament 2002). Indeed, this was a partial recognition that Parliament's debates and resolutions on breaches of human rights and the rule of law frequently had a significant impact, especially *outside* Europe. The reformulated ground rules for topical and urgent debates introduced into Parliament's rules in 2002 maintain the possibility for genuine extraordinary debates held at short notice and provide a mechanism for dealing with human rights questions (PE 304.283 2002:amendment 22; European Parliament 2002:Rule 50). The intention behind the rule changes was to prevent plenary time from being expended on fairly routine and mundane matters – often high in rhetoric and short on substance – which could more effectively be addressed in other ways.

Rules 37 and 38 allow the Commission, Council and European Council to make statements. These are frequently requested by MEPs and the expectation is that the Commission will explain its actions in debate on a very regular basis. At the discretion of the EP's President the statement may be followed by a full debate or by 'thirty minutes of brief and concise questions from Members' (Rule 37). Rule 38, introduced in 1999, sought to ensure that the EP was informed as a priority (especially in advance of any press statement) of any significant Commission decisions.

In Chapter 6 the constraints imposed upon spontaneity and comprehension in debate by the simple practicalities of interpretation were noted. But the stuntedness of debate in plenary was further exacerbated by the EP's procedures and practices relating to debate. In spring 2000 a report produced by the EP's Vice-President, James Provan, criticized the 'fixed allocations of speaking time to groups, pre-arranged lists of speakers and the consequent ritual recital of largely unrelated set-piece interventions' (quoted in *European Voice* 25–30 May 2000). In particular, the time limit of three minutes placed upon individual speeches also encouraged the widespread practice of MEPs reading out preprepared written statements. The result of the combined language and procedural problems was 'lamentably-attended and lack-lustre debates in the chamber' (*European Voice* 25–30 May 2000). At the beginning of June 2000 the EP's Conference of Presidents considered the Provan report and its specific recommendations for abandoning the system of referral to committees for opinion and the making of introductory statements in plenary, and the dropping of the systematic scheduling of a debate on every committee report. More radically still, Provan proposed that the enlarged Bureau of Parliament should act as a committee of the whole to vote on amendments to reports, with the plenary subsequently only ratifying its decisions. He did, however, consider it appropriate to continue to concentrate major debates on Strasbourg, with Brussels being used to conclude more routine business.

Bailer and Schneider (2000:20) demonstrate how debates in the EP can be used strategically to alter the policy status quo. They point to a 'shaming strategy' whereby a cohesive Parliament can 'take a public stance that the other actors [Commission and Council] can only disregard at the risk of losing face'. Indeed, on the issue of enlargement, Bailer and Schneider (2000:31) maintain that the result of the EP's deliberations had some influence on the decisions reached at the Luxembourg Council in December 1997. While the actual impact of the EP upon the final outcome is difficult to determine, the important point for the present discussion is that 'the European Parliament ... in the ... enlargement debate largely profited from the oldest of all resources that are in the hands of a parliament – words' (Bailer and Schneider 2000:31).

Hearings

The capacity of the EP to gain (and disseminate) information has been enhanced through the procedure of public hearings. Such hearings are convened by the EP's committees with the permission of the Bureau (European Parliament 2002:Rule 166, interpretation). The purpose of hearings is to invite experts and interested organizations to provide evidence and engage in dialogue with committee members. Representatives of the Commission and Council attend the hearings, and the Commission is frequently invited to respond to the views expressed during the course of the hearing. In 2000 17 hearings were convened, and 25 hearings were held in 2001. Indeed, in the first 10 months of 2002, 32 hearings were held and ranged across topics such as breast cancer, tobacco advertising and sponsorship, the future of European tourism, and sport and audiovisual rights.

The main advantages of public hearings are that they help committee members to familiarize themselves with a particular policy (either in terms of detail or the broader context). One dimension is that they provide a procedure whereby MEPs can engage in 'exploratory dialogue' and 'forward thinking' and so raise issues for consideration by the other EU institutions. Another dimension of hearings is that they provide MEPs with supplementary sources of advice and information from independent experts, organized interests and NGOs with which to assess the outcomes of the Commission's own pre-legislative consultations. Thus, for example, the hearing on tobacco advertising and sponsorship in April 2002 included speakers from public health interest groups (the Standing Committee of European Doctors, the European Cancer Leagues and the European Heart Network), from the tobacco industry (Imperial Tobacco, the Italian Association of Tobacco Producers and the Group of European Tobacco Industries (GITES)), as well as from academic experts and the recipients of tobacco sponsorship.

Judicial review

Throughout its history the EP has instigated legal action both to advance and to defend its legislative role under the treaties (see Chapter 2). Litigation has been used by the EP to determine the choice of the correct legal basis for legislation, the right to be consulted, its institutional autonomy, and the clarification of parliamentary prerogatives. The Treaty of Nice extended the EP's prerogatives still further by enabling Parliament to bring court actions directly (on an equal footing with member states and the other EU institutions) without having to demonstrate specific concern. It also gained the power to ask the Court of Justice to provide an opinion on the compatibility of international agreements with the treaty (Article 300(6)). The significance of these amendments was judged by Yataganas (2001:278) to 'have given a massive boost to Parliament's role as a real co-decision maker in the Community's decision making process'. One irony of this position as 'a real codecision maker' is that Parliament's traditional role is reversed. The EP becomes a co-defendant in cases brought to the Court as a result of legislation passed under the codecision procedure. In the case of the directive on Advertising and Sponsorship of Tobacco Products (Directive 98/43/EC), for example, the Council and the EP defended, unsuccessfully, their legislation in a case brought by the German government. The Court annulled the directive in October 2000 (Case C-376/98).

Conclusion

In reviewing the formal powers of the EP it is apparent that it now wields significantly more powers than it did just over two decades ago after the first direct elections in 1979. Chapter 2 charted the increments of power over time, and this chapter has examined their cumulative standing in the early 2000s. What is apparent from this examination is the fact that the EP now has the capacity to 'compel' the Council and Commission to take its views into account when processing significant areas of EU legislation. In this sense the EP has an array of 'constraints' which prevent the other EU institutions from taking unilateral policy decisions. In its formal capacity to modify and reject executive proposals the EP thus fulfils Mezey's requirements for categorization as a parliament with 'strong policy-making power' (Mezey 1979:26). Confirmation of this position can also to be found in Bergman and Raunio's (2001:122) assessment that under codecision2 the EP 'ranks high' in its ability to shape policy.

Such global assessments of formal power need to be qualified, however, by the recognition that in certain important policy areas the EP's ability to constrain the dual executive's actions (under the consultation procedure) remains limited. Moreover, even where the EP has the right of veto and the capacity to modify executive proposals (under codecision2), its use of these powers is contingent upon the ability to construct political majorities out of, often, divergent partisan and national perspectives and interests. These contingencies and limitations will be examined in Chapter 8; for the time being, however, it is sufficient to note that over 70 per cent of the EU's legislative output is subject to the codecision procedure (Maurer 1999b: 60) and hence subject to 'constraints' wielded by the EP.

In addition, the EP exercises formal power, through deliberation and questioning, to require the institutions of the dual executive to account publicly for their actions. However, too much should not be made of the exercise of these powers. On the one side, the procedures of debate and of oral and written questions suffer from many of the same limitations that are apparent in national legislatures. On the other, a secular decline in their appeal as instruments of control over the Commission and Council has also been identified (see Maurer 1999b:6). Indeed, Maurer (1999b) observes that these procedures may be losing their appeal precisely because the use of other 'constraints' by the EP has increased (especially its formal legislative powers). Nonetheless, these inquisitorial powers still embody the classic oversight and cathartic functions traditionally associated with legislatures (see Chapter 1).

In terms of budgetary powers, the EP has been adroit in maximizing available procedures. From exercising only limited powers in the original EC treaty, the EP has incrementally enhanced its influence over the EU's budget by challenging the distinction between compulsory and non-compulsory expenditure and by seeking simultaneously to increase the size of the latter. The 1999 interinstitutional agreement marked the latest increment in EP power and was designed to ensure that the twin arms of the EU's budgetary authority moved away from contestation to a more consensual relationship. The cumulative result has been a transformation of the budgetary power of the EP. While the formal power remains as specified in Article 272, the practice is such that the EP has moved significantly toward 'real codecision on the EU budget' (former MEP Detlev Samland, quoted in Maurer 1999b:47). Nonetheless, it should be remembered that the right to codecide remains limited, however, to the expenditure of the EU. The ability to influence decisions on the raising of revenue to fund that spending remains largely beyond the EP's grasp. In this sense the EP 'is far from being a true parliament in the traditionally recognised sense of that term' (Westlake 1994a:121).

Similarly, the extent to which the EU represents a 'parliamentary system' in the 'traditionally recognised sense of that term' is tempered by the limitations observable in the formal powers available to the EP in relation to the selection, control and dismissal of the Commission. From having no direct input into the appointment process, Parliament has gradually secured the dual right to be consulted upon the choice of the Commission President, and also to assent to the choice of the

College of Commissioners as a whole. In this context, commentators refer to the 'parliamentarization' of the Commission (Majone 2002) or of an evolution 'towards a parliamentarian model' (Muntean 2000:14) given the enhanced powers of the EP in the appointment process of the Commission. Yet even after Nice the 'parliamentarization' of the Commission remains an aspiration. As will be seen in the next chapter, the EU still lacks several of the fundamental and interconnected characteristics normally associated with a parliamentary system of government.

Indeed, as Chapter 1 made clear, assessment of the EP as a 'parliament' and as part of a broader 'parliamentary system' requires recognition of the interconnected, interinstitutional and contextual elements of the exercise of formal powers. Chapter 8 moves beyond the specification of the EP's formal powers to examine the actual influence it wields in the early twenty-first century.

Chapter 8

Influence and Decision-Making

Despite the many and varied changes noted in earlier chapters of this book, the European Parliament still suffers an image problem. Some standard student texts on the EU still find it difficult to reconcile the changed post-Amsterdam and post-Nice world with a general academic dismissiveness of parliamentary power and a specific dismissal of the EP. Thus, Peterson and Bomberg (1999:43), for example, while acknowledging the upgrading of the EP's powers under codecision, nonetheless prefer to emphasize Parliament's 'weakness in dealing with highly technical matters' and to suggest that, even under codecision, MEPs are left with 'more interest than power' (1999:45). Later the same authors (2000:36) maintain that despite 'steady institutional advances' the EP continued to experience difficulties in 'wielding its powers'. Yet, in contrast, specialist scholars of parliaments argue that 'the European Parliament is now a serious player in EU law making' (Scully 2000a:235) and that 'Today the EP deserves to be considered a "transformative" legislature capable of significantly impacting the decision-making and policy processes of the European Union' (Kreppel 2002:1).

Given these divergent views, this chapter reviews the evidence – both quantitative and qualitative – on the *legislative influence* of the EP. In trying to assess the extent of this direct influence, attention is also paid to the formal models of the EU's legislative process, as much of the academic debate has revolved around a rather sterile discussion of the relative merits of variants of rational choice models. Returning to the 'real world' the chapter also examines the notion that the EP is able to wield legislative influence indirectly through the 'prior authorization' of the Commission's broad legislative programme as well as of specific policies. This form of indirect influence is often referred to as

245

influence over the executive and is examined in the second section of this chapter.

This chapter reiterates the contention of Chapter 1 that any assessment of the EP's role (in this case its direct and indirect legislative influence) needs to be *interinstitutional* – to take account of the EP's relation with other institutions; *contextual* – to take account of the systemic context; and *interconnected* – to take account of Parliament's multifunctional nature.

Assessing legislative influence

While there is widespread agreement that the legislative role of the EP has increased significantly since the introduction of the cooperation procedure and, especially, since codecision, there still remain fundamental disputes about the exact extent of EP influence. A vital indicator of enhanced influence is the capacity of the EP to amend legislative proposals. Certainly, as Table 8.1 reveals, the cumulative totals of 'successful' parliamentary amendments under the cooperation procedure over a ten-year period are striking. In comparison to national parliaments in the member states the ability of the EP to amend legislation under cooperation was far greater, in quantitative terms at least. As the Commission itself recognized, soon after the introduction of the cooperation procedure, the volume of successful EP amendments was such that: 'No national parliament has a comparable success rate in bending the executive to its will' (ISEC/23/94 Commission Press Release 15 December 1994, quoted in Earnshaw and Judge 1996:96).

Cooperation procedure, 1987–97

On the basis of the figures presented in Table 8.1 Maurer (1999b:39) concludes that: 'the "success rate" of the European Parliament amendments … was impressive'. During this period the EP tabled 6,008 amendments at first reading to 400 procedures. Of these amendments 54 per cent were accepted by the Commission and 41 per cent by the Council, and at second reading the respective percentages were 43 and 21. Clearly, therefore, the cooperation procedure was a 'significant event for the EP' (Tsebelis *et al.* 2001:578) and, as early as 1992, the EP's own Committee on Institutional Affairs concluded that the legislative

TABLE 8.1   *Cooperation procedure, 1987–97 (n = 400)*

	Number of amendments	*% accepted by the Commission*	*% accepted by the Council*
First reading	6,008	54	41
		(+0.6 in part)	(0.4 in part)
Second reading	1,593	43	21
		(+4 in part)	(+3 in part)

Source: Maurer (1999b:40).

role of the EP had been 'transformed' by the cooperation procedure (in Earnshaw and Judge 1995a:7). Yet still, the exact degree
of transformation and the true significance of EP amendments
under the cooperation procedure could not be determined by
a quantitative analysis alone (see below).

After the introduction of the codecision1 procedure under the
Maastricht Treaty the debate about the legislative influence of
the EP intensified still further. While MEPs and most academic
analysts believed that codecision1 was a considerable enhancement of the legislative powers of the European Parliament, a few
strident, persistent and dissenting voices could be heard from
political scientists working within rational choice/game theoretic
frameworks. Despite their small numbers, their rational choice
zealotry came to dominate the academic assessment of the new
procedure. Consequently, much heat was generated by the claim
that, from a 'theoretical point of view' the codecision1 procedure had the 'potential to actually reduce the legislative influence of the EP compared to the cooperation procedure' (Kreppel
2000b:8). This simple claim, based upon assumptions derived
from rational choice/game theoretic models, effectively dominated and detoured the academic assessment of the legislative
impact of the codecision1 procedure (see below).

MEPs and parliamentary officials could only look on in
bemusement as their 'reality' of increased legislative influence
under the codecision1 procedure was challenged by the desic-
cated assumptions of a game theoretic model. As Richard
Corbett (MEP, former EP official and a leading analyst of the
EP) noted, the conclusions based upon such models were 'the

opposite of the opinion of almost every practitioner' (Corbett 2000:373). Quite why this should be so will be examined below, but in the first instance the available quantitative data on the operation of the codecision1 procedure will be examined.

Codecision1 procedure

One reason why Corbett (2000:373–4) believed that the assessment of some rational choice scholars of the relative impact of the two legislative procedures was 'wrong' was because the 'statistics on the number of amendments accepted by the Commission and Council under each procedure ... imply that Parliament's influence on legislation is greater under codecision than under cooperation' (see Table 8.2).

In the period 1 November 1993 to 30 April 1999 there were 165 completed codecision1 procedures with 40 per cent ($n = 66$) subject to conciliation under Article 189b of the Maastricht Treaty. Agreement was not reached in three of the 66 conciliation procedures. In the remaining 63 cases, 913 amendments were adopted by the EP at second reading (see Table 8.3).

Overall some 27 per cent of the EP's second reading amendments were accepted unchanged. This represents an increase on the 21 per cent acceptance rate under the cooperation procedure (see Table 8.1). A further 36 per cent of amendments were accepted after the negotiation of compromises that were close to the EP's original position. Cumulatively, therefore, 63 per cent of

TABLE 8.2   *Codecision1, November 1993–July 1997 ($n = 82$)*

	Number of amendments	% accepted by the Commission	% accepted by the Council
First reading	1,777	52.5	42.7
		(+3.9 in part)	(3.7 in part)
Second/third reading	520	61	46.9
		(+1.9 in part)	(+12.5 joint) compromise

Source: Maurer (1999b:40).

amendments accepted at the conciliation stage reflected the EP's wishes closely, and 74 per cent of amendments in total were 'more or less' compatible with Parliament's position at second reading.

It should be acknowledged, however, that over the period 1993–99 there was a pronounced trend for successful amendments to represent compromises negotiated between the EP and Council in conciliation. In 1994, 26 per cent of amendments were accepted as compromises, whereas by 1999 the corresponding figure was 59 per cent. Similarly, in 1999 only 8 per cent of the EP's second reading amendments were accepted unchanged, whereas in 1994 the figure had been 44 per cent (PE 230.998 1999:11). This pattern emerged after a protracted struggle between the Council and Parliament with both parties eventually recognizing the advantages to be gained through negotiating strategies designed to secure compromise. Thus, for example, the EP sought to avoid reproducing amendments at second reading which already had been incorporated *de facto*, if not precisely, into the common position. On the Council's side, it moved from an initial bargaining strategy of offering the EP a single package which combined those amendments it was willing to accept along with those it rejected to one that distinguishes between those amendments it can accept, those it cannot, and those upon

TABLE 8.3 *Amendments in conciliation, 1 November 1993–30 April 1999*

Second reading amendments	Number	%
Accepted unchanged	244	27
Accepted in compromise close to amendment	328	36
Accepted in compromise with a future commitment	59	6
Accepted in compromise, adding a declaration	45	5
Already covered by another part of common position	35	4
Not accepted at end of negotiations	202	22
Total	913	100

Source: PE 230.998 1999.

250

TABLE 8.4 *Codecision2, 1999–2001*

Second reading amendments	1999–2000 Number of amendments	1999–2000 % accepted	2000–01 Number of amendments	2000–01 % accepted
Accepted unchanged	66	23	51	18
Accepted in compromise close to amendment	165	59	176	61
Accepted in compromise with a future commitment	–	–	–	–
Accepted in compromise, adding a declaration	16	6	27	9
Not accepted at end of negotiations	34	12	34	12
Total	281	100	288	100

Source: European Parliament 2000a; PE 287.593 2001.

which a compromise might be found. In addition, the publication in the *Official Journal* of interpretative declarations, or statements of future legislative intent by the Commission or Council, became alternative means of resolving interinstitutional disputes over certain amendments (see below).

Codecision2

Of a total of 65 codecision2 procedures concluded between 1 September 1999 and 31 July 2000 20 per cent ($n = 13$) were concluded at first reading on the basis of the EP's position, 54 per cent ($n = 35$) were concluded at second reading, and 26 per cent ($n = 17$) went to conciliation (European Parliament 2000a). The corresponding figures for the period 1 August 2000 to 31 July 2001 were 66 procedures, 29 per cent ($n = 19$) of which were concluded at first reading on the basis of the EP's position, 41 per cent ($n = 27$) were concluded at second reading, and 30 per cent ($n = 20$) were adopted following conciliation (PE 287.593 2001:7). The innovation, introduced by the Amsterdam Treaty, of enabling the adoption of an act on first reading, allowed nearly one-quarter (24.4 per cent, $n = 32$) of procedures to be concluded at this early stage.

Of the amendments tabled by Parliament at second reading, 23 per cent were adopted as they stood in the first year of codecision2 and 18 per cent in the second. At the other end of the process, only 12 per cent of amendments were withdrawn or deleted at the end of conciliation. In comparison with codecision1, therefore, the codecision2 procedure resulted in fewer amendments being accepted unchanged by the Council. Equally, however, fewer amendments failed to be accepted at the end of the conciliation process. In between, far more amendments were accepted on the basis of compromises reached in conciliation (see Table 8.4).

Both Parliament and Council made strenuous efforts to seek agreement during the early stages of the codecision2 procedure. Michael Shackleton, as Head of the EP's Conciliations Secretariat, provides an insider's view as to why this increased willingness to compromise came about. He argues that after Amsterdam:

The era of discrete, bounded contacts between Parliament and Council, essentially concentrated on the conciliation procedure, has come to an end. All institutions now see code-cision as an interlinked, continuous procedure where it is essen-tial and normal that there be intensive contacts throughout the procedure from first reading onwards. (Shackleton 2001:5)

Certainly, the formal procedural changes effected by the Amsterdam Treaty reoriented attention to the earlier stages of the process. Equally, however, there was also recognition by the respective co-legislators of the need to develop new informal working patterns to expedite the processing of codecision pro-cedures. In Shackleton's view this amounted to the development of a 'behavioural norm' in favour of early conclusion of the leg-islative procedures. This norm impacted particularly on the Council (see Shackleton 2001:5–7). It also found reflection in the Joint Declaration of May 1999 (OJ C 148, 28 May 1999:1) on practical arrangements for the post-Amsterdam codecision procedure, and in an interinstitutional seminar organized in Brussels in November 2000 on 'the functioning of the codeci-sion procedure after the treaty of Amsterdam'. Indeed, a joint press release, drafted with the intention of being issued at the end of the conference, not only pointed to the effective opera-tion of the procedure but also drew attention to 'a new legisla-tive culture between the co-legislators'. However, reservations were still expressed within the EP as to the advisability of devel-oping a too 'consensual' approach at the early stages of the pro-cedure. Thus, at the conclusion of the interinstitutional seminar, Dagmar Roth Behrendt (leading Socialist MEP and, signifi-cantly, PSE coordinator on the Environment Committee) voiced the opinion that the EP's political demands should continue to take precedence over and above any desire to reach early agree-ment with Council.

Playing with numbers

Aggregate statistics on the adoption of amendments alone tell us little of the legislative impact of 'successful' amendments. As Kreppel (1999:522) notes: 'Certainly not all amendments are created equal; some may have clear political significance while others are technical and non-controversial in nature'. For this reason, recent empirical analyses of the EP's legislative influence have engaged in some qualitative assessment of the relative degree of acceptance and the substantive significance of amendments (see Kreppel 1999; Tsebelis *et al.* 2001). Even with such methodological refinement, however, the results are not radically different. Thus, Amy Kreppel's analysis of 512 amendments to 24 proposals under the cooperation procedure between 1988 and 1996 confirms that 'the EP is a significant legislative actor and that it is able to amend successfully EU legislation in a way that is politically substantive' (1999:533). Similarly, Tsebelis *et al.*'s examination of 2,866 amendments under cooperation and 2,038 under codecision produced summary statistics which paralleled those of the EP presented above (2001:585). The period covered for the analysis of cooperation procedures was 1988 to 1996, and for codecision was 1994 to 1997. The percentage of 'essentially accepted amendments' at first reading was 40 under cooperation and 39 under codecision. At second reading the respective percentages were 32 and 59 (2001:585). In other words the data of Tsebelis *et al.* did not 'deviate from what the EP presents' (2001:585).

There was, however, a notable difference between cumulative rejection rates over time: with the rejection rate for amendments under cooperation starting from low levels and gradually increasing over time, while the opposite was true for codecision (Tsebelis *et al.* 2001:589). After detailed investigation of the data Tsebelis *et al.* (2001:595) concluded that under the cooperation procedure the influence of the Commission increased over time, while under codecision it decreased. While their conclusion – that 'all differences in rejection rates are attributable to differences in the influence and the behaviour of the Commission' (2001:597) – is an overstatement, it does underline, nonetheless, the contingent nature of the EP's legislative influence and the changing constellation of interinstitutional relations. A similar analytical point had been made earlier by Earnshaw and Judge (1995b:647–8) who noted that:

> The net result of the dialogue between Parliament and Council [under codecision] is the confirmation of an increasingly bipartite bargaining process and this, in turn, has placed the Commission in a considerably more ambiguous, and weaker, position than in the cooperation or consultation procedures. The ultimate logic of the Commission's position is

that it needs now to act in a more even-handed manner between Parliament and Council in its search for legislative agreement. Unlike the European Parliament, codecision has not strengthened the Commission's role.

Rejection

As noted in Chapter 1, Mezey (1979:25) maintains that a key variable in classifying the policy influence of legislatures is their ability to constrain the activities of executives: 'The most telling constraint that the legislature can place on the policy-making process is the veto. This means that the legislature can reject any proposal.' The significance of the cooperation procedure is that it enabled the EP for the first time to say no to Commission proposals (see Chapter 7). Even then, however, the Council had the right to overturn Parliament's rejection of its common position by a unanimous vote and with the agreement of the Commission. With the introduction of the codecision procedure in the Maastricht Treaty and certainly in its amended form under the Amsterdam Treaty, the EP obtained the right of legislative veto. Thereafter, a rejection of Council's common position by a majority of MEPs meant that the legislation fell. With this power the EP could 'no longer be accused of lacking teeth' (Corbett *et al.* 2000:189). Of course it is one thing to have such formal powers, however, it is entirely another to use them. Thus, throughout the history of both the cooperation and codecision procedures, MEPs have been cautious in the deployment of the power of rejection.

Rejection under cooperation

When MEPs were asked why Parliament had exercised such restraint in rejecting Council's common positions under the cooperation procedure one leading MEP answered:

> Parliament doesn't like rejecting...It follows that the Parliament will always avoid rejection if it can. Parliament comes badly out of rejection if legislation is needed. It's better to have legislation that we regard as partially unsatisfactory or inadequate rather than no legislation at all. (Derek Prag, in Earnshaw and Judge 1995a:21)

Not surprisingly, in the light of this comment, Parliament used its power of rejection sparingly under the cooperation procedure. Only rarely did it seek to reject a common position and on only seven occasions did it succeed. The first rejection came as early as 1988 on a proposed directive on the protection of workers from benzene in the workplace (OJ C 290, 14 November 1988:36). The second came in May 1992 with the rejection of the common position on a proposal for a directive on artificial sweeteners (for details see Earnshaw and Judge 1993). The third rejection came on a proposal relating to energy consumption of household appliances in July 1992 (see Earnshaw and Judge 1996). In October 1993, on the basis of a recommendation by the Committee on Economic and Monetary Affairs, Parliament rejected a fourth common position on the speed, torque and maximum power of motorcycles (see Earnshaw and Judge 1996). The three other rejections concerned the incineration of dangerous waste, the limitation of emissions into the atmosphere from major combustion plants (both rejected in November 1994), and the dumping of dangerous waste (rejected in May 1996). In two of these cases the Commission withdrew its proposal while in the third (major combustion plant emissions) the final text adopted by Council included the provision which had prompted Parliament to reject the common position (PE 259.385/BUR 1997).

In essence, the rejections on sweeteners and on energy labelling revolved around constitutional rather than policy disputes between the EP and Council. In both cases parliamentary scrutiny of the proposals was redirected, on receipt of the common position, away from the policy substance of the proposal before it, to the issue of the constitutional propriety of the Council's actions. The EP's rejection of the sweeteners common position hinged upon the admission by the responsible Commissioner that Council was seeking to bypass Parliament's reconsultation. He went on to reveal (or at least to confirm on the formal record of proceedings) that unanimity would not prevail in Council should the EP reject the common position. The fact that the Commission took upon itself the withdrawal of its own proposal following the EP's rejection of the common position proved not only an important element in the EP's processing of this proposal but also caused constitutional reverberations (see Earnshaw and Judge 1993:113–14). In the case of energy labelling, the constitutional dispute arose over the issue of 'comitology' (see below) and the Council's incorporation of a Type IIIb regulatory committee into the proposal. In so doing, the Commission's implementation role was effectively undermined. The Commission's attitude proved decisive in Parliament's decision to reject.

The European Parliament and comitology

Comitology (sometimes spelt 'commitology') is the term used to describe a complex and often bewildering array of committees which oversee, on behalf of the Council, the implementation powers exercised by the Commission (for details see Nugent 1999:129–33; Hix 1999:41–5; Corbett *et al.* 2000:255–61). What the system of 'comitology' provides for at the EU level, therefore, is a series of committees, composed of representatives from member states and chaired by the Commission, to supervise and regulate the implementing procedures of the Commission.

There are three main types of 'comitology committees': advisory (procedure I), management (procedure II), and regulatory (procedure III). Before 1999 Procedure II and III committees in turn each had two variants (IIa and IIb and IIIa and IIIb), but, after Council's decision of 28 June 1999 (see below) the number of variants was reduced from two to one for each type of committee. As a basic guide, as Hix (1999:42) points out, 'as the number of the procedure rises, the autonomy of the Commission from national governments declines'. The three types of procedures were given formal status, standardized and numbered I, II and III by Council's earlier decision of 13 July 1987. Although the comitology committees were standardized by the 1987 decision (in the wake of the Single European Act) neither the SEA nor the Council decision itself recognized an active role for the EP in the comitology process. Indeed, other than the general requirement, under Article 202, for Parliament to be consulted before the adoption of a decision setting out the 'principles and rules' for comitology, the EP had no participatory rights in the comitology process itself. Yet, the EP was always acutely aware that extensive use of comitology procedures eroded its position in the legislative process.

A protracted interinstitutional dispute thus followed the 1987 decision. Initially, the EP mounted a formal legal challenge to the decision in the European Court of Justice (C-302/87), but the Court ruled that the EP's application was inadmissible. Thereafter, the EP pursued a two-pronged strategy. First, it opposed the creation of regulatory committees, especially type IIIb, which limited the discretion of the Commission (and so limited the Commission's accountability to Parliament) and, in the case of type IIIb, even allowed for no decision to be reached. Second, it sought more transparency of the comitology process – more information on the composition, proceedings and materials sent to the committees.

Over the next two decades the EP campaigned to gain a more equal status with the Council in the comitology process. It did so both by using its formal budgetary and legislative powers (see Chapter 7), by seeking informal arrangements with the Commission, and through broader interinstitutional agreements with the Council and the Commission. In 1988, the then Presidents of the EP and the Commission agreed to the Plumb–Delors procedure. In 1993, the two institutions signed a code of conduct on the implementation of structural policies (the Klepsch–Millan agreement, this being replaced in turn by the Gil Robles–Santer agreement in 1999). In 1994, after the entry into force of Maastricht and the introduction of the codecision procedure, a *Modus Vivendi* was agreed between Parliament, Commission and Council (for details on these agreements see Earnshaw and Judge 1996:116–17; HL 23 1999:paras 40–3; Corbett *et al.* 2000:257–9). In 1996, the *Modus Vivendi* was supplemented by a further agreement between the Commission and Parliament (the Samland–Williamson agreement). The cumulative effect of these agreements and procedures was to increase the information available to the EP on the work of advisory, management and regulatory committees and to enhance the EP's capacity to express its views about the implementation procedures of the Commission.

In 1999 a new Council decision superseded the 1988, 1994 and 1996 agreements, with the EP declaring them 'null and void' in its resolution of 17 February 2000. Under Article 7 of the 1999 decision the EP was to 'be informed by the Commission of committee proceedings on a regular basis'. It was to be provided with committee agendas, lists of representatives, drafts of the implementation measures, the results of voting, and summary records of committee meetings. For the first time also the Commission was instructed to provide a full list of committees in the *Official Journal*. Under Article 8 the EP was empowered to make the Commission reexamine draft measures which in its opinion, as expressed through a resolution in plenary, exceeded the implementing powers provided for in the primary legislative act. The Commission was then required to inform the EP and the comitology committee what action it intended to take and the reasons for so doing. An agreement between the EP and the Commission was reached subsequently for putting the Council decision into effect (PE 232.403 2000). And the 2000 Framework Agreement (see below) underlined the intention of both the EP and the Commission to 'ensure the strict implementation of this agreement' (European Parliament 2000b:annex II).

However, before the placatory pronouncements of the 1999 Council decision, the issue of comitology soured EP–Council relations for most of the preceding decade.

Rejection under codecision1

Between 1 November 1993 and the end of Parliament's 1994–99 mandate, three legislative proposals were rejected by the EP – open network provision (ONP) in voice telephony in 1994, biotechnology patenting in 1995, and a measure to establish a Securities Committee in 1998. (In the case of ONP and biological patenting new directives were subsequently agreed, respectively, in 1995 and 1998; for details see Earnshaw and Wood (1999) and Rittberger (2000).) In two other cases Parliament adopted an intention to reject (engine power 1994 and European Capital of Culture 1999). The fact that there were so few rejections is noteworthy in itself. Indeed, given that there have been so few rejections under the codecision procedure it is worthwhile briefly examining these 'deviant' cases to understand why the normal processes of interinstitutional accommodation broke down on these notable occasions. In essence, conflict replaced the normal processes of compromise: interinstitutional conflict was at the heart of the EP's decisions to reject the ONP and transferable securities proposals, whereas intra-institutional ideational conflict was at the root of the biotechnology patenting rejection.

In the first year of codecision1 a proposal to apply open net-work provision (ONP) to voice telephony services was rejected (for details see Earnshaw and Judge 1996:122–3; Rittberger 2000:565–7). While there was a substantive disagreement between the Council and the EP on the proposal, the decision by Council to add a regulatory committee for the most important aspects of the directive's implementation precipitated the events which culminated in the rejection in plenary by an overwhelming 373 votes to 45 with 12 abstentions. In analysing this rejection, Earnshaw and Judge (1996:122) stressed the fact that 'the issue of comitology became entwined with, and provided the opportunity for, Parliament's assertion of its claim to some equivalence with Council in the implementation of measures'. Rittberger (2000:565) later confirmed the 'crucial importance' of comitology in the ONP rejection:

> 'Comitology' has to be considered an institutional game affecting the 'rules of the game', with Parliament eager to alter them and the Council equally eager to preserve the sta-tus quo. Concessions by either actor would have resulted in a redistribution of institutional power and thus of influence over future policy outcomes. The EP, by demonstrating its readiness to veto legislation, forced the Council to act. (Rittberger 2000:566)

By this logic, the introduction of provisions for a regulatory committee changed the nature of the legislative game. At this point the institutional dimension of the game came to predom-inate over the policy dimension. The EP's rejection of the Council's common position certainly signalled that Parliament was prepared to play the institutional game and to use its procedural rules to do so. As Shackleton (2000:327) notes: 'It was a signal that certainly worked'. Council had been warned that it would have to take the conciliation process seriously.

This point was reinforced in 1998 when Parliament and Council were unable to reach agreement on amending existing directives on capital adequacy and on investment services with a view to establishing a Securities Committee. The Council insisted on establishing a regulatory committee (IIIb) to assist the Commission in implementing the directive. Parliament on the other hand favoured a management committee. The EP's delegation in the Conciliation Committee pointed out that as the comitology system was being overhauled (see above) the choice of a type IIIb committee was particularly inappropriate. In the end, the Council decided, in anticipation of the entry into force of the Amsterdam Treaty, not to reintroduce its common position and hence the proposal was not adopted.

The directive on the Legal Protection of Biotechnological Inventions (commonly referred to as the biotechnology or gene patenting directive COM[93]661) is notable for being the first legislative measure not to have been adopted after agreement had been reached in conciliation. In this rejection intra-institutional conflict – centred on ideological division and party group contestation – undermined the EP's majority voting requirements to frustrate the successful completion of the codecision procedure.

Indeed, from the outset, the proposal on the legal protection of biotechnological inventions was marked by serious substantive differences within Parliament. Thus, for example, it took Parliament's Legal Affairs Committee three attempts for its first reading report to pass through the EP plenary; and the proposal eventually spanned three parliamentary terms before the final declaration of rejection in March 1995 (for details see Earnshaw and Judge 1995b; Earnshaw and Wood 1999). In assessing the significance of the processing of the biotechnology patenting directive Earnshaw and Wood noted the politicization of the issue: 'biotechnology [became] an area of policy characterised by high emotion, public concern and political sensitivity' (1999:305). The initial assumption of the Commission that the directive was a 'technical' measure designed to protect biotechnological inventions throughout the EU was rapidly overwhelmed by 'political' concerns relating to moral values and ethics (see also Langfried 1997; Gold and Gallochat 2001). The EP, as a primary arena for deliberations on the ethical dimensions of the draft directive, reflected the wider ideational cleavages on this issue. The intensity and variability of these cleavages made it difficult for the EP's conciliation delegation to assess the changing constellation of forces within the EP plenary (given an intervening election which impacted upon the weighting of opinion among MEPs, and also intense lobbying of MEPs by outside organizations). In these circumstances 'intra-parliamentary divisions made it difficult for the parliamentary delegation in conciliation to act "strategically", i.e to propose legislation that would be adopted by the parent chamber' (Rittberger 2000:563).

In fact, the EP's conciliation delegation failed to act cohesively, let alone strategically. Four members of the delegation opposed the joint text. Indeed, one of the dissenting members felt moved to submit a formal statement 'reject[ing] the majority position of the EP delegation to the Conciliation Committee' (see PE 211.523 1995:1). Other members of the conciliation delegation argued within their political groups, and later in plenary, for rejection of the text. Outside Parliament there was exceptionally strong lobbying, including noisy demonstrations and picketing of the EP, by opponents of the text agreed in conciliation.

In plenary the joint text was rejected by 240 votes to 188 with 23 abstentions. Splits were evident in most political groups – though Christian Democrats tended to vote in favour of the compromise and Socialists against. The French President in Office of the Council, Alain Lamassoure, responded: 'I regret the European Parliament's rejection of the compromise ... due to an internal problem within that institution. This vote reveals a problem of method in the codecision procedure.' He concluded that: 'The Council delegation spoke for the Council as a whole; the Parliamentary delegation has just been disavowed by the plenary session' (quoted in *Agence Europe* 3 March 1995:5).

Codecision 2: Takeover Bids directive, 2001

Like the biotechnology patenting directive, the 'Takeover Bids' directive (or to give it its formal title: 13th Directive on Company Law, Concerning Takeover Bids) was also rejected by plenary after agreement in the Conciliation Committee. But it was the first rejection of a joint text under the codecision2 procedure. What is also noteworthy is that the joint text was rejected after a tied plenary vote in July 2001 of 273 in favour, 273 against and 22 abstentions. (Parliament's Rules of Procedure hold that if there is a tied vote then the text shall be deemed to be rejected.) Given these unique circumstances it is worthwhile examining this rejection in some detail.

The intention of the draft proposal (COM[95]655) forwarded to the EP in February 1996 was to ensure that the rules in each member state complied with basic principles such as the equal treatment of shareholders in an offeree company; the prohibition of false markets in the securities of offeree companies; and the provision of time and information for sound decisions on bids to be reached. More specific provisions included the designation by member states of a supervisory authority to ensure the practical application of the general provisions of the directive, specific national rules to safeguard the protection of minority shareholders through mandatory bids or equivalent means, and minimum levels of information and publicity to ensure the transparency of bids.

When the proposal was forwarded to the EP, the Legal Affairs Committee's report (rapporteur Nicole Fontaine) concurred with the logic of the proposed framework directive – for limited harmonization – but, amongst other amendments, sought to tighten some definitions and to strengthen the rights of employees and of minority shareholders. A total of 23 amendments were adopted at first reading. (With the entry into force of the Amsterdam Treaty the numbering of the legal base of the proposal changed and with it the EP held another first reading vote in October 1999 in the new parliament.)

While the Commission amended its initial proposal (COM[97]0565) to 'incorporate most of the amendments adopted by Parliament at first reading' (http://wwwdb.europarl. eu.int/oeil/), the Council did not reach agreement on the wording of its common position until 19 June 2000 before forwarding it to the EP in September 2000. In the Council's common position agreed in June 2000, 13 of the EP's first reading amendments were adopted. At second reading on 13 December 2000 MEPs voted to adopt the Legal Affairs Committee's report (rapporteur Klaus-Heiner Lehne) and supported 15 amendments to the common position. The Commission accepted only three, relatively minor, amendments, and when the Council decided that it could not accept all of the EP's amendments a Conciliation Committee was convened. Two formal sessions of the Conciliation Committee were held (29 May and 5–6 June 2001), and these were preceded by three trialogues and three delegation meetings. In these 'pre-meetings' agreement was reached on nine amendments, with two amendments on defensive measures against hostile takeover bids, and four others on workers' rights, carried forward for consideration in conciliation itself.

Eventually, a last-minute agreement was reached on both outstanding issues on the basis of the Commission's compromise proposals. In reality, however, the 'agreement' on 'defensive measures' was only reached after a split vote in the EP's delegation. A majority of eight MEPs voted in favour of the compromise amendment while six others voted to reject the compromise, believing that 'it was too distant from the EP's amendments as tabled' (PE 287.589 2001:7). In fact, in the Committee's Report on the Joint Text, the EP's rapporteur expressed his 'strong dissatisfaction with the solution attained on the main issue at stake' (PE 287.589 2001:7). He went further in the third reading debate by stating: 'To sum up, the Swedish Prime Minister called the directive unique. I agree – in its present form, it is uniquely bad. That is why it must be rejected' (EP Debates 3 July 2001).

Significance of the rejection of the 'Takeover' directive

As noted above the 'Takeover' directive was the first rejection of a joint text under the codecision2 procedure. It was also the first rejection after a tied plenary vote of 273 in favour, 273 against and 22 abstentions. Indeed, the high level of participation in the vote – with 568 MEPs voting – was itself unique. Moreover, the directive also constituted the first codecision procedure during which a member state dissented openly and assertively from a previously agreed Council common position – *and sought explicitly a parliamentary rejection.*

After reaching agreement in Council in June 2000 the German government subsequently withdrew its support in early 2001. The change of position came after intense lobbying of Chancellor Schröder by senior executives of German companies, especially VW and BASF, along with the head of the Mining, Chemical and Energy Workers' Union (*Financial Times* 6 July 2001). Once the German government had dissociated itself from the common position then the process of conciliation became complicated by the fact that:

> The Council was then in the position of being unable to concede anything to Parliament by way of negotiation ... Had it done so, all 14 Member States would have felt cheated, having already conceded much to achieve a common position. For one Member State to achieve something, having withdrawn from the common position, would have caused

the Council great difficulty in future negotiations. (James Provan, EP Debates 3 July 2001)

In these circumstances the Council 'dug its heels in over the key issue in its common position, and was absolutely unwilling to budge a single centimetre' (Klaus-Heiner Lehne, EP Debates 3 July 2001). Consequently, the joint text agreed on 6 June 2001, in the EP's rapporteur's opinion at least, was 'not so much a compromise as a capitulation by the majority of the Parliament delegation in the face of Council's position' (Klaus-Heiner Lehne, EP Debates 3 July 2001).

The fact that a vote was taken within the EP's delegation raised several related procedural issues. First, there was concern over the number of MEPs participating in the Conciliation Committee. Although formally the EP delegation is composed of 15 members selected from the party groups, the smaller political groups do not always nominate representatives. As a result, since 1999, the average participation rate has been 13 members (PE 287.593 2001:Annex 5). Given the deep divisions within the parliamentary delegation, the issue of exactly how many of the 15 MEPs actually participated in the 'Takeover' conciliation sparked a wider debate about participation levels. A decision was taken by the Vice-Presidents of the EP that, in future, where a political group failed to appoint their representatives at the constituent meeting of the delegation, a letter would be sent reminding them of the need to designate appropriate representatives (PE 287.593 2001:16). Moreover, on the advice of Parliament's Legal Service, it was also established, for the first time, that an absolute majority (of eight votes) was required on a vote of agreement on a joint text. (The EP's 1999 Rules of Procedure, Rule 82(7), merely noted that 'the delegation shall decide by a majority of its members'.) In the event, eight votes in favour of the directive were secured in the delegation. However, it was hoped that the confirmation that an absolute majority was needed to approve a joint text would serve to 'ensure that more members of the delegation attend meetings and [secure] greater involvement of the political groups in the designation of members' (PE 287.593 2001:16).

Concern about the size of majority was also linked in the 'Takeover' conciliation with the national composition of the EP's delegation, especially at the final meeting of the Conciliation Committee. In practice, who attended the meeting of the Conciliation Committee was important both for opponents of the directive (especially those from Germany) and for its supporters. The final vote in the conciliation delegation was controversial, with only the smallest of majorities in favour (eight for and six against). It would only have required one of the members in favour to have failed to make the journey to Luxembourg to vote and a German substitute to have voted in his place, for the vote to have gone the other way. As it was, the substitute member concerned, from Germany, could only speak, not vote. Ultimately the basic division within Parliament's delegation to the Conciliation Committee was amplified in the third reading vote in plenary itself. This vote revealed that there was an almost exact bifurcation of Parliament. Indeed, the chairman of Parliament's delegation argued that in view of the fundamental divide within the delegation: 'it would have been wrong for half of the delegation to have rejected this directive late one night in Luxembourg, without the full Parliament having the opportunity of the third reading' (James Provan, EP Debates 3 July 2001).

After intense lobbying of German MEPs – by the German government, leading German companies and trade unions – they voted overwhelmingly as a single national bloc irrespective of EP party group. Similarly, MEPs from Italy's ruling coalition voted en masse against the measure. As the *Financial Times* noted (6 July 2001): 'In a rare display of unity, the German government and opposition, along with leading business associations and trade unions all welcomed the vote.' Conversely, Frits Bolkestein, the Commissioner with responsibility for the 'Takeover' directive, had no doubts that the blame for failure rested 'squarely on Germany' (*Financial Times* 5 July 2001).

The rejection of the 'Takeover' directive thus provides an illustration of the continued salience of national factors in decision-making in the EP. A primary determinant of voting on the rejection of the 'Takeover' directive was clearly nationality, not party group. Members' voting intentions were subject to intense scrutiny, and lobbying, not only by affected interests but also by national governments. The latter's attention to their respective national MEPs was in itself tacit acknowledgement of the influence exerted by the EP under codecision and the advantages to be gained from lobbying MEPs accordingly.

Variable legislative influence

Variables

The contingency of the EP's legislative influence is apparent in the case studies of rejection. In these cases the EP's influence was dependent upon the types of issue (institutional or substantive policy), the respective weightings of ideological and national interests and their respective configurations in the Council and the EP, and the legislative 'impatience' of the respective institutions. Beyond instances of rejection, Judge *et al.* (1994) have sought to explain the differentials in the EP's legislative influence in terms of four major variables: first, the type of policy; second, the extent of intergovernmentalism; third, the nature of interinstitutional relations; and, fourth, institutional resources.

In terms of the 'type of policy', Judge *et al.* pointed out that different types of policy generate different patterns of decision-making and hold different potential for Parliament to influence policy outcomes. This echoed the commonly made point that various categories of policy are associated both with different patterns of policy-making and with the differential involvement of varying policy actors at various stages of the policy process. The exact categorization of policy varies from analyst to analyst (see, for example, Lowi 1972; Ripley and Franklin 1982, 1987; Wallace 1996, 2000) but most categorizations subsume four broad types of policy: constituent (or history-making), redistributive, distributive and regulatory. While these categories are not mutually exclusive, with overlaps and spill-overs in practice (see Wallace 2000:525), they do manifest different potentialities for politicization of policies and different constellations of policy actors associated with policy areas. Of particular importance for the discussion of the EP's capacity to influence policy is the observation that decision-making over regulatory policies is often more open to parliamentary and public influence than is the case generally for distributive policies (Judge *et al.* 1994:42). Certainly, the extension of EU regulation has had profound effects not only in terms of policy outcomes but also in terms of the styles of EU policy-making. Protective regulatory policies now constitute a significant area of EU competences whereby activities that are thought to be harmful are restricted (for example, environmental pollution, unsafe working conditions, consumption of tobacco), and others, thought to be beneficial, are promoted (for example, testing food additives and medicines before marketing).

However, Judge *et al.* also note that within the category 'regulatory policy', the EP's ability to exert influence may be conditioned by the type of regulatory policy itself. In making this case they utilized James Q. Wilson's (1974) identification of different policy patterns arising from the concentration of costs and benefits. Wilson identified three patterns: concentrated benefits, diffused costs; second, concentrated benefits, concentrated costs; and third, diffused benefits, concentrated costs. Within the latter category 'one of the striking aspects' of legislation is the important role of legislatures, individual representatives and legislative committees (Wilson 1974:144). When the variable of the concentration of costs is applied to the EP, the general proposition holds that 'the less concentrated they are, the more likely it is that Parliament can affect the outcome' (Shackleton 2000:338).

A second variable was the relative mix of national and supranational dimensions of decision-making. On some issues the EU institutions have treaty-prescribed competences and decisions are reached on the basis of cooperation between national and EU institutions. In these areas the Commission and EP have specified powers and responsibilities. On other issues, however, the characteristic style is one of 'intergovernmentalism', of national governments pursuing national interests, either positively or negatively, in the Council. The decision rules in Council between unanimity and QMV, and the extent of the subsequent linkage between QMV and codecision, reflect these differences (see Chapter 2). Shackleton (2000:338) refines this variable to mean 'the level of legitimacy accorded to EU action by Council members' and notes that the lower the level the less potential impact the EP exercises. What this means in practice is that individual member governments are clearly more resistant to EU policy interventions in some policy areas than in others. Although the areas subject to the codecision procedure were extended successively under the Maastricht, Amsterdam and Nice treaties (see Chapter 2), significant policy areas remain beyond direct EP influence. Thus, under the first pillar, important aspects are subject to what Karlheinz Nuenreither (2001:195) calls the 'humiliating status of mere consultation': agriculture, taxation, certain social policy and employment matters, fiscal aspects of environmental policy, issues of citizens' rights, and important budgetary matters relating to the Community's own resources and rules of budgetary implementation. Even here, however, the informal dimensions of EP influence should not be overlooked. Thus, for example, Council officials have noted the propensity of MEPs to import comparisons in the way they operate under codecision to the consideration of policy areas such as agriculture which, formally, is subject only to consultation. The result, as Farrell and Héritier (2002:13) note, is that 'on the ground, Parliament's decision-makers have been successful in reshaping the policy process, so that decisions in this field [agriculture] and others are increasingly taken "as if" under codecision, according to the informal rules of decision-making and discussion which have come to structure codecision interactions'.

Similarly, the role of Parliament in the second pillar (common foreign and security policy) and the third pillar (justice and home affairs) still remains limited – largely to consultation. While some commentators use these limited formal powers as further evidence of the continued marginalization of the EP, it is worth remembering that many other national parliaments also have restricted involvement in the decision-making processes on foreign affairs. Indeed, as Viola (2000:28) notes, 'the impact of national parliaments on foreign affairs can be even more modest than that of the European Parliament'.

The third variable, linked inextricably with the preceding variables, was the nature of interinstitutional relations pertaining at any particular time. Two major dimensions to these relations can be identified: formal and informal. The formal dimension is concerned with treaty-specified powers and interactions between institutions. Yet, as Chapter 2 revealed, policy-making in the EU, and the EP's own contribution to the policy process, cannot be understood without reference to informal interinstitutional interactions. Through informal practices and procedures the EP has successfully interposed itself into, at the very least, the consciousness of the other institutions and has become linked broadly into the interstices of EU policy-making through such arrangements as trialogues and codes of practice. (Confirmation of the importance of such informal interinstitutional interactions can be found in Farrell and Héritier (2002).)

A fourth variable capable of explaining variations in the influence of the EP concerns the institutional resources available in the performance of its policy role. The general constraints of time, personnel, expertise, staffing and research resources affect the capacity of representative institutions to exert policy influence. In the EP, however, the *timing* of its interventions in the policy process is of particular significance. Certainly, the deadlines imposed by the cooperation and codecision procedures have had both a positive and negative impact upon the EP's legislative influence (see Judge *et al.* 1994:48).

A fifth variable was always implicit in Judge *et al.*'s analysis (1994:28) but not explicitly stated at the time. This was the nature of political group cohesion and coalition formation within the EP and the interlinked matrix relationship with national parties. How the party groups behave under the formal procedures of the EP is of vital importance to the legislative outcomes apparent from case studies of the EP's legislative influence (see below). Chapter 5 highlighted, for example, how variable legislative coalitions have formed around specific policy positions, and how, after 1999, the changed balance towards coalitions of the centre right rather than the centre left impacted upon the legislative outputs of the EP. Clearly, there is a linkage between this variable and the interinstitutional variable. In this sense, the role of ideology – as manifested in intra- and inter-party conflict in the EP to determine what Parliament's position will be – is then reflected in the interinstitutional contest between the EP and the other institutions to determine what the EU's legislative outputs will be (with the Council's position also subject to internal ideological contestation).

Variability: case studies

There is now an impressive number of case studies revealing the variability of EP influence over EU legislation. Earnshaw and Judge have analysed over 20 cooperation procedures (Earnshaw and Judge 1993, 1995a,b, 1996; Judge and Earnshaw 1994) and over 25 codecision procedures (Earnshaw and Judge, 1995b, 1996; Earnshaw and Wood 1999) to provide qualitative data on the varying legislative impact of the EP. Other case studies have been provided by, for example, Hubschmid and Moser (1997), who examined the directive on exhaust emission standards for small cars in order 'to analyse the extent of the EP's influence'; Tsebelis and Kalandrakis (1999), who presented a case study of the EP's contribution to legislative measures protecting the environment from dangerous chemicals; and by Shackleton (2000), who used the examples of the Auto-Oil package and the Fifth Framework Programme for Research and Technology to reveal the substantial influence of the EP over EU legislation. Shackleton then offset these examples with those of the Programme for European Voluntary Service and the directive relating to the protection of personal data to reveal the limitations upon the EP's capacity to influence legislation. Rittberger (2000) has provided a detailed discussion of the directives on biotechnology and ONP, while Friedrich *et al.* (2000) have analysed the contribution of the EP to the Auto-Oil 1 Programme.

In addition to these academic studies of the EP's legislative influence, Parliament itself produces – through the Activity Reports of the Delegations to the Conciliation Committee (PE 230.998 1999; European Parliament 2000a; PE 287.593 2001) – assessments of the impact made by the EP in the codecision procedure. These reports are especially valuable for present purposes because they make qualitative comments on the 'real impact' that the EP's amendments have had upon EU legislation. Thus, the 1999–2000 report drew particular attention to 17 legislative measures where the EP's amendments had 'a genuine impact on the lives of European citizens' (European Parliament 2000a:20–1). In the report for 2000–2001 a further 19 legislative measures were identified where the EP's amendments would have a similar impact (PE 287.593 2001:10–11). In particular, the reports note the significant enhancements secured in a range of directives and regulations dealing with environmental protection and environmental monitoring, inspection and assessment. Plus, as noted above, the development of European companies was significantly and detrimentally affected by the EP's rejection of the 'Takeovers' directive. More positively, however, the adoption of a new 'Tobacco' directive (COD 1999/0244) provided further evidence of the significant legislative impact of the EP and is worthy of further detailed study here.

Codecision2: significant legislative impact – the 'Tobacco' directive

The 'Tobacco' directive (formally entitled the Directive on the Approximation of Laws, Regulations and Administrative Provisions of Member States concerning the Manufacture, Presentation and Sale of Tobacco Products (COD 1999/0244)) was submitted by the Commission to Parliament in January 2000. The prime objective of the proposed directive was to combine and revise three existing directives on the tar content of cigarettes, oral tobacco and labelling of tobacco products. The main provisions of the directive included: a reduction in the tar content of cigarettes; harmonization of ceilings for levels of nicotine and carbon monoxide; more stringent requirements concerning the size and type of health warnings on tobacco packets; an obligation on manufactures and importers to list additives, to explain the reason for such ingredients and to provide toxicological data on additives; a ban on misleading descriptors such as 'light' and 'low tar'; and new review and reporting procedures on the implementation of the directive. Despite the apparently technical nature of these issues, it is important to place the proposal in the political context of increasing concern in Europe over smoking and health.

Political context.   As we will see below, the lobbying of the tobacco industry and health activists was an important part of the processing of the proposal, as was informal interinstitutional contact, and the 'anticipatory' behaviour of MEPs ('anticipatory' in the sense of identifying what was possible in legal terms so as to ensure that legislation was not killed later by litigation on the part of the tobacco industry).

The complexity, as well as the political significance, of the issue was revealed in the nuanced process of lobbying by different organized interests and associations. Thus, for example, the very largest tobacco companies (such as Philip Morris) generally adopted a more supportive position than did the smaller companies. At one level, the largest companies identified certain features of the EU's tobacco legislation – relating to packaging, labelling and advertising – as a potential means by which to maintain their current market shares indefinitely. In addition, from their perspective, such legislation held the possibility of distracting political and public attention from more substantive and, for tobacco companies, more financially damaging threats to smoking.

Another nuance was observable in the attempt of the EP's rapporteur to structure lobbying through the convening of collective meetings of the different groups involved. This highlighted not only the range of interests but also the differences within and between different groups involved in the issue. A further feature of the lobbying process was the entry of the pharmaceutical industry into the debate, and its adoption of a moderately progressive stance in support of the case of health activists. (In part, this was not simply altruism, as some benefit would also accrue from the promotion of their own smoking cessation products.) In addition, Swedish manufacturers of Snus (Scandinavian oral tobacco) sought to use the proposal to lobby against the impending ban on their product. In Sweden, the banning of Snus featured regularly as part of the ongoing discussions about the country's membership of the EU.

The EP's processing of the proposal.   The Commission's proposal was referred to the Committee on the Environment, Public Health and Consumer Policy as the committee responsible, and opinions were sought from the Legal Affairs, Industry and Agriculture Committees. Jules Maaten was appointed rapporteur on 26 January 2000 and the EP adopted his report in its first reading vote on 14 June 2000. Some 44 amendments were adopted at first reading.

In essence, Maaten and the Environment Committee maintained the EP's long-standing support for the Commission's preference for the strict regulation of tobacco products in Europe. Although most of the first-reading amendments might readily be classified as 'technical' in nature, in fact, many went to the heart of how tobacco products should be regulated in Europe and how tobacco is perceived, and followed an approach considerably at odds with that favoured by most of the tobacco industry. Significantly, in this case, there was also an important political motivation underlying the Environment Committee's pursuit of what might be perceived by 'outsiders' as a search for technical perfection rather than political impact. This was simply that the tobacco industry had become an enthusiastic litigant against EU tobacco legislation. (Indeed, the directive resulting from Maaten's report was subject ultimately to three legal challenges.) MEPs were conscious, therefore, that amendments designed to maximize the health objectives of tobacco legislation would precipitate a legal challenge from the tobacco companies on the grounds that the limits imposed by the internal market legal base (Article 95) had been exceeded. This 'anticipation of future action against legislation' was evident in the arguments advanced by the rapporteur and other Environment Committee members. The 'anticipatory' logic was also apparent in Parliament more widely, as well as within the Commission and Council. Institutionally, if health objectives were explicitly advanced, decision-making in Council would have to have been by unanimity rather than QMV – to the detriment of the stringency of the measure likely to result. Unanimity in Council would have led to dilution of the proposal by the most reluctant member states (Germany and Greece). As it was, Germany not only voted against the common position in Council but also launched a case in the Court of Justice against Council and Parliament's adoption of the measure.

The Commission accepted the majority of the EP's first reading amendments 'in whole or in part', in some cases subject to drafting modifications, and included them in its amended proposal. This was hardly surprising as the rapporteur had informally discussed his proposed amendments at length with relevant Commission officials. Indeed, from the start of the EP's processing of the proposal, the rapporteur also maintained close contacts with successive Council Presidency officials responsible for the dossier in the Council's working group. In fact, the Parliament's rapporteur undoubtedly acquired both a detailed knowledge and a strategic vision that equalled, at least, that of member state officials in the Council's working group. If anything, the EP's rapporteur was placed in a possibly advantageous position in relation to his Council interlocutors, because, unlike the Council Presidency, which changed every six months, the rapporteur was able to develop a longer-term perspective on the issue. (Indeed, there were four Council Presidencies during the processing of this proposal, and the rapporteur had to liaise successively with each.)

Of the amendments taken up by the Commission only 15 were accepted wholly or in part by the Council. However, two of the EP's amendments which had not been accepted by the Commission were adopted. These related to the use of terms such as 'low tar', 'light' or 'mild' as product descriptions that suggested that a tobacco product was less harmful than others. The Council did not accept an increase in the size of warnings or yield indications on packaging, nor did it accept the possibility of a transition period until December 2006 for the application of the new provision to cigarettes exported outside of the EU (OJ C 300, 20 October 2000:59–62). In its consideration of the common position the Environment Committee proposed the readoption of many of its first reading amendments.

Included among the reintroduced amendments was one to require the reporting of test results after a deliberate change to a tobacco blend, rather than through an annual reporting system. On the issue of warnings the EP favoured labelling which conveyed a 'serious message rather than simplistic slogans' (PE 293.679 2000:27) but was willing to compromise to take account of the reduced size of warnings. In fact the Environment Committee's recommendation for second reading accepted the Commission's compromise between Parliament's first reading amendment in favour of warnings of 35 to 40 per cent on the front of the packet and 45 to 50 per cent on the back and the preference stated in the common position for 25 to 30 per cent on either side. The Commission suggested, depending on the number of official languages to be used, 30 to 35 per cent on the front of packets and 40 to 50 per cent on the back. Parliament's desire to have larger warnings arose from an acceptance of research findings that the most direct medium for the communication of the dangers of smoking was the cigarette packet itself (PE 293.679 2000:27). Moreover, the EP inserted a new paragraph which enabled member states to require colour photographs or other illustrations of the health consequences of smoking to be displayed as part of the warning. This was modelled on the Canadian model of regulation. On this point the Environment Committee succeeded in stretching – or at least interpreting creatively – Parliament's own Rules of Procedure sufficiently to introduce amendments to the common position which had not been adopted at first reading.

To maximize the effects of these general and additional warnings the first-reading amendment was reintroduced to require such warnings to be displayed on tobacco vending machines also. Parliament also reintroduced its amendments on the harmonization of testing and for the Commission to submit a proposal (by December 2004) for a directive providing for a common list of authorized ingredients (and their addictiveness) for tobacco products.

In considering the EP's amendments, the Commission took into account the Court of Justice's ruling, of 5 October 2000 (C-376/98), annulling the directive on tobacco advertising (98/43/EC). The annulment of the tobacco advertising directive, effectively on the grounds that it exceeded the possibilities available under Article 95 for the EU to act against tobacco advertising, was a constant backdrop during the adoption of the tobacco labelling proposal, and became particularly important during the proposal's second reading.

At second reading a total of 32 amendments were adopted by Parliament. Of these the Commission accepted 22 and modified its proposal accordingly. Council announced that it was unable to approve all the amendments and, accordingly, conciliation followed. After six and a half hours of intense negotiations an agreement was reached at the concluding meeting held on 27 February 2001. Agreement was facilitated by the intensive interinstitutional interactions that had occurred at earlier stages of the process (see *European Voice* 7 December 2000), and by the prior meetings of the EP's delegation and the trialogue held with the Swedish Presidency and the Commission on 6 February 2001 (PE 287.586 2001:6). Indeed, in the trialogue the Council accepted 12 amendments and presented compromise texts for some others.

The main issues for consideration in conciliation, therefore, included the nature of health warnings, prohibition of misleading descriptors, the use of photographs and illustrations, the list of ingredients, and a transitional period for exported tobacco products. Compromises were reached on all of these issues. At this stage, the proponents of tight controls on tobacco made available to the Conciliation Committee (and to all 626 MEPs) Canadian cigarette packets (which were empty!) to demonstrate that strict regulation of the labelling of tobacco products was entirely practical and, indeed, was already in force elsewhere.

The outcome of the conciliation process was judged by the EP's rapporteur to be that 'the agreement reached is an excellent one which goes well beyond what was possible before its second reading' (PE 287.586 2001:8). On health warnings the message was strengthened and the size of health warnings was agreed on the basis of the Commission's compromise (noted above). The possibility of member states authorizing the use of photographs and other graphic material on cigarette packets was conceded and the Commission (much against its own will) was given the task of adopting appropriate rules by December 2002. Agreement was also reached that the descriptors 'mild', 'light' or 'low tar' were to be prohibited. (One result of this provision was that Japanese Tobacco, manufacturers of 'Mild Seven' cigarettes – whose brand and trademark were effectively outlawed in Europe – launched a Court of Justice case against the EP and Council.)

Tobacco companies were to be obliged to submit to authorities in the member states an annual list of ingredients in their products, and the Commission was to initiate a proposal, by the end of 2004, for a list of all ingredients authorized for tobacco products. Compromise was reached on the issue of a transitional period (until 2007) for exported tobacco products to meet the tar and nicotine ceilings as products marketed in the EU. The tobacco industry (especially from the UK) had mounted a high profile, and in the end a quite effective lobby, on the transitional period. Lobbying focused overwhelmingly on the potential threat to employment as a result of the adoption of this provision. In particular, a targeted campaign, ostensibly led by workers in the tobacco industry, was directed at MEPs with cigarette factories in their constituencies. Moreover, the position of MEPs was moderated by a recognition that legislation banning the export of high tar cigarettes from the EU might contravene World Trade Organization rules.

Codecision2: limited influence – the EU's contribution to the Global Health Fund

If the 'Tobacco' directive reveals the extent to which the EP has become a co-legislator with the Council, and capable of making a significant impact upon the final legislative Act, it also needs to be borne in mind that there are other issues upon which the EP has a relatively limited impact, even under codecision2. One such example was provided in the EP's processing of the EU's contribution to the Global Health Fund in 2001. An examination of this decision helps to identify the factors that still serve to limit the legislative impact of the EP.

In July 2001 Commission President Prodi announced that the Commission had agreed to contribute €120 million to a proposed Global Fund to fight HIV/AIDS, tuberculosis and malaria. The Fund had initially been proposed by UN Secretary General Kofi Annan in April 2001. The announcement of the EU's contribution was made on the eve of the Genoa summit, at which G8 leaders intended to focus on the scourge of AIDS and other health crises in the developing world. Indeed, the EU's contribution was significant and second only to that made by the United States.

In part, the contribution was intended to raise the Commission's profile further on an issue which had aroused significant public interest in recent years. Yet, both within and outside the Commission, doubts were expressed about the potential impact of the Fund. It is perhaps of significance that Development Commissioner Poul Nielson was not personally associated with President Prodi's announcement of the EU's contribution. Indeed, Nielson's scepticism about the Fund was well-known.

It was only in October 2001, however, that the Commission came forward with a proposal setting out the financing mechanisms of the EU's contribution to the Fund (COM[2001]0612). The proposal provided a legal base for the contribution as well as recommending that a single one-off contribution be made. The finance was to be provided in two parts: €60 million of the total from the 2001 EU budget, with the remainder coming from the European Development Fund (EDF). The latter portion would thereby necessitate the approval of the EU's African, Caribbean and Pacific (ACP) partner countries. The former portion required a specific legal instrument based on Article 179 of the treaty, and thus was subject to the codecision2 procedure. Of the €60 million, 50 million was to be found from fisheries, and another 10 million from the Asia and Latin American budget lines.

Hence, what had started as a major political statement in July by the President of the Commission about the EU's contribution to the Global Health Fund had become, by October, a 'one-off' EU contribution garnered from both unused resources and from resources over which the Commission did not have sole responsibility. Moreover, the contribution hardly constituted the new and additional resources that had been implied at the time of the Commission President's announcement and in discussion about the Fund more broadly.

The EP's processing of the contribution to the Global Fund.   In submitting its proposal just two months before the end of the budgetary year the Commission severely restricted the time available to the EP to process the matter. In fact the proposal was submitted at the end of October with the Commission expecting a final decision by November. The pressure to reach a rapid response was increased by the awareness that, if the legal base was not established before the end of the year, the resources identified in the 2001 budget would no longer be available. In these circumstances the simple fact that the contribution was processed within the timeframe available was a source of pleasure to Fernández Martín (EPP–ED, Spain): 'we have achieved this in record time, through the codecision procedure, with urgency and at first reading' (EP Debates 28 November 2001). In many respects this 'achievement' was all the more remarkable given that the Development Committee had little experience of the codecision procedure (see Chapter 6).

As the Development Committee was scheduled to meet for only two days in November and for one day in December 2001, the timetable was unduly tight. It would not have been feasible to process the necessary legislation through the full sequence of the appointment of a rapporteur, consideration of a draft report, tabling of amendments, adoption of amendments and referral to plenary if the procedure had needed to go beyond first reading. But the urgency accompanying this particular proposal highlighted the more general issue of the Commission's (and, for that matter, Council's) oft-repeated failure to incorporate the constraints inherent in the working methods of the EP into its procedural thinking and scheduling of legislation.

Parliament's Development Committee placed the Commission's proposal on its agenda for 19 November, and the Director-General of the Commission's DG Development, Koos Richelle, attended in person to explain the proposal. During the exchange of views with the Director-General about the proposal, the strength of dissatisfaction among members about the Commission's approach was notable. Members of the Committee were concerned about the indeterminate nature of the Global Health Fund itself, as its structure was far from settled at the end of 2001. The Commission's proposal for a legal base for the EU's contribution was subject to the criticism that public money was about to be handed to a fund which hardly yet possessed a bank account, let alone had clear rules for spending its resources. Indeed, a note prepared by the EP's Development Committee secretariat observed that: 'Parliament is not at all aware of these arrangements [for financing projects under the Fund] and must be properly informed in order not to give a blank cheque' (European Parliament 2001b:2).

More specifically, in terms of procedure, committee members insisted that the Commission had put Parliament in a 'take it or leave it' position and so had effectively stripped Parliament of its power under codecision. In this regard, Parliament was confronted by a dilemma. On the one side, MEPs resented being confronted with what was tantamount to a *fait accompli*. Yet, on the other side, they were extremely reluctant to be seen to be opposed to the creation of a legal base for the financing of measures to promote access to health care in poor countries. Parliamentarians were well aware of the political imperative for the proposal to be adopted before the end of 2001, and for EU finances to be transferred to the Fund as soon as possible. As Fernando Fernández Martín stated during the later plenary debate: 'I have to say how much we regret that the Council and, especially, the Commission, have put us in such a difficult position' (EP Debates 28 November 2001). In turn Commissioner Nielson acknowledged the difficulties encountered by the EP but thanked it, nonetheless, 'for the cooperative manner in which Parliament has handled this matter in spite of the difficulties we have had'. He did stress however that:

> We still have many unanswered questions. This is the real reason why it has not been easy or possible for the Commission to move this dossier forward in a very nice, elegant and timely manner…I regret that the proposal was transmitted so late in the year to the budget authority but this reflects the fact that we did not have anything good or clear enough before that. (EP Debates 28 November 2001)

In informal negotiations between the committee chairperson, senior members of the EP's Development Committee and officials of the Council Presidency and the Commission's Development DG, a compromise was achieved whereby it was agreed that Parliament would adopt eight amendments to the Commission's proposal. Of these only two were of particular significance. One clarified the fact that the EU's contribution was for 2001 only, thereby not preempting any subsequent contribution which might be proposed during 2002. It did not, however, suggest that a contribution during 2002, or in subsequent years, was likely. This contrasted sharply with Parliament's fundamental starting point in negotiations with Council that the €60 million was only a first contribution, to be followed by an annual contribution decided each year by Council and Parliament as part of the budgetary procedure. A second amendment agreed a recital to the regulation which suggested that the Commission 'should propose a legal basis for future contributions ... including any further contributions to the Global Fund'. This latter change was not only limited to a recital but also failed to specify a timescale for subsequent action. A further amendment sought to require the Commission to submit a report to Parliament and Council on the management and working methods of the Fund.

In the case of the Global Fund, Parliament's impact was clearly very limited. Even so, despite being 'bounced' into a quick decision, Parliament did reach agreement with the Council and the Commission. Some amendment of the Commission's proposal was secured and some sense of the EP's concern over reporting procedures and management procedures found reflection in the final act. The EP's strong political support for the Commission's actual objective meant that despite the procedural hurdles, and limited parliamentary impact, it was possible, nonetheless, to agree legislation under codecision urgently and at first reading.

Formal models of legislative influence

The academic analysis of the legislative influence of the EP has been dominated by a small number of scholars working primarily within the parameters of rational choice theory or more precisely 'non-cooperative game theory applied to spatial models of political competition' (Tsebelis and Garrett 2000:11). In the absence, until very recently, of systematic empirical data on the EP's legislative influence, rational choice theories were advanced to fill what their proponents believed was an empirical void. Indeed, Tsebelis and Garrett, who, individually and jointly, have been at the forefront of modelling and theoretical contestation about the legislative influence of the EP, believe that 'a major reason the theoretical debate goes unresolved is the inadequacy of empirical data' (Tsebelis *et al.* 2001:574). Their aim has been 'to make simple and clear models that lead to specific predictions' and to do so by challenging the 'conventional wisdom' derived from 'too much reliance on case studies and the views of informed insiders' (Garrett and Tsebelis 2001:361).

What is important to remember from the outset, however, is that for a long period the debate has been about *formal models* of decision-making in the EU. Different modes of modelling, based upon different theoretical assumptions, lead to different conclusions about the outcomes of the EU's legislative process. Thus, as Steunenberg (2000:368–9) notes:

> several models have been developed yielding different conjectures about the possible outcomes of this [the EU's decision making] process – the contents of common policy – and the extent to which this outcome resembles the preferences of some actors ... Despite the elegance and complexity of these models, the 'findings' are still conjectures, which might not be empirically true.

The essence of such models is captured in Crombez's (1999:4) summary:

> In spatial models of political institutions and legislative procedures alternative policies are represented by points in a policy space. Each dimension of the policy space stands for a specific policy issue. The relevant political actors have preferences over alternative polices. Often, they are assumed to have Euclidean preferences. That is, each political actor has an ideal policy and prefers policies that are closer to, rather than farther away from, his ideal policy. Policy making can then be thought of as choosing a point in the policy space.

In his early studies of EU decision-making Tsebelis examined the logic and outcomes of the cooperation procedure. From an analysis of the later stages of the cooperation procedure he concluded that:

> the EP has an important power: it can make proposals that, if accepted by the Commission, are easier [for the Council] to

> accept than to modify (only qualified majority being required for acceptance but unanimity, for modification). I call this power the conditional agenda setter. (Tsebelis 1994:128)

Without outlining the complexities of the conditional agenda-setting model, the essence of Tsebelis's position is that under the cooperation procedure the EP could 'offer a proposal that makes a qualified majority of the Council better off than any unanimous decision. *If* such a proposal exists, *if* the EP is able to make it, and *if* the Commission adopts it, then the EP has agenda setting powers' (original emphasis 1994:131). If these conditions were not fulfilled then it lost its agenda-setting power. It is in this sense that the EP's agenda power was deemed by Tsebelis to be 'conditional'.

Throughout successive studies Tsebelis maintained that the EP's conditional agenda-setting power under cooperation was far from trivial (Tsebelis 1994, 1995; Tsebelis and Garrett 1997, 2000). This claim has been challenged however by other analysts working within a rational choice institutional framework. Crombez for example produced a spatial model of three EU legislative procedures (consultation, cooperation and assent) in order to assess 'the workings of EC institutions and procedures, and arguments over the future direction institutional change should take' (1996:201). Unlike Tsebelis, however, he concluded that under cooperation the EP did not have agenda-setting powers. While the EP had a veto power, a unanimous Council could override its veto. Overall, therefore, Crombez concluded that the cooperation procedure did not increase the EP's powers (1996:224). Similarly, Moser disputed the findings of Tsebelis and concluded that under the cooperation procedure the EP had only limited powers and these were derived from 'conditional veto rights' rather than a conditional agenda-setting capacity (Moser 1996:838; 1997).

However, the commonalities and divergences of spatial theories are most evident in analyses of the EU's legislative process under the codecision procedure. Despite empirical evidence to the contrary Tsebelis *et al.* maintained that 'the conditional agenda setting powers accorded to the Parliament by cooperation are more important than the veto powers ascribed by codecision' (Tsebelis *et al.* 2001:573). In analysing codecision1, the procedure after Maastricht, Tsebelis and Garrett (Tsebelis and Garrett 1996,

1997, 2000; Tsebelis *et al.* 2001) claimed that the conditional agenda-setting powers were lost as the EP acquired unconditional veto powers. Their contention was that under cooperation the EP was able to select the compromise closest to its ideal point, while under codecision1 selection was delegated to the Council. Under codecision2, the procedure as modified by the Amsterdam Treaty, the EP became a co-legislator with the Council and became 'unambiguously more powerful than it was under cooperation' (Tsebelis and Garrett 2000:11). The reason adduced by Tsebelis and Garrett was that the Council could no longer overrule the EP and that the two institutions bargain on an equal footing with no *a priori* bargaining advantage inhering to either institution.

Different assumptions, different predictions and different conclusions

While Tsebelis and Garrett's assessment of the EP's legislative impact under codecision2 brings them closer to the empirical and academic mainstream they still maintain that their model of conditional agenda setting correctly identified the Council as an unconstrained agenda setter under codecision1 (Tsebelis and Garrett 2000:23). This brings them into conflict with the conclusions of other analysts using spatial models. Crombez (1999:22) has no doubts that the EP 'becomes a genuine co-legislature equal in stature to the Council'. For Scully (1997:65 emphasis in original), Tsebelis and Garrett's findings were 'invalid even *within* the logic of [their] own model'. These divergent conclusions about the legislative impact of the EP under codecision1 highlight the simple fact that when different assumptions are built into rational choice models they culminate in different predictions (see Rittberger 2000:568–70). For example, whether the entire codecision procedure, or only the last two stages of the procedure, are included in the model has a significant impact upon the predictions of each model (see Crombez 2000:364–5). Equally, predictions are affected by the choice of assumptions: one-dimensional versus *n*-dimensional spatial models; complete versus imperfect information; one shot versus iterated games; and two unitary institutional actors versus one single player (EP) and a non-unitary actor (Council).

Tsebelis and Garrett in defending their conclusions on codecision1, and in defying the practical experience of the procedure itself (see above), invoke the notion of 'backward induction' (1997:80). In translation, this means that the Council can foresee what will happen at each stage of the procedure and so adopt a stance at the outset at the first reading. Or, in Tsebelis and Garrett's words, 'rational actors ... strategise "backwards" from the end of a game-tree to the beginning' (1997:80). Whilst in game theory the logic of backward induction might be 'unimpeachable', one-play extensive form games are rarely encountered 'in real life' (Dowding 2000:131). Certainly, the bargaining processes between Council and EP do not constitute a single game but rather represent 'a series of games over many issues, and bargaining in one game will affect moves in other games' (see Dowding 2000:131).

Just as Tsebelis and Garrett's modelling of interinstitutional bargaining has been deemed deficient, so too has their understanding of the 'real world' of bargaining and procedural manoeuvrings within the EP. Generally, Richard Corbett (2000:378) notes that a 'striking feature' of the writings of Tsebelis and Garrett is 'the apparent lack of knowledge of particular features of EU procedures'. Specifically, Burns (1999:11) maintains that their belief that the Commission did not reconsider the EP's amendments after second reading was 'quite simply incorrect'. Equally damning is Scully's assessment that the actual provisions of third reading in the codecision1 procedure 'bears almost no resemblance' to the bargaining game described by Tsebelis and Garrett' (Scully 1997:102).

Tsebelis and Garrett have also been criticized for missing the nuances of bargaining in the EP. Their model cannot accommodate the reality of informal bargaining (as identified by Judge *et al.* 1994; Earnshaw and Judge 1996; Garman and Hilditch 1998; Shackleton 2000). Moreover, Corbett questions the extent to which their model is based 'on a too literal interpretation of the Treaty that took no account of how the institutions sought to interpret or use the Treaty' (Corbett 2000:374). In other words, the model was not based 'on practical reality'.

In the world of 'backwards induction' and 'endgames' there is undoubtedly merit in Tsebelis and Garrett's work. In the 'real world' of EP decision-making and interinstitutional bargaining, however, the pristine logic of rational choice appears a little tarnished both by the limited modelling of the procedure and by alternative qualitative assessments of the outcomes of the codecision procedure itself. Doubts have been raised as to the value of rational choice modelling when 'much of the empirical evidence flies in the face of the Tsebelis and Garrett theory' (Corbett 2000:373); and when a leading MEP claimed that: 'I do not know anybody who is involved in this business: from the Council side, in the Commission, or in the Parliament, who would argue such a case' (Ken Collins, MEP, quoted in Wurzel 1999:5).

Despite the methodological and modelling disputes (see Moser 1996:834–7; Tsebelis 1996:839–43; Crombez 1996: 207–19; Moser 1997:337–445) and the deficiencies of extant models, the common objective remains the development of consistent rational choice-based explanations of EP legislative influence, and to do so by explicit analysis of interinstitutional relations. There is no dispute that the institutional configuration of the EU, the changing dynamic of interinstitutional relations and the procedural refinements of successive treaties impact on policy outputs. The dispute arises over exactly how much and why the impact varies.

Influence over the executive

> The relationships between the legislature and the executive are the cornerstone of any parliamentary system: as parliaments are regarded as the main providers of legitimacy, executive authority must derive from, and be responsible to, the legislature. (Dehousse 1998:609)

In parliamentary systems, as noted in Chapter 1, there is a basic interconnectedness between the legislative and executive branches of government. This interconnectedness entails both *post hoc* accountability and *ante hoc* 'directedness' (in the sense of influencing future policy preferences). As Chapter 7 observed, the formal powers of dismissal and appointment extended beyond the choice of executive personnel to incorporate the EP's capacities to hold the Commission responsible for its collective and individual actions and also to influence its policy agenda. Of particular significance to the discussion here is the fact that the Maastricht Treaty synchronized the Commission's term of office with that of Parliament. After Maastricht the appointment of the President, and of the Commission as a whole, now coincided with that of a new parliament. The intention was that the coterminous periods of office of the EP and the Commission would facilitate not only parliamentary scrutiny and control and increase the Commission's accountability to Parliament, but would also encourage the 'prior authorization' of the Commission's programme.

There are at least two major dimensions to the notion of 'prior authorization'. The first stems from the logic of 'control through selection'. The reasoning is simple in that it was believed that the new selection process would increase not only the EP's influence over who was appointed as President (and subsequently as Commissioners and to which specific portfolios) but also that it would enhance Parliament's impact on the Commission's policy agenda by securing the 'prior authorization' of the executive's programme. Paradoxically, the logic of maximized parliamentary control over the Commission's agenda rested in a further 'presidentialization' of the Commission itself under the Amsterdam Treaty. Article 219 states that the 'Commission shall work under the political guidance of its President'. In effect there are both positive and negative dimensions to such 'political guidance'. Perhaps, not surprisingly given the events surrounding the resignation of the Santer Commission, the negative dimension of individual resignations and the individual responsibility of Commissioners preoccupied the incoming Commission President in 1999 (see Judge and Earnshaw 2002). However, the positive dimension of presidential 'political guidance' was incorporated in a new right conferred by the Amsterdam Treaty on the President to agree or disagree (by 'common accord' (Article 214)) on member states' nominees for Commission posts. Furthermore, Declaration 32 to the treaty also recorded that 'the President of the Commission must enjoy broad discretion in the allocation of tasks within the College, as well as in any reshuffling of those tasks during a Commission's term of office'. From the EP's perspective, such enhanced presidential authority contributed to a further incremental increase of parliamentary influence over the Commission. Thus, Spence (2000:5–6), for example, identified the EP's ability to vote on the President as 'a way of influencing the Commission's agenda, as parliamentarians could make their ratification of a President conditional on his/her amenability to their programme'. In practice, however, Prodi's personal impact on the choice of Commissioners and the allocation of portfolios continued to be closely delimited by the interests of national governments (see *European Voice* 8–14 July 1999; Spence 2000:7–8).

A second dimension of 'prior authorization' is the acceptance of the Commission's policy programme by a parliamentary majority. In the case of the EU, exactly what constitutes 'authorization' and what is being 'authorized' remains open to wide interpretation. On the one side, the Commission's programme is not the exclusive construct of supranational endeavour but also reflects the priorities of constituent member governments and national organized interests (Peterson 1999:59). On the other, Parliament's assessment of the programme is conditioned by national party considerations and political group perspectives (see Chapter 9). Despite these ambiguities, Romano Prodi, as President-designate, agreed to present to Parliament the Commission's 'policy perspectives for the next five years' (Prodi, Speech to the EP 14 September 1999). The five-year programme was designed to supplement the established practice of the presentation of the annual work programmes by the Commission. The first annual programme had been submitted in 1988, and the system was gradually revised over the years in an attempt to increase its contribution to the planning and monitoring of EU legislation. Even so, the annual programme provided little indication of the priorities of the Commission and tended to be introduced by anodyne statements of good intent. In return, parliamentary deliberation of the programme was characteristically perfunctory and 'mechanical' (for details see Corbett *et al.* 2000:212).

When the EP eventually considered the Commission's policy priorities, as outlined in the document *Strategic Objectives 2000–2005 'Shaping the New Europe'* (European Commission 2000b), at its plenary of 15 February 2000, Mr Prodi was at pains to emphasize that 'a five-year programme is an extremely important undertaking'. Its purpose was to provide the Commission's 'major guidelines for action over the next five years' (EP Debates 15 February 2000). In fact Mr Prodi was willing to liken the programme to 'a political manifesto' (EP Debates 15 February 2000).

From Parliament's side Enrique Barón Crespo, as leader of the PSE, particularly welcomed 'the first ever debate on the Commission's programme for government – the word President Prodi is so fond of; as I am – for the whole legislature' (EP Debates 15 February 2000). In this respect he acknowledged that the five-year programme was 'breaking new ground'. However, he also recognized that the time-lapse of eleven months from Prodi's nomination to the presentation of the programme infringed the notion of 'prior authorization'. In which case he believed that, in future, 'it would be appropriate for the investiture of the next Commission to coincide with the presentation of a legislative programme'.

At least one UK member of the EPP–ED took exception to the use of the term 'government' by Prodi and Barón Crespo, with James Elles being quick to point out that 'The Commission is not in fact today a European Government' and, moreover, it did 'not reflect the majority in this particular Parliament' (EP Debates 15 February 2000). The significance of this statement for the 'parliamentarization' of the EU will be examined in Chapter 9. Here, however, what needs to be noted is that, underpinning the congratulatory statements to the Commission President for honouring his commitment to present a five-year programme to Parliament, there was an undercurrent of concern about the substantive merits of the programme itself. MEPs from the smaller groups were particularly critical, with, for example, Francis Wurtz of the EUL/NGL, expressing concern that the 'weakness of the analysis and the obstacles to the necessary changes have resulted in a project whose scope is severely limited by an overabundance of generalisations, a rather indecisive approach and therefore a lack of impetus' (EP Debates 15 February 2000; see also Gianfranco Dell'Alba (TDI)).

Nonetheless, Prodi 'perceived a broad consensus on the basic lines of our programme' within Parliament (EP Debates 15 February 2000) and from this base sought to effect a more ambitious scheme of policy management in the future. A first stage, in July 2000, was the incorporation of the five-year programme into a new Framework Agreement between the EP and the Commission (European Parliament 2000b). The two institutions agreed that 'an incoming Commission shall present, as soon as possible, its political programme, containing all its proposed guidelines for its term of office, and shall establish a dialogue with the European Parliament' (for details of the Framework see Judge and Earnshaw 2002). The Commission also agreed to six-monthly reports on the implementation of the work programme and regular updates of any changed priorities occasioned by changing political circumstances.

A second stage came in January 2001 when the Commission presented its traditional work programme for the coming year (COM[2001]28 final) but stressed that its 'priority objectives' would now be pursued 'bearing in mind the guidelines laid down by the Commission when it came into office' (COM[2001]28:4). More radically, in February 2001, the Commission also adopted its first Annual Policy Strategy. This document set out the political priorities which required 'special attention in 2002'. It also defined actions stemming from those priorities and sought to allocate resources accordingly (COM[2001]620 final:3). In turn, the introduction of the Strategy had knock-on effects for the presentation of the Commission's work programme to the EP. One immediate result was that the 2002 programme was presented in early December 2001, rather than, as in the past, at the beginning of the calendar year itself. A second consequence was that the work programme sought to assess progress in the current year, to identify the political and economic context for the forthcoming year, to identify the political priorities in light of the Annual Policy Strategy, and then to translate those priorities into practice in 2002 (COM[2001]620 final:3). In this sense it was identified as a 'genuine political programme' (Prodi, EP Debates 11 December 2001).

But the 2002 programme was accompanied by a third stage whereby future work programmes were to be based on 'a more structured dialogue' between the Commission and Parliament programme' (Prodi, EP Debates 11 December 2001). Thus, the 2003 work programme was to entail an initial presentation, in February 2002, of the political priorities approved by the Commission followed by the formal presentation of the programme itself to the EP in November 2002. Moreover, the debate on the 2002 programme was attended by Annemie Neyt-Uttebroeck as a representative of the Belgian Presidency (and a former MEP). But she was anxious to note that, although the Council was 'very interested' in the Commission's work programme, each institution remained, nonetheless, 'autonomous in the drafting of its own work schedule and deciding upon its own priorities' (EP Debates 11 December 2001).

For all the talk of 'a more structured dialogue' there still remained manifest shortcomings in the eyes of MEPs. First, the 2002 work programme was unavailable for preparatory discussions in EP group meetings the week before it was presented to Parliament (Poettering, EP Debates 11 December 2001). Second, the leader of the EPP–ED wondered why – if the programme was that of a self-styled 'government' – the whole College of Commissioners was not present to offer its support in the EP. Third, Barón Crespo voiced doubts that what had been presented by the Commission was a political programme. In his eyes it was a 'working programme' but the PSE also wanted a 'legislative programme' (EP Debates 11 December 2001). The fact that the legislative programme was only forwarded to the EP the night before the debate spoke volumes of the ability of the EP to 'prior authorize' the details of the Commission's programme. The problem of processing, and so influencing, the working programme was highlighted by Pat Cox (then ELDR leader) in his plea: 'The Commission already has a wonderful process of consultation in place with the social partners. Share this process with us [the EP] as well' (EP Debates 11 December 2001). Ultimately, Paul Lannoye (Greens, Belgium) concluded that, in the circumstances surrounding the 2002 programme, 'I think that Parliament is *de facto* deprived of its powers of control and influence' (EP Debates 11 December 2001).

Concern with the presentation, timing and processing of the legislative and work programme led Parliament's Constitutional Affairs Committee to recommend a revised timetable for its preparation and for its consideration by the EP (PE 304.309 2002). The Committee's starting point was an acknowledgement that the annual legislative programme was 'an invaluable tool for the functioning of the European institutions' but that the 'whole legislative cycle is opaque and quite incomprehensible not only to the European Parliament, but also to the citizens and the national parliaments' (PE 304.309 2002:11). By changing the procedures surrounding the preparation of the legislative and work programme the Committee sought to increase interinstitutional cooperation between the Commission and the EP and so increase the influence of the latter in the legislative cycle and in the identification of the priorities of the former institution.

Conclusion

From the evidence presented in this chapter there is little doubt, empirically, that the EP is a genuine co-legislator with the Council under the codecision2 procedure. This is so whether assessed quantitatively, in terms of the numbers of successful amendments, or qualitatively, in terms of the substantive changes effected to legislative proposals. Equally, the significance of the EP's influence is apparent in formal models of the EU's legislative process. What those models reveal, as do the detailed case studies examined above, is the contingency of EP influence. One theme of this book has been that the nature of interinstitutional bargaining, the systemetic context (the nature of multi-level governance) within which those bargains are made, and the multifunctionality of the EP (as representative, legislative and oversight institution) all impact upon the capacity of Parliament to exert influence in the EU's policy process.

A further theme of this chapter, and of this book more generally, has been that the formal dimensions of influence have to be supplemented by recognition of the informal dimensions of the EP's contribution to the EU's decision-making processes. Other scholars have come to acknowledge the inextricable linkage of these formal and informal dimensions (see Farrell and Héritier 2002; Hix 2002), and of how the creative use of the EP's own Rules of Procedure, and interinstitutional innovations – such as trialogues, framework agreements and *modus vivendi* – serve to extend the EP's legislative influence beyond its treaty-prescribed powers. Not only is this a historical phenomenon, as revealed in Chapter 2, but it also constitutes a future strategy. Indeed, the elemental importance of this strategy is recognized by one Council official:

> Parliament wants to be 'top-dog'. They are constantly building, piece by piece, brick by brick, and the trend has been over recent treaties to give them more powers, to give them a greater role ... When you get an informal procedure established with

Parliament, they want to concretize it in the Treaty, or in an inter-institutional agreement. (Quoted in Farrell and Héritier 2002:15)

Simon Hix (2002:261) has recently translated these established perspectives of the incremental advancement of the EP's powers (through small steps and qualitative leaps (see Chapter 2)) into a 'new theory of the development of the powers of the EP'. In so doing, Hix characterizes the development of the EP's legislative powers as a transition from 'consultation to bicameralism' (2002:261) and its powers over the appointment of the Commission as a transformation of the EU 'from international organization to parliamentary government' (2002:264). While Hix formulates these 'transitions' as mere statements, they are in fact contentions that need to be analysed. This we intend to do in Chapter 9, and in this regard, Hix's 'transitions' provide us with a neat pivot by which to turn from the specific focus of this chapter with legislative influence to the more general concern of the next chapter with the 'parliamentarization' of the EU.

Chapter 9

A Parliamentary Europe?

Introduction

An essential part of the analysis of this book has been to examine the extent to which the EP can be understood in terms of the universal roles ascribed to 'parliaments'. Established analyses of comparative legislatures have been used to assess the merits of arguments about whether the EP constitutes a 'true', 'proper' or 'normal' parliament; and discussions about whether the EU can be identified as a parliamentary system and the prospects for further 'parliamentarization' have been set within a broader examination of the notion of a 'parliamentary model' (see Chapter 1).

Manifestly the primary focus of this book has been the European Parliament itself. Yet, throughout the preceding chapters, the connections between the parliamentary processes at national level have intruded into the analysis of the supranational EP. Moreover, conceptions of what sort of political system the EU is – whether 'type 1 governance' or 'type 2 multi-level governance' (see Chapter 1) – have provided a subconscious structuring of the debate. That the sources of legitimation within the EU are multi-level is widely accepted, as is the idea of a 'dual legitimacy' rooted in representative parliaments at both national and EU levels. Indeed, as we will see below, the EU has consciously sought to develop dual legitimation in practice, through an acknowledgement that both national parliaments and the European Parliament have roles to play in providing authorization, representation and accountability in the Union. Thus, as we noted in Chapter 3, much of the political debate surrounding the future political order in Europe revolves around parliaments and further parliamentarization of the EU's political process.

Part of the purpose of this chapter, therefore, is to examine exactly what further 'parliamentarization' means and the forms that this process takes. A further purpose is to reveal the complexities and ambiguities entailed in that process. But,

293

equally, this chapter also aims both to monitor the normative debate about the deepening of legitimation through parliamentary institutions and to examine the practical steps taken to enhance legitimation through coordination of the activities of national parliaments and the EP. If the 'future of Europe' is 'parliamentary', we need to understand what 'parliamentarization' entails and the extent to which the interinstitutional connections between national parliaments and the EP contribute to such a process.

The EP and national parliaments compared

Chapter 1 introduced typologies of how legislatures could be ranked in terms of their policy influence. As was noted there, Mezey (1979:36) produced a threefold categorization of those parliaments with strong, modest, or little or no policy-making power or impact, and Norton (1990:178) offered a parallel typology of policy-*making*, policy-*influencing*, or little or no policy impact. Chapter 2 then proceeded to chronicle how successive enhancements of the formal and informal powers of the EP had transformed the categorization of the EP over time. At its inception the Common Assembly had no legislative powers and no direct democratic legitimacy, and so was easily located in Mezey's categorization as having 'little or no legislative influence'. In the early 1980s, in the wake of the *Isoglucose* ruling, the EP began to edge away from the lowest category of legislative influence towards the modest influence/power category. After Maastricht, and certainly after Amsterdam and Nice, the EP – with its capacity to 'modify and reject executive proposals' under codecision2 – can now be located in Mezey's category of legislatures with 'strong policy-making power'.

If the policy influence of the EP has increased diachronically (making a comparison across over half a century), how does the EP rank in comparison with other national parliaments in the early twenty-first century? Two recent attempts to answer this question have been provided by Scully (2000a) and Bergman and Raunio (2001). Both assessments are acutely aware of the difficulties entailed in measuring influence and producing comparative rankings (see Scully 2000a:235–6; Bergman and Raunio 2001:120) yet both conclude that the EP ranks highly in comparison to other West European legislatures.

In reaching their assessment Bergman and Raunio disaggregate the analysis of influence and provide three separate rankings based, respectively, upon a 'transformer-arena' scale, an 'agenda-power' scale, and a 'lobby attractiveness' scale. The first scale measures a legislature's policy influence relative to that of the executive. On this scale, the EP (under codecision) ranks sixth in a list of West European legislatures (Bergman and Raunio 2001:121). This ranking is based upon the EP exerting high policy influence while lacking a formal right to initiate legislation in its own right and not possessing the ability to control a single executive. On the agenda-setting scale the EP fares even better and is ranked jointly in second place with the Italian parliament behind the Dutch parliament. On the third scale the EP is ranked in terms of its 'attractiveness' to lobbyists. Bergman and Raunio (2001:123) maintain that 'There is no question that lobbyists find the EP attractive' and so position the EP in second place just behind the Austrian parliament. Overall, therefore, Bergman and Raunio (2001:123) conclude that 'MEPs probably have more direct impact on policy output at the EU level than many national MPs have on national-level policy'. This assessment supports our own analysis in Chapter 8, and finds further support in Scully's (2000a:238) conclusion that '*in toto ...* the policy influence wielded by the EP is surely far greater than that of most national chambers in the EU'.

A Europe of parliaments: the European Parliament and national parliaments

In Chapter 3 the concept of 'dual legitimation' was raised. This idea simultaneously grounded legitimacy, at one level, in the directly elected representative institutions of the member states and, at a second level, in the directly elected European Parliament. The importance of this concept was underlined in 2002 in the report of the EP's Constitutional Affairs Committee on relations between the EP and national parliaments:

> The Union is based on a two-fold democratic mandate, as a Union of States and a Union of peoples. The European Parliament and the national parliaments, since they are both directly elected by the citizens, are equally representative of

the peoples in the European Union ... [Legitimacy rests] on two pillars, the European Parliament and the national parliaments. The European Parliament must be fully aware of this, taking care not to cultivate a simplistic attitude, increasingly seeing itself as the exclusive representative of the citizens and guarantor of democracy in relations with the other Union institutions. It must not concern itself exclusively with acquiring greater powers, ignoring recognition of the role of the national parliaments. (PE 304.302 2002:11)

The obverse of the notion of 'dual legitimacy', however, is the idea of a 'dual democratic deficit' in the EU (see Judge 1995). Here the problem of the EU's 'democratic deficit' is identified not solely as a failure by the European Parliament to exert adequate control over the Commission and the Council (the first deficit), but also a failure of national parliaments to exert sustained control over their own national executives (the second deficit). Leaving aside the contention that the EU suffers not simply from a dual but a *multiple* legitimacy crisis (see Chapter 3), one common solution to the perceived deficits is framed in terms of further 'parliamentarization' of the EU.

An important part of such a process of parliamentarization is believed to be the simultaneous strengthening of the respective control and oversight functions of the EP and of the national parliaments. Thus, in the opinion of the EP's Constitutional Affairs Committee, what is required is, first, close 'collaboration, a common vision, and a joint commitment' between parliaments in the EU; and, second, a recognition that 'the quality of relations between the European Parliament and the national parliaments is of fundamental importance for the overall democratic nature of the Union' (PE 304.302 2002:12). This echoed the conclusion of an earlier report by the Institutional Affairs Committee that 'the most productive way of tackling the democratic deficit lies in intensified cooperation between the national parliaments and the European Parliament, and for their relationship to be characterised by partnership rather than rivalry' (PE 221.698 1997:23).

Certainly, rivalry has underpinned the relationship between the EP and some national parliaments (see Judge 1995), but, equally, enhanced cooperation has resulted from three significant interparliamentary initiatives. The first is the Conference of

European Affairs Committees (COSAC), the second is parliamentary assizes and conventions, and the third is the facilitation by the EP of national parliamentary involvement in EU activities.

Conference of European Affairs Committees (COSAC)

COSAC is the French acronym for the Conference of European Affairs Committees. The Conference was established in 1989, following a French-led initiative to convene regular meetings of representatives of the respective European Affairs committees of national parliaments and representatives of the EP. At its first meeting in Paris in November 1989, COSAC agreed to increase the exchange of information among parliaments, and to meet twice a year in the country holding the Presidency of the Council to discuss issues of common concern. In 1991 specific rules of procedure were adopted to regulate COSAC meetings, and these were amended at the meetings in Athens and Rome in 1994 and in Helsinki in 1999.

Writing before the Amsterdam Treaty, Martin Westlake (1994a:60) maintained that COSAC's 'principal and enduring achievement has been to create and encourage sustained inter-parliamentary reflection on how best to overcome the "democratic deficit" '. However, the Protocol on the Role of National Parliaments appended to the Amsterdam Treaty moved beyond this reflective and 'expressive' role and gave COSAC treaty status and empowered it to:

> make any contribution it deems appropriate for the attention of the EU institutions, in particular on the basis of draft legal texts which Representatives of Governments of the Member States may decide by common accord to forward to it, in view of the nature of its subject matter.
>
> ... examine any legislative proposal or initiative in relation to the establishment of an area of freedom, security and justice which might have a direct bearing on the rights and freedoms of individuals.
>
> ... address to the European Parliament, the Council and the Commission any contribution which it deems appropriate on the legislative activities of the Union, notably in relation to the application of the principle of subsidiarity, the area of

freedom, security and justice as well as questions regarding fundamental rights. (Treaty of Amsterdam 1997)

Yet, despite its enhanced status, the actual impact of COSAC remains limited. Its most useful function is as 'a forum and an opportunity for those MPs most involved in EU issues in their national parliaments to meet and network' (HL 48 2001:memorandum by Richard Corbett MEP). Beyond this networking role some of COSAC's members see relatively few positive outcomes from its work. For example, the UK's House of Lords Select Committee on the European Union expressed disappointment that:

> There is no consensus among national parliaments about COSAC's priorities or functions, or its future role. The Agenda usually consists of extremely broad debates reflecting the priorities of the Presidency of the day. Topics are so wide that many subjects are raised and debates become a series of set speeches...COSAC meetings also aim to adopt conclusions...but the text adopted is often at the lowest common denominator, given the need to secure agreement in the text in a very limited time, often without prior consultation or discussion. (HL 48 2001:para. 73)

The Committee's overall assessment was that COSAC was 'an opportunity missed' in terms of strengthening parliamentary scrutiny within the EU's system of governance (HL 48 2001:75). This view was echoed later by the UK's House of Commons European Scrutiny Committee in its view that the potential of COSAC had been 'largely squandered' (HC 152-xxxiii 2002: para. 149).

However, a more optimistic assessment of COSAC was provided by the EP's Constitutional Affairs Committee. Whilst noting that the full potential of COSAC had not yet been exploited, the Committee went on to identify a crucial role for COSAC in facilitating dialogue among parliaments on matters of the common foreign and security policy (CFSP), European Security and Defence policy, economic and monetary union, and constitutional affairs (PE 304.302 2002:7). Moreover the Constitutional Affairs Committee proposed an interparliamentary agreement between the EP and national parliaments in order to systematize cooperation through reciprocal commitments on organizing programmes of meetings and for the exchange of information and documents (PE 304.302 2002:7).

Yet no matter how often their meetings or systematic their cooperation, the European Affairs committees of national parliaments – comprised as they are of national parliamentarians with their own national priorities, national concerns and prejudices, and with no common institutional perspective – will find it difficult to reach collective outputs that extend much beyond a lowest common denominator, or in fact to perform more than a general 'talking shop' role. The sheer pace, depth, breadth and significance of EU decision-making limits the capacity of national parliamentarians to control, or to participate effectively in, that process. Thus, while COSAC is undoubtedly of use in providing an educative and developmental forum for national parliamentarians to enhance their understanding of the EU and of its policies and functioning, its contribution to the 'democratization' of the EU is inherently limited. Indeed, the same generic constraints face the various institutional experiments with assizes and conventions, to which we now turn.

Assizes and conventions

In addition to the routinized meetings of COSAC, representatives from national parliaments and the EP have also met together in one parliamentary 'assizes' (derived from a traditional French term) and, more recently, in two 'conventions'. The assizes were held in Rome in November 1990 on the eve of the Maastricht IGC. The formal proposal for the assizes was contained in the Martin I Report (OJ C 96, 14 March 1990) which recommended that a conference of parliamentarians should be held before national governments convened intergovernmental conferences to discuss further EC treaty amendment. Indeed, Corbett (1998:296) concluded that the assizes was a 'highly significant' event as 'Never before has a major international negotiation been preceded by a conference of the very parliaments that would later have to approve the outcome of the negotiations'. Despite the successful outcome of the assizes for the EP (marked by the adoption of a declaration which endorsed all of the EP's proposals for treaty reform (see Chapter 2)), MEPs strongly resisted the regularization of such assizes in the future. Equally, a French proposal at the IGC for the creation of a new 'Congress', which would bring together delegates from national parliaments and the EP to be consulted on major EU policy options, was opposed. In the end, this proposal was negotiated out of contention and a more ano-dyne proposal was annexed to the Maastricht Treaty in Declaration 14:

> The Conference invites the European Parliament and the national parliaments to meet as necessary as a Conference of the Parliaments (or 'assises').
>
> The Conference of the Parliaments will be consulted on the main features of the European Union, without prejudice to the powers of the European Parliament and the rights of national parliaments. (Declaration 14, Treaty of Maastricht)

Nonetheless, despite opposition within the EP to the institutionalization of 'assizes', an ad hoc convention was established in December 1999 to draft the Charter of Fundamental Rights. The convention consisted of 16 MEPs, 30 representatives of national parliaments, 15 representatives of the Heads of State and Government and a representative of the President of the Commission. The EP's Constitutional Affairs Committee provided the basis of a mandate for collective action by the EP's representatives in its report (PE 232.648 2000:8). No such mandate was available, however, for the diverse members of national parliamentary delegations (HL 67 2000:paras 35–6). As one participating MEP noted: 'the national parliamentary 30 ha[d] no framework or steering within which they [could] function so [they were] pretty much all over the place' (HL 67 2000:Q106, Andrew Duff).

Overall, however, the Lords EU Committee concluded that: 'The composition of the "Convention" is ... welcome: representation from national parliaments and the European Parliament provides the opportunity for a more direct input from elected representatives than is the norm at EU level' (HL 67 2000: para. 152). Similarly, the EP acknowledged that the Convention was 'an original and extremely valuable experience' (PE 304.302 2002:16).

Pre-2004 IGC Convention on the Future of Europe

In the Declaration on the Future of the Union annexed to the Treaty of Nice a process of 'wide-ranging discussions with all interested parties' was outlined. For its part, the EP maintained that such discussions should be conducted within 'a body such as the tried and tested Convention' (PE 304.302 2002:17). Thus, from expressing concern at any institutionalization of an assizes model a decade earlier, by 2002 the convention model was now accepted as 'tried and tested'. Of particular importance in reconciling the EP to such a model was a recognition that the convening of a pre-IGC convention would mean:

> moving towards assigning to the national parliaments – who hitherto have merely been called upon to say yes or no during ratification – and the European Parliament – which hitherto has not even been entitled to give its assent to revisions of the Treaties – *joint constituent power*, i.e. a constituent power shared with the national governments. This would mark a new chapter in the role of parliaments in European integration. (PE 304.302 2002:16)

The motion for resolution produced by the Constitutional Affairs Committee in January 2002 underlined the significance of the Convention as it allowed 'not only ... effective preparation of reform of the treaties but would also give European integration efforts greater legitimacy and would thus mark a new chapter in the role of parliaments in European integration by introducing a major institutional innovation' (PE 304.302 2002:17). Nonetheless, despite these blandishments, a convention or assizes model holds relatively few opportunities for a practical reduction of the democratic deficits in the daily operations of the EU.

National parliaments

While the EP has always recognized that the modes of scrutiny of EU policies employed by national parliaments is entirely a matter of national responsibility (PE 221.698 1997:7), nonetheless it has maintained that there were measures which could be adopted at an EU level which would facilitate national parliamentary scrutiny. Thus, for example, recent treaty amendments have encouraged the greater involvement of national parliaments in the activities of the EU. In this manner, for the first time, the Maastricht Treaty acknowledged the role of national parliaments and that the exchange of information between the EP and national parliaments was vital. To this end Declaration 13 proposed that national governments should ensure that their respective parliaments should 'receive Commission proposals for legislation in good time for information or possible examination'. This commitment to the timeous provision of Commission proposals was reiterated in Protocol 20 of the Amsterdam Treaty. The protocol also stipulated that there should be a six-week period between a legislative proposal being made available and the date when it is placed on the Council agenda for decision.

Modification of the protocol on the role of national parliaments was urged by COSAC in the run-up to the Nice Treaty. At its meeting in Versailles in October 2000 COSAC recommended: the electronic transmission to each national parliament of all consultation documents and proposals for legislation from the European Commission; that the six-week time period should be extended to CFSP proposals; and that a minimum 15-day time period, or one week in urgent cases, should be observed between the final reading of a text by COREPER and the Council decision (COSAC 2000). However, the 2000 IGC did not consider COSAC's proposals and the EP's Constitutional Affairs Committee was left to urge that the 2004 IGC should consider the implementation of the recommended procedures (PE 304.302 2002:14). Equally, the Committee noted the urgent need to examine how adequate information could be transmitted to national parliaments about comitology procedures and the activities of conciliation committees.

While a number of leading politicians, in the period before the Nice summit, made speeches about the need to involve national parliaments more closely in the EU's decision-making processes, no new text on their role was incorporated into the treaty itself.

Predictably, the role of national parliaments resurfaced in the deliberations of the European Convention in 2002. In its working group on national parliaments, in its discussion papers (see, for example, CONV 67/02 2002), and in its plenary deliberations (see especially 6 and 7 June 2002, CONV 97/02 2002) the case for greater involvement of national parliaments in the

EU's activities was explored. The precise means for enhancing this involvement ranged from suggestions to increase their political scrutiny of national governments, through treaty amendment to effect compulsory consultation of national parliaments, to various changes to the EU's institutional architecture. Amongst numerous suggestions in this latter respect were: a strengthened role for COSAC; the establishment of a permanent congress (as envisaged by the Rome assizes of 1990); and the creation of a second chamber either alongside or within the European Parliament (CONV 67/02 2002).

A second parliamentary chamber for Europe

A recurring proposal for the 'parliamentarization' of the EU, through greater involvement of national parliaments in the EU decision-making processes, has been the creation of a second chamber of the European Parliament. As early as 1953 the Assembly of the ECSC, in its draft treaty for a European Political Community, included provision for a bicameral legislature. Alongside a Chamber of Peoples representing 'the peoples united in the Community' would be a Senate to represent 'the people of each state' and with senators selected by national parliaments (HL 48 2001:para. 9). These proposals fell with the failure of the draft treaties for the European Political and the European Defence Communities themselves (see Chapter 2). However, the early years of the twenty-first century witnessed a marked revival of interest in the notion of a bicameral European Parliament. In rapid succession leading politicians in France, Germany and the UK, alongside MEPs and individual EU Commissioners, advanced the case for a second chamber (for details see HL 48 2001:paras 13–16; HC 152-xxxiii 2002:paras 122–8). In May 2001 the French Prime Minister, Lionel Jospin, suggested that a Congress of National Parliaments should be established to monitor the application of the principle of subsidiarity. A year earlier the German Minister for Foreign Affairs, Joschka Fischer, had called for a bicameral European Parliament to reflect both 'a Europe of nation states and a Europe of citizens'. He suggested the second chamber could either draw its members equally from each member state in a small 'senate'; or, alternatively, have variable representation from each member state according to size. Nearly a year later, in April 2001, the German President, Johannes Rau, also called for a second chamber but this time composed of ministers from the member states. Rau's proposal, in turn, echoed a scheme that had been articulated by the German Chancellor Gerhard Schröder in November 2000. Schröder proposed that the Council of Ministers should be transformed as a second legislative 'Chamber of States' to operate alongside the existing EP. But a speech made by the UK's Prime Minister, Tony Blair, in Warsaw in October 2000, particularly ignited the debate about a second chamber in the EU.

For Mr Blair and the UK government the stated attraction of a second chamber was that it would: serve to connect national parliaments and parliamentarians more directly with decision-making in Brussels; help to define what could be best done at a European level and what could best be achieved at a national level; review implementation of the Commission's annual work programme; and provide collective oversight of EU activities neither currently nor adequately controlled by the EP such as the CFSP and justice and home affairs (HL 48 2001:Memorandum by the Foreign and Commonwealth Office, paras 3–6). In his Warsaw speech Mr Blair stated that:

the time has now come to involve representatives of national parliaments more on such matters, by creating a second chamber of the European Parliament ... A second chamber ... would not get involved in the day-to-day negotiation of legislation – that is properly the role of the existing European Parliament. Rather, its task would be to help implement the agreed statement of principles; so that we do what we need to do at a European level but also so that we devolve power downwards. Whereas a formal Constitution would logically require judicial review by a European constitutional court, this would be political review by a body of democratically elected politicians. It would be dynamic rather than static, allowing for change in the application of these principles without elaborate legal revisions every time ... Such a second chamber could also, I believe, help provide democratic oversight at a European level of the common foreign and security policy. (Quoted in HC 152-xxxiii 2002:para. 122)

Certainly, as the House of Lords EU Select Committee concluded: 'At the root of all the proposals for a second chamber there seems to lie a perception that there is a problem with the democratic legitimacy of the EU and its institutions' (HL 48 2001:para. 26).

Proponents of bicameralism believe that the existence of a nationally based second chamber would better connect European citizens to EU institutions and decision-making. These ideas were neatly summarized in a French Senate Report (HL 48 2001:Appendix 4) which maintained that a second chamber would 'anchor Europe better in each country'. It would 'allow the restoration of the link between the national parliaments and the European Institutions which was weakened with the election of the European parliament by direct elections'. In the context of an enlarging EU, a second chamber would also assuage the fears of smaller member states that their contributions to the EU decision-making process were being reduced in the institutional changes attendant upon the Amsterdam and Nice treaties. The positive effect of establishing a second chamber 'where all the member states would be represented on an equal footing, by its very nature [would] make the achieving of consensus between the member states easier'. A third advantage identified in the French Senate Report would be a 'rebalancing of the EU institutions'. By this argument a second chamber would 'by its nature rebalance the institutional arrangements as a whole by placing, beside the European Parliament which is rather cut off from daily life, a counterbalance directly linked to national realities'. In addition, a second chamber would offset the centripetal tendencies of EU institutions in Brussels with a centrifugal dynamic within a nationally focused assembly. In this sense the second chamber would be a living embodiment of the principle of subsidiarity.

In part, the emphasis upon subsidiarity is an attempt to distance the second chamber from becoming a 'third' legislative chamber. Most proponents do not envisage a legislative role for the second chamber. Indeed, in an attempt to defuse the criticisms that a new chamber would be 'one institution too far' (HL 48 2001:para. 36) its primary role is often envisaged, therefore, in restricted terms of examining Commission proposals in order to determine whether they conform to the principles of subsidiarity and proportionality (see, for example, HL 48 2001:Appendix 4; CONV 67/02 2002:14). For opponents, however, the practical difficulties involved in integrating second chamber scrutiny into the existing legislative procedures – of ensuring agreement as to the precise boundaries of the levels of competencies in the EU, or of identifying a discrete role that was not already performed by the EP or by national parliaments – seemed to outweigh many of the other potential benefits a second chamber might contribute to EU governance (HL 48 2001:para. 54; HC 152-xxxiii 2002:para. 127).

In particular it is feared that the creation of a new chamber has the potential to generate more institutional conflict. If the decision-making processes of the EU already had a 'Byzantine reputation' then Sir William Nicoll, for one, feared that a second chamber could be yet another 'roadblock' that the other EU institutions would have to 'spend time and effort to circumvent' (HL 48 2001:memorandum by Sir William Nicoll, para. 31).

If the second chamber was to move beyond issues of subsidiarity and to become involved in CFSP or Justice and Home Affairs matters then this would be 'tantamount to declaring war on the EP, which has consistently demanded that it should not be excluded from these Pillars' (HL 48 2001:memorandum by Sir William Nicoll, para. 34). Not surprisingly, in these circumstances, 'The European Parliament views a second chamber as a threat to its own position' (HL 48 2001:memorandum by Lord Norton of Louth). Overall, opponents found it difficult to see what 'added value' another chamber would contribute to the EU's decision-making processes (HL 48 2001:Q181). More pointedly, Andrew Duff MEP could only speculate 'why it is that, just when a directly elected European Parliament is maturing steadily and its powers of codecision are settling down along come [proposals] to recreate alongside it, cuckoo style, its former, unelected predecessor' (HL 48 2001:memorandum by Andrew Duff, para. 3).

Parliamentarization of the EU: executive–legislative roles

In outlining a 'parliamentary model' in Chapter 1 the fusion of executive and legislative roles was noted. In the EU there is certainly a fusion of executive and legislative roles but there is no corresponding unambiguous differentiation of executive and legislative institutions. In other words there are no clear and determinate institutional boundaries in the EU. This is made clear in Michael Rocard's statement:

> The originality of the European system lies in the fact that it does not reproduce a national democratic model articulated between executive and legislative, or still more between government and parliament. The Commission shares the governmental function with Council. The Council shares the legislative function with the Parliament (when it does not exercise it alone). (HL 48 2001:memorandum by Michel Rocard)

Thus, whereas it is relatively easy to identify discrete executive and legislative institutions within each member state, in the EU 'institutions are profoundly and inescapably interdependent' (Peterson and Shackleton 2002:9). The best way of understanding the EU's institutions (specifically the EP in the case of this book), therefore, is in terms of their interinstitutional interactions. They are part of complex, interwoven and overlapping institutional networks. There are no singular institutional structures, only plural institutional forms. Thus, there is no single executive but rather a 'dual executive' of Commission and Council (see Hix 1999:54–5; Christiansen 2001:106). Similarly there is no single legislature but a series of interconnected 'legislative bodies' (see Hayes-Renshaw and Wallace 1997:4, 16). Manifestly the EP is a legislature but it also shares legislative functions with the Council and the Commission.

The significance of all of this for present purposes is that the initial conceptualization of interinstitutional relations in the EU affects the proposals that are subsequently made for the further 'parliamentarization' of the EU.

The Council and bicameralism

In outlining schemes for a second parliamentary chamber in the EU (see above), the proposals for a transformation of the Council of Ministers into a second legislative 'Chamber of States' were briefly noted. The logic of such proposals was to make explicit the position of the Council as a legislative body, and so to formalize what for many already exists – a bicameral

EU. Indeed, many academics, campaigning organizations and politicians alike have no hesitation in identifying a bicameral model at the EU level. American academics Tsebelis and Money (1997), for example, treat the Council as an upper chamber in a bicameral legislature, and maintain that the conciliation procedure under codecision constitutes 'a conference committee of a bicameral parliament' (1997:203). Similarly, Hix believes that 'the EU has evolved into something that would be familiar to observers of two-chamber parliaments in other democratic political systems' (1999:98). The Federal Trust regards the EU legislative process as a 'simple structure' whereby the Commission makes proposals which are then 'approved by two chambers, the European Parliament and the Council of Ministers' (HL 48 2001:memorandum by the Federal Trust). French politician Michel Rocard reinforces this view in his statement that: 'European bi-cameralism already exists, with the Parliament and the Council' (HL 48 2001).

While these statements emphasize the 'familiarity', 'simplicity' and 'certainty' of bicameralism in the existing EU institutional configuration, there are countervailing arguments which challenge the bicameral nature of EU legislative politics. The first is that there is nothing 'familiar' about the institutional form of the Council. While the Council has a singular legal status, in practice it has met in up to 20 different formations of national ministers depending on subject area (though the Seville European Council in June 2002 agreed to reduce this number to nine 'Council configurations' (SN 200/02 2002:23)). Moreover, the 'variable geometry' of the EU complicates definitions of exactly what constitutes 'the Council' at any particular time. Second, the Council is also part of the executive, and so, unlike national second chambers, is responsible not only for scrutinizing legislation but its members are also involved in the implementation of EU legislation. The need to distinguish between the Council in its legislative mode and in its executive mode was acknowledged in 2001 in Jacques Poos' report for the EP on the reform of the Council (PE 294.777 2001:7). This distinction was deemed necessary if transparency was to be brought to the legislative activities of the Council. While it is generally accepted that the processes of intergovernmental bargaining and negotiation are eased by confidentiality in the Council when it acts in an executive capacity, there are widespread calls for greater transparency and more open access when it acts as a legislative body (see HL 48 2001:para. 60; PE 294.777 2001:9; CONV 97/02 2002:8–9). Indeed, the force of such calls was acknowledged at the Seville European Council, where it was agreed that the debates of Council, when acting under codecision, would be open to the public during the initial stage of the procedure and during the final stage – of voting and explanations of voting (SN 200/02 2002:25).

Indeed, the need to separate the executive and legislative functions of the Council becomes even more essential in the arguments of those pressing for the Council to act formally as a second chamber (see, for example, HL 48 2001:Q104; PE 294.777 2001:18). Commissioner Michael Barnier made the point forcefully that: 'If the Council of Ministers is to [be] recognised as a second chamber, a chamber of states … then you have … to separate the work of the Council between its executive work and its legislative tasks' (HL 48 2001:Q129; see also HC 152-xxxiii 2002:para. 105). In performing the latter tasks the Council would effectively then become exclusively a 'Council of Legislative Affairs'.

Yet exactly how, if at all, the two decision-making functions could be separated constitutes a considerable stumbling bloc for the transformation of the Council into a second legislative chamber. Moreover, as presently constituted, if the Council is perceived as being 'at the core of the executive' (HL 48 2001:Q141) it cannot simultaneously perform the legislative oversight functions normally ascribed to legislatures. If 'Parliaments are supposed to control the operation of the executive' (Dehousse 1998:598), then clearly the Council, constituted as a second chamber, would have the task of controlling itself.

Alternatively, democratic control and the reconnection of the peoples of Europe with EU government might be achieved by the direct election of the President of the European Council. Just such a proposal had been advanced by French ex-President Giscard d'Estaing who, before presiding over the Convention, had favoured the direct, European-wide election of the President of the Council. (This is a more radical proposal than the initiative launched by British Prime Minister Blair, Spanish Prime Minister Aznar and French President Chirac, in June 2002 prior to the Seville European Council, for a 'President of Europe' chosen by the European Council, and with a two-and-half- to five-year term of office.) If, however, the proposal for a directly elected President by universal franchise is, as Vernon Bogdanor (HL 48 2001:memorandum, part IV) believes, 'too utopian in present circumstances' then the election of the President of the Commission by the European Parliament may prove to be a more attainable alternative in the shorter term.

Parliamentarization of the Commission

Election of the Commission President

In national parliamentary systems, political executives normally depend upon a parliamentary majority for their appointment and continuance in office. There is thus a mediated linkage between parliamentary elections and the choice and sustenance of a government. In the EU, however, there has been no such linkage (let alone indirect linkage) between EP elections and the choice of a Commission.

Yet there are those who argue that the ability of the EP to vote on the nominated Commission President immediately after EP elections introduces an indirect connection between the selection of the Commission and the election of the EP itself (Hix 2000b:97). Indeed, it was widely anticipated before the 1999 EP elections that the EP-induced resignation of the Commission would simultaneously raise the profile of the EP amongst European electorates and stimulate increased turnout at the June elections. Julie Smith (1999:68), for example, argued in early 1999 that the changes in the appointment procedure incorporated in the Maastricht and Amsterdam treaties marked 'a considerable advance towards an elective [authorization] function and one which could be expressed to the voters in relatively simple terms, potentially giving them a greater interest in EP elections'. In the event, as the June 1999 election demonstrated, that potential remained unfulfilled.

The simple fact is that the institutional framework of the EU, even post-Amsterdam, does not allow voters to determine who holds (or does not hold) executive office in the EU. To date, EP elections have not been about who holds EU executive power. As revealed in Chapter 3, elections to the European Parliament have been dominated by national political issues, national parties, and the political standing of national governments at the time.

One consistent proposal underpinning calls for the 'parlia-mentarization' of the EU, therefore, has been to provide a direct connection between EP elections and the choice of the Commission President. Over a decade ago, David Martin, MEP (1990:26), recognized that: 'At present, European elections are genuinely about electing a Parliament, but the affect of casting one's vote is less immediately perceptible to the voter. To allow the Parliament to elect the President of the Commission would go some way to rectifying that situation.' More recently, before the 1999 election, Dietmar Nickel (1998:3), Director-General, Secretariat-General of the EP, speculated upon the effects of a 'partisanization' of the Commission selection process:

> Imagine one of the two big European parties (either the PES or the EPP) deciding to put up in its electoral campaign for the 1999 direct election a top candidate common to all the member states, declaring this candidate at the same time their candidate for the Commission presidency. If one party were to do so, the other would be obliged to follow... The party obtaining a majority (even a relative majority) in the newly elected Parliament will, of course, expect governments to honour the views of the electorate and to present the top candidate as their proposal for Commission president.

The impact of connecting the selection of the President to the party composition of Parliament would be profound. First, Nickel maintains that the 'electoral campaign would be brought alive by a union-wide personality'; second, the future President would be drawn from the ranks of the majority coalition within the EP, and so would reflect the votes of a European electorate.

Nickel's speculation about 'partisanization' contains the two basic characteristics of a parliamentary model of EU executive appointment identified by Hix (2000b:99). First, EP elections would provide a choice between rival candidates for the Commission President, or at least between competing party pol-icy programmes for EU action. Second, the investiture of the Commission's President would be determined by an electoral majority as reflected in the composition of the EP.

Support for the election of the Commission President was also evident in the 2002 Convention and in associated discussions on the Future of Europe. However, ideas about who would elect the

President, and how, separated the proponents of election. Those who favoured direct election were confronted with several choices. One was to hold separate elections for the President on the same day as the EP elections (see HC 252-xxxiii 2002:35; CONV 27/02 2002:36). A second was to elect some MEPs (possibly 60) on the basis of a transnational, cross-border electoral list, with the highest placed candidate becoming Commission President. This was the personal preference of Commissioner Michel Barnier (see HC 252-xxxiii 2002:Q117). Another proposal – which followed the logic of Nickel (see above), as well as echoing an earlier suggestion of Jacques Delors – was that each main European transnational political family would designate a candidate for President of the Commission with actual nomination secured on the basis of the outcome of the European election (Lamy and Pisani-Ferry 2002:78).

An alternative to direct election would be for the Commission President to be elected by a vote in the European Parliament. Such a view found strong support from within the EP (see, for example, PE 232.758 2000:7; PSE 2002:8; Klaus Hänsch MEP HC 152-xxxiii 2002:Q157) and from without (see Hoffman 2002). A further proposal, designed to reflect the dual legitimation afforded by the EP and national parliaments, was for the convening of a congress of representatives from the EP and national parliaments to elect the President of the Commission (CONV 97/02 2002:10). Mr Prodi himself was reported as supporting the nomination of his successors by MEPs and MPs but with the Council's formal approval (*Financial Times* 29 July 2002).

However, any linkage of the election of the Commission President to the EP (and national parliaments) would require a fundamental shift in the relationship between national and European parties, with the former relinquishing to the latter the choice of presidential candidates. Moreover, as Nickel (1998:3) observes, '[national] governments may not like the idea too'. Clearly, this is an understatement. The very intensity of intergovernmental bargaining over the choice of Commission President and the allocation of Commission portfolios reveals the continuing dominance of national interests in the selection process and the jealous guarding of this monopoly by national governments. If anything, the gradual increase in the significance of EU policy has increased the intensity of national bargaining and the tenacity with which member states seek to maintain their monopoly. Without a seismic shift in the balance between national and EU party politics, and without the linkage of the presidency appointment process to the partisan composition of the EP, 'parliamentarization' in the sense of the electoral connection of the Presidency of the Commission to a parliamentary majority is likely to remain an aspiration rather than a practical reality.

Responsibility of Commissioners to the EP

As noted in Chapter 7, the responsibility of the Commission to the EP remains embryonic in form. While Article 201 empowers the EP to force the collective resignation of the Commission there is no corresponding formal power to enforce the resignation of individual Commissioners (see Chapter 7). Nonetheless, the Framework Agreement on Relations Between the European Parliament and the Commission (European Parliament 2000b) did address, for the first time, the question of the individual responsibility of Commissioners. This had been one of the issues that had been at the centre of the 'Commission crisis' in 1999 and its inclusion in the agreement reflected the lessons learned by the EP and the importance it attached to ensuring the Commission's future accountability to Parliament. Points 9 and 10 of the agreement explicitly addressed the responsibility of individual Commissioners, while still maintaining that collective control rested with the Commission President:

9. Without prejudice to the principle of Commission collegiality, each Member of the Commission shall take political responsibility for action in the field for which he or she is responsible.

10. The Commission accepts that, where the European Parliament expresses lack of confidence in a Member of the Commission (subject to the substantive and representative nature of the political support for such a view), the President of the Commission will examine seriously whether he should request that Member to resign. (European Parliament 2000b)

In essence, these points reflected a compromise between the insistence of the Commission President on the continued principle of collegiality and the desire of some MEPs to ensure the responsibility of individual Commissioners.

A two-way street: Commission–EP relations

At the same time as the EP has considered the 'parliamentarization' of the Commission, so in turn the Commission has also reexamined its relations with the EP. Thus, for example, in July 2000, Michael Barnier, the Commissioner responsible for the IGC, while sharing the EP's vision of a strong Commission presidency responsible to a strong Parliament, raised the prospect of institutional changes that would redirect the flow of accountabilities between executive and legislature. In this respect, Barnier (2000:10) argued that 'To balance the European Parliament's right to censure the Commission, provision should be made for the right to dissolve the assembly, either by the President of the Commission following approval by the European Council, or by the Council on the basis of a proposal by the President of the Commission'. The idea was taken up subsequently by Spanish Prime Minister José Maria Aznar, who proposed that the European Council should have the right to dissolve Parliament, on the basis of a proposal from the Commission (*Agence Europe* 22 May 2002).

These proposals were a direct echo of Lijphart's (1984:72) observation that 'A logical corollary of the legislature's power to dismiss the cabinet in a parliamentary system is the prime minister's right to dissolve parliament and call new elections'. In this regard, Barnier's thoughts tapped into an historic vein of parliamentarism and served as a reminder to the EP and commentators alike that the relationship between the executive and the legislature in a parliamentary system is interconnected and reciprocal. The assertion of parliamentary power precipitated, therefore, a counter-response in calls for a reassertion of executive power in the EU.

'Deeper and wider debate about the future of the European Union'

The fact that the institutions of the EU are relatively new in historical terms, constantly realigning themselves in interinstitutional terms and essentially *sui generis* in nature, has generated a reformist institutional dynamic (see Chapter 2) yet simultaneously has failed to produce an agreed and unambiguous blueprint for institutional reform. As Chapter 1 maintained, how the institutional structure of the EU is conceived also determines conceptions of how the institutional structure should develop in the future. The fact that there is little agreement as to how to classify the existing institutional configuration of the EU makes it all the more difficult to reach, and, indeed, unreasonable to expect, consensus as to how that configuration will develop in the future.

Nonetheless – given imminent enlargement to a Union of 25 member states and extensions of EU competences – reflection upon, and reform of, the institutional structure of the EU has become a preoccupation of all three major institutions – Commission, Council, and Parliament – in the twenty-first century. This preoccupation was evident in Declaration 23 appended to the Treaty of Nice which stated that 'the institutional changes necessary for the accession of new Member States to the European Union' had been completed, and that the time was thus propitious for 'a deeper and wider debate about the future of the European Union'. A particular concern identified for this debate was how to improve 'the democratic legitimacy and transparency of the Union'.

This concern was amplified in the Commission's White Paper on European Governance published in July 2001 (COM[2001]428 final), the Conclusions of the Laeken European Council in December 2001 (PE 313.424 2001), and, as we have seen above, in the deliberations of the post-Nice, pre-IGC 2004 Convention on the Future of Europe. Each, in turn, provide benchmarks as to the conceptualization of 'improved' democratic legitimacy and transparency. What concerns us here, however, is the relative emphasis placed upon 'parliamentarization' in these parallel debates.

The Commission's White Paper on European Governance

The starting point of the White Paper was the Commission's commitment to the revitalization of the Community method (COM[2001]428 final:29). The Commission was anxious to see a return to the original treaty-prescribed tasks for each institution (see Chapter 2), and a return to a position where 'everyone should concentrate on their core tasks'. In effect it was a plea to return to a simpler era where the 'Commission initiates and executes policy' and the 'Council and the European Parliament decide on legislation and budgets' (2001:29). In this vision the independence of the Commission would be asserted (2001:8). But to achieve this in practice would mean 'disentangling the institutions from one another and guaranteeing the Commission the pre-eminent role as co-ordinator of EU policy' (Wincott 2001:902). In this sense the White Paper clearly emphasized the Commission's distinct executive status and the 'Community method' over and above any notions of the further parliamentarization of the EU. Indeed, there was no mention of an elected Commission President responsible to the EP; and further enhancement of the role of the EP was restricted to, first, 'control on the execution of EU policies and the implementation of the budget', second, to a review of the areas covered by codecision, and, third, to greater activity in jointly organizing, with national parliaments, public debate on the future of Europe and upon EU policies (2001:29–30).

When talking of enhancing democracy the White Paper did not envisage a further parliamentarization of the EU's decision-making process. Instead, other channels of functional and regional representation were to be nurtured alongside parliamentary representation (2001:13–19). In seeking a 'reinforced culture of consultation and dialogue' the Commission seemed to conceive of the EP's role primarily in terms of amplifying the concerns of organized associations through its system of 'public hearings'. What was absent was direct acknowledgement of the EP's importance as the direct representation of the citizens of Europe.

The emphasis upon consultation 'upstream' in the decision-making process was linked in turn to a concern with effective implementation 'downstream'. A technocratic ethos pervaded the Commission's conception of the EU policy process, with the need for 'better and faster regulation' (2001:20) often appearing to outweigh the need for democratic representation and accountability. In this sense, the emphasis was placed upon 'substantive legitimacy' or 'output legitimacy' (see Chapter 1; Lord and Beetham 2001:444).

Not surprisingly, however, this technocratic vision was challenged by the EP in the Report of the Constitutional Affairs Committee on the White Paper (PE 304.289 2001). In its motion for resolution the Committee advised caution in the introduction of 'elements of participatory democracy' and counselled that the 'recognised principles of and structural elements of representative democracy' (PE 304.289 2001:7) should not be infringed. In 'reiterating its confidence in the Community method' and advocating the maintenance of 'the institutional balance' the EP assumed that the principles of parliamentarism would be paramount. Thus, in the EP's conception of 'method' and 'balance', democratic legitimacy was provided jointly by the EP and the parliaments of member states. The parliamentary vision of legitimacy 'presupposes that the political will underpinning decisions is arrived at through parliamentary deliberation; this is a substantive and not merely a formal requirement' (PE 304.289 2001:9). In which case:

> consultation of interested parties with the aim of improving draft legislation can only ever supplement and can never replace the procedures and decisions of legislative bodies which possess democratic legitimacy; only the Council and Parliament, as co-legislators, can take responsible decisions in the context of legislative procedures. (PE 304.289 2001:10)

In its view that participation and consultation based upon 'organized civil society' would 'inevitably' be 'sectoral' – and so could not 'be regarded as having its own democratic legitimacy, given that representatives are not elected by the people and therefore cannot be voted out by the people' (PE 304.289 2001:10) – the EP reflected one strand of academic opinion (see Judge 1999:121–48, 176–7; Lord and Beetham 2001:453–8).

Equally, the EP was anxious that the principles of 'parliamentarization' should not be undermined by increasing delegation of decision-making powers to regulatory agencies (PE 304.289 2001:12). Nor should the creation of expert and scientific groups detract from the accountability and transparency requirements of representative democracy. Similarly, the EP was wary of the Commission's suggestion that there should be greater use of 'framework directives' and primary legislation where the executive was empowered to fill in the technical details 'via implementing "secondary" rules'

(COM[2001]428: 20). The use of delegated legislation would only be supported by the EP if 'adequate mechanisms of democratic control' were put in place, in particular time-limited, call-back mechanisms (PE 304.289 2001:14).

Generally, the Commission was warned against taking reformist initiatives in the legislative process without full, prior consultation of the EP. More specifically, the EP endorsed the principle that:

> the 'parliamentarisation' of the Union's decision-making system presupposes increased transparency of the work of the Council and that the involvement of both the European and national parliaments constitutes the basis for a European system with democratic legitimacy and that only regional, national and European institutions which possess democratic legitimacy can take accountable legislative decisions. (PE 304.289 2001:9)

Laeken European Council: Future of Europe

Whilst welcoming the Commission's White Paper on Governance, the Laeken European Council of December 2001 proceeded to issue its own Declaration on the Future of the Union (PE 313.424 2001). In convening a Convention to consider the future development of the EU the Laeken Council identified one of the major issues as the need to 'increase the democratic legitimacy and transparency of the present institutions' (PE 313.424 2001:35). Three fundamental questions were posed for the Convention to consider: first, how democratic legitimacy and transparency could be increased; second, what role should national parliaments play; and, third, how institutional performance and efficiency of decision-making could be improved. A number of sub-questions were also listed and these are reproduced in Box 9.1.

Earlier in this chapter some of the Convention's attempts to answer these questions have been noted, but the significant point is that the questions were raised at all. Some fifty years after the creation of the institutional form of the ECSC, the complexity of institutional development prevents simple answers being provided for the most elementary questions. The most basic of all, for present purposes, is what is the scope for the 'parliamentarization' of the EU.

BOX 9.1 Laeken Declaration on the Future of the European Union

Increasing the democratic legitimacy and transparency of the present institutions

- How should the President of the Commission be appointed: by the European Council, by the European Parliament or should he [sic] be directly elected by the citizens?
- Should the role of the European Parliament be strengthened?
- Should we extend the right of co-decision or not?
- Should the way in which we elect the members of the European Parliament be reviewed?
- Should a European electoral constituency be created, or should constituencies continue to be determined nationally? Can the two systems be combined?
- Should the Council act in the same manner in its legislative and its executive capacities?
- With a view to greater transparency, should the meetings of the Council, at least in its legislative capacity, be public?
- How, finally, should the balance and reciprocal control between the institutions be ensured?

The role of national parliaments

- Should national parliaments be represented in a new institution, alongside the Council and the European Parliament?
- Should they have a role in areas of European action in which the European Parliament has no competence?
- Should they focus on the division of competence between Union and member states, for example through preliminary checking of compliance with the principle of subsidiarity?

The efficiency of decision-making and the workings of the institutions

- Is there a need for more decisions by a qualified majority?
- How is the co-decision procedure between the Council and the European Parliament to be simplified and speeded up?
- What is the future role of the European Parliament?

Source: PE 313.424 2001:35.

Conclusion

Indeed, it is fitting perhaps to end this book with the last question hanging in the air: 'what is the future role of the European Parliament?' The first fifty years of the EU have been exercised by this question, and, undoubtedly, the same question will feature significantly in the next fifty years. The fact that there is neither a simple nor a consensual answer reflects both the contested nature of the EU as a system of governance and the different perceptions of the role of the EP within that system. What this book has sought to do is to locate the EP within conceptions of the EU and within notions of what parliaments 'are' and 'do'. It is up to the reader then to use these locational coordinates to answer the questions posed in Box 9.1. In the study of the European Parliament, where you start from determines where you finish.

References

Note: European Parliament committee reports appear in this bibliography with 'PE' as author and are listed numerically by PE number, rather than by year of publication.

Abromeit, H. (2002) 'Contours of a European Federation', *Regional and Federal Studies*, 12, 1, 1–20.

Andersen, S. S. and Burns, T. (1996) 'The European Union and the Erosion of Parliamentary Democracy: A Study of Post-Parliamentary Governance', in S. S. Andersen and K. A. Eliassen (eds), *The European Union: How Democratic Is It?*, London, Sage.

Attina, F. (1990) 'The Voting Behaviour of the European Parliament Members and the Problem of Europarties', *European Journal of Political Research*, 18, 3, 557–79.

Bach, S. (1999) 'The Office of Speaker in Comparative Perspective', *Journal of Legislative Studies*, 5, 3/4, 209–54.

Bailer, S. and Schneider, G. (2000) 'The Power of Legislative Hot Air: Informal Rules and the Enlargement Debate in the European Parliament', *Journal of Legislative Studies*, 6, 2, 19–44.

Barnier, M. (2000) 'Europe's Future: Two Steps and Three Paths', A Personal Note, Brussels, European Commission.

Beetham, D. (1992) 'Liberal Democracy and the Limits of Democratization', *Political Studies*, 40, 5, 40–53.

Beetham, D. and Lord, C. (1998) *Legitimacy and the European Union*, London, Longman.

Bergman, T. and Raunio, T. (2001) 'Parliaments and Policy Making in the European Union', in J. Richardson (ed.), *European Union: Power and Policy-Making*, 2nd edn, London, Routledge.

Blondel, J. (1970) 'Legislative Behaviour: Some Steps Towards a Cross-national Measurement', *Government and Opposition*, 5, 1, 67–85.

Blondel, J. (1973) *Comparative Legislatures*, Englewood Cliffs, NJ, Prentice-Hall.

Blondel, J., Sinnott, R. and Svensson, P. (1998) *People and Parliament in the European Union: Participation, Democracy and Legitimacy*, Oxford, Clarendon Press.

Bowler, S. and Farrell, D. M. (1993) 'Legislator Shirking and Voter Monitoring: Impacts of European Parliament Electoral Systems upon Legislator–Voter Relationships', *Journal of Common Market Studies*, 31, 1, 45–70.

Bowler, S. and Farrell, D. M. (1995) 'The Organizing of the European Parliament: Committees, Specialization and Co-ordination', *British Journal of Political Science*, 25, 2, 219–43.

Bowler, S., Farrell, D. M. and Katz, R. S. (1999) 'Party Cohesion, Party Discipline and Parliaments', in S. Bowler, D. M. Farrell and R. S. Katz, *Party Discipline and Parliamentary Government*, Columbus, Ohio State University Press.

Brzinski, J. B., Ginning, H., Haspel, M. and Saunders, K. (1998) 'Understanding Defection in the European Parliament', Paper presented at the Annual Meeting of the American Political Science Association, September, Boston.

Bullen, R. and Pelly, G. (eds) (1986) *Documents on British Policy Overseas*, Series II, Vol. 1, No. 114, London, HMSO.

Burns, C. (1999) 'Measuring Power and Influence: Does Conditional Agenda Setting Tell the Full Story about European Parliament Powers', Paper presented to the Fourth UACES Research Conference, University of Sheffield, 8–10 September.

Burson-Marsteller (2001) *Guide to Effective Lobbying of the European Parliament*, Brussels, BKSH.

Butler, D. and Westlake, M. (2000) *British Politics and European Elections 1999*, Basingstoke, Palgrave Macmillan.

Caporaso, J. A., Marks, G., Moravcsik, A. and Pollack, M. A. (1997) 'Does the European Union Represent an *n* of 1?', *ECSA Review*, 3 (Fall), 1–5.

Capotorti, F., Hilf, M., Jacobs, F. and Jacqué, J. P. (1986) *The European Union Treaty: Commentary on the Draft Adopted by the European Parliament on 14 February 1984*, Oxford, Clarendon Press.

Carrubba, C. and Gabel, M. (1999) 'Roll Call Votes and Party Discipline in the European Parliament: Reconsidering MEP Voting Behaviour', Paper presented at the Annual Meeting of the American Political Science Association, 2–5 September, Atlanta, Georgia.

Cautres, B. and Sinnott, R. (2002) 'The European Parliament Elections and the Political Culture of European Integration', in P. Perrineau, G. Grunberg and C. Ysmal (eds), *Europe at the Polls: The European Elections, 1999*, New York, Palgrave.

Christiansen, T. (2001) 'The European Commission: Administration in Turbulent Times', in J. Richardson (ed.), *European Union, Power and Policy-Making*, 2nd edn, London, Routledge.

Chryssochoou, D. N. (1994) 'Democracy and Symbiosis in the European Union: Towards a Confederal Consociation?', *West European Politics*, 4, 3, 1–14.

Chryssochoou, D. N. (1997) 'New Challenges to the Study of European Integration: Implications for Theory Building', *Journal of Common Market Studies*, 35, 4, 521–42.

Chryssochoou, D. N., Tsinisizelis, M. J., Stavridis, S. and Ifantis, K. (1999) *Theory and Reform in the European Union*, Manchester, Manchester University Press.

COD 1999/0244 *Directive on the Approximation of Laws, Regulations and Administrative Provisions of Member States concerning the Manufacture, Presentation and Sale of Tobacco Products.*

COM[93]661 (1993) *Proposal for a European Parliament and Council Directive on the Legal Protection of Biotechnological Inventions*, Brussels, Commission of the European Communities.

COM[95]655 (1995) *Proposal for a 13th European Parliament and Council Directive on Company Law Concerning Takeover Bids*, Brussels, Commission of the European Communities.

COM[97]0565 (1997) *Amended Proposal for a 13th European Parliament and Council Directive on Company Law Concerning Takeover Bids*, Brussels, Commission of the European Communities.

COM[97]510 final (1997) *Motor Insurance: Civil Liability, Fourth Directive (Amend. direct. 73/239/EEC, 88/357/EEC, 92/49/EEC)*, Brussels, Commission of the European Communities.

COM[2000]898 final (2001) *Proposal for a Council Regulation on the Statute and Financing of European Political Parties*, Brussels, Commission of the European Communities.

COM[2001]0612 (2001) *Combating AIDS, Tuberculosis and Malaria: Community Contribution to the Global Fund*, Brussels, Commission of the European Communities.

COM[2001]28 final (2001) *The Commission's Work Programme for 2001*, Brussels, Commission of the European Communities.

COM[2001]428 final (2001) *European Governance: A White Paper*, Brussels, Commission of the European Communities.

COM[2001]620 final (2001) *The Commission's Work Programme for 2002*, Brussels, Commission of the European Communities.

Committee of Three (1979) *Report on European Institutions*, Luxembourg, European Council.

CONV 27/02 (2002) 'Contribution from Mr John Bruton, Member of the Convention', CONTRIB 10, Brussels, Secretariat, European Convention.

CONV 67/02 (2002) 'The Role of National Parliaments in the European Architecture', Information Note from Praesidium to Convention, Brussels, Secretariat, European Convention.

CONV 97/02 (2002) 'Note on the Plenary Meeting, 6 and 7 June', Brussels, Secretariat, European Convention.

Copeland, G. W. and Patterson, S. C. (1994) *Parliaments in the Modern World: Changing Institutions*, Ann Arbor, Michigan, University of Michigan Press.

Corbett, R. (1992) 'The Intergovernmental Conference on Political Union', *Journal of Common Market Studies*, 30, 3, 271–98.

Corbett, R. (1993a) *The Treaty of Maastricht, from Conception to Ratification: A Comprehensive Reference Guide*, London, Longman.

Corbett, R. (1993b) 'Governance and Institutional Development', in N. Nugent (ed.), *The European Union 1993: Annual Review of Activities*, Oxford, Blackwell.

Corbett, R. (1994) 'Representing the People', in A. Duff, J. Pinder and R. Pryce (eds), *Maastricht and Beyond*, London, Routledge.

Corbett, R. (1995) 'Governance and Institutional Developments', *Journal of Common Market Studies, Annual Review 1995*, 34, 29–42.

Corbett, R. (1998) *The European Parliament's Role in Closer European Integration*, London, Macmillan – now Palgrave Macmillan.

Corbett, R. (2000) 'Academic Modelling of the Codecision Procedure: A Practitioner's Puzzled Reaction', *European Union Politics*, 1, 3, 373–81.

Corbett, R. (2001) 'Evaluating Nice', Speech in the Committee on Constitutional Affairs, 9 January, European Parliament.

Corbett, R., Jacobs, F. and Shackleton, M. (1995) *The European Parliament*, 3rd edn, London, Cartermill.

Corbett, R., Jacobs, F. and Shackleton, M. (2000) *The European Parliament*, 4th edn, London, John Harper.

COSAC (2000) 'Analytic Report, XXIIIrd COSAC, Versailles, 16–17 October 2000', Brussels, Conference of Community and European Affairs Committees.

Cotta, M. (1974) 'A Structural–Functional Framework for the Analysis of Unicameral and Bicameral Parliaments', *European Journal of Political Research*, 2, 3, 201–24.

Cotta, M. and Best, H. (2000) 'Between Professionalization and Democratization: A Synoptic View on the Making of the European Representative', in M. Cotta and H. Best (eds), *Parliamentary Representation in Europe 1848–2000*, Oxford, Oxford University Press.

Cox, G. and McCubbins, M. D. (1993) *Legislative Leviathan: Party Government in the House*, Berkeley, University of California Press.

Cram, L. (2001) 'Integration Theory and the Study of the European Policy Process', in J. Richardson (ed.), *European Union: Power and Policy-Making*, 2nd edn, London, Routledge.

Crombez, C. (1996) 'Legislative Procedures in the European Community', *British Journal of Political Science*, 26, 199–228.

Crombez, C. (1999) 'The Treaty of Amsterdam and the Codecision Procedure', Paper delivered at the Annual Meeting of the American Political Science Association, 2–5 September, Atlanta, Georgia.

Crombez, C. (2000) 'Codecision: Towards a Bicameral European Union', *European Union Politics*, 1, 3, 363–81.

Curtice, J. and Steed, M. (2000) 'Statistical Appendix', in D. Butler and M. Westlake (eds), *British Politics and European Elections 1999*, Basingstoke, Palgrave Macmillan.

Darcy, R., Welch, S. and Clark, J. (1994) *Women, Elections and Representation*, 2nd edn, Lincoln, University of Nebraska Press.

de Haan, J. and Eijffinger, C. W. (2000) 'The Democratic Accountability of the European Central Bank', *Journal of Common Market Studies*, 38, 3, 393–408.

Dehousse, R. (1998) 'European Institutional Architecture After Amsterdam: Parliamentary System or Regulatory Structure?', *Common Market Law Review*, 35, 595–627.

de Witte, B. (2002) 'The Closest Thing to a Constitutional Conversation in Europe: The Semi-Permanent Treaty Revision Process', in P. Beaumont, C. Lyons and N. Walker (eds), *Convergence and Divergence in European Public Law*, Oxford, Hart.

Dinan, D. (1999) *An Ever Closer Union: An Introduction to the European Community*, 2nd edn, London, Macmillan – now Palgrave Macmillan.

Dowding, K. (2000) 'Institutionalist Research on the European Union', *European Union Politics*, 1, 1, 125–44.

Duff, A. (2001) 'The Treaty of Nice: From Left-Overs to Hangovers', http://www.andrewduffmep.org/Press%20Releases/newnice.rtf.

Earnshaw, D. (1985) 'The European Parliament's Quest for a Single Seat', *Journal of European Integration/Revue d'Intégration Européenne*, 8, 1, 77–93.

Earnshaw, D. and Judge, D. (1993) 'The European Parliament and the Sweeteners Directive: From Footnote to Inter-Institutional Conflict', *Journal of Common Market Studies*, 31, 1, 103–16.

Earnshaw, D. and Judge, D. (1995a) 'Prelude to Codecision: A Qualitative Assessment of the Cooperation Procedure in the 1989–94 European Parliament', Political Series W-11, Directorate General for Research, Luxembourg, European Parliament.

Earnshaw, D. and Judge, D. (1995b) 'Early Days: the European Parliament, Codecision and the European Union Legislative Process Post-Maastricht', *Journal of European Public Policy*, 2, 4, 624–49.

Earnshaw, D. and Judge, D. (1996) 'From Co-operation to Co-decision: The European Parliament's Path to Legislative Power', in

J. Richardson (ed.), *European Union: Power and Policy Making*, London, Routledge.

Earnshaw, D. and Judge, D. (1997) 'The Life and Times of the European Union's Co-operation Procedure', *Journal of Common Market Studies*, 35, 4, 543–64.

Earnshaw, D. and Wood, J. (1999) 'The European Parliament and Biotechnology Patenting: Harbinger of the Future?', *Journal of Commercial Biotechnology*, 5, 4, 294–307.

Elazar, D. J. (1991) 'Introduction', in D. J. Elazar (ed.), *Federal Systems of the World: A Handbook of Federal, Confederal and Autonomy Arrangements*, London, Longman.

Eulau, H. and Karps, P. (1977) 'The Puzzle of Representation: Specifying Components and Responsiveness', *Legislative Studies Quarterly*, 2, 3, 233–54.

European Commission (1999) General Report on the Activities of the European Communities 1999, Brussels, Commission of the European Communities, http://europa.eu.int/abc/doc/off/rg/en/ 1999.

European Commission (2000a) General Report on the Activities of the European Communities 2000, Brussels, Commission of the European Communities, http://europa.eu.int/abc/doc/off/rg/en/ 2000.

European Commission (2000b) *Strategic Objectives 2000–2005 'Shaping the New Europe'*, Brussels, Commission of the European Communities.

European Parliament (1978) *Powers of the European Parliament*, London, Information Office of the European Parliament.

European Parliament (1979) *Rules of Procedure*, Brussels, European Parliament.

European Parliament (1987) *Rules of Procedure*, 4th edn, Brussels, European Parliament.

European Parliament (1994) *The European Parliament and Codecision: The Fourth Framework Programme*, Working Paper W-11, Directorate-General for Research, Luxembourg, European Parliament.

European Parliament (1997a) European Parliament Directorate-General for Committees and Delegations, Committee on Institutional Affairs, 'The European Parliament as it would be affected by the Draft Treaty of Amsterdam of 19 June 1997', Brussels, European Parliament, http://www.europarl.eu.int/dg7/treaty/en/epchange.htm.

European Parliament (1997b) General Secretariat Working Party Task Force on the Intergovernmental Conference: The Coordinator, *Note on The European Parliament's Priorities for the IGC and The New Amsterdam Treaty: Report and Initial Evaluation of the Results*, Brussels, European Parliament.

European Parliament (1997c) *Legislation Governing Elections to the European Parliament*, Political Series, DGIV Working Paper W13, Luxembourg, European Parliament.

European Parliament (1998) Discussion Paper on the Revision of the Committee Structure, Ken Collins MEP, Conference of Committee Chairmen, Brussels, European Parliament.

European Parliament (1999) *Rules of Procedure*, 14th edn, Brussels, European Parliament.

European Parliament (2000a) *Activity Report of the Delegations to the Conciliation Committee*, 1 May 1999 to 31 July 2000, 418584EN.doc., Delegations to the Conciliation Committee, Brussels, European Parliament.

European Parliament (2000b) *A Framework Agreement on Relations between the European Parliament and the Commission*, European Parliament minutes, 5 July, C5-03498/2000, Brussels, European Parliament.

European Parliament (2001a) *Conciliations Handbook*, 3rd edn, 449191EN.doc., Conciliations Secretariat, Brussels, European Parliament.

European Parliament (2001b) First Comments on the Global Health Fund Proposal, Development Committee Secretariat, 24 October 2001, Brussels, European Parliament.

European Parliament (2002) *Rules of Procedure*, Amended Text, provisional edition, July 2002, Brussels, European Parliament.

Evans, C. L. (1999) 'Legislative Structure: Rules, Precedents, and Jurisdictions', *Legislative Studies Quarterly*, 24, 4, 605–42.

Farrell, H. and Héritier, A. (2002) 'Formal and Informal Institutions Under Codecision: Continuous Constitution Building in Europe's Parliament', *European Integration online Papers*, 6, 3; http://eiop.or.at/texte/2002-003a.htm.

Featherstone, K. (1994) 'Jean Monnet and the "Democratic Deficit" in the European Union', *Journal of Common Market Studies*, 32, 2, 149–70.

Fieschi, C. (2000) 'European Institutions: The Far-Right and Illiberal Politics in a Liberal Context', *Parliamentary Affairs*, 53, 3, 517–31.

Fitzmaurice, J. (1975) *The Party Groups in the European Parliament*, Farnborough, Saxon House.

Fitzmaurice, J. (1988) 'An Analysis of the European Community's Co-operation Procedure', *Journal of Common Market Studies*, 26, 4, 389–400.

Fitzmaurice, J. (1994) 'The European Commission', in A. Duff, J. Pinder and R. Pryce (eds), *Maastricht and Beyond: Building the European Union*, London, Routledge.

Franklin, M. (2001) 'European Elections and the European Voter', in J. Richardson (ed.), *European Union: Power and Policy-Making*, 2nd edn, London, Routledge.

Franklin, M., van der Eijk, C. and Marsh, M. (1996) 'Conclusions: The Electoral Connection and the Democratic Deficit', in C. van der Eijk and M. Franklin (eds), *Choosing Europe? The European Electorate and National Politics in the Face of Union*, Ann Arbor, Michigan University Press.

Freedman, J. (2002) 'Women in the European Parliament', *Parliamentary Affairs*, 55, 1, 179–88.

Friedrich, A., Tappe, M. and Wurzel, R. (2000) 'A New Approach to EU Environmental Policy-Making: the Auto-Oil 1 Programme', *Journal of European Public Policy*, 7, 4, 593–612.

Frognier, A. P. (2002) 'Identity and Electoral Participation: For a European Approach to European Elections', in P. Perrineau, G. Grunberg and C. Ysmal (eds), *Europe at the Polls: The European Elections, 1999*, New York, Palgrave Macmillan.

Gabel, M. and Hix, S. (2002) 'The Ties that Bind: Partisanship and the Investiture Procedure for the EU Commission President', in M. Hosli, A. van Deemen and M. Widgrén (eds), *Institutional Challenges in the European Union*, London, Routledge.

Garman, J. and Hilditch, L. (1998) 'Behind the Scenes: An Examination of the Importance of the Informal Processes at Work in Conciliation', *Journal of European Public Policy*, 5, 2, 271–84.

Garrett, G. and Tsebelis, G. (2001) 'Understanding Better the EU Legislative Process', *European Union Politics*, 2, 3, 353–61.

Gold, E. R. and Gallochat, A. (2001) 'The European Biotech Directive: Past as Prologue', *European Law Journal*, 7, 3, 331–66.

GPC (2000) *All Change: The European Parliament One Year On*, Brussels, Government Policy Consultants.

Gray, M. and Stubb, A. (2001) 'Governance and Institutions 2000: Edging Towards Enlargement', in G. Edwards and G. Wiessala (eds), *The European Union: Annual Review of the EU 2000/2001*, Oxford, Blackwell.

Greenwood, J. (1997) *Representing Interests in the European Union*, London, Macmillan – now Palgrave Macmillan.

Greenwood, J. (1998) 'Regulating Lobbying in the European Union', *Parliamentary Affairs*, 51, 4, 587–99.

Greenwood, J. and Thomas, C. S. (1998) 'Regulating Lobbying in the Western World', *Parliamentary Affairs*, 51, 4, 487–99.

Grunberg, G. and Moschonas, G. (2002) 'The Disillusionment of European Socialists', in P. Perrineau, G. Grunberg and C. Ysmal (eds), *Europe at the Polls: The European Elections, 1999*, New York, Palgrave Macmillan.

Guyomarch, A. (2000) 'The June 1999 European Parliament Elections', *West European Politics*, 23, 1, 161–74.

Hallstein, W. (1972) *Europe in the Making*, London, Allen & Unwin.

Hayes-Renshaw, F. and Wallace, H. (1997) *The Council of Ministers*, London, Macmillan – now Palgrave Macmillan.

HC 152-xxxiii (2002) *Democracy and Accountability in the EU and the Role of National Parliaments*, 33rd Report of the House of Commons European Scrutiny Committee, London, The Stationery Office.

Henig, S. and Pinder, J. (1969) *European Political Parties*, London, George Allen & Unwin.

Héritier, A. (1999) 'Elements of Democratic Legitimation in Europe: An Alternative Perspective', *Journal of European Public Policy*, 6, 2, 269–82.

Herman, V. (1980) 'Direct Elections: The Historical Background', in V. Herman and M. Hagger (eds), *The Legislation of Direct Elections to the European Parliament*, Farnborough, Gower.

Herman, V. and Lodge, J. (1978) *The European Parliament and the European Community*, London, Macmillan – now Palgrave Macmillan.

Hibbing, J. R. and Patterson, S. C. (1986) 'Representing a Territory: Constituency Boundaries for the British House of Commons of the 1980s', *Journal of Politics*, 48, 992–1005.

Hirst, P. (1990) *Representative Democracy and Its Limits*, Cambridge, Polity Press.

Hix, S (1997) 'Executive Selection in the European Union: Does the Commission President Investiture Procedure Reduce the Democratic Deficit?', *European Integration online Papers*, 1, 21; http://eiop.or.at/eiop/texte/1997-021a.htm.

Hix, S. (1998a) 'The Study of the European Union II: The "New Governance" Agenda and Its Rival', *Journal of European Public Policy*, 5, 1, 38–65.

Hix, S. (1998b) 'Elections, Parties and Institutional Design: A Comparative Perspective on European Union Democracy', *West European Politics*, 21, 3, 19–52.

Hix, S. (1999) *The Political System of the European Union*, London, Macmillan – now Palgrave Macmillan.

Hix, S. (2000a) 'How MEPs Vote', Briefing Note 1/00, ESRC One Europe or Several Programme, London, ESRC.

Hix, S. (2000b) 'Executive Selection in the European Union: Does the Commission President Investiture Procedure Reduce the Democratic Deficit?', in K. Neunreither and A. Wiener (eds), *European Integration After Amsterdam: Institutional Dynamics and Prospects for Democracy*, Oxford, Oxford University Press.

Hix, S. (2001a) 'Legislative Behaviour and Party Competition in the Post-1999 European Parliament: An Application of NOMINATE to the EU', Paper delivered at the One Europe or Several Programme Conference, April.

Hix, S. (2001b) 'Legislative Behaviour and Party Competition in the Post-1999 European Parliament: An Application of NOMINATE to the EU', *Journal of Common Market Studies*, 39, 4, 663–88.

Hix, S. (2002) 'Constitutional Agenda Setting Through Discretion in Rule Interpretation: Why the European Parliament Won at Amsterdam', *British Journal of Political Science*, 32, 2, 259–80.

Hix, S. and Lord, C. (1996) 'The Making of a President: The European Parliament and the Confirmation of Jacques Santer as the President of the Commission', *Government and Opposition*, 31, 1, 62–76.

Hix, S. and Lord, C. (1997) *Political Parties in the European Union*, London, Macmillan – now Palgrave Macmillan.

Hix, S., Noury, A. and Roland, G. (2002) 'A "Normal" Parliament? Party Cohesion and Competition in the European Parliament, 1979–2001', European Parliament Research Group Working Paper No. 9, available at http://www.lse.ac.uk/Depts/eprg/working-papers.htm.

Hix, S., Raunio, T. and Scully, R. (1999) 'An Institutional Theory of Behaviour in the European Parliament', Paper presented at the Joint Sessions of the European Consortium for Political Research, March, Mannheim.

HL 23 (1999) *Delegation of Powers to the Commission: Reforming Comitology*, Third Report, House of Lords European Union Committee, London, The Stationery Office.

HL 67 (2000) *EU Charter of Fundamental Rights*, House of Lords Select Committee on European Union, Eighth Report, Session 1999–2000, London, The Stationery Office.

HL 48 (2001) *A Second Parliamentary Chamber for Europe: An Unreal Solution to Some Real Problems*, House of Lords Select Committee on European Union, Seventh Report, Session 2001–2, London, The Stationery Office.

Hoffman, L. (2002) 'Linking National Politics to Europe – an Opposing Argument', London, Federal Trust, available at www.fedtrust.co.uk.

Holland, M. (1994) *European Integration: From Community to Union*, London, Pinter.

Hooghe, L. and Marks, G. (2001) 'Types of Multi-Level Governance', *European Integration online Papers*, 1, 2; http://eiop.or.at/eiop/texte/2001-011a.htm.

Höreth, M. (1999) 'No Way Out for The Beast? The Unsolved Legitimacy Problem of European Governance', *Journal of European Public Policy*, 6, 2, 249–68.

Hubschmid, C. and Moser, P. (1997) 'The Cooperation Procedure in the EU: Why Was the European Parliament Influential in the

Decision on Car Emission Standards', *Journal of Common Market Studies*, 35, 2, 225–41.

Humphreys, J. (1997) *Negotiating in the European Union*, London, Random House.

Jachtenfuchs, M. and Kohler-Koch, B. (1997) 'The Transformation of Governance in the European Union', Mannheim, MZES Arbeitspapier AB III, Nr. 11, available at http://userpage.fu-berlin.de/~jfuchs/current/transfo.htm.

Jacobs, F. B. (1999) 'Nominations and Appointments: An Evolving EU Model', Paper presented to the ECSA Sixth Biennial Conference, June, Pittsburgh, Pa.

Jewell, M. E. (1983) 'Legislator–Constituency Relations and the Representative Process', *Legislative Studies Quarterly*, 8, 303–37.

Judge, D. (1981) *Backbench Specialisation in the House of Commons*, London, Heinemann Educational Books.

Judge, D. (1993) ' "Predestined to Save the Earth": The Environment Committee of the European Parliament', in D. Judge (ed.), *A Green Dimension for the European Community*, London, Frank Cass.

Judge, D. (1995) 'The Failure of National Parliaments', in J. Hayward (ed.), *The Crisis of Representation in Europe*, London, Frank Cass.

Judge, D. (1999) *Representation: Theory and Practice in Britain*, London, Routledge.

Judge, D. and Earnshaw, D. (1994) 'Weak European Parliament Influence? A Study of the Environment Committee of the European Parliament', *Government and Opposition*, 29, 2, 262–76.

Judge, D. and Earnshaw, D. (1999) 'Locating the European Parliament', Paper presented to the ECSA Sixth Biennial Conference, June, Pittsburgh, Pa.

Judge, D. and Earnshaw, D. (2002) 'The European Parliament and the Commission Crisis: A New Assertiveness?', *Governance*, 15, 3, 345–74.

Judge, D., Earnshaw, D. and Cowan, N. (1994) 'Ripples or Waves: The European Parliament in the European Policy Process', *Journal of European Public Policy*, 1, 1, 27–52.

Katz, R. S. (1997) 'Representational Roles', *European Journal of Political Research*, 32, 2, 211–26.

Katz, R. S. (1999) 'Role Orientations in Parliaments', in R. S. Katz and B. Wessels (eds), *The European Parliament, the National Parliaments, and European Integration*, Oxford, Oxford University Press.

Katz, R. S. and Wessels, B. (eds) (1999) *The European Parliament, the National Parliaments, and European Integration*, Oxford, Oxford University Press.

Kiewiet, D. R. and McCubbins, M. D. (1991) *The Logic of Delegation*, Chicago, Ill., University of Chicago Press.

Kirchner, E. and Williams, K. (1983) 'The Legal, Political and Institutional Implications of the Isoglucose Judgments 1980', *Journal of Common Market Studies*, 32, 2, 173–90.

Kohler-Koch, B. (1997) 'Organised Interests and the European Parliament', *European Integration online Papers*, 1, 9; http://eiop.or.at/eiop/texte/1997-009a.htm.

Kohler-Koch, B. (2000) 'Framing: The Bottleneck of Constructing Legitimate Institutions', *Journal of European Public Policy*, 7, 4, 513–31.

Kornberg, A. and Clarke, H. D. (1992) *Citizens and Community: Political Support in a Representative Democracy*, Cambridge, Cambridge University Press.

Krehbiel, K. (1991) *Information and Legislative Organization*, Ann Arbor, University of Michigan Press.

Kreppel, A. (1999) 'The European Parliament's Influence Over EU Policy Outcomes', *Journal of Common Market Studies*, 37, 3, 521–38.

Kreppel, A. (2000a) 'Rules and Ideology and Coalition Formation in the European Parliament: Past, Present and Future', *European Union Politics*, 1, 3, 340–62.

Kreppel, A. (2000b) 'Procedure and Influence: An Empirical Analysis of EP Influence under the Codecision and Cooperation Procedures', Paper presented to the Annual Meeting of the American Political Studies Association, Washington, DC.

Kreppel, A. (2002) *The European Parliament and the Supranational Party System: A Study in Institutional Development*, Cambridge, Cambridge University Press.

Kreppel, A. and Tsebelis, G. (1999) 'Coalition Formation in the European Parliament', *Comparative Political Studies*, 32, 8, 933–66.

Ladrech, R. (1996) 'Political Parties in the European Parliament', in J. Gaffney (ed.), *Political Parties in the European Union*, London, Routledge.

Laffan, B. (1992) *Integration and Co-operation in Europe*, London, Routledge.

Laffan, B. (1997) 'The IGC and Institutional Reform of the Union', in G. Edwards and A. Pijpers (eds), *The Politics of European Treaty Reform: The 1996 Intergovernmental Conference and Beyond*, London, Pinter.

Laffan, B. and Shackleton, M. (1996) 'The Budget', in H. Wallace and W. Wallace (eds), *Policy Making in the European Union*, Oxford, Oxford University Press.

Laffan, B. and Shackleton, M. (2000) 'The Budget', in H. Wallace and W. Wallace (eds), *Policy Making in the European Union*, 2nd edn, Oxford, Oxford University Press.

Lamy, P. (2002) *L'Europe en première ligne*, Paris, Editions du Seuil.

Lamy, P. and Pisani-Ferry, J. (2002) *L'Europe de nos volontés*, Les Notes de la Fondation Jean-Jaurès, 27, January, Paris, Fondation Jean-Jaurès.

Langfried, C. (1997) 'Beyond Technocratic Governance: The Case of Biotechnology', *European Law Journal*, 3, 3, 255–72.

Laursen, F. (1997) 'The Lessons of Maastricht', in G. Edwards and A. Pijpers (eds), *The Politics of European Treaty Reform: The 1996 Intergovernmental Conference and Beyond*, London, Pinter.

Lazar, M. (2002) 'The Communist and Extreme Left Galaxy', in P. Perrineau, G. Grunberg and C. Ysmal (eds), *The European Elections, 1999*, New York, Palgrave Macmillan.

Lijphart, A. (1984) *Democracies: Patterns of Majoritarian and Consensus Government in Twenty-one Countries*, New Haven, Conn., Yale University Press.

Lijphart, A. (1991) 'Introduction', in A. Lijphart (ed.), *Parliamentary versus Presidential Government*, Oxford, Oxford University Press.

Lodge, J. (1982) 'The European Parliament After Direct Elections: Talking-Shop or Putative Legislature', *Journal of European Integration*, 5, 3, 259–84.

Lodge, J. (1983) 'The European Parliament', in J. Lodge (ed.), *Institutions and Policies of the EC*, London, Pinter.

Lodge, J. (1984) 'European Union and the First Elected European Parliament: The Spinelli Initiative', *Journal of Common Market Studies*, 22, 4, 377–402.

Lodge, J. (1989) 'The European Parliament from "Assembly" to Co-Legislature: Changing the Institutional Dynamics', in J. Lodge (ed.), *The European Community and the Challenge of the Future*, London, Pinter.

Lodge, J. (1993) 'EC Policymaking: Institutional Dynamics', in J. Lodge (ed.), *The European Community and the Challenge of the Future*, 2nd edn, London, Pinter.

Lodge, J. (1994) 'The European Parliament and the Authority–Democracy Crises', *Annals of the American Academy of Political and Social Sciences*, 531, January, 69–83.

Loewenberg, G. and Patterson, S. C. (1979) *Comparing Legislatures*, Boston, Mass., Brown & Co.

Longley, L. D. and Davidson, R. H. (1998) 'Parliamentary Committees: Changing Perspectives on Changing Institutions', *Journal of Legislative Studies*, 4, 1, 1–20.

Lord, C. (1998) *Democracy in the European Union*, Sheffield, UACES, Sheffield Academic Press.

Lord, C. and Beetham, D. (2001) 'Legitimizing the EU: Is There a "Post-Parliamentary Basis" for its Legitimation?', *Journal of Common Market Studies*, 39, 3, 443–62.

Lowi, T. (1972) 'Four Systems of Policy, Politics and Choice', *Public Administration Review*, 32, 4, 298–310.

Lupia, A. and McCubbins, M. D. (1994) 'Who Controls? Information and the Structure of Legislative Decision Making', *Legislative Studies Quarterly*, 29, 3, 361–84.

Lupia, A. and McCubbins, M. D. (1998) *The Democratic Dilemma*, Cambridge, Cambridge University Press.

McAllister, R. (1997) *From EC to EU*, London, Routledge.

McElroy, G. (2002) 'Committees and Party Cohesion in the European Parliament', European Parliament Research Group Working Paper, No. 8, available at http://www.lse.ac.uk/Depts/eprg/working-papers.htm.

Majone, G. (2002) 'The European Commission: The Limits of Centralization and the Perils of Parliamentarization', *Governance*, 15, 3, 375–92.

Mamadouh, V. and Raunio, T. (2000) 'Committees in the European Parliament: The Distribution of Reports and Rapporteurships', Paper presented at the Fourth Workshop of Parliamentary Scholars and Parliamentarians, Wroxton College, 5–6 August.

Manin, B. (1997) *The Principles of Representative Government*, Cambridge, Cambridge University Press.

Marks, G., Hooghe, L. and Blank, K. (1996) 'European Integration in the 1980s: State Centric v. Multi-level Governance', *Journal of Common Market Studies*, 34, 3, 341–78.

Marsh, M. (1998) 'Testing the Second-Order Election Model after Four European Elections', *British Journal of Political Science*, 28, 591–607.

Marsh, M. and Norris, P. (1997) 'Political Representation in the European Parliament', *European Journal of Political Research*, 32, 2, 153–64.

Marsh, M. and Wessels, B. (1997) 'Territorial Representation', *European Journal of Political Research*, 32, 2, 185–210.

Martin, D. (1990) *European Union and the Democratic Deficit*, West Lothian, John Wheatley Centre.

Mather, J. (2001) 'The European Parliament – a Model of Representative Democracy?', *West European Politics*, 24, 1, 181–201.

Mattson, I. and Strøm, K. (1996) 'Parliamentary Committees', in H. Döring (ed.), *Parliaments and Majority Rule*, Frankfurt, Campus Verlag.

Maurer, A. (1999a) *What Next for the European Parliament?*, Federal Trust Series, Future of European Parliamentary Democracy 2, London, Federal Trust.

Maurer, A. (1999b) 'Co-Governing After Maastricht: The European Parliament's Institutional Performance 1994–99', Working Paper Political Series, POLI 104/rev.EN, Directorate-General for Research, Luxembourg, European Parliament.

Mayo, H. B. (1960) *An Introduction to Democratic Theory*, Oxford, Oxford University Press.

Mazey, S. and Richardson, J. (2001) 'Interest Groups and EU Policy-Making: Organisational Logic and Venue Shopping', in J. Richardson (ed.), *European Union. Power and Policy-Making*, 2nd edn, London, Routledge.

Mezey, M. (1979) *Comparative Legislatures*, Durham, NC, Duke University Press.

Mill, J. S. [1861] (1910) *Considerations on Representative Government*, London, Dent.

Milward, A. (1984) *The Reconstruction of Western Europe*, London, Methuen.

Monnet, J. (1978) *Memoirs*, New York, Doubleday.

Moravcsik, A. and Nicolaidis, K. (1998) 'Federal Ideas and Constitutional Realities in the Treaty of Amsterdam', in G. Edwards and G. Wiessala (eds), *European Union 1993: Annual Review of Activities*, Oxford, Blackwell.

Moser, P. (1996) 'The European Parliament as a Conditional Agenda Setter: What Are the Conditions', *American Political Science Review*, 90, 4, 834–8.

Moser, P. (1997) 'A Theory of the Conditional Influence of the European Parliament in the Cooperation Procedure', *Public Choice*, 91, 333–50.

Muntean, A. M. (2000) 'The European Parliament's Political Legitimacy and the Commission's "Misleading Management": Towards a Parliamentarian European Union?', *European Integration online Papers*, 4, 5; http://eiop.or.at/texte/2000-005a.thm.

Murphy, W. F. (1993) 'Constitutions, Constitutionalism and Democracy', in D. Greenberg, S. N. Katz, M. Oliviero, and S. C. Wheatley (eds), *Constitutionalism and Democracy: Transitions in the Contemporary World*, Oxford, Oxford University Press.

Nentwich, G. and Falkner, M. (1997) 'The Treaty of Amsterdam: Towards a New Institutional Balance', *European Integration online Papers*, 1, 15; http://eiop.or.at/eiop/texte/ 1997-015a.htm.

Neuhold, C. (2001) 'The "Legislative Backbone" Keeping the Institution Upright? The Role of European Parliament Committees in the EU Policy-Making Process', *European Integration online Papers*, 5, 10; http://eiop.or.at/eiop/texte/2001-10a.htm.

Neunreither, K. (1994) 'The Democratic Deficit of the European Union: Towards Closer Cooperation Between the European Parliament and the National Parliaments', *Government and Opposition*, 29, 299–314.

Nickel, D. (1998) 'The Amsterdam Treaty – a Shift in the Balance Between the Institutions!?', *Jean Monnet Papers*, 14, Cambridge,

Mass., Harvard Law School, http://www.law.harvard.edu/Programs/JeanMonnet/papers/98/98-14.html.

Nickel, D. (1999) 'Beyond Treaty Revision: Shifts in the Institutional Balance?', Paper presented to the ECSA Sixth Biennial Conference, June, Pittsburgh, Pa.

Nicoll, W. (1994) 'The European Parliament's Post-Maastricht Rules of Procedure', *Journal of Common Market Studies*, 32, 3, 403–10.

Nicoll, W. and Salmon, T. C. (2001) *Understanding the European Union*, London, Longman.

Noël, E. (1989) 'The Single European Act', *Government and Opposition*, 24, 1, 1–14.

Norderval, I. (1985) 'Party and Legislative Participation among Scandinavian Women', in S. Basevkin (ed.), *Women and Politics in Western Europe*, London, Frank Cass.

Norris, P. (1996) 'Woman Politicians: Transforming Westminster?', *Parliamentary Affairs*, 49, 1, 89–102.

Norris, P. (1999) 'Recruitment into the European Parliament', in R. S. Katz and B. Wessels (eds), *The European Parliament, the National Parliaments, and European Integration*, Oxford, Oxford University Press.

Norris, P. and Franklin, M. (1997) 'Social Representation', *European Journal of Political Research*, 32, 2, 185–210.

Norris, P. and Lovenduski, J. (1989) 'Women Candidates for Parliament: Transforming the Agenda', *British Journal of Political Science*, 19, 1, 106–15.

Norris, P. and Lovenduski, J. (1995) *Political Representation: Gender, Race and Class in the British Parliament*, Cambridge, Cambridge University Press.

Norton, P. (1990) *Legislatures*, Oxford, Oxford University Press.

Norton, P. and Wood, D. M. (1993) *Back From Westminster: British Members of Parliament and Their Constituents*, Lexington, University Press of Kentucky.

Nuenreither, K. (2001) 'The European Union in Nice: A Minimalist Approach to a Historic Change', *Government and Opposition*, 36, 2, 184–208.

Nugent, N. (1999) *The Government and Politics of the European Union*, 4th edn, London, Macmillan – now Palgrave Macmillan.

Packenham, R. A. (1970) 'Legislatures and Political Development', in A. Kornberg and L. Musloff (eds), *Legislatures in Developmental Perspective*, Durham, NC, Duke University Press.

PE 155.236 (1992) *Notice to Members*, Committee on the Environment, Public Health and Consumer Protection, Brussels, European Parliament.

PE 167.189 (1997) *Institutional Aspects of Budgetary Control, Briefing Budgetary Affairs No. 2*, Directorate-General for Research, Luxembourg, European Parliament.

PE 200.405 (1992) *Proposals for the Enlarged Bureau: With a View to Laying Down Rules Governing the Representation of Special Interest Groups at the European Parliament*, Committee on the Rules of Procedure, the Verification of Credentials and Immunities, Rapporteur Marc Galle, Brussels, European Parliament.

PE 211.523 (1995) *Legal Protection of Biotechnological Inventions, Statement by Mrs Breyer, Member of the Delegation, following the Meeting of 22 February 1995*, Parliament's Delegation to the Conciliation Committee, Brussels, European Parliament.

PE 216.869 (1996) *Report on Lobbying in the European Parliament*, Committee on the Rules of Procedure, the Verification of Credentials and Immunities, Rapporteur Glyn Ford, Brussels, European Parliament.

PE 221.698 (1997) *Report on Relations between the European Parliament and the National Parliaments*, Committee on Institutional Affairs, Brussels, European Parliament.

PE 226.077 (1998) *Report on Postponement of the Discharge to be Given to the Commission in Respect of the Implementation of the General Budget of the European Community for the 1996 Financial Year*, Committee on Budgetary Control, Brussels, European Parliament.

PE 229.204 (1999) *Report on the Amendments to be Made to the Rules of Procedure*, Committee on the Rules of Procedure, the Verification of Credentials and Immunities, Brussels, European Parliament.

PE 229.285 (1998) *Report on Giving Discharge to the Commission in Respect of the Implementation of the General Budget of the European Communities for the 1996 Financial Year*, Committee on Budgetary Control, Rapporteur James Elles, Brussels, European Parliament.

PE 230.998 (1999) *Activity Report of the Delegations to the Conciliation Committee, 1 November 1993 to 30 April 1999. From Entry into Force of the Treaty of Maastricht to Entry into Force of the Treaty of Amsterdam. Codecision Procedure Under Article 189b of the Treaty of Maastricht*, Delegations to the Conciliation Committee, Brussels, European Parliament.

PE 231.873 (1999) *Report on the Preparation for the Reform of the Treaties and the Next Intergovernmental Conference*, Committee on Constitutional Affairs, Brussels, European Parliament.

PE 232.403 (2000) *Report on the Agreement Between the European Parliament and the Commission on Procedures for Implementing the New Council Decision of 28 June 1999 – 'commitology' (1999/468/EC) (ACI 1999/2202)*, Committee on Constitutional Affairs, Brussels, European Parliament.

PE 232.648 (2000) *Report on the Drafting of a European Union Charter of Fundamental Rights*, Committee on Constitutional Affairs, Brussels, European Parliament.

PE 232.649 (2000) *Report on the Convening of the Intergovernmental Conference*, Committee on Constitutional Affairs, Brussels, European Parliament.

PE 232.758 (2000) *Report on the European Parliament's Proposals for the Intergovernmental Conference*, Committee on Constitutional Affairs, Rapporteurs Giorgos Dimitrakopoulos and Jo Leinen, Brussels, European Parliament.

PE 232.762 (2000) *Report on Amendments to Parliament's Rules of Procedure to Ensure Balanced Rights Between Individual Members and Groups*, Committee on Constitutional Affairs, Rapporteur Richard Corbett, Brussels, European Parliament.

PE 232.976 (2000) *Report on the Guidelines for the 2001 Budget*, Committee on Budgets, Brussels, European Parliament.

PE 259.385/BUR (1997) *Reply to question 39/97 by Richard Corbett, pursuant to Rule 28(2) of the Rules of Procedure, to the President: Rate of Acceptance of EP Amendments in Codecision Procedures*, Brussels, European Parliament.

PE 287.586 (2001) *Report on the Joint Text Approved by the Conciliation Committee for a European Parliament and Council Directive on The Approximation of the Laws, Regulations and Administrative Provisions of the Member States Concerning the Manufacture, Presentation and Sale of Tobacco Products*, European Delegation to the Conciliation Committee, Brussels, European Parliament.

PE 287.589 (2001) *Report on the Joint Text by the Conciliation for a European Parliament and Council Directive on Company Law Concerning Takeover Bids*, Brussels, European Parliament.

PE 287.593 (2001) *Activity Report of the Delegations to the Conciliation Committee, 1 August 2000 to 31 July 2001*, Delegations to the Conciliation Committee, Brussels, European Parliament.

PE 289.524 (2000) *Report on the Estimates of Revenue and Expenditure of Parliament for the Financial Year 2001*, Committee on Budgets, Brussels, European Parliament.

PE 289.603 (2000) *Report on the Draft General Budget of the European Union for the Financial Year 2001*, Committee on Budgets, Brussels, European Parliament.

PE 293.679 (2000) *Recommendation for Second Reading on the Council Common Position for Adopting a European Parliament and*

Council Directive on *The Approximation of the Laws, Regulations and Administrative Provisions of the Member States Concerning the Manufacture, Presentation and Sale of Tobacco Products*, Committee on the Environment, Public Health and Consumer Policy, Brussels, European Parliament.

PE 294.737 (2001) *Draft Treaty of Nice (Initial Analysis)*, Directorate-General for Committees and Delegations, Committee on Constitutional Affairs, Brussels, European Parliament.

PE 294.755 (2001) *Report on the Treaty of Nice and the Future of the European Union*, Committee on Constitutional Affairs, Brussels, European Parliament.

PE 294.777 (2001) *Report on Reform of the Council*, Committee on Constitutional Affairs, Brussels, European Parliament.

PE 300.037 (2001) *Report on the Estimates of Revenue and Expenditure of Parliament for the Financial Year 2002*, Committee on Budgets, Rapporteur Kathalijne Maria Buitenweg, Brussels, European Parliament.

PE 303.546 (2001) *Report on the Treaty of Nice and the Future of the European Union*, Committee on Constitutional Affairs, Brussels, European Parliament.

PE 304.283 (2001) *Second Draft Report on the General Revision of the Rules of Procedure (2001/204[REG])*, Committee on Constitutional Affairs, Brussels, European Parliament.

PE 304.283 (2002) *Report on the General Revision of the Rules of Procedure*, Committee on Constitutional Affairs, Rapporteur Richard Corbett, Brussels, European Parliament.

PE 304.289 (2001) *Report on the Commission White Paper on European Governance*, Committee on Constitutional Affairs, Brussels, European Parliament.

PE 304.302 (2002) *Report on Relations between the European Parliament and the National Parliaments in European Integration*, Committee on Constitutional Affairs, Brussels, European Parliament.

PE 304.309 (2002) *Report on the European Commission's Legislative and Work Programme (Amendment of Rule 57 of Parliament's Rules of Procedure) (2001/2110(REG)*, Committee on Constitutional Affairs, Brussels, European Parliament.

PE 305.659 (2002) *Report Concerning Discharge in Respect of the Implementation of the General Budget of the European Union for the 2000 Financial Year*, Committee on Budgetary Control, Brussels, European Parliament.

PE 313.424 (2001) *European Council Laeken. Conclusions of the Presidency, 14 and 15 December 2001, Bulletin 17 December 2001, Annexes*, Brussels, European Parliament.

Peterson, J. (1995) 'Decision-making in the European Union: Towards a Framework for Analysis', *Journal of European Public Policy*, 2, 1, 69–93.

Peterson, J. (1999) 'The Santer Era: The European Commission in Normative, Historical and Theoretical Perspective', *Journal of European Public Policy*, 6, 1, 46–65.

Peterson, J. and Bomberg, E. (1999) *Decision-Making in the European Union*, London, Macmillan – now Palgrave Macmillan.

Peterson, J. and Bomberg, E. (2000) 'The European Union after the 1990s: Explaining Continuity and Change', in M. Green Cowles and M. Smith, *The State of the European Union, Vol. 5: Risks, Reform, Resistance, and Revival*, Oxford, Oxford University Press.

Peterson, J. and Shackleton, M. (2002) 'The EU's Institutions: An Overview', in J. Peterson and M. Shackleton (eds), *The Institutions of the European Union*, Oxford, Oxford University Press.

Phillips, A. (1995) *The Politics of Presence*, Oxford, Clarendon Press.

Pitkin, H. (1967) *The Concept of Representation*, Berkeley, University of California Press.

Pryce, R. (1994) 'The Treaty Negotiations', in A. Duff, J. Pinder and R. Pryce (eds), *Maastricht and Beyond*, London, Routledge.

Pryce, R. and Wessels, W. (1987) 'The Search for An Ever Closer Union: A Framework for Analysis', in R. Pryce (ed.), *The Dynamics of European Union*, London, Croom Helm.

Pridham, G. and Pridham, P. (1981) *Transnational Party Co-operation and European Integration: The Process towards Direct Elections*, London, Allen & Unwin.

PSE (2002) 'A Successful Convention on the Future of Europe: Our Essentials', Brussels, Parliamentary Group of the Party of European Socialists.

Raunio, T. (1996a) *Party Group Behaviour in the European Parliament*, Tampere, University of Tampere.

Raunio, T. (1996b) 'Parliamentary Questions in the European Parliament: Representation, Information and Control', *Journal of Legislative Studies*, 2, 4, 356–82.

Raunio, T. (1997) *The European Perspective: Transnational Party Groups in the 1989–1994 European Parliament*, Aldershot, Ashgate.

Raunio, T. (1999) 'The Challenge of Diversity: Party Cohesion in the European Parliament', in S. Bowler, D. M. Farrell, and R. S. Katz (eds), *Party Discipline and Parliamentary Government*, Columbus, Ohio State University Press.

Raunio, T. (2000) 'Losing Independence or Finally Gaining Recognition?', *Party Politics*, 6, 2, 211–23.

Raunio, T. (2002) 'Political Interests: The EP's Party Groups', in J. Peterson and M. Shackleton (eds), *The Institutions of the European Union*, Oxford, Oxford University Press.

Reif, K. (1985) 'Ten Second-Order Elections', in K. Reif (ed.), *Ten European Elections: Campaigns and Results of the 1979/81 First Direct Elections to the European Parliament*, Aldershot, Gower.

Reif, K. and Schmitt, H. (1980) 'Nine Second-Order Elections: A Conceptual Framework for the Analysis of European Election Results', *European Journal of Political Research*, 8, 3–44.

Richardson, J. (2001) 'Policy-Making in the EU: Interests, Ideas and Garbage Cans of Primeval Soup', in J. Richardson (ed.), *European Union: Power and Policy-Making*, 2nd edn, London, Routledge.

Riker, W. (1982) *Liberalism Against Populism*, San Francisco, Freeman & Co.

Ripley, R. B. and Franklin, G. A. (1982) *Bureaucracy and Policy Implementation*, Chicago, Ill., Dorsey Press.

Ripley, R. B. and Franklin, G. A. (1987) *Congress, the Bureaucracy and Public Policy*, 4th edn, Chicago, Ill., Dorsey Press.

Rittberger, B. (2000) 'Impatient Legislators and New Issue-Dimensions: A Critique of the Garrett–Tsebelis "Standard Version" of Legislative Politics', *Journal of European Public Policy*, 7, 4, 554–75.

Romer, H. (1993) Guidelines for the Application of the Rule Changes, Secretariat, Group of the European People's Party, Brussels, Group of the European People's Party.

Rosamond, B. (2000) *Theories of European Integration*, Basingstoke, Palgrave Macmillan.

Sartori, G. (1987) *The Theory of Democracy Revisited*, Chatham, NJ, Chatham House.

Schumpeter, J. A. [1943] (1976) *Capitalism, Socialism and Democracy*, 5th edn, London, Allen & Unwin.

Scully, R. (1997) 'The European Parliament and the Codecision Procedure', *Journal of Legislative Studies*, 3, 3, 58–73.

Scully, R. (2000a) 'Democracy, Legitimacy, and the European Parliament', in M. Green Cowles and M. Smith (eds), *The State of the European Union: Risks, Reform, Resistance and Revival* (Vol. 5), Oxford, Oxford University Press.

Scully, R. (2000b) 'Conditional Independence: Understanding MEP-National Party Relations', Paper presented to the Annual Meeting of the American Political Science Association, August, Washington, DC.

Scully, R. and Farrell, D. M. (2001) 'Understanding Constituency Representation in the European Parliament', Paper presented at the Conference of the European Community Studies Association, Madison, Wisconsin, 31 May–2 June 2001.

Shackleton, M. (1998) 'The European Parliament's New Committees of Inquiry: Tiger or Paper Tiger?', *Journal of Common Market Studies*, 36, 1, 115–30.

Shackleton, M. (2000) 'The Politics of Codecision', *Journal of Common Market Studies*, 38, 2, 325–42.

Shackleton, M. (2001) 'Codecision Since Amsterdam: A Laboratory for Institutional Innovation and Change', Paper presented at the ECSA Seventh Biennial Conference, Madison, Wisconsin.

Shephard, M. (1999) 'The European Parliament: Getting the House in Order', in P. Norton (ed.), *Parliaments and Pressure Groups in Western Europe*, London, Frank Cass.

Shephard, M. and Scully, R. (2002) 'The European Parliament: Of Barriers and Removed Citizens', in P. Norton (ed.), *Parliament and Citizens in Western Europe*, London, Frank Cass.

Smith, J. (1999) *Europe's Elected Parliament*, Sheffield, UACES/ Sheffield Academic Press.

SN 200/02 (2002) Presidency Conclusions, Seville European Council, 21 and 22 June 2002, Brussels, European Council.

SN 400/00 (2000) Presidency Conclusions: Nice European Council Meeting 7, 8 and 9 December 2000, Brussels, European Council.

SN 533/1/00/REV1 (2000) *Treaty of Nice*, Brussels, European Council.

Spence, D. (1993) 'The Role of the National Civil Service in European Lobbying: The British Case', in S. Mazey and J. Richardson (eds), *Lobbying in the European Community*, Oxford, Oxford University Press.

Spence, D. (2000) 'Plus ça change, plus c'est la même chose? Attempting to Reform the European Commission', *Journal of European Public Policy*, 7, 1, 1–25.

Steunenberg, B. (2000) 'Seeing What You Want to See: The Limits of Current Modelling on the European Union', *European Union Politics*, 1, 3, 368–72.

Strøm, K. (1995) 'Parliamentary Government and Legislative Organisation', in H. Döring (ed.), *Parliaments and Majority Rule in Western Europe*, Frankfurt, Campus Verlag.

Strøm, K. (1998) 'Parliamentary Committees in European Democracies', *Journal of Legislative Studies*, 4, 1, 21–59.

Thomassen, J. and Schmitt, H. (1999) 'Partisan Structures in the European Parliament', in R. S. Katz and B. Wessels (eds), *The European Parliament, the National Parliaments, and European Integration*, Oxford, Oxford University Press.

Tindemans, L. (1976) 'European Union: Report to the European Council', *Bulletin of the European Communities*, Supplement 1, No. 1, Bull. EC1-1976, Brussels, European Commission.

Treaty of Amsterdam (1997) Luxembourg, Office for Official Publications of the European Communities.

Treaty of Paris (1952) Luxembourg, Office for Official Publications of the European Communities.

Treaty of Rome (1957) Luxembourg, Office for Official Publications of the European Communities.

Treaty on European Union (1992) Luxembourg, Office for Official Publications of the European Communities.

Tsebelis, G. (1994) 'The Power of the European Parliament as a Conditional Agenda Setter', *American Political Science Review*, 88, 1, 128–42.

Tsebelis, G. (1995) 'Conditional Agenda-Setting and Decision-Making Inside the European Parliament', *Journal of Legislative Studies*, 1, 1, 65–93.

Tsebelis, G. (1996) 'More on the European Parliament as a Conditional Agenda Setter: Response to Moser', *American Political Science Review*, 90, 4, 839–44.

Tsebelis, G. and Garrett, G. (1996) 'Agenda Setting Power, Power Indices and Decision Making in the European Union', *International Review of Law and Economics*, 16, 3, 345–61.

Tsebelis, G. and Garrett, G. (1997) 'Agenda Setting, Vetoes, and the European Union's Co-decision Procedure', *Journal of Legislative Studies*, 3, 3, 74–92.

Tsebelis, G. and Garrett, G. (2000) 'Legislative Politics in the European Union', *European Union Politics*, 1, 1, 9–36.

Tsebelis, G. and Kalandrakis, A. (1999) 'The European Parliament and Environmental Legislation: The Case of Chemicals', *European Journal of Political Research*, 36, 1, 119–54.

Tsebelis, G. and Money, J. (1997) *Bicameralism*, Cambridge, Cambridge University Press.

Tsebelis, G., Jensen, C. B., Kalandrakis, A. and Kreppel, A. (2001) 'Legislative Procedures in the European Union: An Empirical Analysis', *British Journal of Political Science*, 31, 3, 573–99.

Urwin, D. W. (1991) *The Community of Europe: A History of European Integration Since 1945*, London, Longman.

Viola, D. M. (2000) *European Foreign Policy and the European Parliament in the 1990s*, Aldershot, Ashgate.

von Weizsäcker, R., Dehaene, J.-L. and Simon, D. (1999) *The Institutional Implications of Enlargement*, Report to the European Commission, Brussels, European Commission.

Wahlke, J. C., Eulau, H., Buchanan, W. and Ferguson, L. C. (1962) *The Legislative System*, New York, Wiley.

Wallace, H. (1993) 'European Governance in Turbulent Times', *Journal of Common Market Studies*, 31, 3, 293–304.

Wallace, W. (1996) 'Government Without Statehood: The Unstable Equilibrium', in H. Wallace and W. Wallace (eds), *Policy-Making in the European Union*, 3rd edn, Oxford, Oxford University Press.

Wallace, W. (2000) 'Collective Governance: The EU Political Process', in H. Wallace and W. Wallace (eds), *Policy-Making in the European Union*, 4th edn, Oxford, Oxford University Press.

Wallace, W. and Smith, J. (1995) 'Democracy or Technocracy? European Integration and the Problem of Popular Consent', in J. Hayward (ed.), *The Crisis of Representation in Europe*, London, Frank Cass.

Weiler, J. H. H. (1997) 'Legitimacy and Democracy of Union Governance', in G. Edwards and A. Pijpers (eds), *The Politics of European Treaty Reform: The 1996 Intergovernmental Conference and Beyond*, London, Pinter.

Weiler, J. H. H. (1999) *The Constitution of Europe*, Cambridge, Cambridge University Press.

Wessels, B. (1999) 'European Parliament and Interest Groups', in R. S. Katz and B. Wessels (eds), *The European Parliament, the National Parliaments, and European Integration*, Oxford, Oxford University Press.

Wessels, W. (1991) 'The Institutional Strategies Toward Political Union', in L. Hurwitz and C. Lequesne (eds), *The State of the European Community: Policies, Institutions and Debates in the Transition Years*, Boulder Col., Lynne Rienner/Longman.

Wessels, W. (1996a) 'The Modern West European State and the European Union: Democratic Erosion or a New Kind of Polity', in S. S. Andersen and K. A. Eliassen (eds), *The European Union: How Democratic Is It?*, London, Sage.

Wessels, W. (1996b) 'Institutions of the EU System: Models of Explanation', in D. Rometsch and W. Wessels (eds), *The European Union and Member States*, Manchester, Manchester University Press.

Wessels, W. (1997) 'An Ever Closer Fusion? A Dynamic Macropolitical View on Integration Processes', *Journal of Common Market Studies*, 35, 2, 267–99.

Wessels, W. (2001) 'Nice Results: The Millennium IGC and the EU's Evolution', *Journal of Common Market Studies*, 39, 2, 197–220.

Wessels, W. and Diedrichs, U. (1997) 'A New Kind of Legitimacy for a New Kind of Parliament – the Evolution of the European Parliament', *European Integration online Papers*, 1, 6; http://eiop.or.at/eiop/texte/1997-006a.htm.

Wessels, W. and Diedrichs, U. (1999) 'The European Parliament and EU Legitimacy', in T. Banchoff and M. P. Smith (eds), *Legitimacy and the European Union: The Contested Polity*, London, Routledge.

Wessels, W. and Rometsch, D. (1996) 'Conclusion: European Union and National Institutions', in D. Rometsch and W. Wessels (eds), *The European Union and Member States*, Manchester, Manchester University Press.

Westlake, M. (1994a) *A Modern Guide to the European Parliament*, London, Pinter.

Westlake, M. (1994b) 'The Commission and Parliament', in G. Edwards and D. Spence (eds), *The European Commission*, London, Cartermill.

Westlake, M. (1995) 'The European Parliament, the National Parliaments and the 1996 Intergovernmental Conference', *Political Quarterly*, 66, 1, 59–73.

Westlake, M. (1998) 'The European Union's "Blind Watchmakers": The Process of Constitutional Change', in M. Westlake (ed.), *The European Union Beyond Amsterdam: New Concepts of European Integration*, London, Routledge.

Wilson, J. Q. (1974) 'The Politics of Regulation', in J. W. McKie (ed.), *Social Responsibility and the Business Predicament*, Washington, DC, Brookings Institution.

Wincott, D. (2001) 'The Commission and the Reform of Governance in the EU', *Journal of Common Market Studies*, 39, 5, 897–911.

Wood, D. M. and Young, G. (1997) 'Comparing Constituency Activity by Junior Legislators in Great Britain and Ireland', *Legislative Studies Quarterly*, 22, 2, 217–32.

Wurzel, R. (1999) 'The Role of the European Parliament: Interview with Ken Collins MEP', *Journal of Legislative Studies*, 5, 2, 1–23.

Yataganas, X. A. (2001) 'The Treaty of Nice: The Sharing of Power and the Institutional Balance in the European Union – a Continental Perspective', *European Law Journal*, 7, 3, 242–91.

Index